T0326332

Law, Liberty and the Constitution

Law, Liberty and the Constitution

A Brief History of the Common Law

HARRY POTTER

THE BOYDELL PRESS

First published 2015
The Boydell Press, Woodbridge
Paperback edition 2020

ISBN 978 1 78327 011 8 hardback
ISBN 978 1 78327 503 8 paperback

The Boydell Press is an imprint of Boydell & Brewer Ltd
PO Box 9, Woodbridge, Suffolk IP12 3DF, UK
and of Boydell & Brewer Inc.
668 Mount Hope Ave, Rochester, NY 14620–2731, USA
website: www.boydellandbrewer.com

A catalogue record for this book is available
from the British Library

The publisher has no responsibility for the continued existence
or accuracy of URLs for external or third-party internet websites
referred to in this book, and does not guarantee that any content
on such websites is, or will remain, accurate or appropriate

This publication is printed on acid-free paper

For Alfie

Contents

Illustrations

Abbreviations

Full details of the following will be found in the bibliography.
Cases not to be found in the *State Trials* are given their reported references.
These may be found in specialist law libraries.

Blackstone	*Commentaries on the Laws of England*
Bracton	Thorne, S.E., ed., *Bracton: On the Laws and Customs of England*
EHD	*English Historical Documents*
Glanvill	Hall, G. D. G., ed, *The Treatise of the Laws and Customs of England commonly called Glanvill*
GRA	Malmesbury, William of, *Gesta Regum Anglorum*, ed. R. Mynors *et al.*
Henry	Huntingdon, Henry of, *History of the English People 1000–1154*, ed. D. Greenway
LHP	Downer, L. J., ed, *Leges Henrici Primi*
Niger	Anstruther, R., ed., *Chronicles of Ralph Niger*
OHLE	*Oxford History of the Laws of England*
OV	Chibnall, M., ed., *The Ecclesiastical History of Orderic Vitalis*
P&M	Pollock, Frederick and Maitland, Frederic, *The History of English Law*
ST	Howell, T. B., ed., *State Trials*
SWEC	Coke, Edward, *Selected Writings of Sir Edward Coke*, ed. Steve Sheppard

Introduction

Woe unto you lawyers! for ye have taken away the key of knowledge.
                                                            Luke ii. 52

A competent knowledge of the laws ... is the proper accomplishment
of every gentleman and scholar, an highly useful ... part of a liberal and
polite education.   Blackstone, *Commentaries on the Laws of England*

When the BBC asked me to present a series on the history of the English
legal system – broadcast under the title of *The Strange Case of the Law* – like
many other lawyers, I knew little about the subject. I have tried to make up
for that deficit. It struck me that the story of the law should be better known,
and that a short selective history was called for, devoid of jargon, replete
with good stories, a restitution of the key of knowledge. This is the result:
breaking no new ground, but providing a new approach to the telling of
legal history, distilling the efforts of others in a way palatable to the educated
layperson. There is no legal history quite like this. It is certainly panegyric,
but with justification. The eulogy, however, at least so far as public law is
concerned, may be an elegy.

England is a law-abiding country: parliament enacts laws; courts enforce
and interpret them; citizens on the whole obey them. What is sought is
justice beyond the rigidities of legalism or the letter of the law, justice that
is blind and impartial, justice that is done by judges who are expected to be,
and largely have been, the disinterested champions of law and of right, and
by independent jurors who bring in the verdicts they choose. English law,
legal procedures, the quality of the judiciary, trial by jury, and the championing of freedom, justice and equality under the rule of law are rightly
recognised throughout the world.

In two respects the common law of England is not common at all.
Firstly, unlike legislation, it is not the creation of the common people or
of the community, but of kings and their judiciary. Secondly it is not at all
common, but is unique – in its inception as in its development. It is peculiarly English, but not insular, as its reach has spread widely throughout the
world – as indeed has that of its great continental rival, Roman or civil law
– first as a result of colonisation and empire, and latterly because of the its
intrinsic excellence. It is a law unto itself.

This is the story of how a system devised to limit feuds, to settle disputes over land, and to ensure order among the early Germanic and Scandinavian settlers in this country grew into perhaps the most sophisticated legal system the world has ever known. The origins of the English common law are to be found in Anglo-Saxon times and on these island shores. While Germanic and Nordic practices have influenced its creation, it owes relatively little to Roman or continental exemplars. England was on the edge of Europe, it had been populated by successive waves of people from Europe, but it was, and remained, distinct from Europe, an island apart. For good or ill, English law was common to England and to nowhere else on the Continent.

Thanks to its reputation for fairness, its protection of the rights of the individual, its combining the certainty of precedent with systematic procedure, and lawyerly professionalism with the active participation of the wider public in the form of juries, the common law has served as a model for legal systems all over the globe.

The secret of its success in England is that it was never imposed as an immutable code on a reluctant nation. Rather, the common law emerged from local customs, was forged into a national entity by kings and judges, has asserted its authority by consensus as well as by compulsion, and has, over many centuries, grown in sophistication and evolved to meet ever-changing circumstances. It is essentially conservative, not revolutionary. It looks back to earlier custom, its reliance on precedents anchors it in the past, and it reveres and revives the wisdom of earlier times.

Yet the law is vital, in both senses of the word. Essential to English society is the rule of law. It runs through the national story as veins through a body. It has proved both robust and adaptable. It has had to be. Since medieval times the common law has been confronted with no shortage of challenges or challengers.

In 1470 Serjeant Catesby declared that the common law had been in existence since the creation of the world. This was somewhat of an exaggeration. The antiquity of the common law was later championed for political purposes in the seventeenth century when parliamentarians and lawyers depicted it as being in existence before the 'Norman Yoke', and as pre-dating rather than being created by the monarchy. In fact the common law of England, elements of which harked back to monarchical activism in Anglo-Saxon times, was forged in the twelfth century as a powerful centralised system of justice by kings. Royal justices developed and administered general rules common to the whole of England, as distinct from local customs, peculiarities and variations. By common law is meant the 'settled law of the king's court, common to all free men in the sense that it is available to them in civil causes if they will have it, and applicable against them in serious criminal causes whether they like it or not'.[1] This unified system of law pre-dates that of any other European country. It was predicated on a strong monarchy ruling a compact island, and the English monarchy was more powerful than any other in Europe during the critical period from 1000 to 1200. The common law has been exalted as 'one of the glories of England, and ... perhaps the chief legacy of the middle ages'.[2]

In their eulogies of the common law writers have deployed a variety of metaphors: a river fed by many streams; a tree with myriad roots and branches; a garden, fertile and fruitful. But there is another metaphor equally apposite. The common law was royal in its conception and upbringing, but by the seventeenth century this royal offspring – *Oedipus Lex* it could be called – was capable of emasculating its father, and ultimately of regicide. Since then it has also had a sometimes querulous relationship with its step-father, that institution upon which the regal mantle of supreme power has since reposed – parliament.

I shall not deal with all aspects of legal development such as land law, contract and tort, important as they are, but with the salient legal develop-ments, features, cases and personalities relating to the constitution, criminal jurisprudence and civil liberties. I shall describe chronologically and in some detail the creation and development of the law from Anglo-Saxon times to 1215. From then on the text is more thematic and episodic, discoursing on the great constitutional conflicts of the seventeenth century, the rise of advocacy and its pre-eminent practitioners, and on curious cases relating to slavery, insanity, necessity, obscenity and miscarriages of justice, all illustra-tive of how the common law grows or flounders. Finally, the extension of the law into the international arena of the prosecution of war criminals and of the protection of universal human rights will be counterposed with threats to the rule of law and liberty that come from coercive moralism and the over-reaction to national emergencies and, latterly, to terrorist threats. The concluding chapter covers other problems facing, primarily, the criminal justice system.

The term 'common law' has been used in various distinct senses. Origi-nally the term was used by canonists as denoting the general law of the Church, as distinct from divergent local customs in different parts of Chris-tendom. In England, after the secular curtailed the sphere of the ecclesi-astical, it came to mean the unwritten law of the whole land, originating

---

[1] *Glanvill*, p. xi.
[2] G. R. Elton, *England Under the Tudors*, Folio Society edn (London, 1997), p. 63.

from ancient usages and developed by judges, applicable everywhere and to everyone, as distinct from enduring local customs, statute law, or the legal systems of other countries. Any common law system, such as that of the United States, is the child of the English common law, and is one that is primarily developed by judges on the basis of precedent, in contrast to a civil law system based on Roman law and codification. It is malleable, flexible and capable of accommodation. Even equity, which grew up to remedy the defects of the common law, in as much it is administered by the same courts, has been accommodated within it.

This unwritten law is distinct from, though married to, the written law of the statute book. Judge-made law has been called 'subordinate legislation, carried on with the assent, and subject to the supervision, of parliament'.[3] Statute law, which has long rivalled, if not supplanted, precedent as creating, or reinvigorating and rejuvenating, the law, is still construed by, and implemented according to, common law principles. The fundamentals – the right to a fair trial before an impartial judge and, in criminal cases in particular, by a jury of your peers – are not dependent on parliament but on precedent, hallowed by antiquity.

The sovereignty of parliament – king, lords and commons – replaces that of the Crown. It derives from the constitutional upheavals of the seventeenth century, from common law,[4] from parliament's own assertion of supremacy, and from the longstanding, popular and universal assent to this proposition. It is, however, a political and juridical construct, not a force of nature. Its effect is considerable. The great constitutional lawyer Albert Venn Dicey did more than any other to establish it. Writing during the halcyon days of Queen Victoria he gave his authoritative judgment: 'it is a fundamental principle with English lawyers, that parliament can do everything, but make a woman a man and a man a woman'.[5] With recent developments in gender-reassignment surgery even this is not now beyond the untrammelled power of parliament.

But even parliament cannot, in practice, be above the common law, and it was virtually inconceivable – until recent years – that it should pass legis-

---

3 A. V. Dicey, *Lectures Introductory to the Study of the Law of the Constitution* (London, 1886), p. 56.

4 Edward Coke, *Institutes of the Laws of England*, 4 parts (London, 1817), IV, p. 36; Blackstone, I, pp.156ff; Dicey, *Lectures Introductory to the Study of the Law*, p. 35.

5 Dicey, *Lectures Introductory to the Study of the Law* (p. 39) derived this bon mot from the *Constitution d'Angleterre* by the Swiss political theorist Jean Louis De Lolme, who in turn had taken it from a speech by Philip Herbert, the 4th Earl of Pembroke, made on 11 April 1648.

lation which undermines the basic principles of fairness, liberty, equality and justice. Should parliament turn tyrant and exceed the unspoken bounds to its authority, for instance by outlawing all redheads, or imprisoning all Sikhs, or denying the right to a fair trial, these enactments would be lawful in the sense that they would be enforceable in the courts, but there would be a constitutional crisis: judges would refuse to enforce such legislation, and the common law's assertion of right and justice would prevail. As one of England's greatest jurists often said, 'Be you never so high, the law is above you.'[6] That ultimately includes parliament.

England's common law, however imperfectly, ensures justice and liberty, and in that respect equals anything the English have achieved in the arts and sciences. This is its story.

---

6 Lord Denning, quoting from Thomas Fuller's volume, *Gnomologia: Adagies and Proverbs, Wise Sentences and Witty Sayings, Ancient and Modern, Foreign and British*, no. 943 (London, 1732).

PART I

LAYING DOWN THE LAW
600–1500

CHAPTER I

The Promulgation of the Law
in Anglo-Saxon England

Christian men are not to be condemned to death for altogether too little; but otherwise one is to devise lenient punishments for the people's benefit, and not ruin for little God's handiwork, and his own merchandise, that he so dearly bought.
Archbishop Wulfstan, Aethelred's Code V

Revenge is a kind of wild justice, which, the more Man's nature runs to, the more ought law to weed it out.   Francis Bacon, 'Of Revenge'

THE Angles and Saxons were invaders of the land later called England who fought, conquered and stayed, as the Romans had done before, and the Vikings and the Normans would do after. They migrated from Germany in the fifth and sixth centuries and established a number of kingdoms, most notably Kent, Wessex, East Anglia and Mercia. Anglo-Saxon law, which took root in England, has often been portrayed as part of the history of this receding Germanic past almost unchanging in the five hundred years from the code of Aethelbert to the laws of Henry I, and as the province not of royal power but of popular liberties.[1] This is fallacious in at least two respects.

Certainly the law that prevailed in England immediately before the Norman Conquest owed little if anything to the Celts or Romans. Older Anglo-Saxon codes, especially those of Kent and Wessex, owed much to their Germanic inheritance. From their inception, however, they did not stagnate but began to grow, and other influences – notably Scandinavian – began to impinge on, or infiltrate, the legal landscape.

Secondly, royal involvement was crucial in the development of Anglo-Saxon codes. English law and its universality sprang not primarily from the field and the hearth, but largely from the power and reach of its early Christian kings. Its vitality survived their deposition; it did not succumb to the so-called 'Norman Yoke'. It was instead nurtured by the successors of the Anglo-Saxons. The common law was eventually hammered into shape and

---

[1] Patrick Wormald, *The Making of English Law: King Alfred to the Twelfth Century* (Oxford, 1999), p. 27.

erected into a national structure by an Angevin king, but the components he used had been forged by his pre-Norman predecessors. They were made to last.

Over the centuries, the Anglo-Saxon kings produced numerous bodies of laws – or 'dooms' as they were called – almost exclusively to do with criminal law and procedure. In the early codes tariffs of fines are predominant, while in the later ones, with royal influence in the ascendancy, this compensation culture is superseded by dispossession, outlawry, and corporal and capital punishment. As the centuries pass the penalties become ever more severe.

The earliest extant code comes from the reign of King Aethelbert of Kent and was issued probably between 597 and 602.[2] Traditional laws stemming back to Germanic roots already existed but were transmitted orally. This was no problem in a small fledgling kingdom. Aethelbert, however, had ambitions. He likely attained the status of Bretwalda (overlord), and his influence extended beyond his own kingdom, as far north as the Humber. He had imperial ambitions 'over the southern territories'.[3] The maintenance of law and order was a predominant duty of any king, and fixed money payments could undermine the prime source of disorder: the feud. There was another incentive for regal involvement however: the enforcement of the law was a major source of royal revenue.

It is no coincidence that Aethelbert set down his code shortly after Augustine arrived in Canterbury, and converted him to Christianity. The missionaries brought 'law with them in a stronger form than the Anglo-Saxons recognised'.[4]Augustine was an emissary of Latin Christianity. He came from Rome where lawmaking and law codes had a long and distinguished history, and he brought the Bible which begins with the Mosaic laws, extols the forensic wisdom of Solomon and the advocacy of Jesus, and ends with the Last Judgment. Conversion brought Aethelbert within this double tradition. As the first Christian Anglo-Saxon monarch he may have wanted to symbolise his acceptance into this world, and immortalise his renown, by

---

[2]   *EHD*, I, pp. 391–4. The text is contained in the *Textus Roffensis*, compiled in the early twelfth century in Rochester on the instructions of the bishop, an indication of how the Normans were determined to preserve this ancient heritage. So finely wrought was the 'Rochester Book' that it survived, virtually unscathed, an eighteenth-century dunking in the Thames. The ink on the vellum did not run. This priceless volume is held in a safe in the featureless concrete building that stores the Medway Council archives. It may soon have a more fitting display in the cathedral.

[3]   Bede (the Venerable), *History of the English Church and People*, II.5, Folio Society edn (London, 2010), p. 74.

[4]   *OHLE*, I, p. 2.

EXPLANATION of the FRONTISPIECE. *On the Fore-Ground:* S.t Augustine *the* 1.st Arch-Bishop *of* Canterbury, *converting* Ethelbert *the* 1.st K. *of* Kent. On *the second-Ground,* King Lucius *sending* Elvanus *and* Medvinus *to* Rome, *where they are Baptis'd and Ordain'd; the* 1.st *made a* B.P *the other a Teacher. At a distance* S.t Alban *the* 1.st Christian Martyr. *In the Far-Scheit, The Cathedral Church of Canterbury.*

1. Aethelbert and Augustine: Church and state at one in the creation of the first English law code.

aping the legislative endeavours of his most eminent European predecessors, Clovis and Justinian.[5] According to the Venerable Bede, Aethelbert created a written code of laws *iuxta exempla Romanorum* – 'after the examples of the Romans'. It may be that the use of the plural – *exempla* – implies that Bede had in mind contemporary Frankish 'exemplars, the actual law-codes of still more or less recognisably "Roman" regimes'.[6] Whatever the precise meaning of Bede's elliptic phrase it is clear that Aethelbert's contact with the traditions of Rome and its heirs inspired emulation, and the code was the result. It was a joint act of Church and state. Augustine, indeed, may well have had the dominant hand in drafting it, which would explain why the first seven clauses deal with compensating the Church.

Law-giving as well as law enforcement was a royal function for a Christian king. In Aethelbert's reign, and thereafter, the Church sought to infuse royal legislation with Christian principles. Since archbishops drafted much of it, this infusion was secured. Lawmaking had royal and divine imprimatur: 'these are the dooms which King Aethelbert set in Augustine's time' is how the code begins, and, although this rubric is later than the code itself, it rightly encapsulates the congruence of Church and state. The code probably did not innovate, but encased old laws 'in a new legislative frame'. By causing them to be written down the king made them his own.[7]

The medium in which Aethelbert had his code promulgated was distinctive, even eccentric. Unlike his continental precursors, he did so not in the *lingua franca* and the traditional language of law – Latin – but in the local tongue: the Anglo-Saxon, the Old English, of his subjects. Why he did so is not obvious.[8] Aethelbert's is not merely the first law code in English, but is the oldest extant English document written in the vernacular. There is something rather appropriate that the earliest English law was accessible to everyone, for the role of laypeople, most importantly as jurors, has been a defining characteristic of the English legal system.

Emulation of the Roman way of creating law codes was a major inspiration for Aethelbert's creation, but the actual text is singularly free from the influence of Roman legislation. Instead, the influence was German. Nor were the contents of the code innovative. It looked back to traditional customs,

---

5   *GRA* I.9.2. The first Salic Code was published between 507 and 511, and reissued by Clovis's successors. Justinian produced his Codex in 529.
6   Bede, *History of the English Church* II.5, p.73. Wormald, *Making of English Law*, pp. 29f, 93–101.
7   J. M. Wallace-Hadrill, *Early Germanic Kingship in England and on the Continent* (Oxford, 1971), pp. 40ff.
8   Wormald, *Making of English Law*, p. 101, suggests possible explanations.

did not constitute general legislation, and was concerned almost entirely with safeguarding the Church and establishing stability within the realm by the setting of pecuniary penalties for criminal offences. This emphasis may again reflect the influence of the Church. Establishing a legitimate alternative to feud and reprisal was 'one of the goals of the Church at the time'.[9] Pope Gregory, who had dispatched Augustine in the first place, had a far more charitable approach to crimes such as theft from churches than Roman law had, or later Anglo-Saxon laws would come to have. He distinguished between those who stole from greed and those who took from need, and believed that different penalties should reflect different circumstances and different intent. Charity was to monitor correction. Restitution should be the hallmark of justice, rather than retribution or reprisal.[10] This is an early expression of what we would call 'restorative justice'. It is no coincidence that in Aethelbert's code it is *bote* – compensation paid, or restitution made, for injuries – that predominates.

Not only did every person have financial worth which varied according to status – from king to slave – but every part of them did too, from big toes to testicles. The loss of a big toe cost ten shillings, while severing a foot cost fifty, no mean sum as a shilling was the price of an ox in Kent.[11] The penalty for 'damaging the kindling limb' – the genital organ or penis – was set at three 'person prices' or 300 shillings, much more than for any other injury.[12] A person price – *leodgeld* – was a price paid for a life; killing a royal official, for instance, merited merely one person price.[13] The fact that in this instance the injured party got thrice that amount was to compensate not merely for the injury and insult to his manhood but for the children he would not be able to sire, the generation he could not 'kindle'. For a snip to the scrotum, falling short of emasculation, a mere six shillings would suffice. Even the least disfigurement merited three shillings.[14] Pulling someone's hair was cheapest of all, costing only fifty sceattas in restitution.[15] The layout of the code, with

---

9   *OHLE*, I, p. 36.
10   *Ibid.*, pp. 6f.
11   H. Munro Chadwick, *Studies on Anglo-Saxon Institutions* (Cambridge, 1905), p. 61. 'Shilling' is of Germanic derivation, and once referred to a piece cut from a golden ring.
12   Clause 64: Lisi Oliver, *The Beginnings of English Law* (Toronto, 2002), pp. 75, 99.
13   Clause 13. *Leodgeld*, a Kentish term, likely synonymous with wergild, had a monetary value of 100 shillings: *ibid.*, p. 65b.
14   Clause 60: *ibid.*, p.73.
15   Clause 33. Sceatta literally means 'wealth' or 'property'. At the time of Aethelbert it referred to a small unit of gold whose weight equalled that of a grain of barley corn. Twenty sceattas made a shilling. The silver penny was not in use until at least seventy-

the injuries listed from the crown of the head to the toes of the feet, making them easier to remember, suggests an oral precursor. Aethelbert was putting in writing the ancient custom of his people, so that from then on there could be no dispute as to the amount to be paid, either in full, or by barter.

The victim and his family were the enforcers, not yet the king. Disputes could be sorted out 'by the book'. A culture of compensation had much to commend it: in a society where everyone carried staves, knives, or just farming implements, quarrels could easily lead to blows, and blows to death. Killing the killer could merely make matters worse, causing feuds to proliferate. Being able to settle a dispute, or draw a line under a grievance, was therefore crucial in the early Anglo-Saxon era when the greatest threat to the social fabric came not from external enemies but from internal feuding. The king – and the Church – had no prospect of banning blood feuds, but also no desire to stir them up. Regulation with compensation was the appropriate way to limit and constrain this routine means of restoring the status quo. Nor did Aethelbert wish to deprive the community of the labour or military service of able young men by hanging large numbers of them. He had few enough subjects as it was. Fines, in addition to compensating the loser or the family of the victim and helping maintain the peace of the realm, also benefited the royal coffers. A law code such as this was thus invaluable to an ambitious Christian king.

Later in the seventh century, Kings Hlothhere, Eadric and Wihtred in Kent, and, in the eighth, Offa in Mercia, enacted their own codes, suffused with Christianity, which protected the Church and enforced its precepts, and also punished crime.[16] To the Anglo-Saxon mind, as to many others, neglect of God and the commission of crime were linked. Lawlessness was to be restrained, and self-help in the form of feuds discouraged. This was royal fiat. It was the king who laid down the law: 'the demand for due process came initially not from the subject but the ruler. It is the voice of organised authority.'[17]

From the first, however, the king did not act alone, nor did he act arbitrarily. Aethelbert, Bede relates, sought 'the consent of his councillors'.[18] Wihtred specifically convened a 'consiliary assembly of great men', including Brihtwold, 'archbishop of Britain', and Gefmund, bishop of Rochester. At

five years later and is erroneously known as a sceatta: Anna Gannon, *The Iconography of Early Anglo-Saxon Coinage* (Oxford, 2003), p. 12.

16 *EHD*, I, pp. 394–407.
17 Warren, W. L., *King John* (New Haven and London, 1997), p. 178.
18 Bede, *History of the English Church*, II.5, p. 74.

this assembly, 'with the consent of all, the leading men devised these decrees and added them to the lawful usages of the Kentish people'.[19] In lawmaking, therefore, the kings were consulting counsellors, consolidating customs, and at most adding 'to the law which their forefathers had made'.[20] They were improving on the past, rather than imposing novelties on their people; amending rather than innovating. This was conservation and adaptation. It was not revolution.

Increasing royal involvement in the administration of justice resulted in an increasing severity of punishments. Serious crimes could be deemed *boteless* or unemendable, and punishment for these could not be avoided merely by compensating victims or their kin. The notion of the king's peace began to emerge, and to break it was to offend not just against your neighbour but against your king, and even against God. A crime was now deemed an offence against the Crown (as it is today) and so merited severe penalties, including mutilation and execution. In addition, by acting as the guarantor of justice, the king could claim the fines and forfeitures levied on the living or the dead.

In the late eighth century the Vikings began to invade England, eventually to settle in an extensive area that was to become known as the 'Danelaw': the Scandinavian impact on English legal development had begun.[21] The regions unoccupied by the incoming Scandinavians remained separate entities, and it fell to the lot of one man to begin the unification of these disparate Anglo-Saxon groupings into a kingdom of England. This constituted 'the most obvious and the most important change affecting legal development in the later Anglo-Saxon period'.[22]

Alfred, the only English king awarded the appellation 'Great', defeated the Vikings decisively at Edington in 878, and saved his kingdom of Wessex. In the following years he expanded his influence, becoming overlord of Mercia and capturing London, as a result of which all the English people not under the subjection of the Danes submitted to him. Alfred also devoted himself to restructuring his kingdom, culturally, militarily and legally, showing wherein his true greatness lay: he could create as well as destroy; he could keep his kingdom in peace, internally as well as externally, and he could both elevate and ornament it. Alfred was formidably able, and deeply devout.

---

[19] *EHD*, I, p. 396.
[20] *Ibid.*, p. 394; Oliver, *Beginnings of English Law*, p. 127.
[21] 'Law' derives from the Scandinavian *lagu*.
[22] *OHLE*, II, p. 244.

He recognised that he had triumphed only with God's help, and that God's continuing help had to be ensured for the kingdom by a godly emphasis on learning, literacy and the law.

Alfred won a well-deserved reputation for being a wise and just king. Many of his subjects sought his intervention in their disputes and his judgments were lauded. However, he could not be everywhere in his realm, nor could he deal with every case personally. His judicial powers therefore had to be delegated. Wisdom, not professional expertise, was the attribute he most valued in those he appointed for the task. According to Alfred's contemporary biographer, the Welsh cleric Asser, when ignorant and illiterate ealdormen and reeves, the decisions of whom had been found wanting, were brought before the king, he ordered them either to study and apply wisdom, or abjure the office and status of wise men.[23] Just as he insisted on literacy among his officials and nobles, so he insisted on written instructions that had to be obeyed throughout the land. Writing them in English, and having enough of his subjects capable of both reading and promulgating them, were vital.

As a king with imperial ambitions, Alfred wanted a more lasting legal legacy than a reputation for doing justice. He too wanted to be associated with the righteous lawgivers of the past, stretching from the divinely inspired Moses himself, to the great continental and Christian emperor Charlemagne, who had reigned gloriously between 768 and 814. Alfred yearned for 'the wise and understanding heart' that God had given Solomon to 'discern judgment',[24] and aspired to be as great in peace as in war. So it was to prove, and 'peaks of legislation [matched] peaks of royal aspiration'.[25] Something extraordinary was taking place in a small kingdom on a small island off the coast of Europe.

Alfred's growing dominion required some degree of legal harmonising, and the increasing stature of his kingdom demanded it. Justice was central to his vision of his people as a new chosen race, heirs to the Israelites, for the

---

[23] I Kings 3. 7–14; Simon Keynes and Michael Lapidge, eds, *Alfred the Great: Asser's Life of King Alfred and Other Contemporary Sources* (London, 1983), p. 109. Wormald, *Making of English Law*, pp.118–25, provides a compelling case for the authenticity of Asser's final chapter, concluding that he 'wrote the most circumstantial and arresting account of a king's sense of responsibility for justice in the entire historical literature of the early mediaeval West'. Ealdormen were major landowners and royal officials administering one or more shires, and were responsible for law, order and justice. Towards the end of the tenth century the title was gradually replaced by the Danish word *jarl*, which in turn evolved into the English earl. The reeve was an official of high rank having administrative responsibilities.

[24] Keynes and Lapidge, eds, *Alfred the Great*, p. 92.

[25] *OHLE*, II, p. 25.

chosen had to know and observe their obligations. Sometime in the second half of his reign – probably around 890 – after consulting the earlier examples of Kent, Wessex and Mercia, Alfred enacted his own impressively large and resonant law code – or *domboc* – based on these researches.[26] It is quite likely he was the actual author, as tradition maintains. Alfred was a Christian king, legislating in the biblical tradition: the Old and New Testaments were the portals to his legislation. Quotations from the words of God to Moses in Exodus prefaced the work, and the Golden Rule of St Luke's Gospel was paraphrased and affirmed:

> A man can think on this one sentence alone, that he judges each one rightly; he has need of no other law books. Let him bethink him that he judge no man what he would not that he be judged to him, if he were giving the judgment on him.[27]

Despite this assertion that no law book was needed, Alfred produced by far the largest Anglo-Saxon code and for this reason, in Angevin times, was heralded as the founder of English law. Yet his was not an attempt to create a code for all the English, nor was it comprehensive. It sought to impose uniformity in certain spheres. Much was borrowed from his precursors and in particular from Ine, who had reigned in Wessex a hundred and fifty years before, but at times Alfred expressly innovated. Mediation and compensation were encouraged, sanctuary was to be respected, and feuding was further regulated: attacking an adulterer caught 'under the same blanket' should not spark a vendetta.[28] Compensation was still very much in the ascendancy. All first offences could be dealt with by fines, except for treachery against one's lord or king, which was a capital offence. Yet even those so accused could clear themselves by an oath equivalent to the lord's or king's wergild, or price.[29] A Christian king in a Christian land could assume that even traitors would not take such an oath lightly. Similarly, a Christian king would not kill lightly, nor execute the innocent. Only the clearest guilt would merit the most severe punishment, and a few examples would provide a deterrent. Later, Alfred was extravagantly praised for spreading 'peace throughout the province, so that even on public highways he would order bracelets of gold

---

[26] *EHD*, I, pp. 407–16; Wormald, *Making of English Law*, pp. 265–85; Keynes and Lapidge, eds, *Alfred the Great*, p. 304.

[27] *EHD*, I, p. 408.

[28] *Ibid.*, p. 415; Richard Fletcher *Bloodfeud: Murder and Revenge in Anglo-Saxon England* (Oxford, 2003), p. 115.

[29] *EHD*, I, p. 410. A king's wergild was at least 6,000 shillings. An oath equivalent to that would be one sworn by a number of individuals whose collective wergilds would equal that sum: *Laws* §4, Keynes and Lapidge, eds, *Alfred the Great*, p. 307 note 13.

to be hung up at crossroads, to mock the greed of passers-by, for no one dared steal them.'[30]

Alfred's initiatives were possibly intended to replace the existing regional laws with a body of law of general application throughout his growing and unified kingdom. According to William of Malmesbury it was Alfred who subdivided the land into hundreds and tithings, making every man responsible for the behaviour of his neighbour.[31] He picked what he liked from the laws of his predecessors and rejected what displeased him, doing so specifically with the help and acquiescence of 'all [his] councillors'.[32] His laws, to be intelligible to all of his subjects who could read or listen, were written in the vernacular: Alfred turned Aethelbert's Kentish aberration into an English tradition. His itch to legislate was imitated by his successors, and as the hegemony of the kings grew so too did the reach of their laws. This legal activism was without parallel in Europe.

In the tenth century, under Alfred's grandson Aethelstan, the kingdom of Wessex came to predominate, not just in Anglo-Saxon England, but in the whole of Britain. Aethelstan was hailed as a paragon of royal virtue by the twelfth-century historian William, a monk of Malmesbury Abbey. William recorded that 'there is a vigorous tradition in England that he was the most law-abiding and best-educated ruler they have ever had'.[33] On Aethelstan's tomb is inscribed, probably in William's words, the epitaph: 'Path of rectitude, Thunderbolt of justice, Model of purity.'[34] William of Malmesbury had a certain self-interest in as much as the king was buried in his abbey, but his judgment is vindicated in contemporary sources and by modern research.

Largely neglected until recent times, Aethelstan was no less important than his grandfather in the history of England and of English law. Deeply devout, he also conceived of kingship in sacral terms, and was the first Anglo-Saxon king to be later depicted at his coronation wearing a crown rather than a helmet, and carrying a sceptre not a sword. But he could wield a sword with the best. He was an outstanding warrior prince, winning a stunning victory in 937 at Brunanburh over the combined Scots and Viking forces leagued

---

[30] *GRA* II.122.2.

[31] *Ibid.* The name hundred first appears in the mid-tenth century when Edmund's third code refers to it as an organised body. The Hundred Ordinance of Edgar (957–975) set down its procedure: EHD, I, pp. 429f. Given Alfred's gift for administration it is probable that it was he who brought in this subdivision or regulated a pre-existing unit.

[32] *EHD*, I, pp. 408f.

[33] *GRA* II.132.

[34] Sarah Foot, *Aethelstan, The First King of England* (New Haven and London), p. 188.

against him. By means military, diplomatic and dynastic, he managed to woo and subdue the whole of England, and of Scotland too, until he could style himself on his coins (immodestly if not inaccurately) as *Rex Tot Brit – Rex Totius Britanniae*, 'King of All Britain'.

Imperial pretensions, as in the reign of Alfred, would again provide the impetus for legislative activity.[35] It is no surprise that Aethelstan was a feverish lawmaker who, in his short reign, promulgated several law codes for his expanding realm, in which his determination to eradicate criminality was equalled by his desire to keep his kingdom united. The consistent and savage enforcement of the law was aimed at securing both ends. Moneyers caught counterfeiting coins bearing the king's image were guilty of subverting the kingdom, and faced exemplary and apt punishment. They were to have their offending hands struck off and 'set upon the money-smithy'. Theft, a common enough offence, obsessed Aethelstan throughout his reign: one third of all occurrences of the word 'thief' in the entire corpus of Anglo-Saxon law occur in his codes. Theft was a manifestation of social break-down, a breach of the king's peace, an affront to God, and so constituted the ultimate disloyalty to the person of the monarch, the heir of Moses, the embodiment of the law.[36]

If crime went undeterred and unpunished, it was believed that anarchy would result. Royal enactments became increasingly severe, but to little effect. At one point the king tried a different tack, offering an amnesty for those who confessed their crimes and made amends, though he soon reverted to draconian measures. Under his last code, issued at Thunderfield, all thieves, and not just those caught in the act, would suffer death and the public display of their corpses. Those who harboured thieves were just as culpable and faced the same fate. Stoning was stipulated for male thieves, burning for female, while free women could be pushed off a cliff, or drowned. Savage justice, however, was tempered by a degree of Christian charity, at least so far as the young were concerned. Perhaps under the influence of Wulfhelm, his archbishop of Canterbury, Aethelstan limited capital punishment for thieves to those over fifteen years of age who stole more than twelve pence, saying he could not countenance the execution of so many children for relatively minor offences. He had not always felt so: in Aethelstan's first legislative foray the age was twelve and the amount eight pence.[37] Even after his change

---

35 Wormald, *Making of English Law*, p. 444.
36 Foot, *Aethelstan* p. 140.
37 *EHD*, I, p. 417.

of heart, second offenders aged twelve or more –considered to be adults – would still end up on the gallows.

In Aethelstan's short dynamic reign the royal stamp on justice was everywhere evident, but at such a pitch that no ruler thereafter could sustain the momentum. Continuity would be preserved, but royal activism was more restrained.[38]

In 939 the childless Aethelstan was succeeded by his younger brother Edmund, who in turn issued a legislative ordinance, the overwhelming concern of which was, again, the limitation of blood feuds: kinsfolk could disavow a killer and so exempt themselves from a feud; 'wise men' would arbitrate; while those who killed in the course of feud were barred from access to the royal courts until they had made penance. To feud with those who pursued thieves was to align against royal authority. Once the warring sides had settled, the king himself guaranteed the enforcement of compensation agreements. To break trust and breach the peace was to offend against the king, who personified good order and answered for it to God.[39]

Ironically Edmund would not enjoy his regnal peace for long. In May 946 he was celebrating the feast of St Augustine at Pucklechurch when he received a fatal stab wound, not in chivalric battle, but in an attempt to apprehend a thief who had had the temerity to attend.

The last major pre-Norman lawmaker was not Anglo-Saxon but a Dane. Canute – Cnut or Knut – became king of England in 1016 and reigned until 1035. Both ruthless and wise,[40] he was a precursor of Duke William of Normandy as an invader and conqueror of all England, but he did not transform the landscape, displace the Anglo-Saxon aristocracy, nor draw divisions within the people he ruled. His chief minister, and the inspiration behind his lawmaking, was Wulfstan, the archbishop of York whom he had inherited from his predecessor, Aethelred the Unready. This was crucial as Wulfstan was 'the new English kingdom's main exponent of the biblical ideal that God's People be ruled in accordance with His will: the pre-eminent ideal of Charlemagne's kingship'.[41] With archiepiscopal help the new king tried to

---

38 Wormald, *Making of English Law*, pp. 305–8.
39 *EHD*, I, pp. 427f.
40 The story of his attempt to hold the sea back was not a demonstration of his folly or arrogance, but the reverse. He was showing his sycophantic followers the limits of temporal power.
41 Wormwald, *Making of English Law*, p. 27.

'expiate by justice and mercy the dark deeds of his bloodstained youth; trying (and not in vain) to blend the two races over which he ruled'.[42]

Canute legislated within his realm for the protection of his English and Danish subjects without distinction, while acknowledging the differing customs of the Danelaw, Wessex and Mercia. His laws were territorial not personal, common to all, not just for his Danes. He promulgated a series of legal enactments for the first time specifically prohibiting idolatry and witchcraft, and dealing with ecclesiastical as well as secular matters. Monks, who had forsaken their 'kin-law when [they bowed] to [monastic] rule-law' could not demand or pay compensation in a feud, but secular clergy could.[43] The code included the protection of the forests, which covered a third of the land. Outlawry, a sort of secular damnation, was introduced, a judgment only the king could remit. Raising revenue, eradicating heathenism, discouraging criminality and protecting life and property were paramount concerns. The tariff of punishments was clear: compensation to the victim and fines to the king were appropriate for most first offences. Second or third infractions merited increasingly severe forms of mutilation: punishing the body but preserving the soul.

Canute's code, issued in the early 1020s, built on those of his Anglo-Saxon predecessors rather than erased them,[44] and emphasised continuity. Specifically he invoked 'Edgar's law', which had taken on a talismanic quality like that later ascribed to the laws of Edward the Confessor. Both King Edgar and Canute shared similar concerns, they had similar priorities, and the foundations they had laid were easy to build upon as the Anglo-Saxons were relatively sophisticated in their edicts and procedures. But despite all this repeated intervention by the government, regional variations still prevailed and local custom often trumped central legislation.[45]

Wulfstan, through the king, sought to proclaim the Christian standards that all should observe – ruled and ruler – and held up godly kingship as an exemplar. The effect of this is seen in Canute's extraordinary instruction to his officials, contained in a letter written in 1027, on how the law was to be administered. Canute admitted that 'through the intemperance of youth' he had not always done right, but he pledged to do so, 'to rule faithfully [his] kingdoms and peoples and to maintain equal justice in all things'.

42　Charles Kingsley, Prelude to *Hereward the Wake* (London, 1866).
43　Fletcher, *Bloodfeud*, p. 118.
44　*EHD*, I, pp. 454–67.
45　The compilers of Domesday Book refer to the law of Wessex, of Mercia and of the Danelaw as separate entities.

I enjoin upon and command my counsellors ... that on no account, either from fear of me or to secure the favour of any powerful person, shall they henceforward consent to any injustice, or suffer it to flourish in all my realm. I also command all the sheriffs and reeves throughout my kingdom, as they wish to enjoy my goodwill or their own prosperity, to use no unjust violence against any man, rich or poor, but that impartial justice may be enjoyed by all, noble and common, rich and poor, but that all men ... shall have the right to secure justice under the law, from which they shall in no way deviate, either to obtain the king's favour, or out of respect for any powerful person, or for the sake of amassing money for me, for I have no need of money accumulated by iniquitous exactions.[46]

A just king, ruling within the law, was what Canute aspired to be in his latter years, not a tyrant. Unfortunately for the monarchy, some subsequent kings of England – most notably John and Charles I – were not averse to ignoring or abusing the law of the land to raise lucre for the royal treasury.

---

[46] GRA II.183.5–6.

CHAPTER 2

The Enforcement of the Law in Anglo-Saxon England

Mankind should be should be governed by wise laws well-administered.
Thomas Babington Macauley, *History of England*

Pagan and Christian alike realized that the law should be at once the recognition of an eternal truth and the solution by a community of one of its temporal problems. Rebecca West, *The New Meaning of Treason*

M ANY – perhaps most – disputes in Anglo-Saxon England would
have been settled between the parties without bothersome recourse to law, on the sensible basis that 'agreement trumps law, and love trumps judgment'.[1] Some were not. Courts were necessary to hear cases and make determinations, but also to mediate, or broker compromise. Over time the Anglo-Saxons developed a sophisticated network of assemblies, the hierarchy extending perhaps from manor and village courts, certainly through *burh* (or borough), hundred, and shire courts to the royal court – the *witanagemot* – where the king alone or with his ealdormen gave the final judgment in person.

Shires were largely mapped out before the Norman Conquest as Wessex, where they originated, imposed its authority on more and more of England. By the year 1000 there were thirty-two shires. Some such as Kent and Sussex were ancient kingdoms, others new creations. Many of the latter grew up around, and took their name from, *burhs*, fortified strategic points in which permanent markets found security. This network of territorial units, created by the kings, was placed under royal officials: ealdormen, and their deputies in each shire called 'shire-reeves' or sheriffs. It has been said that 'if the courts were the backbone of government, the king's reeves were the spinal cord'.[2] Each shire, at least from the tenth century when the smaller unit was first attested, was subdivided into hundreds, so-called because each one contained roughly a hundred homesteads, or provided a hundred fighting

---

[1] *LHP*, ch. 49, l. 5a: *Pactum enim legem vincit et amor iudicium.*
[2] Alan Harding, *The Law Courts of Medieval England* (London, 1973), p. 30.

men, or comprised a hundred hides (enough land to support a hundred families). They consisted of a group of villages, from ten to twenty in some areas to a mere two in Kent. Depending on population density they could vary from one square mile to several hundred square miles. Reflecting this, in the south there were up to ten times more hundreds than in the north – where under Danelaw they were called *wapentakes*. Hundreds formed the basic unit of local governance, each one boasting its own church, court and place of execution.

For a century before 1066, and for a century after, most of the ordinary judicial and administrative work was transacted in the hundred court.[3] It was central to resolving property disputes, and to maintaining the king's peace. It met monthly to conduct all sorts of business and biannually to review tithings so as to ensure that every free man was pledged and that crimes were being presented. Responsibility for the court lay with the reeve, whose tasks included collecting royal revenue as well as conducting judicial business, and whose jurisdiction often overlapped with that of the grander ealdorman. They could cooperate or compete. The hundred courts were usually open-air affairs, conveniently situated near bridges, fords or crossroads. Attendance by free men over the age of twelve was expected, even demanded. How often is not clear, but it was quite an imposition, emphasising the extraordinary importance Anglo-Saxon society placed on active involvement in the legal process, not just for the litigant but for the populace as a whole. Whose cause was just, who had committed the crime, what land belonged to whom, were matters decided by local laymen obliged to perform a community duty. Decisions were made by them and not by a judge.

By the time of King Edgar, borough courts met thrice a year and shire courts twice. The former presumably dealt with borough business, the latter with important regional matters, although the extent of their overlap with hundred courts is unclear.[4] Sheriffs presided over shire courts, and thegns, the local aristocracy, were active in giving judgment. It was here that they would learn and pass on traditional local customs. Sometimes the court was held in a townhouse, the hall of a castle, a monastery, or sometimes outdoors.[5] An assembly such as the shire court of Berkshire, meeting atop the Ridgeway at an Iron Age barrow known as Scutchamer Knob – sometimes

---

3   Abolished only in 1867.
4   *OHLE*, II, pp. 64f, 282.
5   P&M, II, pp. 555f; John Hudson, *The Formation of the English Common Law* (London, 1996), p. 35.

cruelly corrupted to Scotsman's Nob – would have been visible for miles around.

Some cases – particularly those concerning the king and his property, treason, or complaints from litigants aggrieved that they had not received justice from the lower court – came before a loftier tribunal: the king and his council. The king, under advice, could pronounce judgment in person. Although all these courts did not constitute an integrated system and many of their functions overlapped, by the tenth century England had a legal and administrative infrastructure unmatched in Europe.

In the transaction of the law there was no rigid division between Church and state. No separate system of ecclesiastical justice, as was to come into being in Norman and Angevin times, yet existed and there was no ecclesiastical court. While Church litigation could take place in synods, most routine disputes over tithes and marriages were heard in the hundred courts. Bishops and clergy were expected to participate with the laity in the administration of justice. Clergy were integral to trial by ordeal. Prelates together with magnates were expected to preside over shire and hundred courts as, for instance, Ealdorman Aethelwine and Bishop Aeswig did at Whittlesford in East Anglia.[6] These dignitaries, representing Church and state, were to administer both the secular and ecclesiastical law and ensure the smooth running of the business of the court. They were integral to the administration of justice. Whether or not they decided cases is unclear. There is evidence that bishops could give judgments, and impose harsh penalties, such as when Bishop Aelfheath of Winchester had an inveterate thief whipped and put in the stocks. They were also instrumental in reconciling parties and in the exercise of mercy. Canute instructed his reeves not only to govern justly, but to 'practise such mercy as the bishop of the diocese thinks just, and as can be supported'.[7]

Legal proceedings began in one of two ways. An accusation – later called an appeal of felony[8] – or a claim made orally by the aggrieved, and formally denied by the accused, was one. The other consisted of locals sworn for the purpose presenting the names of those suspected of criminality in their area. This system known as friborg or frankpledge – 'peace-pledge' – existed in all but three counties south of the Humber. It pre-dated the Conquest, can

---

6   *OHLE*, I, p. 17 note 56.

7   *EHD*, I, p. 453; *OHLE*, II, pp. 31ff, 49.

8   Appeal derives from the French *appeler* and amounts to an accusation. A felony was an offence so heinous as to break the bond between lord and vassal and justify the forfeiture of the felon's goods, and later of his life: John Langbein, Renée Lettow Lerner and Bruce Smith, *History of the Common Law* (New York, 2009), p. 29.

be traced back to Canute, and may have originated earlier.[9] It was a form of self-policing, of peer pressure: the compulsory sharing of responsibility. Free men over the age of twelve were formed into quasi-kinship groups of ten or twelve called tithings. They pledged neither to commit nor to consent to crime, and on pain of amercement – being fined – to bring before the court those suspected of wrongdoing. This was not a case of 'twelve good men and true', but as with so many things in English law it was a seed capable of future growth.

There remained the major problem of apprehending the malefactor. If he was not caught red-handed, but his identity was known, the victim or witnesses could raise the 'hue and cry', obliging every able-bodied man to do all in his power (*pro toto posse suo*[10]) to chase and catch the suspect. Those who successfully fled justice were declared outlaws. In a phrase of the time, they 'wore the wolf's head': they could be hunted like wolves, cornered, and killed at will.[11] While self-help such as this was utilised but regulated, feuding was restrained and vengeance was channelled into justice.

For those brought to trial there was not much examination of witnesses and little testing of evidence. This was no great loss. In many cases there were no witnesses to question and no evidence to test. It was a matter of accusation and denial, and judgment by those locals who had been summoned to attend the court, judgment based on repute. By contrast, in cases concerning land, charters, documents and local knowledge could be produced as evidence. If such were available there may have been no need to have recourse to the two other methods of proof commonly employed: oath or ordeal. These were imposed when conciliation failed or only suspicion persisted. Both were aspects of the *judicium dei*, God's judgment. In the context of a society deeply infused with religious belief and the terrors of hell, they were as effective a means of administering justice as could be found. They were beyond dispute, and had the added advantage of joining temporal justice to divine.

Where there was no more than neighbourhood suspicion that a person had committed a crime, the accused's own oath of exculpation, if he were of good repute, might suffice. In other cases where the suspect was 'untrustworthy' his oath could be tested by compurgation. If he swore that he was innocent and found the requisite number[12] of compurgators – or oath helpers

---

9   Frankpledge first appears in 1114 but the English term of the same meaning, *friborg*, is probably older: *OHLE*, II, pp. 169ff, 391f.

10   From which 'posse' derives.

11   *Leges Edwardi* in *OHLE*, II, p. 414.

12   The number was at the discretion of the judge, the participants the choice of the defendant: *OHLE*, I, p. 615.

– to swear to his character, he was acquitted. Oath helpers first appear in the Kentish laws of Hlophere and Eadric, and compurgation persisted for hundreds of years. This was not a method for thwarting justice, but the reverse. The oath, indeed, was akin to a form of ordeal, but one which depended for its efficacy on delayed divine judgment. Without eyewitness evidence, how could a court ever know if an accused was guilty or innocent, unless, of course, God Himself demonstrated it, either by His own direct devices, or by witnesses who knew the accused swearing on oath to his good character and 'oathworthiness'? The opinion of neighbours was important both in implicating an individual and in exonerating him. Compurgation was simple but often effective. It was not easy to persuade people to risk their immortal souls by perjury, or endanger their own reputation by testifying on behalf of ne'er-do-wells. Christian writers repeatedly warned of the extreme 'peril' involved in swearing false oaths.[13] Often the sworn testimony would be made upon holy relics, a mighty deterrent against false testimony. In many cases criminals could not obtain the prescribed number of compurgators.[14] In some cases, of course, bribery, sympathy with the accused, or his outstanding character might lead to the guilty going free, but that does not undermine the general utility of this mode of proof.

Oaths could also be used to settle property disputes. One good example is what happened at Scutchamer Knob in 990. A wealthy woman called Wynflaed laid claim against one Leofwine to the estates of Hagbourne and Bradfield in Berkshire. Her suit, at the insistence of Leofwine, was heard at the shire court before two bishops. She mustered an impressive array of illustrious oath helpers, including three least likely to lie and most likely to appeal to clerical judges: the abbot of Abingdon and the abbesses of Nunnaminster and Reading. In the end their oaths were 'left aside' (not needed) as the matter was resolved in her favour by arbitration. Just as well since otherwise 'there would afterwards be no friendship [between the parties]'.[15] In most disputes, civil or criminal, one side, or both, had to be lying. Perjured evidence would poison relations indefinitely and could lead to the perjurer being denied burial in consecrated ground: it was a portal to

---

13 James Whitman, *The Origins of Reasonable Doubt: Theological Roots of the Criminal Trial* (New Haven and London), p. 75.

14 Hudson, *Formation of the English Common Law*, p. 76.

15 A. J. Robertson, *Anglo-Saxon Charters* (Cambridge, 1939), pp. 137ff; Peter Hunter Blair, *Anglo-Saxon England* (Cambridge, 1956), pp. 218–19; Wormald, *Making of English Law*, pp. 151ff. Some 40% of extant Anglo-Saxon legal disputes ended this way, as do many civil cases to this day.

Hell. Oath-helping is one precursor of the jury system. Compurgators were called *juratores* in Latin and were usually numbered in twelves.[16]

Sometimes, especially if witnesses were reluctant to swear on oath, either because they feared feud, or for their immortal souls, the proof took a physical form – the ordeal. Trial by ordeal was not peculiar to England. The custom probably originated with the Franks, and it did so before their conversion to Christianity. It was first mentioned in the Salic Law of c.510, but was to spread throughout most of Europe. Pagan in origin, it thrived under Christianity for four hundred years. The first mention of its use in England dates to the tenth century, although there may be a reference to trial by cauldron in the laws of Ine c.690.[17]

It does not seem to have been a common procedure in Anglo-Saxon times, but was a last resort when all other contemporary methods of ascertaining the truth had failed. In the code of Canute it was applied to those untrustworthy souls who could not find compurgators. The ordeal was essential for those 'situations in which certain knowledge was impossible but uncertainty was intolerable', or 'where suspicion was considerable but guilt was not unquestionable'.[18] It afforded those maligned a chance of redeeming themselves, though even those who passed the ordeal were still stained by the accusation: it was the medieval equivalent of the Scots' 'not proven' verdict.[19] When deployed it was almost exclusively in criminal cases, including murder, arson, forgery, theft and witchcraft, and predominantly it was confined to the lower orders. Another distinction was that of all the varieties of ordeal only three regularly occurred in England: hot cauldron, hot iron, and cold water.[20] It was neither torture nor punishment but a means of discovering the truth, and of deterring crime.

---

[16] Harding, *Law Courts of Medieval England*, pp. 225f.

[17] Robert Bartlett, *Trial by Fire and Water, the Medieval Judicial Ordeal* (Oxford, 1986), pp. 4, 7.

[18] *Ibid.*, pp. 33, 64.

[19] In England and Wales a jury can bring in a verdict either of 'guilty' or 'not guilty'. In Scotland they have a third option of 'not proven', implying that the accused has escaped conviction only because of some slight doubt or technical inadequacy of evidence. No punishment accompanies such a verdict, other than the stigma of suspicion which may long linger.

[20] Others supposedly included the ordeal of the cross (in which the two adversaries stood with arms outstretched in the shape of a cross until one could maintain the pose no longer); the ordeal of walking on hot ploughshares (in which Queen Emma, mother of Edward the Confessor, triumphed with the help of St Swithun, but the account was apocryphal: Bartlett, *Trial by Fire and Water*, pp. 10f, 17f); the consumption of sanctified bread (upon which Earl Godwin of Wessex choked to death in 1053, having been accused of murder: Harding, *Law Courts of Medieval England*, pp. 27f).

Since God was intrinsic to this device, the ordeal was both sanctioned and administered by the Church. It could take place only at an episcopal see or other significant venue designated by a bishop. Because defendants were believers, only the truly innocent were likely to choose to endure trial by ordeal with the prospect of mutilation or execution following failure, and eternal damnation for the guilty who successfully passed. Guilty defendants would likely confess, run away or settle cases instead. Those who did opt for the ordeal were in for a highly regulated and lengthy procedure, and with a high chance of coming through it with success.

Free men and women were rarely put to the physical ordeal and when they were it was usually because they were deemed outside the legal world of oaths and compurgation, either because they were 'foreigners or the friendless',[21] or because they were of ill repute, and so were not 'oath worthy'. For them it was the ordeal of hot iron or water. In the former a metal bar was placed on the altar before Mass. The priest called down God's blessing: 'Bless, O Lord, through the strength of your power, this metal, removing every demonic falsehood and dispelling the magic and trickery of unbelievers, so that in it the truth of a most truthful judgment may be made clear to believers.'[22] Before the ordeal itself the priest prayed that 'the righteousness of justice should be manifested', and that God would deign to send his 'holy and true blessing on this iron, so that it should be a pleasing coolness to those who carry it with justice and fortitude, but a burning fire to the wicked'. The accused then had to walk a number of paces holding the hot iron, the hand was bound, and after three days inspected to see if it were healing cleanly. Similarly, in the latter, the hand would be plunged into a cauldron of boiling water to retrieve a stone, and then be bandaged.[23] A miracle acquitted the accused; to fester was a disaster.

The ordeal of cold water was reserved for male serfs. It was considered indecent for women and degrading for free men. The accused was taken to church at Vespers on the Tuesday preceding the ordeal, dressed in penitent's clothes and made to fast for three days, hearing matins and Mass. On the Saturday the priest began Mass and then told the accused he was not to take the sacrament if he had done the deed. If he did not confess, the Mass continued. The accused was led from the church to a pit twenty feet wide

---

21 So stated in the laws of Aethelred and Canute.

22 Quoted in Robert Bartlett, *England Under the Norman and Angevin Kings, 1075–1225* (Oxford, 2000), p. 181; *The Pontifical of Magdalen College*, ed. H. A. Wilson (London, 1910), pp. 179f.

23 *Decree concerning Hot Iron and Water*, in Andrew Reynolds, *Later Anglo-Saxon England: Life and Landscape* (Stroud, 1999), pp. 101f.

and twelve deep, bound with his hands under his knees, and with a rope tied around the loins. The priest blessed the water. A knot was made in the rope at a distance of the length of his hair and 'he shall be let down gently into the water so as not to make a splash. If he sinks down to the knot he shall be drawn up and saved.'[24] If he sank, the water had received him and he was innocent. If he floated he was guilty, and convicted by a miracle: the holy water, by rejecting him, was repelling evil.

In the Angevin period, when trial by ordeal, either by hot iron or cold water, was relatively commonplace, of the recorded cases 17% were tried by the former, and 83% – serfs – were tried by the latter. For both groups, just under two-thirds passed. On one occasion, twelve were subjected to the iron and twelve triumphed.[25] There is no reason to doubt that the pass rate was any lower in Anglo-Saxon times. What explains this high rate of acquittal? Some twelfth-century contemporaries believed that the rise of the confessional distorted the outcome of the ordeal. A guilty but contrite felon might confess and be absolved. If he then went to the ordeal, God would have to demonstrate his guiltlessness. Another explanation is that some priests may have not only supervised but ameliorated the ordeal – heating the iron moderately for instance – to produce the outcome they, as judges, deemed right. It was thought that most of those taking part in an ordeal were likely to be innocent – or why participate? – and so deserved to pass. In this the clergy were merely ensuring that the divine will was done and the means vindicated. Faith was a force for justice. Others may have succumbed to intimidation, or been seduced by bribery. How often they may have given God a helping hand we shall never know.

What is clear is that the system of ordeal ensured that the Church for four hundred years had a central role in the dispensation of justice. So successful was ordeal by fire and water that it survived undiminished until 1215, and only then was it killed off by the Church itself, when the Fourth Lateran Council prohibited clerical participation. With the divine sanction and imprimatur gone this method of proof was rendered useless. The same fate would befall judicial hanging many centuries later.[26]

The 'suitors' – those under a duty to attend the court – and in particular the thegns, delivered judgment, or announced a settlement. Goods would

---

24 W. L. Warren, *Henry II* (London, 1991), p. 283, note 1. The procedure described here is Angevin but is likely to be similar to that used in earlier times.

25 Bartlett, *Trial by Fire and Water*, pp. 79f; Bartlett, *England Under the Norman and Angevin Kings*, pp. 183f.

26 Harry Potter, *Hanging in Judgment: Religion and the Death Penalty in England from the Bloody Code to Abolition* (London, 1993).

be restored, and punishments pronounced. As kings increased their involvement in local justice, punishments were prioritised over compensation. As time went on they increased in severity, and hanging or beheading, as well as mutilation – ranging from branding to blinding and castration – became much more prominent. The death penalty was the ultimate punishment and went back to at least the seventh century when Ine's code mentions it for the first time, and archaeological evidence supports its use. Thieves were the most likely to be executed, as a deterrent to a prevalent crime, and offending slaves suffered the worst. Forfeiture could accompany outlawry or death.

Capital punishment was still kept within narrow bounds however. It was not appropriate for the very young, or for minor, or many first, offences. There was no desire to kill all and sundry nor to impose a 'bloody code'. That would wait a thousand years. A balance had to be kept between the dreadful exactions of justice and deterrence, and the need to preserve as well as punish the predominantly young men who committed most crimes. They were often at the peak of their productivity in a society which had much land to cultivate but which did not have a surfeit of idle and unemployed youths. Of the surviving Anglo-Saxon lawsuits only six record a death sentence.[27] The other striking feature is that Anglo-Saxon execution sites are consistently located on the boundaries of hundreds, boroughs or shires – on the edge of, but outside, civilised society.

One grisly example illustrates both aspects. A cemetery was found just off the Roman approach to the old Wessex capital of Winchester at a place called Harestock – meaning 'heads on stakes' – on the borough and hundred boundary. It comprised thirteen graves containing at least eighteen bodies of executed felons. The burials spanned from the second half of the ninth to the eleventh century, perhaps one every ten years. Other sites suggest a similar frequency.[28] Occasional executions served as an exemplar and a warning. An outlaw was taken to a prominent place on the border between civilisation and the wilderness, forced to kneel down with his hands behind his back, and beheaded. The severed head was displayed on a stake for the edification of passers-by. Sometimes for added effect the whole carcase would be gibbeted:

> One shall ride the high gallows and upon his death hang until his soul's treasury, his bloody bone-framed body, disintegrates.... He suffers his lot,

---

[27] Andrew Reynolds, 'Crime and Punishment', *The Oxford Handbook of Anglo-Saxon Archaeology* , ed. Helena Hamerow, David Hinton and Sally Crawford (Oxford, 2011), p. 895.

[28] *Ibid.*, p. 910.

pallid upon the beam, enveloped in the mist of death. His name is damned.[29]

Finally, the remains of the executed outcasts would be buried, from the tenth century at least, in unconsecrated ground. This landscaping of executions had no parallel in contemporary Europe. Once again an aspect of the criminal justice system seems unique to England.

From the tenth century the law of English kings intruded into their subjects' lives to an extent that had no Anglo-Saxon precedent or European parallel. While the English had laws, as yet there was no law of all England. But the infrastructure for a more unified and uniform legal system was coming into being. It is in criminal matters in particular, where royal involvement and responsibility was greatest, that 'we may detect the beginnings of law common to the whole kingdom'.[30] The maintenance of law and order, the strength of royal justice and the effective punishment of offences 'were a crucial contribution of the Anglo-Saxon period to the development of English law', which 'was moving to a position where, metaphorically if not literally, the king's writ would run throughout the realm'.[31] But it would do so in diverse ways, and localism with its varying customs was tolerated, accepted or even encouraged. Edgar stipulated that it was his will that 'among the Danes such good laws should be valid as they best appoint'. The law codes of Aethelred the Unready applied solely to those who lived in the Danish areas of the realm, and within his kingdom there were differing laws for Wessex, Mercia and the Danelaw.[32] They probably did not differ much except in detail.

Eleventh-century England was perhaps the best-run state in Europe, with a sound currency, an efficient tax structure, and a highly developed judicial system. The land was inhabited largely by different groups, hailing from different parts of Europe, subject in theory to one king, living harmoniously together, but possessing local customs and laws of their own. Anglo-Saxon England seemed a land at ease with itself. All that would suddenly change.

---

[29] W. S. Mackie, *The Exeter Book*, 2 vols (Oxford, 1934), I, p. 29.
[30] J. H. Baker, *An Introduction to English Legal History*, 4th edn (London, 2002), p. 9.
[31] *OHLE*, II, p. 199; Wormald, *Making of English Law*, pp. 27, 483.
[32] Hudson, *Formation of the English Common Law*, p. 17.

CHAPTER 3

A Norman Yoke?

Norman saw on English oak,
On English neck a Norman yoke:
Norman spoon in English dish,
And England ruled as Normans wish.

Walter Scott, *Ivanhoe*

The Saxon is not like us Normans. His manners are not so polite.
But he never means anything serious till he talks about justice and right.
When he stands like an ox in the furrow with his sullen set eyes on your own,
And grumbles, 'This isn't fair dealing', my son, leave the Saxon alone.

Rudyard Kipling, 'Norman and Saxon, A.D. 1100'

I N 1066 Duke William of Normandy landed at Pevensey Bay in East Sussex, and killed Harold, the last Anglo-Saxon king, at the battle of Hastings. England was conquered. Two meteors had collided. Edmund Burke called it 'the great era of our laws' when the poor stream of English jurisprudence was replenished 'as from a mighty flood'.[1] Later, F. W. Maitland, our pre-eminent legal historian, in a memorable phrase stated that 'the Norman conquest is a catastrophe which determines the whole future of English law'.[2]

Well was it and did it? Yes and no. The effects of the Norman Conquest are debated to this day. Certainly immigration, insemination and assimilation were nothing new. The Normans were the last in a long line of conquering invaders, from the Romans, through the Anglo-Saxons themselves, to the Vikings. They themselves were only just French, having been Norse raiders – or 'pirates' – until the early tenth century when they were granted settlement rights in what became the Duchy of Normandy. Nor were they strangers to England. Edward the Confessor's mother was Norman – she was William's great-aunt – Edward himself spent his youth in Normandy, and Norman clerics already held some ecclesiastical positions in England.

William 'the Conqueror' is somewhat misnamed, and it is not an appellation coined in his time – contemporaries called him 'the Bastard'. He did not see himself as conquering a foreign country, but as claiming, as King

---

[1] Edmund Burke, *Writings and Speeches*, 12 vols (New York, 2008), VII, pp. 487f.
[2] P&M, I, p. 79.

William I of England, his right – as lawful heir – to the throne of the Anglo-Saxons, a right usurped by Harold. Legitimacy was predicated on law and the continuity of law. William advanced on London slowly, more 'a royal progress than an enemy advance'.[3] He was crowned *Rex Anglorum* – King of the English – and made the same coronation promises to preserve peace, protect the Church, exercise justice with mercy, and uphold the old laws of England as his predecessors had done. He was coming into his own, not just despoiling a vanquished enemy. The Normans had not come to destroy and eradicate, but to displace and exploit. The conquerors were few, maybe ten thousand in a country with a population of perhaps two million. Of these, not all were Norman as some had come from other parts of France or Flanders. To ensure he remained on the throne, William needed them to stay in his new realm. Endowing them with land as he did, rather than paying them with gold, secured their continuing presence in England as his military muscle. They were warriors, but untutored. They could suppress a kingdom, but could they run it?

The English viewed these French invaders very differently from their Norse predecessors. The newcomers were aloof, and unwilling to assimilate or even treat the Anglo-Saxons as equals. Antagonism erupted into insurrection, and as a result England was changed enormously. The English could not be trusted. The Normans took increasing control: Anglo-Saxon aristocrats were virtually eradicated, and their lands seized and dispersed; native bishops were dispossessed; English sheriffs were replaced; the rebellious North was devastated and its inhabitants were left to starve; cathedrals were built to dominate the landscape and castles to intimidate the land; Norman names replaced Anglo-Saxon ones; English was dislodged as the language of literature and of the lawcourt. As a result of this fatal disaster, England became 'the residence of foreigners and the property of strangers'.[4]

Not all was lost. The English survived and their language and laws with them.[5] William and his heirs would specifically affirm the 'Law of Edward [the Confessor]', their Anglo-Saxon inheritance. The laws of England, 'which

---

3   *GRA* III.247.

4   *Ibid.*, 245.

5   It took a long time for English to reassert its dominance in the law courts. In 1362 parliament enacted that pleadings should be in English, and in 1650 that all judicial records should be printed, and all legal proceedings be conducted, in the vernacular. At the Restoration this was reversed until 1731, when, in almost identical wording, parliament decreed that all proceedings in the law courts were to be 'in the English tongue and language only, and not in *Latin* or *French*'. *EHD*, IV, p. 483; V(b), p. 1231; X, p. 237.

had served as a fixed point amidst the disruptions of the 1016 conquest could ... be reassembled as one anchor in the cyclonic conditions created by that of 1066'.[6] If the Norman Conquest had not taken place legal developments would have been different, but to what extent and in what ways we cannot know. Would England have undergone a different indigenous development, or capitulated to Roman jurisprudence? The former is inevitable, the latter unlikely. Ironically, having been conquered by a continental power, England, in contrast to her unconquered neighbour Scotland, did not adopt a continental legal system. The Conquest was the fertile womb in which was conceived that mixed-race offspring of Anglo-Saxon and Norman parentage called the English common law.

The Normans had no written law of their own making, nor could they readily borrow one from their French neighbours. Their invasions occurred in the 'very midnight of the legal history of France'; indeed, 'they brought the midnight with them'.[7] They arrived in a kingdom better administered than any other in Europe, and whose basic structures of government William inherited and gratefully adopted. England's laws and legal infrastructure were Anglo-Saxon in origin, but had been tempered by Viking settlers, Norsemen like the Normans themselves. Those laws intruded into everyday life to an extent unparalleled elsewhere. Why eradicate the most sophisticated and lucrative legal system in Europe? The English had proved better at running their country than defending it.

The king remained central to the law. Although he was occasionally obliged to supplement it, William proclaimed that he was upholding the law of his Anglo-Saxon predecessor. He was conscious of being the fount of justice and that he had inherited a creative and directional role regarding the law. He continued to hear cases that impacted on himself. He continued to adjudicate between the senior clergy or nobility, or between them and their tenants, especially over land. Absentee as he often was, William relied increasingly on terse written instructions under the royal seal, called writs. It was an important development, but whether it was contingent on the Conquest is uncertain as writs pre-dated the Conquest. William initially continued issuing writs in English, but from the 1070s, as the king was forced by rebellion to rely increasingly on foreigners to serve him in place of untrustworthy Englishmen, Latin became the norm. The language of the writs may have changed, but their form and meaning continued to reflect the authoritarianism of Anglo-Saxon government. William greatly increased

6   Wormald, *Making of English Law*, pp. 481f.
7   P&M, I, p. 65.

their use in commanding local courts to hear cases, and extended their remit, from initiating proceedings in matters concerning the Crown to bringing disputes between subjects into the shire courts.[8] He garnered a reputation for being a just ruler and one who kept 'good order' in – or cowed – the land so that 'a young girl, laden with gold, could travel unharmed through the kingdom'.[9] If he did replace capital punishment with blinding and castration for criminal offences such as rape, this was not suggestive of mercy. It was to provide a walking or crawling deterrent. Many preferred to die than to live dismembered and disfigured.

The 'Norman Yoke', the supposed suppression of traditional English freedoms under an alien heel, is largely myth. Freedom was far from the birthright of all in Anglo-Saxon England. It had been a slave-holding culture. Domesday Book recorded that slaves made up between one tenth and one quarter of the rural population. In contrast, their numbers declined after the Conquest and petered out by 1135.[10] Nor had there been equality before the law. From Aethelbert of Kent to Edward the Confessor, status mattered for credibility and compensation. In Mercia the oath of a thegn was reckoned to be worth that of six ceorls (lower-ranking freemen). Canute's laws penalised the violation of the king's protection at five pounds, that of an archbishop or aetheling (prince) at three, and that of an ealdorman at two.[11] The biggest distinction, of course, was between the free and the enslaved. How much the lower strata of society were adversely affected by the Conquest is questionable.

Nonetheless, after the Conquest, in nervous reaction to the continuing resistance of the English, there was a short period of unparalleled oppression. The only contemporary writer specifically to use the term 'yoke' was the Anglo-Norman Orderic Vitalis, born in Shropshire 1075, who did so twice in one page. He wrote that 'the English were groaning under the Norman yoke, and suffering oppressions from the proud lords' who 'oppressed all the native inhabitants ... and heaped shameful burdens on them'. The worst offenders were the vice-regents, the king's own half-brother Bishop Odo, and kinsman William FitzOsbern, who 'were so swollen with pride that they would not deign to hear the reasonable plea of the English or give them impartial judgment.' They protected their own men, even if guilty of murder

---

8   M. T. Clanchy, *Early Medieval England*, Folio Society edn (London, 1997), p. 30; OHLE, II, pp. 258f; Marjorie Chibnall, *The Debate on the Norman Conquest* (Manchester, 1999), pp. 92f.

9   *EHD*, II, p. 164; *Henry*, p. 32.

10   OHLE, II, pp. 424ff.

11   *Ibid.*, pp. 202f.

or rape, and punished instead their accusers. Injustice and inequality were at the very heart of the complaint, and so 'the English groaned aloud for their lost liberty and plotted ceaselessly to find some way of shaking off the yoke that was so intolerable and unaccustomed'.[12] This yoke, he acknowledged, was later lifted. An eyewitness to the events he related, Orderic contrasted the dispossessed magnates and starving peasants he had seen in his youth with a land that was peaceful and prosperous less than fifty years later, under Henry I.[13] Another mixed-race and near-contemporary historian, Henry of Huntingdon, largely supported this contention. While viewing the Norman invaders as surpassing all others in savagery, sent by God to 'wipe out the English nation', in the longer term he considered that, having suddenly and completely subdued the land, they had granted the conquered their life, liberty, and their ancient laws.[14]

Consequently the Conquest did not result in any lasting division between laws for the conquerors and conquered, even though there is evidence of separate jurisdictions persisting for a time, hardly conducive to the creation of a common law. In 1075 the rebel Earl Waltheof was tried for treason under English law, while his Breton and Norman co-conspirators were subject to 'the laws of the Normans'.[15] The former was put to death, the latter were imprisoned.

Draconian and divisive laws were, however, introduced by the Norman kings to extend their precious woodlands and protect their game from being exploited, or enjoyed, by the locals. Vast tracts of land extending far beyond the royal demesne were considered to be part of the royal forest – a hundred years or more after the Conquest it still constituted one third of the realm. Much was ordinary land declared to be forest, thereby allowing the king a monopoly over the management and use of its resources, rights previously enjoyed by local landowners. In William's creation, the New Forest, people were evicted, villages rooted up, and the hunting and snaring of game prohibited, so that 'the habitation of wild beasts' could be enlarged and preserved intact for Norman sport, as well as for wood-felling and mineral extraction. No unlicensed hounds were allowed within the forests and in Henry I's time the feet of dogs merely living nearby were hambled – lamed so as to make them unfit for hunting.[16] These designated areas were subject to the forest

---

12 *OV*, II, p. 203.
13 *Ibid.*, V, pp. 294ff.
14 *Henry*, p. 31.
15 *OV*, II, pp. 314–18.
16 *OV*, VI, p. 100.

laws, which could vary from place to place. Penalties, pecuniary or corporeal, for infractions were severe, and included capital punishment under William Rufus for poaching stags, and blinding and castration under Henry I for forest offences. Only such savage measures could ensure obedience to such unpopular laws. Not only unpopular, they were also exceptional, based not on the 'common law of the realm but upon the will and disposition of the monarch, in such wise that whatsoever has been done in accordance with its laws may be termed not *absolutely* just, but *just according to the law of the forest*.[17] This was personal law protecting privilege, not common law upholding justice.

Initially, the invaders, worried by their vulnerability in a hostile land, divided the nation along racial lines: the *Franci* and the *Anglici*. The former developed a distaste for being ambushed and killed by the latter. The law was deployed as a deterrent. Before the Conquest *murdrum* was the name given to any 'secret killing': out of sight and hearing, and where the slayer was unknown. Not so afterwards. To murder was to kill a Norman – all murder victims were presumed to be French. Should the killer remain unknown, or unapprehended, the hundred within which the corpse was found would have to pay the hefty *murdrum* or murder fine. A coroner would convene a jury of men over twelve years of age from four or more neighbouring vills. They viewed the body, recorded the wounds, and determined if the death were natural, accidental or felonious. They also received any 'presentment of Englishry', which would obviate the murder fine by rebutting the presumption that the victim was French.[18] This division in death would persist until Henry II oversaw that great amalgamation into one united realm, neither Anglo-Saxon nor Norman. When all at last spoke a common tongue, and all thought of themselves as English, the *murdrum* fine would be extended to cover *all* unexplained deaths of freemen.[19] All freemen in England would be subject to the same law, the law common to all England.

One Norman innovation was the introduction of trial by battle, an early example of adversarial justice.[20] Found in the early law codes of many Germanic peoples though not in those of the Anglo-Saxons, this means of proof was imported as an alternative to ordeal in criminal accusations – especially treason – and in property disputes. In the latter, paid champions

---

[17] The late twelfth-century *Dialogue of the Exchequer, EHD*, II, p. 528.
[18] A similar payment may have been made in Canute's day for the slaying of a Dane. *OHLE*, II, pp. 407ff.
[19] *EHD*, II, p. 523.
[20] *Ibid.*, pp. 399f.

could stand in for the contesting parties. In the former, accused and accuser battled it out themselves, if the accused demanded it. It did not have a sacral character, since it did not involve priestly participation in a ritualised ceremony, nor miraculous intervention to make natural elements behave in unnatural ways. Nor was it chivalrous: more a brutal brawl between peasants with hammers or sharpened sticks than a duel between beautifully attired and expensively armed gentlemen.[21] No holds were barred, and recourse was routinely had to wrestling, gouging and biting. After all, as one contemporary expert noted, good incisors 'are of great assistance in winning a fight'.[22] This rather militated against justice as some accusers – especially those suffering from dental decay – were put off pursuing a grievance or accusation.

The most detailed account of one such bloody encounter dates to 1221, but it is likely to reflect proceedings in the preceding century and a half. One Thomas, of Eldersfield near Tewkesbury in Gloucestershire, was accused by George, a drinking companion and local lord of the manor, of burglary and wounding. Thomas denied both accusations and refused to pay compensation. The jury of neighbours decided that there was a case to answer, and so the matter was sent to Worcester for trial. The accusation dated back to 1217 but the trial could not take place until it could be held before the royal justices, since burglary amounted to the breach of the king's peace. Thus in 1221 on Kingsmead meadow near the cathedral, the two men fought it out armed with clubs and shields, but resorting to teeth and nails. His right eye half out, it was Thomas who cried 'craven', admitting defeat. In mercy, the judges did not order his hanging as well they might, merely his castration and exoculation, thus enabling him to save his soul by penance. The punishment was carried out by the victor and his friends in front of a large crowd of eager spectators. They set to with gusto, 'moved more by the pleasure of revenge than the love of justice', gouging out his eyeballs and tossing Tom's testicles into the watching crowd, where the local lads kicked them at the girls for sport. There was a happy ending to this story though: after ten days of incessant prayer a miracle restored his missing parts, or so the tale goes.[23]

Despite preserving some significant legal distinctions between themselves and the subject populace, the Normans were content to accept important elements of English custom. Life went on in England and English law with it. Some hundred courts were absorbed into the private jurisdiction of great

---

[21] Hudson, *Formation of the English Common Law*, p. 75.

[22] *Bracton*, II, p. 410.

[23] F. W. Maitland, ed., *Pleas of the Crown for the County of Gloucester 1221* (London, 1884), no. 87, pp. 21f, 141f.

lords, but this fate did not befall the majority, while shire – or county – courts were preserved as vehicles of royal authority. Henry I directed that '*my* counties and hundreds' meet in the same places and at the same times as in the days of King Edward and not otherwise, and that they be utilised just as before.[24] The survival of Anglo-Saxon infrastructure under royal control was crucial to the development of the common law and is in stark contrast to the loss of control of equivalent courts by the kings of post-Carolingian France.[25] Vitally, the procedures of local justice were largely untouched, and were still administered by the sheriff. He was the lynchpin of royal local administration, a 'precious Anglo-Saxon legacy, one of those "good things" of the Old English monarchy which the new dynasty carefully preserved'.[26] While the native Anglo-Saxon office-holders were increasingly replaced by Normans, many of whom were barons, the sheriff continued to act according to the old and differing customs prevailing throughout the realm.

The persistence of these Anglo-Saxon institutions, the apparatus of royal bureaucracy which deployed writs to communicate with the sheriff, and Domesday Book, William I's great national survey, were all crucial to what was to prove the single most innovative and significant legal contribution that the Normans were to make: the transformation of land tenure. For them, landowning and lordship were intertwined. Legally the Conquest marked a new start: no one other than the king had a title to property that pre-dated 1066. Every landholder held directly from the king or from a lord who held from the king. All entitlement stemmed from the Conquest. The distribution of the spoils among the victors ensured that this new concept of tenurial dependance on the king would be established irrevocably in England.

Created twenty years into William's reign, Domesday Book was integral to the project in two ways. It attempted to disguise the radical novelty of tenurial dependance by assuming it was long-established, and it provided an inventory of the entire kingdom and of the holding and value of the land in it, both in the time of Edward and of William. Designed to be used by royal administrators in raising revenue, Domesday's primary concern was with royal properties and with tenants-in-chief. It also benefited the magnates in giving them something akin to a written title to their lands. It was astonishingly detailed and thorough, even recording the fines or alternative punishments locally imposed for offences. The brewer of bad beer

---

[24] *OHLE*, II, p. 273.
[25] *Ibid.*, p. 284.
[26] R. C. Van Caenegem, *The Birth of the English Common Law*, 2nd edn (Cambridge 1988), p. 13.

in Chester, for instance, unless he paid four shillings to the reeves, would end up *in cathedra stercoris* – 'in the shit-seat'. The way and speed with which the facts were compiled showed how the Normans were prepared and able to utilise existing Anglo-Saxon institutions and how much information those institutions could quickly provide. Domesday has no parallel in the history of medieval Europe. The king dispatched justices to every shire to make enquiry of juries, half French and half English, the latter being local people familiar with English customs, who could swear on oath as to how much arable land there was, the revenues expected from river, marsh and wood, and when and by whom such a piece of land was sold or let or bequeathed.[27] Long before they were incorporated into criminal trials, juries were becoming fundamental to civil litigation. This had begun before the Conquest but continued thereafter.

One other crucial change William made was to separate temporal from spiritual jurisdictions, as was common continental practice. In an ordinance, issued probably in the 1070s, he declared that henceforth no bishop or archdeacon was to engage in pleas involving ecclesiastical law in the hundred court, and that criminal cases falling foul of Church laws were to be tried by a bishop in a place of his choosing and 'according to the canons and episcopal laws'. No royal official could interfere 'with the laws that pertain to the bishop'.[28] William's legacy would have far-reaching if unintended effects in the years to come. He had severed secular matters from ecclesiastical ones. Canon law, which became the first law common to all England, took a different tack. It separated lay people from clerics: while the former were still subject to Church courts for spiritual offences, the latter were no longer subject to temporal courts at all.

William himself had no trouble keeping the Church in check and the clergy under control. Notably the odious Odo had been put on trial in the secular court – to salve clerical scruples Lanfranc, the canny archbishop of Canterbury, provided the excuse that it was not the bishop of Bayeux who was being tried but the earl of Kent.[29] Such sleight of hand would not long prevail. In succeeding reigns the ecclesiastical courts would become the preserve and protection of the clergy, a refuge for dangerous criminal elements. To be deemed a cleric was to remove the miscreant from the jurisdiction of the civil authorities, who would execute punishment without mercy, and to place him under the bishop who would merely ensure that his

[27] *Henry*, p. 30.
[28] *OHLE*, I, pp. 108f; II, pp. 297f.
[29] *OV*, IV, pp. 42f.

sin was purged. Many serious offences were dealt with by penance. William of his own volition had unwittingly deprived his successors of their prey.

England was transformed by the Normans and the Normans by England. Ultimately the conquerors were conquered: in time and through inter-breeding they too became English; in time they were accepted as such. Assimilation and acquiescence would take a hundred years. It had happened before – the Normans were not merely conquerors, they were chameleons. Their tenth-century Viking forebears had been granted Normandy – 'North-man's land' – and a century later referred to themselves as *Franci*, French. Within a similar period of time these erstwhile *Franci* would become *Anglici*, English. The loss of Normandy in 1204 was merely the final sloughing off of an old skin.

So far as the law was concerned, Norman rule was anything but a disaster. It was a catalyst. Gradually, the blending of slowly developing customs on both sides of the Channel, and the combination of Norman discipline and flair for strong government with Anglo-Saxon sophistication and infrastruc-ture produced a legal system very different from elsewhere in Europe. In embryo the 'methods and characteristics of a common law were beginning to emerge'.[30] The Norman kings allowed their English subjects to pursue their varied and ancient legal traditions in the context of a stability engendered by strong, stable government and a sound administration. Kings were both the unifying force and symbols of continuity.

William the Conqueror died in 1087, and was succeeded in turn by two of his sons, William II and Henry I. The former was damned in his own day – and according to contemporaries for all eternity, being buried 'on the day after his perdition' – as an unjust, rapacious and exploitative despot under whom 'England was miserably stifled and could not breath.'[31] This appraisal is currently and successfully being challenged. His great monument is West-minster Hall, built around 1097 and by far the largest building of this sort in western Europe, upon which he spared no expense 'to secure an effect of open-handed splendour'.[32] In that, Rufus was conspicuously successful. He did not know it, but this was to be his lasting legal legacy.

By contrast, Henry I was, and is, generally considered to be a great king, renowned for his wisdom, fulfilling the prophecy of Merlin as 'the lion

---

[30] Chibnall, *Debate on the Norman Conquest*, pp. 92, 105.
[31] *Henry*, p. 48.
[32] *GRA* IV.321.

of justice at whose roar the dragons tremble'.[33] He was also ruthless, and successful. He knew the importance of uniting his kingdom under a strong king. By wedding, within months of his accession, Matilda, the daughter of the king of Scots and great-granddaughter of Edmund Ironside, he married into the old English royal line, and their progeny would be Anglo-Norman. In the person of their son William it was thought that 'the hope of England, once cut down like a tree, was again to blossom and bear fruit, so that one might hope the evil times were coming to an end'.[34] That hope was dashed on the rocks when this headstrong teenager was drowned off Barfleur in 1120, but for thirty-five years Henry was to prove a unifying and steadying force for a fractured land.

In 1100 Henry inaugurated his reign by circulating a 'Coronation Charter', a manifesto of good intent, in which the new king promised to 'abolish all the evil customs by which the kingdom of England has been unjustly oppressed', and promised neither to exploit his subjects nor impoverish them. He saved his wrath for 'moneyers' who debased the coinage and upon whom 'true justice' would be visited.[35] He was particularly lauded, as his father and Anglo-Saxon forbears had been, for the 'inflexible standard' of that justice: 'At the beginning of his reign, so that by fearful example he might make a lasting impression on evildoers, he was more inclined to mutilation of limbs, later to require monetary payments.'[36]

After twenty-four years on the throne Henry's inclination, at least towards the bugbear of corrupt moneyers whose actions impoverished the people, remained the same: during the Christmas festivities in Normandy he sent orders to England to have all moneyers deprived of their testicles and right hands. Mercifully they were allowed to enjoy the festive season, as the orders were not executed until the New Year.[37] To enhance his authority, Henry emphasised that he was one in a long line of English kings who had preserved and perpetuated the laws of their predecessors. It was a golden age for historians, and pedlars of myth, whose task it was to resurrect the past and to connect it to the present. From early in his reign Henry upheld continuity. He stipulated that shire and hundred courts should be held in the same places and on the same terms as in Edward's day. Both the *Textus Roffensis*,

33 Geoffrey of Monmouth, *History of the Kings of Britain*, Folio Society edn (London, 2010), p. 101.
34 *GRA* I.419.2.
35 *EHD*, II, pp. 400ff.
36 *GRA* V.411.
37 *EHD*, II, p. 192; *Henry*, p. 58.

and the *Leges Henrici Primi* date from his reign. The former preserved on vellum the ancient codes of England's infancy. The latter reflected the chaotic legal practices at the time of its composition. It is a confusing ragbag collection of old legal traditions, rooted in the dooms of Anglo-Saxon kings, and modified by the Anglo-Normans. The author tries, stumbles, despairs, but hardly succeeds in integrating them into England's first legal treatise.

With royal authority re-established, the royal grip was tightened. Henry raised 'from the dust men of common stock' – men who were his creatures. He asserted the central control of the *curia regis* – the king's council – over the administration of the kingdom, including the enforcement of justice. He intervened where local justice was wanting, summoning litigants before a royal court, or ordering settlement by royal writ. Sometimes, at the expense of barons, he appointed loyal officers of his household as sheriffs. In addition he strikingly innovated in despatching 'justices in eyre'[38] around the land to preside over shire courts, hearing cases of concern to the king, and dispensing the hard imprint of royal justice. Many justices were also sheriffs. One such was Ralph Basset. In the ominous days before Christmas in 1124 he held court in Leicestershire and hanged 'there more thieves than had ever been hanged before, forty-four men altogether, and six who were deprived of their eyes and testicles'.[39] Such visitations as took place in the reign of Henry I may have been sporadic and restricted in range, and did not overturn the role of the local people in delivering judgments, but they were an assertion of royal dominance, dramatic, and pregnant with potential.

Henry not only maintained the law of Edward the Confessor – and so of his Danish and Anglo-Saxon forebears – 'strengthened as it was by the reforms introduced by his blessed father', but improved it 'with his own laws'. The shire courts were central to the rule of law, before which were heard most serious criminal cases and most land disputes, especially between vassals of different lords. Over and above these and all other courts stood 'the pleas of the royal court', which preserved 'the use and custom of its law at all times and in all places and with constant uniformity'. There were references in this period to the 'law of the realm' and the 'law of the land': the country was once again becoming more united, the laws more uniform. In the autumn of content at the end of Henry's long days, peace and prosperity, law and order reigned in England.

---

[38] Itinerant Justices – eyre deriving from an Old French word meaning a journey or wandering.
[39] *EHD*, II, p. 191.

Then disaster. On 1 December 1135 Henry died after gorging on the indigestible delicacy, lampreys.[40] He left no legitimate male heir, but two bickering claimants: his daughter Matilda and his nephew Stephen. The latter struck first and usurped the throne. Civil war ensued. The prolonged conflict, called the Anarchy or the Nineteen-Year Winter, was a pitiless time when, according to the Anglo-Saxon Chronicle (another survival of the Conquest), 'Christ and his saints slept.' Their somnolence coincided with a breakdown in law and order and an erosion of royal power concomitant with the growth of that of the barons. Where they did not rob, or burn, or kill, these warlords levied taxes on the villages, calling it 'protection money'.[41]

Vitally, however, the period of disruption was too short to sustain a loss of royal control over local justice. The survival of Henry I's legacy ensured that future legal development would be built on the foundations of 'a long-established and specifically English system'.[42] Matilda's son would be that builder, but he would do more than merely reconstitute what had gone before. He would construct a system more uniform, more centralised, more dependent on the king's courts and his representatives. He would construct a uniform law for a united realm.

---

[40] *Henry*, p. 64.
[41] *EHD*, II, p. 200.
[42] Wormald, *Making of English Law*, p. 266.

4

Henry II and the Creation of the Common Law

Justicia regnorum fundamentum – Justice is the foundation of kingdoms.
Latin proverb

Wisdom enough he had for his work, and work enough for his wisdom.
Thomas Fuller, *Church History of Britain*

Hope reposed in the twenty-one-year-old Henry of Anjou. His ascension to the throne in 1154 was anticipated in words Shakespeare would later echo: 'England, long numbed by mortal chill, now you grow warm by the heat of a new sun.'[1] The thaw came just in time. Much of the kingdom, including the legal system, was in jeopardy, and justice was administered in a haphazard and arbitrary manner. The proliferation of laws and the combination of Anglo-Saxon and Norman practices had led to overlapping jurisdictions, delay and confusion. The recent troubles had left courts prey to subversion by powerful noblemen, who were often laws unto themselves in their localities. Increasingly, subjects, despairing of the maze of feudal, communal and ecclesiastical courts and laws, placed their hope in royal intervention. The king alone could deliver them from the legal mire. This king could and would.

The young and vigorous Henry II had a kingdom to pacify, disputes that had grown gangrenous during the civil war to resolve, revenue to raise, and a continental empire to run. He had also to be a law-maker and law-enforcer. He took very seriously his coronation oath to ensure justice and peace for the realm. Henry had no need to invent completely new laws and procedures, but to consolidate, and to build upon proven existing ones. He abolished nothing, but succeeded in combining all the local customary laws into a law common to the country as a whole. The transformation was effected by setting up an alternative system of justice, in which old practices were rationalised and selected precedents fused together with 'the transmuting touch of intelligence'.[2] He swung into frantic and meddlesome action. First he had to regain control of the localities. He did this by two means: reining in the

---

[1] *Henry*, p. 96.
[2] Warren, *Henry II*, p. 317; Hudson, *Formation of the English Common Law*, p. 22.

sheriffs by disciplinary action, and reasserting royal authority by regularly despatching his own men around the realm to administer his business and enforce his laws.

His efforts at cowing the sheriffs began in 1155 when the king removed twenty-one of them, and culminated in 1170 with the 'Inquest of Sheriffs', which delved into the extent of their exploitation of the country. As a result Henry removed the great majority, replacing most of them with officials of the Exchequer who had neither regional loyalties nor independent power bases. They were accountable to the king alone, and could be removed at will. Their powers would be eroded as those of royal justices increased, as evidenced particularly in the 1176 Assize of Northampton. The king had reversed the tendency of sheriffs 'to drift from being royal appointees to being local grandees, as had happened with the counts and viscounts of France and Germany earlier in the Middle Ages'.[3]

To extend the imprint of royal authority over the whole kingdom depended on delegation, the development of which is one of the greatest achievements of the Norman and Angevin kings.[4] It arose out of necessity, a necessity most acute in the reign of Henry II. He had imperial pretensions, and vast French estates. Because the king was often abroad, or busy on other business, the practice arose of having a chief justiciar to deputise in his absence. Robert de Beaumont, earl of Leicester, and Richard de Lucy were probably the first such appointees, though some would give this distinction to Roger, bishop of Salisbury, in the reign of Henry I. They held vice-regal power, administering the financial and legal business of the kingdom. But more needed to be done to make royal authority everywhere ever-present, and there was a precedent. The practice of visitations by justices in eyre introduced by Henry I, although falling into disuse during the 'Anarchy', was a device that his namesake could use to his advantage. Henry II revived and extended it. Ostensibly this was part of his conservative restoration of everything as it was in the time of his grandfather. In reality it was innovation cloaked in tradition. It took time to hone this tool of royal resurgence. It was not until twelve years into his reign that the king was in a position to impose his will on the whole country.

In 1166, a date according to Maitland more significant than 1066, Henry II, after consulting his bishops and barons, promulgated the Assize of Clarendon, the first of the great legislative enactments of his reign, the earliest evidence for the great administrative changes he had introduced, and

---

3 Bartlett, *England Under the Norman and Angevin Kings*, p. 150.
4 Baker, *Introduction to English Legal History*, p. 19.

a landmark in the history of the jury. 'For the preservation of peace and the maintenance of justice', itinerant justices were to make enquiries through the old juries of presentment, consisting of twelve lawful men from each hundred and four from each vill. These were not jurors as we would understand them. They did not weigh up evidence and reach a verdict. Instead they were 'to speak the truth' and name those in their area who had been 'accused or notoriously suspect of being a robber, murderer or thief', or had 'received' any such 'since the lord king has been king'. Sheriffs were to cooperate in hunting down and arresting those suspected 'through the oath of this assize'. They were to bring them to trial before the royal justices, without any regard to the rights and privileges claimed by the holders of franchises – individuals or corporations authorised by royal mandate to hold courts. Lords who enjoyed franchisal rights, and privileged communities such as boroughs, and even 'the honour of Wallingford', were forbidden to exclude the sheriff, as they normally did, and to claim jurisdiction over the criminals arrested. Instead they were ordered to assist the sheriffs in making arrests.[5] The king was firmly in control.

Those caught red-handed and of ill repute, and those who admitted their offence, should have 'no law' and were to be punished without trial. Others accused of robbery, murder or theft, either by individual appellors or by communal accusation delivered by juries of presentment, were to be tried not as the shire court saw fit, but in a specified way and under royal judges. A case could be proved by inquisition, battle or ordeal. The near-contemporary treatise on the laws and customs of England (*De Legibus et Consuetudinibus Angliae*), known as *Glanvill*, considered that battle was the routine method of proof between male appellors and male accused unless old age or serious injury precluded it. In such cases the recourse was to ordeal. The assize mentioned only one form: water, a method previously reserved for serfs, but with the major advantage of giving immediate results, and so preferable to hot iron when dealing with a multitude of offenders. For *Glanvill*, however, the type of ordeal was still determined by social status: hot iron for the free, cold water for the villein. The plea rolls from 1194 to 1214 show the use of both, with water greatly predominating.[6] The use of the ordeal was being greatly extended, well beyond the hard cases for which it had previously

---

5   *EHD*, II, p. 408. There is a precursor of such compelled accusation in a law from the time of Aethelred the Unready requiring twelve thegns to denounce all 'malefactors' in their community.

6   *Glanvill*, ch. xiv; Hudson, *Formation of the English Common Law*, p. 177; Bartlett, *Trial by Fire and Water*, p. 66.

been deployed. Those who failed the test were either hanged or suffered the amputation of a foot.[7] A boon for the treasury, the guilty also forfeited their chattels to the king.

By the 'revising' Assize of Northampton in 1176, 'for the sake of stern justice', the right hand was added to the limbs to be severed, exile within forty days was included in the punishment, and arsonists and forgers were added to the Clarendon list of serious offences, as were those guilty of the undefined 'any other felony.' Some or all felonies constituted 'Pleas of the Crown', another fluid category but denoting serious matters touching the king and so coming under the sole jurisdiction of his justices. Those caught and condemned for felonies would die, and those who fled would be outlawed. Even those who were 'cleared of guilt at the water', but had been accused of 'murder or some other base felony by the common report of the county and of the lawful knights of the country' were forced to abjure the realm. Should they return they would be outlaws. Those less notorious had merely to find sureties for good behaviour. Despite divine exoneration, therefore, a strong presumption of guilt was held to reside in those accused and of ill repute.[8] Bad character was of increasing significance to the law.

But bad character could be put to good use: notorious criminals who were caught, confessed and were condemned could be induced to implicate and convict their fellows by a promise that their lives would be spared. These reprobates were called 'approvers' because they had to prove the case against one or more of their accomplices in trial by battle. If they won they received a degree of mercy, although exile would be imposed or mutilation inflicted. If they were defeated they were hanged. As in later days such men were reviled, and it was often thought that they would be prone to accuse innocent parties who were least able to defend themselves.

As the first-fruits of Clarendon, Richard de Lucy and Geoffrey de Mandeville, earl of Essex, were sent out on a grand tour of inspection. This was the first such visitation of Henry II's reign and probably the first since the death of Henry I. They rode far and wide. When they reached Carlisle the earl rather inconveniently died, but before his demise they had visited many a shire, with dramatic results. In Lincoln, 105 cases came before these royal officials. A lesser offence, such as when a man called Hugo de Kirketon absented himself from a judicial duel, merited a one mark fine; a middling one, twenty shillings; a more serious, forty shillings or even five pounds.

---

7   These punishments are not found in the Assize of Clarendon, but are referred to as being so at the beginning of the Assize of Northampton: *EHD*, II, p. 411.

8   *EHD*, II, p. 411.

In all, £250 was owed to the king, no mean sum as it was enough to pay for twenty knights or 165 foot soldiers for a year.[9] County records show the effectiveness of these itinerant justices in eradicating or at least stemming an age-old problem: how to deal with notorious and persistent offenders. In 1166 the sheriff of Lincolnshire reported that thirty-nine felons had either fled or failed their ordeals, while Norfolk and Suffolk reported 101 and York-shire 127. Those counties not yet visited showed meagre results. Hampshire had brought four felons to justice, Wiltshire three, Worcestershire one, and Shropshire none. All told around 600 were put to the ordeal and failed, or fled at the prospect. Flight became increasingly normal, resulting in fewer convictions, but indicative of the success of the system, and of the fear it induced.

So successful were these early visitations that from around 1175 the king made them both systematic and national. They became 'general eyres', country-wide visitations by groups of royal officials, transformed into judges – *iusticiarii in itinere* – and armed with specific powers and duties, going on one of the several circuits into which England was newly divided. The number of circuits and the frequency of eyres varied from time to time. By the 1180s the system was working on a regular basis and on average some twenty justices were sent on eyre in the provinces. By 1189 there were at least thirty-five itinerant justices, a massive increase on the half dozen of Henry I's time. Each circuit could be assigned between seven and nine justices.

The justices would arrive at a county town or other important local centre, hear the Pleas of the Crown and other matters within their jurisdiction, and move on. They performed a remarkable variety of tasks listed for them in the articles of the eyre. None survives from Henry's reign, but their later development was an elaboration and refinement of a basic pattern already evolved in the 1180s. The justices were to promulgate and enforce new legislation, assess taxes on towns and royal manors, review how the authorities of shire or vill were performing their duties; and impose penalties on the lax or corrupt. Now and again they were instructed to perform special tasks. In 1176, for instance, they were ordered to take oaths of fealty after war. The work of the justices was thus at once judicial and financial, political and administrative, supervisory and executive. The twelfth century did not distinguish between such functions. Government was as yet indivisible.

The general eyre was a powerful engine of that government. It was to run, much developed and enlarged for over a century until, weighed down by the multifarious tasks laid upon it, it was brought to a halt. Alternatives

---

9   Warren, *Henry II*, pp. 284f.

were sought in a variety of commissions of more limited scope culminating in the assize-court system, established by Edward I, which also served a country divided into circuits.[10] But none was to prove so effective a means of imposing central control throughout the land as the general eyre which Henry II had fashioned.[11] Royal authority, re-established by Henry II, was unchallenged throughout England, unchallenged that is by all except those subject to a higher authority, the clergy.

---

[10] Initially in 1273 it was six circuits, but the number fluctuated from four to nine. In its developed form, assize judges were given commissions of 'oyer and terminer' – to try serious criminal cases; or of 'gaol delivery' – to try all those imprisoned for any offence and thus clear the gaols. They could also hear civil cases under commissions of *nisi prius*. Twice a year those so commissioned visited the main towns of each circuit to hold the assizes. In London the Old Bailey exercised the criminal jurisdiction of assizes until it was superceded by the Central Criminal Court in 1834, which in turn was no more than a restyling and extension of its sessions. The assize system was finally abolished in 1971 when it was replaced by Crown Courts, permanent centres in major towns and cities with resident judges trying cases throughout the year.

[11] Warren, *Henry II*, pp. 298ff; *OHLE*, II, pp. 546f.

5

Becket and Criminous Clergy

You are Englishmen, and therefore will not judge anyone without hearing both sides of the story.   T. S. Eliot, *Murder in the Cathedral*

THE common law was triumphantly created by regal power. In its emergence, that law and that power were already locked into a dangerous struggle with a rival system: canon law and the power of the Church, embodied in the person of Thomas Becket, archbishop of Canterbury. Becket asserted that secular courts had no jurisdiction over clergymen because it was the privilege of clergy not to be accused or tried for crime except before an ecclesiastical court. The Church was attempting to exempt a substantial part of the population from the jurisdiction of royal justice. Canon law was setting up as a rival to common law and threatening to undermine the universal sweep of the latter.

During the reigns of the Conqueror and his sons, English bishops had not been unduly protective of clerics, and in some cases had degraded malefactors and handed them over for secular punishment. Italian ecclesiastical jurisprudence refined but essentially supported that stance. In Bologna around 1140 the jurist Gratian published his *Decretum*, a compilation and codification of canon law that included a provision of the Second Lateran Council designed to protect the clergy from physical attack. Gratian's followers expanded this protection to create a coherent theory of clerical immunity.[1] Clerks were not to be tried in a secular court, but there were exceptions. Ecclesiastical crimes were the exclusive preserve of the Church, but grave secular crimes committed by criminous clergy could lead to punishment by secular judges after the culprit had been deprived of his orders. This was not very different to the prevailing English custom.

During Stephen's reign, however, the power of the undivided Church in a fragmented kingdom was in the ascendancy, and by the time of his death the clergy had become more distinct as a separate order in society. Holy orders were construed as indelible, and crimes committed by clerics could not be

---

[1]   *OHLE*, I, p. 505.

tried in secular courts. This was the *privilegium fori,* known as 'benefit of clergy' in England.

Reasserting royal authority, Henry would have none of this largely English aberration. To his mind an ecclesiastical process that eschewed the ordeal and relied on compurgation, which most clerics passed, and the imposition of mild sanctions, such as public penance or imprisonment, on the few who did not, fostered crime and crippled justice. There were cases where clerics and laymen were co-accused, and where the latter fled rather than face trial but the former felt no need to do so.[2] The problem was exacerbated by the fact that the title cleric could be claimed by perhaps as many as one in six of the male population: basic literacy or the ability to recite simple oaths could enable you to make this assertion. Thus the better educated or better connected could escape savage secular justice altogether by claiming on the flimsiest grounds to be a cleric, thus removing their sanctified souls from the grasp of secular power into the jurisdiction of ecclesiastical authority, where their sin was purged.

Unsurprisingly, lawless acts by clerks and men who masqueraded as clerks were seen to be on the increase. Robert de Monte lamented:

> England is at this time infested by a kind of robbers unheard of until our days. They go about under the disguise of religion; and having dressed themselves up in the garment of monks, they join travellers; and when they have arrived in some lone road or in some forest, they summon their companions by signal, murder the travellers and plunder them of their money and goods.[3]

When such felons were caught they pleaded clerical immunity and demanded trial in the ecclesiastical courts. A large body of 'headless clerks' (those who had no superiors) roamed about the country and complaints against them were commonplace. For Henry, the problem of criminous clerks was part of the wider problem of how to master prevalent crime, and his intention was stern repression and condign punishment for all such evildoers whatever their status.

The most serious of offences committed by clerics could escape temporal justice. At the beginning of his reign, Henry had learnt the hard way to regret making concessions to the Church. He had conceded both the trial and punishment of clergy to Theobald, archbishop of Canterbury. Shortly thereafter, in 1156, Archdeacon Osbert of York was accused of murdering his archbishop, William. The trial showed the deficiencies of the ecclesiastical courts in reaching prompt and effective judgments. In this serious case

---

2　*Ibid.*, pp. 624f; II, p. 747; P&M, I, p. 455.
3　Richard Winston, *Thomas Becket* (London, 1967), p. 143.

the trial dragged on for over a year and no determination was ever made. Theobald conceded that the case faltered 'owing to the subtlety of the laws and the canons'.[4] In 1158 a burgess of Scarborough complained to the king at York that a rural dean and archdeacon had taken twenty-two shillings from him to withdraw an accusation of adultery against his wife. The corrupt clerk was brought before the king, the archbishop, the bishops of Durham and Lincoln, the treasurer of York, the justiciar Richard de Lucy and other barons. The clergy and barons were to decide the case. The punishment proposed by the clerics was that he repay the money he extorted and be committed for punishment to the mercy of the archbishop of York. Because the rural dean was a cleric, the king would get nothing. Richard de Lucy refused to sustain such a sentence and walked out of the room in disgust; Henry furiously turned on Theobald, denounced the sentence as perverse and ordered a rehearing. He was, however, called away to the Continent before the matter could be resolved, and remained there for five years. By the time of his return there was a new archbishop of Canterbury, one elevated to the position largely by the king's own insistence, one called Thomas Becket.

Initially Becket tried to appease the absent king by imposing, on his own authority, more severe punishments. He had a clerk who stole a silver chalice from St Mary Le Bow branded and degraded. Such acts of severity could scarcely be justified under canon law, and by such acts Becket was usurping the authority committed only to royal justices. The problem could not be resolved by these discretionary interventions outside the law, and his archbishop's arrogant and arbitrary actions merely provoked Henry to react.

On his return in July 1163 Henry convened a council at Woodstock. There he received many complaints about the inadequacy of ecclesiastical discipline. He was told that more than a hundred murders had been committed by clerks since 1154, and that there had been innumerable cases of theft and robbery. He commanded that clerks convicted of great crimes should be deprived of the protection of the Church and handed over to his officers. He was not demanding trial in a secular court but merely the secular punishment of a former clerk, tried and found guilty by a Church court, and who had been degraded from his orders. In other words, that someone who had been shown by his proven turpitude to be no longer worthy of holy orders should be excluded from ecclesiastical protection, and exposed to the full rigour of the law of the land. Becket responded with a flat refusal and a long diatribe. He could have temporised, admitted that canon law was uncertain

4   John of Salisbury, in Warren, *Henry II*, p. 464.

on this, and appealed to Rome for the answer, but he did not. He knew that Rome would not back him.

Cases brought to Henry's attention infuriated him further, especially when his own authority was impugned. Shortly after the council had concluded, a clerk in the diocese of Worcester was accused of raping a young girl and murdering her father. The king, going much further than he had demanded at Woodstock, ordered trial in a secular court. Becket interfered, commanding Bishop Roger of Worcester to put the clerk in the episcopal prison and not allow royal officials to touch him. Another notorious case was that of a canon of Bedford, Philip de Brois, who was tried, on a charge of murdering a knight, by the bishop of Lincoln's court. There he had cleared himself by compurgation. Simon FitzPeter, the sheriff and itinerant justice in Bedfordshire, reopened the case and ordered Philip to be tried once more. Philip openly abused him, and the justiciar reported this contempt of court to the king. Henry demanded that Philip be tried both for homicide and for abusing a royal official. Becket intervened, took Philip under his protection, and personally retried him solely for abusing the official. For that misdemeanour Philip was publicly flogged. Henry was outraged by the leniency, demanding 'by the eyes of God now you will swear to me that you judged a just judgment and did not spare the man because he is a clerk'.[5]

In October 1163 at the council at Westminster Henry returned to the issue. He declared that the peace of the kingdom was being disturbed by a host of clerics who committed rape, robbery and murder, and that men who thought so little of their sacred orders were unlikely to tremble at the threat of spiritual penalties. He had consulted those skilled in both civil and canon law and they agreed that the proper course was that followed in the time of Henry I. He demanded that Thomas and his bishops agree to the customs of the realm that governed relations between the royal and ecclesiastical authorities, and that clerks caught committing crimes or who confessed them, be degraded, deprived of the protection of the Church, and handed over to the royal courts for punishment. Becket refused to comply. He pointed out that double punishment (degradation followed by corporeal punishment) was against canon law. He denounced such customs as abuses if they ran counter to the law of God. The bishops would only agree to the customs 'saving their order', that is with the reservation that anything contrary to canon law was excluded from that assent.

The following year at the council of Clarendon, Henry tried again to define jurisdictional competence with a clarity that the Conqueror's ordi-

---

5   Winston, *Thomas Becket*, pp. 145f.

2. Henry II and Thomas Becket: Church and state at odds over the development of the law.

nance had lacked, to set restrictions on the procedures of the ecclesiastical courts, and to protect royal prerogatives.[6] He reduced to writing what he said were 'the customs, liberties and privileges … and of other things which ought to be observed and maintained in the realm'. These 'Constitutions', as they were called, gave the king the upper hand. In particular, clause 3 stated that

> Clerks cited and accused of any matter shall, when summoned by the king's justice, come before the king's court to answer there concerning matters which shall seem to the king's court to be answerable there, and before the ecclesiastical court for what shall seem to be answerable there.[7]

The king's justices, in other words, were to have the last word in deciding jurisdiction. If the ecclesiastical court tried the case, it would do so under the

[6] *OHLE*, I, pp. 115f.
[7] *EHD*, II, pp. 718ff.

eye of a royal official, and if the clerk were convicted he would automatically be degraded and returned as any layman to royal justice for punishment.

Henry was inflexible, and in the Constitutions was giving malleable custom the rigidity of law. He was obdurate with the bishops, demanding that they observe these customs of the realm without reservation. The bishops' riposte was to stigmatise the ancient customs as ancient abuses, quoting Gratian's dictum that 'the Lord never said "I am the custom" but "I am the truth"'. Initially Becket and the bishops stood firm, but on the third day Becket, for reasons unknown, caved in. His capitulation forced the hands of his colleagues, and he and the others swore 'in good faith, without deceit and according to law' to observe the customs of the kingdom enshrined in the Constitutions. Henry had triumphed. Or had he?

Becket soon repented this weakness, donned a penitent's garb, and, in a tantrum, excommunicated his erstwhile friend. Fearing reprisals, he went into exile. King and archbishop were immoveable and implacable, and shouted catcalls at each other across the Channel. It was all very unedifying. Eventually they managed to reach some sort of accord, even to rekindle some of the old intimacy, but no sooner had Becket stepped foot again in England than he reverted to his old high-handed ways. It is not hard to understand why Henry got more than a little exasperated with his archbishop's obduracy, and demonstrated his frustration by an intemperate outburst to the effect of, 'will no one rid me of this turbulent priest?' Unfortunately for Henry, someone would.

On the night of 29 December 1170 the recently returned archbishop was at evening prayer in his cathedral at Canterbury when he was confronted by four knights loyal to the king. They struck him down with repeated blows from their swords. Such was the ferocity of the attack that they sliced off the crown of Becket's head and, in a words of a eyewitness, 'the blood white with the brain, and the brain no less red from the blood, dyed the floor of the cathedral'. Ironically, his assassins were safe from secular retribution as only the Church could punish the slaying of an ecclesiastic. They faced excommunication but not execution, an absurdity that was to persist for another eight years.[8]

It is hard to feel much sympathy for the egotistical Becket. Martyred he may have been, but saint he was not. To defend the independence of the Church from secular intrusion was one thing; to protect literate murderers, robbers, and rapists from the full rigours of the law was quite another. Henry, not Becket, gave voice to the outrage of the people at the leniency shown

---

[8] Winston, *Thomas Becket*, pp. 358ff; Warren, *Henry II*, p. 539.

to those clerical hypocrites who should have suffered the most. The later history of ecclesiastical protection for errant clergy does not add lustre to the martyr's crown Becket sought to put on. The clerical child abuse scandals of recent years are arguably Thomas's lasting legacy.[9]

In the short term, Henry was to be frustrated. The scandal of the murder of an archbishop in his own cathedral – the victim of royal *in*justice as it was viewed throughout Europe – forced the king to abandon his unilateral incursion into the ecclesiastical sphere. In particular he had to relinquish clause 3 of the Constitutions. Criminous clerks thereafter were to enjoy benefit of clergy – Becket's touchstone of ecclesiastical independence – even though that claim had to be made in a secular court to the satisfaction of a royal justice.[10] By contrast, despite efforts by the Church to include them within the *privilegium fori,* civil cases remained differentiated on the basis of the nature of the litigation, in accordance with the Conqueror's ordinance.[11] In the event, benefit of clergy in criminal matters was to enjoy a long life and encompass many unlikely 'clerics'.

As it has been aptly put, Becket's posthumous victory was 'a triumph for his reputation not the triumph of his cause'.[12] Henry had been checked in his plans but not ultimately thwarted. The removal of Becket allowed for constructive and fruitful dialogue to take place, and in 1178 the king made a final settlement with the pope. It was a matter of give and take, but in the event Henry took more than he gave. He had to make concessions about which he cared little, such as exempting the clergy from participating in judicial duels, but in return was allowed to make significant inroads into their exclusivity: those accused of forest offences or litigating about non-ecclesiastical land would be subject to the secular law, and the killers of clerks would finally be tried before, and punished by, a royal judge. All this was done with the consent of the Church and not under compulsion, which was an important concession by Henry.

Ultimately Henry II had created a uniform system of national justice, administered by royal officials, accessible and applicable to all but the clergy, which would survive the archbishop's murder, the king's own death, and even the reigns of his wayward sons. Henry had built on rock and built to last.

---

9 *OHLE*, I, p. 118; cf. p. 603: In 1102 Archbishop Anselm had prohibited English priests from having wives. To Henry of Huntingdon (p. 50), in words that still resonate, 'there seemed a danger that if they sought a purity beyond their capacity, they might fall into terrible uncleanness, to the utter disgrace of the Christian name.'

10 Warren, *Henry II*, pp. 538ff.

11 *OHLE*, I, p. 110.

12 Warren, *Henry II*, p. 518.

A Note on Benefit of Clergy

Over the centuries a privilege of ecclesiastical jurisdiction and a way for an ordained cleric, monk or nun to evade secular justice was slowly transformed into a means by which all first-time offenders could obtain partial clemency and escape the noose.[13] Initially it could be pleaded early in the proceedings in order to have the case transferred to an ecclesiastical court for trial, but later it came to be pleaded only after conviction but before sentencing. It did not nullify the conviction, but rather changed the sentence for first-time offenders from probable hanging to some lesser sanction, or no sanction at all.

Consequently, over time, the requirements to prove 'clergy' were relaxed by the judiciary. The benefit became laicised. In the thirteenth and first half of the fourteenth century, judges would often disallow the claim if the supposed 'cleric' were not wearing clerical attire, did not have the tonsure, or could not read. In 1350 secular clerks, such as subdeacons or even doorkeepers, were accorded the benefit.[14] By the later fifteenth century clerical dress or tonsure no longer mattered. Literacy, or even the appearance of literacy, became the sole requirement.[15] The ability to read a biblical passage, in Latin, chosen at the discretion of the judge, sufficed.[16] Even this requirement was reduced over time, and the frisson accompanying judicial serendipity removed, by allowing felons to claim the benefit if they were sufficiently educated or intelligent enough to read, or memorise, the same verse, and for them to do so in English. This was the first verse of Psalm 51 – known aptly as the 'neck verse' – 'Have mercy upon me, O God, according to thy lovingkindness: according to the multitude of thy tender mercies blot out my transgressions.' As more and more people became subject to the death penalty, judges were often inclined to indulge the merest hint of competency. Education was elastic and subject to merciful judicial stretching. In effect, the educated, or those with a semblance of literacy, would not be executed. Nor should the aristocracy, however ignorant: in 1547 parliament granted illiterate peers a privilege which was equivalent, though not identical, to benefit of clergy.[17] Those of

---

13 Blackstone, IV, ch. 28, especially pp. 364f; James Fitzjames Stephen, *A History of the Criminal Law in England*, 3 vols (London, 1883), I, pp. 458ff.
14 Stephen, *History of the Criminal Law*, I, p. 461.
15 Baker, *Introduction to English Legal History*, p. 514.
16 *OHLE*, VI, p. 532.
17 Stephen, *History of the Criminal Law*, I, p. 462.

high birth would not suffer on account of poor education or stupidity, but their low-born comparators were more expendable.

In the face of such laxity and lenity on the part of the judiciary, the Tudors tried to restore some balance. In 1489, parliament, at Henry VII's bidding, enacted that literate laymen should be allowed the privilege, but only once: those claiming clergy, but not able to prove it through documentation, were branded on the thumb with 'M' for manslayer and 'T' for thief. This mark of Cain disqualified them from pleading the benefit in the future. Treason was exempt from the benefit, and the concept of treason was stretched to include desertion and the murder of masters by their servants. Temporarily in 1512, and permanently in 1531, parliament further restricted the benefit by making offences such as premeditated murder and some forms of robbery 'unclergyable'. As expressed in many statutes, they were 'felonies without benefit of clergy'. Some statutes, such as that of 1489, did not apply to actual clergymen, who still enjoyed the protection and pampering of the Church. In 1534 benefit of clergy was withdrawn from those who refused to enter a plea. In the 1530s parliament added offences such as piracy and buggery to the list of non-clergyable offences, and this time genuine clergy were not spared the same 'pains and dangers' as the laity. In the 1540s, sorcery, horse-stealing, and 'remaining in the country as a gypsy' were added to the list of exemptions. Benefit of clergy had become a universal male privilege, subject to, and restricted by, the law of the land. By the end of the sixteenth century nearly half of all the men convicted of felony successfully claimed benefit of clergy. On the other hand, half could not.[18]

Legislation in the seventeenth and eighteenth centuries attempted to be balanced. It further increased the number of people who could plead benefit of clergy, but decreased the benefit of doing so. In 1624 women acquired a privilege analogous to clergy in the case of larceny of goods valued up to ten shillings, although it was not until 1691 that they were put on an equal footing with men who could plead clergy for thefts of up to forty shillings. In 1706 the reading test was abolished, and the benefit became available to all first-time offenders of lesser felonies, although the sentence that could be imposed was increased to up to twenty-four months hard labour. Under the Transportation Act of 1718, those who pleaded benefit of clergy could be sentenced to seven years' exile to North America.[19]

18 *OHLE*, VI, pp. 536–40.
19 Stephen, *History of the Criminal Law*, I, pp. 462ff; Theodore Plucknett, *A Concise History of the Common Law*, 5th edn (London, 1956), pp. 439ff; Langbein, Lerner and Smith, eds, *History of the Common Law*, pp. 619f. Each gives slightly different dating.

Thus by the beginning of the eighteenth century, anyone charged with a 'clergyable felony' was entitled to be excused from capital punishment for a first offence. It was to be the high point of the device. In the later years of the eighteenth century an increasing crime rate prompted parliament to exclude many seemingly minor property crimes from benefit of clergy. Eventually housebreaking, shoplifting goods worth more than five shillings, and the theft of sheep and cattle all became felonies without benefit of clergy and earned their perpetrators automatic death sentences. If mercy was to be shown it had to come from parliament with its ability to repeal capital statutes, or from the jury with its capacity to acquit or condone. Parliament, under Robert Peel's reforming influence, finally abolished this medieval hangover in 1827.

6

The Achievement of Henry II

> Not only must royal power be furnished with arms against rebels and
> nations which rise up against the king and the realm, but it is also fitting
> that it should be adorned with laws ... so that in time of both peace
> and war our glorious king may so successfully perform his office that,
> crushing the pride of the unbridled and ungovernable with the right
> hand of strength and tempering justice for the humble and meek with
> the rod of equity, he may both be victorious in wars with his enemies
> and also show himself continually impartial in dealing with his subjects.
>
> *Glanvill*, Prologue

IN THE early twelfth century the legal lieutenants who were responsible
for the king's justice in the localities had limited authority. As the passive
representatives of an absent king they presided over special sessions of a
county court where others – local worthies or suitors following local custom
– passed judgment. Henry II transformed their status and power. From 1176
the royal justices in eyre made judgments themselves in what was a local
session of a national royal court.[1] They were becoming fully-fledged judges
with the beginnings of an independent authority, not the mere mouthpieces
of the king. For the first time, judgment-making was not subject to the
vagaries of local politics, popularity or influence. The judges were royal
appointees with no local roots or allegiances.

The first stirrings of a judicial professionalism were being seen, and royal
justices would soon have their own headquarters at Westminster Hall and
a law manual in *Glanvill*. The fact that so many early manuscripts of this
vademecum survive suggest that each royal justice may have had one.[2] Much
of the common law was to be judge-made. If it originated in royal diktat, it
developed as a result of a combination of a sensible, if circumscribed, discretionary power which Henry II had conferred on his justices, with their own
sense of the importance of consensus and collective wisdom. Royal justices
were becoming a corporate body: the judiciary.

---

1 Van Caenegem, *Birth of the English Common Law*, p. 13; Paul Brand, *The Making of
   the Common Law* (London, 1993), pp. 80–4.
2 The chronicler and royal justice Roger of Howden certainly had a copy along with
   other legal texts: *OHLE*, II, p. 530.

In 1178 an ordinance provided that five judges were to remain in Westminster to hear claims. Westminster had a number of benefits. Suits were heard there more quickly than in the shires. Fees went straight into the king's coffers, although they were relatively modest – Henry tried to keep justice affordable. This ordinance, however, did not mark the beginning of what would be either the Court of the King's Bench or the Court of the Common Pleas, and may have been little more than one of the king's experiments in the allocation of personnel. The dean of St Paul's, Ralph de Diceto, observed that the king was prone to experiment: 'unchanging in his purpose, he again and again made changes in personnel ... making use now of abbots, now of earls, now of members of his household, now of those closest to him, to hear and judge cases'.[3]

A new court was established at Westminster, probably in the reign of Richard I. It was severed from the old court at the Exchequer to deal with matters not relating to finance. It acquired the name 'the Bench', which may have referred to a particular area within the court. Six or seven justices from a wider pool were present at any one time, a core of whom appeared regularly. Whether they were of knightly rank or more, whether they were lay or clerics, most came from families with a tradition of royal service. Their prime duty was to the king, as was their loyalty.

The functions of this new court overlapped with the court *coram rege*. For centuries this had been a large body composed of magnates sitting with the king in judgment. In Henry II's later years it became a more compact body, comprising the king and a selection of his justices. A core of increasingly experienced legal experts, albeit not yet permanent and not yet professional, serving with the king in person, or in the Exchequer or in eyre, and often in both, was emerging, 'ensuring that a uniform and general "custom of the king's court" developed and was observed' in both the Exchequer and in eyre.[4] From wherever they had been plucked, these justices would begin to build up a body of special expertise and professional cohesion. By travelling around the country they gained practical understanding of how things worked and of what things worked. With increasing confidence they were prepared to preserve some old customs and jettison others. On their return to Westminster they would confer in the great hall, and discuss or debate among themselves the finer points of legal practice and forensic problems. Between sessions, or even just socially, they would share their experiences and anecdotes. They used all this to shape their rulings, fashioned out of

---

3 Cited in *OHLE*, II, pp. 519f.
4 Brand, *Making of the Common Law*, p. 93.

their common interests and common experience.[5] They were the common law made flesh.

What was starting to emerge was a body of judges as we would recognise them now, serving both in Westminster and on circuit. They were royal officials, not regional magnates. They were largely laymen, not clergy, although Hubert Walter was made chief justiciar in 1193 when he was also archbishop of Canterbury. The law they administered and enforced was the same law for all free men throughout the kingdom, English and Norman alike.

Judges were not yet bound by precedent. No earlier case constituted binding authority, but was at most illustrative of the custom and conclusions of the court, helpful but not determinative. Their judgments could be informed by the wisdom of their predecessors, if it were known and if it were relevant. Many cases involved little law, many were never decided (as the parties took the hint and settled), most were never reported, and judges did not have to give reasoned judgments. Sometimes the King's Bench and the Common Pleas came up with contradictory decisions, and the answer to a particular issue depended on which end of Westminster Hall was asked.[6] Sometimes equitable principles, developed by the chancellors to ensure justice, would be deployed to overturn judgments. Consequently, there was, as yet, no theory of the relationship between enacted and unenacted law, between law and custom, between conflicting jurisdictions, and between the law as it was and law as it ought to have been. But a kernel was beginning to grow: the common law was not just about consistency across the realm, it was also about being consistent with the past.

The king and his judges were creating a strikingly innovative system of justice. English legal practice was transformed

> by the practical decisions of busy men responding intelligently to practical problems that were nothing new in themselves but which had never encountered an authority that made a habit of asking not simply what needed to be done but how it could be done better. Better meant more simply, more rationally, more efficiently and more effectively. This attitude was yeast to the dough of an English legal system which for all its hoary virtues was immensely complicated, and frequently irrational, clumsy and slow.[7]

The common law was Henry's instrument, created to control and cajole his kingdom.

---

5   J. H. Baker, *The Law's Two Bodies* (Oxford, 2001), pp. 79ff.

6   *Ibid.*, pp.13–17, 22–4, 77.

7   Warren, *Henry II*, p. 317.

He did not, however, act in a vacuum. Henry was a man of his time and had a continental empire and a cosmopolitan outlook, and it is a truism that the distinctiveness of his Angevin legal system derived in part from Norman and ecclesiastical influences as well as from Anglo-Saxon. This legal system too was a product of its time, and of a country that was both an island and part of an empire. Nonetheless, it was unique. While the

> Latin learning of the schools … the ecclesiastical and canonical world of [the time], the values of French courtly and feudal society, and the eclectic political dominance of Henry II, were all strands in the formation of the common law [those strands] were woven into the existing fabric of custom and organisation which was Anglo-Saxon in origin…. Without the sheriffs, counties and hundreds, and without the habit of thinking of the king as lord of all free men (barons and knights, cleric and lay) and of all England, there could have been no common law.[8]

Henry II, cosmopolitan as he was, had not turned primarily to principles of Roman law and distorted English traditions by grafting on alien institutions. The king chose to take English customary law, fragmented and localised, no longer adequate to the needs of a changing society, and to 'trim it, knead it, reshape it and give it the transforming touch of genius'.[9] The best of local laws could be applied throughout the land. The result was a basic system of law that both drew on tradition but – unlike customary law – was also capable of being built upon, and expanded or adapted in the future. Now England did not just have regional laws; it had a legal system common to the whole kingdom. A king born in France had laid the foundations upon which the immense structure of English law could be built.

To be accepted, to be effective, legal redress had to be accessible and cheap, respected and feared, and had to be seen to be free from external control, either by great lords or by the king himself. Expectations were raised that royal justice would have high standards and that it would be implemented in a systematic and fair way. Judges boasted a striking impartiality. No judge, it was said, was 'so shameless or audacious as to presume to turn aside at all from the path of justice, or to digress in any respect from the way of truth'. Lowly status should be no bar to justice: in the royal courts 'a poor man is not oppressed by the power of his adversary, nor does favour or partiality drive any man away from the threshold of judgment'.[10] Admittedly this applied only to free men and women – those adults who did no

---

8 Clanchy, *Early Medieval England*, pp. 110ff.
9 Warren, *Henry II*, p. 360; Brand, *Making of the Common Law*, pp. 101f.
10 *Glanvill*, Prologue.

servile work for a lord – who constituted only a small proportion of the population. But the free, be they barons or bakers, were supposed to be treated equally. In practice, of course, money and power were likely still to have considerable effect. Sometimes the justices in eyre were 'referred to as errantes, "wandering", a pun on their itinerant nature and deviation from justice'.[11] This is no more than one expects from English humour, and is not indicative of any widespread discontent, let alone resistance. The usage became so accepted as to be employed in official records.

Henry's zeal for rationalisation was not constrained to crime. Indeed, some of his greatest achievements were elsewhere. The new writs and procedures he introduced have been called 'the very foundation of the common law'.[12] Writs were written instructions emanating from the king himself either authorising, or commanding, that such and such a thing be done. Before Henry's time writs had long been used to initiate litigation, but were not the sole means. His royal courts were competent to hear only cases so initiated. Henry standardised writs, made their form more precise, and made enforcement more likely. In civil matters – which were often very uncivil in the way the parties conducted themselves – writs were no longer to be personally served on the defendant, which could be a risky business. Now they were addressed to the sheriff, and he had the responsibility of bringing the dispute to trial. Standard writs and standard procedures were all conducive, even essential, to a standardised or common law. They were also conducive to the growth of legal argument about technical defects, factual errors, or spelling mistakes in the writ. The era of 'legal technicalities' had begun.

The reality of the changes Henry brought about can be seen in the 'law books' straddling his reign: the *Leges Henrici Primi*, written c.1115–18, and *Glanvill*, composed probably between 1187 and 1189. Whereas the valiant author of the earlier work despaired of his attempt to write a text book of contemporary law because there is 'so much perversity in human affairs and so much profusion of evil ... the precise truth of the law or a settled statement of the legal remedy can rarely be found', and advised his readers to avoid 'the utterly whimsical dice of pleas altogether',[13] the author of the latter took a completely different stance. He was proud of the rational and national legal system, brought about during his own lifetime, that he could now describe. Confusion and conflict had yielded to system and consistency, and it had done so within the space of two reigns and half a century.

---

11 *OHLE*, II, pp. 576, 844.
12 By Hall in *Glanvill*, p. xii.
13 *LHP*, ch. 6, l. 4; ch. 6. l. 6.

It is no coincidence that this seminal work could be, and was, produced within a decade of the 1178 ordinance, during the chief justiciarship of Ranulf de Glanvill who held that post from 1180 until Henry's death in 1189. Whether or not it was actually written by this senior royal official or, under his influence or inspiration, by his nephew, Hubert Walter, or by some justice or clerk of lesser status, is unknown, although the first seems the least, and last the most, likely.[14] Whoever was responsible, from the thirteenth century the treatise was commonly called *Glanvill*. As Maitland said, the question of authorship is

> interesting rather than important, for though we would gladly know the name of the man who wrote our first classical text-book, it is plain that he was one who was very familiar with the justice done in the king's court during the last years of Henry II. We may go further, we may safely say that it was not written without Glanvill's permission or without Henry's.[15]

This first systematic treatise on the law as administered by the royal courts was rendered possible by the nascent common law.

The author must have been intimately involved in, or been an astute observer of, the legal revolution going on around him. The success of his work mirrored that of the legal system it described. It met a need as well as a demand, as there was an increasing unease that England had no written laws. Local customs might be passed on orally from generation to generation, but national laws emanating from the king should, it was felt, be preserved on durable vellum, just as the laws of imperial Rome had been in the Codex of Justinian. *Glanvill*'s prologue states that 'although the laws of England are not written it does not seem absurd to call them laws'; this book was an attempt to rectify matters. Not that the author could reduce all the laws and customs to writing, but he could provide an exposition of the 'general rules frequently observed in the king's court', an enterprise 'not presumptuous, but rather very useful for most people and highly necessary to aid the memory'.[16] Royal justice, fixed and uniform, was elevated high above variable local custom. In time it would entirely displace it.

That a short, simple book of such clarity could be written, describing a law that was rational, precisely formulated and common to the whole country is a measure of the achievement of Henry II's reforms. Unsurprisingly, it speaks warmly of the new common law system as expediting justice and making it much more accessible and affordable. A work composed 'when justice was

---

[14] *Glanvill*, pp. xxx–xxxiii; *OHLE*, II, p. 872.
[15] P&M, I, pp. 164f.
[16] *Glanvill*, pp. 2f.

under the direction of the illustrious Ranulf Glanvill, the most learned of that time in the law and ancient customs of the realm'[17] and presumably with his imprimatur, was also instrumental in ensuring the system it described in such glowing terms became an actuality. Glanvill, as Roger de Howden, a contemporary royal justice, said, was the man 'whose wisdom established the laws we call English'. The book bearing his name did so too.

Perhaps inadvertently Henry II's reforms, intended to reassert royal authority by portraying the king as the guarantor of justice, began a process of limiting it. The rule of law was to be more powerful than any ruler, and the surest antidote to the abuse of power. Justice would rapidly be seen not as the king's gift but as his subjects' right. A confident, strong and effective ruler such as Henry II could let go of his creation. He could devolve power with equanimity. He could also take it back at will. Henry's 'tyranny' – as one contemporary traducer typified his reign[18] – was a tyranny only of one who had the legal system under his control. No strong king, such as Henry, wanted to have his ability to act swiftly and decisively restricted. He could not allow himself to be limited by custom or by the law. Henry could enforce, and at the same time act outside, his own law and the legal system he had created.

But how would a less secure, less able, less lucky and more vindictive monarch who did the same, or worse, fare? The reign of Henry's own youngest son, John, which was seen by some as a punishment for his father's murder of an archbishop,[19] was to provide the answer, climaxing on a water meadow in 1215. Not for the last time would the legislators find themselves subject to a higher power: the law of unintended consequences.

---

[17] *Ibid.*, Prologue.

[18] *Niger*, p. 168. Ralph Niger, a theologian who had served Becket in exile and who again fled abroad after his master's murder, perhaps unsurprisingly was hostile to Henry as a ruler as well as to his legal reforms. In his warped assessment, Henry was not a purveyor but 'a seller and delayer of justice'.

[19] David Carpenter, *The Struggle for Mastery: Britain 1066–1284* (London, 2003), p. 295.

7

Magna Carta

And still when Mob or Monarch lays
Too rude a hand on English ways,
The whisper wakes, the shudder plays,
Across the reeds at Runnymede.
And Thames, that knows the mood of kings,
And crowds and priests and suchlike things,
Rolls deep and dreadful as he brings
Their warning down from Runnymede!
Rudyard Kipling, 'The Reeds of Runnymede'

THE extraordinary year 1215 has an unparalleled significance in English law and culture, and for two reasons: the proclamation of Magna Carta and the abolition of trial by ordeal. The former is by far the more famous, but the latter is just as significant.

The momentous confrontation at Runnymede between the barons and the king stemmed from need coupled with suspicion, and from the flawed personality of the king. In temperament John was unsuited to kingship. He had cunning but lacked confidence. He exercised power through the prism of paranoia. He thought others as base as himself, distrusting all the world and being distrusted in return. W. L. Warren says 'he had the mental abilities of a great king, but the inclinations of a petty tyrant.'[1] Most would go further. John is generally considered to be the worst king England has ever had, and no other has ever borne his name.[2] His failure was all the more apparent when contrasted with the enduring successes of his father Henry II, and with the martial reputation of his eldest brother Richard the Lionheart.

John succeeded to the throne in 1199 when Richard was killed at the height of his fame and in the midst of a siege. John proceeded precipitously to lose the Angevin empire his father had painstakingly built up and his brother had defended. He embarked on disastrous military ventures in France, which within five years had left him shorn even of Normandy itself. He desperately

---

[1] Warren, *Henry II*, p. 259.

[2] When in 1377 the barons toyed with the idea of promoting the third son of Edward III as successor to the throne, one of the chief arguments against his accession was his name: John of Gaunt. There could not be another King John.

needed money to win it back, but doubted the barons' loyalty. Need and suspicion coalesced. Rather than placating them for their continental losses, he demanded that the nobility finance the losing war. Confined to England by the loss of his possessions in France, John was constantly on their backs. He used royal courts to levy fines, often on spurious grounds. He put many in debt to the Crown, with their lands forfeit should they not repay, and compelled some to 'buy his favour' at exorbitant rates. John also had an unfortunate proclivity to covet not just their goods, but their wives. Despite the king accumulating enormous sums of cash, all his enterprises climaxed in defeat, and by 1214 he had squandered his barons' money and lost their French possessions as well as his own. By his carelessness this worst of kings had created 'this sceptred isle'.

Through his endeavours John had alienated the major part of the aristocracy, fashioning thereby what he most feared: a disgruntled nobility who despised their sovereign. He had been defeated time and again. God, they believed, had rejected him. He had to be stopped before he wrecked the kingdom. In addition, the barons realised that the Angevin reforms of land law had afforded considerable protection to their subtenants but not to themselves as tenants-in-chief. With a mixture of motives, they rebelled the following year and seized the rich and well-fortified city of London. The king could not attack the city, let alone take it, but equally the barons could not defeat John and his mercenary army in the field.

Both sides were compelled to negotiate, but the barons had the edge. Archbishop Langton, sympathetic to their cause, acted as an intermediary, and it is to him we chiefly owe the composition of Magna Carta. In his view the king had to be bound to the law, and peace between John and his nobility restored. This was a sacred task and the undertakings were to be made to last – John would make them 'by the inspiration of God, for the good of [his] soul ... to the honour of God and the exaltation of holy Church, and the improvement of the kingdom'.[3] John's word, however, could not be trusted, and so the terms of any peace treaty had to be in writing and had to be disseminated.

On 15 June 1215, on neutral ground on the banks of the Thames, the two sides met in what was later called 'the parliament of Runnymede'.[4] In that consciously judicial setting they came to an uneasy understanding.[5] The

---

3   From the preamble of Magna Carta.
4   An echo of this early definition of parliament as the king and his councillors acting as the supreme judicial body is preserved in the term the High Court of Parliament.
5   *EHD*, III, pp. 316–24.

compromise, grudgingly – or cunningly[6] – conceded by John constitutes one of the most significant documents in English history, setting down in writing the limitations of royal power. It was also one of the earliest attempts to do so, though not perhaps the first.[7] It is, however, a statement of liberties rather than an assertion of Liberty. The rebels were not propounding, even in embryo, anything we should call 'human rights', unless 'human' excludes most of the populace. Even the change from the first draft of 'any baron' to 'any free man' was not much of an extension, as the number of 'free men' was pretty limited.

The rebels primarily wanted to safeguard their own position and possessions by ending arbitrary rule. They did not want the end of royal justice, but more –it was a good thing, but should not be abused, nor evaded by anyone, not even by the king. Henry II may not always have abided by his own rules, but the barons now insisted that his successors should: the source of law should be subject to law. 'Instead of law there was tyrannical will', lamented a chronicler. 'Right and justice', asserted a contemporary tract, 'ought to reign in the kingdom more than depraved will.'[8] But this was true only in part. The tyrannical and depraved will had not been directed at all and sundry but at the barons. The king had been assiduous in administering justice to his lesser subjects without fear or favour, and was well respected for it.[9] Justice for all under the law was what was needed, and that included the barons.

The legal changes that had taken place under Henry II were admirable and irreversible. They had engendered high expectations. Royal justice was now favoured as the first resort, a guarantor of law and order and defender of property rights. The Charter was restorative, not revolutionary. The provisions did not seek to limit royal justice but to make it more regular, equitable and accessible, as it had been prior to John. Clause 17 stipulated that 'common pleas' should not follow the king's court, but for public convenience should

---

6　As recent commentators, led by J. C. Holt, have suggested.

7　The earliest recorded pact between an English ruler and his subjects, the first time a king had to agree to conditions before he was allowed to resume his rule, was two hundred years earlier, but we do not know if the demands, terms or pledges were put in writing. The *Anglo-Saxon Chronicle* states that in 1014 Aethelred the Unready was restored to the throne after pledging that 'he would be a gracious lord to [his people], and reform all the things which they all hated': *EHD*, I, p. 247. The Charter of Liberties, issued by Henry I at his coronation in 1100, also constitutes a direct written progenitor of Magna Carta: *EHD*, II, pp. 400ff.

8　Carpenter, *The Struggle for Mastery*, pp. 292f.

9　W. L. Warren, *King John* (New Haven, 1997), pp. 141–4.

be held 'in some predetermined place',[10] which in practice usually meant Westminster. Clause 18 stipulated that two itinerant justices were to hold county court sessions four times a year to deal with civil actions, namely the writs of *novel disseisin*, *mort d'ancestor* or *darrein presentment*.[11] Four times a year proved aspirational as it was well beyond the capacities of government to ensure and, in the reissue of 1217, the commitment was reduced to once a year. Clause 45 insisted that all those appointed as justices and sheriffs be men who knew what could properly be called 'the law of the realm' and wanted to maintain it.

Amidst these, and other transitory clauses such as those regulating fish weirs and measures of ale, were two of enduring significance:

> 39. No free man shall be arrested or imprisoned or disseised [dispossessed] or outlawed or exiled or in any way victimised, neither will we attack him nor send anyone to attack him, except by the lawful judgment of his peers or by the law of the land.
> 40. To no one will we sell, to no one deny or delay right or justice.[12]

These celebrated clauses guaranteed due process, taxation by consent, and the rule of law, all aspects of government that had already impressed themselves on the English consciousness. Guaranteeing the charter were twenty-five barons chosen for the task, a body elected to ensure that the king complied with the law. Although it would not last, for a time 'the king was virtually reduced to the role of executive officer of the law under the supervision of a baronial committee'.[13] When John put his seal of authentication on Magna Carta, Magna Carta put the seal of approval on the principles upon which the common law was grounded.

Even in its own day the Great Charter was considered very significant. Of forty-odd original copies – or 'exemplifications' – sent to every shire in England, four have survived the course of eight hundred years:[14] the provisions were made to outlast the reign of one king and were to be disseminated

---

10 The Latin is '*in aliquo loco certo*', usually translated as 'in some fixed place'. As the eyre could hear common pleas, this phrase must mean that the sitting of the court is predictable and not that it is permanently in one place.

11 *Novel disseisin* was available to those who felt they had been unlawfully dispossessed of land; *mort d'ancestor* to those who claimed to be the lawful inheritors of land; *darrein presentment* to those disputing patronage over churches.

12 This clause is etched into the doors of the library of the new Supreme Court.

13 Warren, *King John*, p. 239.

14 Salisbury and Lincoln each have a copy, the British Library has two. Winston Churchill was prepared to let the Americans keep the Lincoln copy, which was on tour in the United States during the Second World War, as an inducement to enter the fray. Lincoln Cathedral declined to make the ultimate sacrifice.

3. These words prominently displayed in the United Kingdom's new Supreme Court demonstrate the continuing relevance of Magna Carta and the continuity of English law.

far and wide throughout the realm. Its title, however, was not a sign of greatness. Calling it 'Magna' was merely to distinguish the bigger charter from its smaller companion, the Charter of the Forest.[15] The barons referred to it as 'the common charter of the realm'.

While the provisions of Magna Carta were being promulgated throughout the kingdom, John was reneging on the deal and winning the support of the pope, who declared it null and void.[16] Within eight months the king was again at war with the rebels, and in one of the few glorious moments

---

[15] *EHD*, III, pp. 337–40.
[16] *Ibid.*, pp. 324ff.

of his troubled reign, seized their stronghold of Rochester. Had he lived long thereafter he might have reversed the concessions wrung out of him at Runnymede. But Rochester was to be a hollow victory. John succumbed to dysentery the following year, leaving a minor as his heir. The king died; the Charter lived. Moreover, John's son Henry III, insecure in his minority, was induced to give it new life by reissuing modified versions in 1216, 1217 and 1225.

The 1225 version became law, the first statute, and three of its clauses have never been repealed.[17] It was becoming fundamental law. 'This was not a fiction of the seventeenth century or even of the fourteenth' but 'was implicit in the original purpose of the Charter', for only fundamental law could ensure such a grant of liberties in perpetuity. The sapling had survived and was set to grow huge in the history of England and its future colonies.[18] Its growth was precocious. The Confirmation of the Charters in 1297 expanded it to cover major extensions of royal policy. In the reign of Edward III (1327–77) no fewer than six acts of parliament further expanded the meaning of Magna Carta, to encompass trial by jury, due process, and everyone 'of whatever estate or condition he may be'.[19]

The myth of Magna Carta was becoming even more potent than the actuality, and it was myth that gave this rather stolid medieval charter immortality. As Samuel Johnson later wryly observed, the Great Charter 'was born with a grey beard'. By the early seventeenth century the beard was full grown and the Charter was elevated for political purposes to an unassailable status no other document has held in English history. It is not surprising that this happened in the reign of Charles I, a king who lacked success in war, was constantly in need of money, and who was prepared to impose his unceasing demands on his begrudging subjects – a king who was coming to look more and more like 'Bad King John'. That this final transmutation had not taken place earlier is perfectly demonstrated by the fact that Shakespeare in his play *King John*, which was written before 1598 in the time of 'Good Queen Bess', makes no mention of what is now considered the most significant event of John's reign.

This emergence in the seventeenth century of the 1225 version of Magna

---

[17] (1) the English Church shall be free, and shall have its rights undiminished, and its liberties unimpaired; (2) the city of London shall enjoy all its ancient liberties and free customs ... all other cities, boroughs, towns and ports shall enjoy all their liberties and free customs; (3) to no one will we sell, to no one deny or delay right or justice.

[18] J. C. Holt, *Magna Carta*, 2nd edn (Cambridge, 1992), p. 14; Bartlett, *England Under the Norman and Angevin Kings*, p. 65.

[19] 28 Edward III, cap. 3.

Carta as the source, or more precisely the succour, of all ancient English liberties was achieved largely as a result of the exertions of that great champion of the common law, Edward Coke, who pointedly portrayed it as 'such a fellow that he will have no sovereign'. Coke was building an extension, not a house. The foundations for his erection were laid in the thirteenth and fourteenth century in the restatements and developments of the Charter. It was in the context of bitter rivalry between an alien Stuart king and parliament, and on the authority of a legal titan, that it became the embodiment of 'fundamental incontrovertible law',[20] enshrining forever the age-old rights and liberties of all the English, whatever their status. A statute protecting specific liberties was in effect proclaiming 'Liberty'. In particular, Clauses 39 and 40 were hailed as the origins of *habeas corpus*, trial by jury, and the liberties of the subject generally. These claims maybe somewhat specious – for instance, *habeas corpus* was part of the royal prerogative and originated as a writ issued in the royal courts – but the clauses had been 'felicitous phrases' that 'gradually entered the common law and worked their rhetorical magic down the centuries'.[21]

But so what? The myth has not distorted the reality, merely expanded it. These two succinct clauses were supremely adaptable and so could sustain many interpretations and much development. They were intended to protect all 'free men', not just the barons, against the kinds of arbitrary conduct which a particular king, John, had been committing against the latter. Why should these clauses not be invoked against tyrannous power everywhere and in every time? Why should the term 'free men' – a fairly limited group in the thirteenth century – not be expanded to include everyone? Magna Carta 'meant more than it said'. It was a code of law established by royal charter at the prompting of the king's subjects. As such, 'it opened the way to periodic revisions of custom and law and implied that government could not be conducted to the damage of the governed. Moreover merely by existing it was a standing condemnation of the rule of arbitrary will.'[22]

On two occasions of the greatest historical moment, Magna Carta would become a clarion call for liberty against overweening government. Preceding the English Civil War it was cited, as we have noted, by parliamentarians contesting the arbitrary rule of Charles I. In the eighteenth century, it inspired the Fathers of the American Revolution and provided the basis for the United States' Constitution, and has been accorded a sacred status in that

[20] Holt, *Magna Carta*, p. 4.
[21] Geoffrey Robertson, *Crimes Against Humanity* (New York, 1999), pp. 2f.
[22] Warren, *King John*, p. 240.

country, even greater than in England. Maitland, with all the authority of the *fons et origo* of the study of the history of English law, pontificated that 'for all its faults, this document becomes and rightly becomes a sacred text, the nearest approach to an irrepealable "fundamental statute" that England has ever had … for in brief it means this, that the king is and shall be below the law.'[23] When the need arose and the crisis came, Magna Carta was Excalibur waiting to be drawn from the stone.

---

[23] P&M, I, p. 173.

8

From Ordeal to Jury

Thou shalt not tempt the Lord thy God   Matthew 4.7

IF 1215 was the year in which the law outgrew the king, it was also the
year it outgrew that rival power in the land, the Church. This institution had not only enjoyed its own separate legal system, but maintained a
strong foothold in the common law: only a cleric could preside over trial by
ordeal, only a cleric could judge the result. To possess an ordeal pit and the
accoutrements of ordeal conferred dignity and status, but in addition priests
were paid handsomely for their participation. The ordeal, despite those who
doubted its efficacy, or questioned its rationale, remained strong throughout
the twelfth century. Then suddenly in 1215 that all changed.

The Fourth Lateran Council prohibited clerical participation in, and
thus in effect abolished, trial by ordeal.[1] Why Pope Innocent III wanted to
prohibit ordeals is not clear. To do so ran against clerical interests and influence. This high-minded decision would have been a conjunction of many
things: theological disdain for dragging God into mundane affairs at the
beck and call of mortals demanding a miracle on each and every occasion;
concern that ordeal was uncanonical, being found neither in Scripture nor
in Roman law, but was part of 'custom', a term becoming a dirty word for

---

[1]   An exception was trial by battle which did not have the character of a *iudicium dei*,
did not require the presence of a priest, was restricted to those who chose it, and was
usually reserved for disputes over land. Even so, it began a rapid slide into insignifi-
cance other than in cases of treason, being finally abolished by parliament in 1819,
fifteen months after the notorious but misunderstood case of *Ashford* v. *Thornton*, in
which the brother of a dead girl claimed the archaic right of 'appeal of murder' which
permitted the relatives of murder victims to appeal a 'not guilty' verdict and request
a retrial. The acquitted man, Thornton, claimed his equally archaic right of 'trial by
battle', one-to-one combat with his accuser, William Ashford. The latter declined to
fight, and Thornton went free: Robert Megarry, *A New Miscellany-at-Law* (Oxford,
2005), pp. 57–79. The ordeal of water saw an extra-judicial comeback in England and
elsewhere in the late sixteenth century for supposed witches, who were first bound
and thrown into water to see if they sank or swam. The practice of the 'swimming of
witches' continued, despite official disapproval, throughout the seventeenth century,
and survived in Virginia, for example, until 1706: Bartlett, *Trial by Fire and Water*,
pp. 146f.

the Church; the pollution of the clergy by being involved in 'judgments of blood'; and doubts about the efficacy of ordeals, especially for those who had confessed and been absolved. Whatever the reasons, the withdrawal of the Church from this procedure was fundamental. The ordeal was killed in its prime. Without it how do you secure a verdict in those difficult cases which were not amenable to other modes of proof?[2]

It was a pivotal moment when English criminal procedure could have been merged with, or been submerged by, the system based on Roman precedent and created following the demise of the ordeal that was to become dominant on the Continent in the thirteenth century, a system designed to extract confessions or other evidence – by intimidation routinely, by torture if necessary – the Inquisitorial System. This did not attempt to prove guilt or innocence, but to find out the truth of the matter by the creation of a dossier of evidence. Often the best source of evidence was the accused, who could either endure unremitting torture or confess. He had no way out, and, unless of indomitable fortitude, no real chance of an acquittal. The use of torture was predicated on guilt, and guilt was usually established. As Robert Bartlett puts it 'torture, a judicial procedure in human hands, was more unrelenting than the judgment of God'.[3] And the hands were not just ordinary human hands, but those of specialists employed by the state. Justice was the preserve of experts, it was professionalised. This was the rival system the common law eschewed. Torture was rejected in favour of the judgment of peers. England continued along her own exceptional path which led to juries – already long deployed in civil cases – trying criminal matters. This refusal to countenance torture has been crucial throughout the development of the English legal system right down to the present day, when governments cannot be, or cannot admit to being, complicit in 'extraordinary rendition'.

The end of the ordeal proved not so much a threat to the newly forged common law, but an opportunity. The involvement of the Church – that great rival to the throne – in the secular law of the land was at a stroke removed, and the law survived this amputation. After forty years or so of judicial experience of getting at the truth of the matter by the rational means of hearing testimony, the government of England felt confident in leaving the problem of proof to the discretion of the justices in eyre. They were

<hr />

2   Danny Danziger and John Gillingham, *1215: The Year of Magna Carta*, (London, 2003), pp. 196f; Whitman, *Origins of Reasonable Doubt*, pp. 53, 83–90. The oath and compurgation survived and passed into the common law, being abolished in 1833. A version of the former still survives in the statutory declaration.

3   Bartlett, *Trial by Fire and Water*, p. 141.

accustomed to asking juries of presentment or accusation – grand juries – why they suspected those named in the indictments, or to empanelling a jury from those who lived in the locality and were present in court to speak to some point of fact material to the case. The jury took an oath to give a 'truthful answer' or verdict – a *veredictum* in medieval Latin or *voir dit* in Old French – to a question put to them by an authority. It was short step to put to the jurors the question of whether the suspect was guilty as charged, to bring in a verdict. The practice increased of summoning a second, or petty jury, of twelve free men for this task. The jury could take on the responsibility of determination, leaving the judge free from 'the agonies of decision'.[4]

Thus when Henry III in 1219 sent out instructions to his justices to find some new means of criminal proof, 'since the Church has forbidden the judgments of fire and water', within the year they had settled on jury trial.[5] The transition from trial by ordeal to trial by jury for criminal matters was as fast as it was seamless. The last record of trial by ordeal in England was in 1219, and the first record of a criminal jury trial was in 1220 in Westminster. A woman called Alice was condemned for murder. She in turn accused five others of criminality. They submitted themselves to the judgment of their neighbours, 'putting themselves for good or ill upon a verdict'. The truthful answer given – the verdict – was that one was innocent and went free, and four were guilty and went to the gallows.

Trial by jury soon became the norm. It was cheap and effective, and by making ordinary lay people central to the system of justice it was revolutionary. It was the obverse of feuding, of people taking the law into their own hands. The jury was a regulated mob, in which private revenge was turned into public justice. The function of these early jurors was not to weigh evidence but to decide facts on the basis of their own local knowledge or the general belief of the district, and they were – decreasingly – entitled to do this for centuries to come. Unlike jurors of today, they came to their task with knowledge of the case. Having sworn an oath, they would be guilty of perjury if they gave a false verdict, and could themselves be tried. This verdict was as decisive as it was inscrutable. It was not given individually. It did not involve giving reasons. It was not subject to question. Even so, to assuage tender consciences in criminal trials, jurors could bring in special verdicts, determining specific facts and leaving the legal consequences to the judge, or they could rely on benefit of clergy to mitigate the severity of the consequences of their decision.

4 *OHLE*, VI, pp. 47f.
5 *EDH*, III, pp. 340f.

But a legal revolution had taken place. The decision on guilt or innocence was no longer made by God, nor did it revert to the king, nor to agents of the state. It was the preserve and responsibility of a more mundane tribunal: the people. The offender was convicted in public by members of the public. The jury, the institution that most defines English criminal justice truly began here.[6]

England thus took a distinctly different route from the rest of Europe. No forced inquisition, no regular recourse to torture, no coerced self-incrimination, no state control of the result. Instead resort was made to the compulsion of witnesses to secure evidence and the judgment of peers to decide the issue. It was a vastly significant distinction, and it had the virtues of suppleness and adaptability as well as anonymity in numbers. By the fourteenth century, for instance, the rule was established that the verdict had to be unanimous, and by the fifteenth century the distinction between law and fact, judge and jury was arising.

Only in those cases of felony where trial by jury was thwarted because a defendant refused to plead was there recourse to something akin to torture, not to get a confession, nor to implicate accomplices, but to induce a plea.[7] From 1275 until 1772 the defiant were subjected to *prison* – corrupted to *peine – forte et dure*, during which they were pressed by weights until they pleaded or died. Only an accused found guilty at trial was subject to forfeiture. Those who did not plead but endured to the end could not be put on trial, and therefore in their demise had the comfort of knowing that they had preserved their estate. They could be killed but not convicted.[8]

Thus between 1160 and 1220 the administration of English law and justice had been transformed. Juries had replaced ordeal in all criminal matters. Litigation over land was now primarily conducted in royal courts. A body of professional justices was just beginning to emerge who would administer technical, uniform legal procedures at Westminster and in the counties.

---

6   The history of the jury in neighbouring Scotland is uncertain, but it is thought to have derived from Anglo-Norman influence which began to spread throughout Scotland in the eleventh and twelfth centuries. It may have been inspired by an English progenitor but it developed in a markedly different way and has retained its distinctiveness, having fifteen rather than twelve jurors, and a verdict based on a simple majority: Ian Willock, *The Origins and Development of the Jury Trial in Scotland* (Edinburgh, 1966), pp. 20–30.

7   High treason and misdemeanours were exempt. Standing mute in those cases was deemed to be the equivalent of a conviction: Blackstone, IV, p. 320.

8   It was abolished in 1772, and a conviction substituted. Since 1827 a plea of 'not guilty' is imposed on a defendant who is fit to plead but refuses to do so, remaining 'mute of malice'. Jury trial no longer requires the consent of the accused.

Rights and liberties which would be cherished by the English and others down the centuries were in embryo. The Anglo-Saxon legacy of strong local government, judicial procedures, and the involvement of the populace, coupled with the powerful Anglo-Norman monarchy culminating in Henry II, ensured that the womb of England would be fertilised. From it the English common law had been born.

9

Legal Eagles

You have a gift, sir (thank your education),
Will never let you want, while there are men,
And malice, to breed causes.   Ben Jonson, *Volpone*

I could have been a judge, but I never had the Latin for the judgin'. I
never had it, so I'd had it, as far as being a judge was concerned.
Peter Cook, 'Sitting on the Bench'

H AVING been hatched, the law grew fast and fit, and soon took flight.
Originally the king's council had carried out executive as well as
legislative and judicial functions. Over time, royal courts split off from the
council and were established as separate entities at Westminster Hall. Built
by William Rufus, and later enlarged and re-roofed by Richard II, its enormous dimensions – three hundred feet long with a high, beamed roof –
could accommodate a plethora of royal courts. By the mid 1160s ordinary
litigation was being transacted before the king's justices at Westminster.
But there could be lengthy absences. It was not until 1339, after a six-year
interlude in York, that the location of the royal courts in Westminster Hall
became permanent.

The first department of state established there was the Exchequer, which
took its name from the chequered table at which it sat. Moving from
Winchester to Westminster at the end of the twelfth century, it took up
residence in a separate chamber adjoining the Hall. In its judicial role the
Exchequer originally dealt with disputes over Crown revenues, but gradually
extended its jurisdiction to disputes between individuals on many subjects.
Its meticulous work required written records. From 1130 it got them in the
form of pipe rolls. The other royal courts would follow suit, producing the
plea rolls.

Near the entrance of the Hall was the Bench or Common Bench, later
called the Court of the Common Pleas. It was the main royal court for
ordinary civil litigation and by far the busiest. It developed out of the Court
of Exchequer, separating from it in the 1190s.[1] In the thirteenth century

---

[1] Brand, *Making of the Common Law*, p. 136.

it acquired its place against the west wall of the Hall, not far from the Exchequer. Pleas of the Crown – civil matters affecting the king, actions of trespass alleging violation of the king's peace, and criminal cases – were heard in the Court of the King's Bench, which sometime after 1230 was situated on the south side of the stairs. By 'writ of error' it had the power to review judgments of the Common Pleas. Both the Common Pleas and the King's Bench had a Chief Justice and several judges attached to them, and both occupied a space marked out by a wooden bar at which counsel stood before those judges who sat on a raised platform or bench against the wall.

From the end of the fourteenth century a new court, the Court of Chancery (named after the wooden screens or *cancelli* behind which its clerks worked), emerged from the king's council, and at some point assumed an independent jurisdiction under the chancellor. It joined the other royal courts in Westminster Hall, ultimately to be situated opposite the King's Bench. It had the power to inhibit, through injunctions, the proceedings of the common law courts.[2] In 1348 a new chamber was built in front of the Hall for the exercise of the council's judicial and other delegated functions. Gilded with stars set in an azure ceiling, from 1366 it was known as *Camera Stellata*, or Star Chamber.

The courts were partitioned off from each other but this hardly masked the noise all around, and the voices of pleaders in one court must have carried to the other. Round the walls, and adding to the hugger-mugger, huddled temporary booths and shops selling writing materials, wax, ink, spectacles and other tools of the trade, although there is no mention of any law booksellers before 1640. 'Men of straw' congregated there, the straw displayed in their shoes a sign that their testimony could be bought. Every so often, for occasions of State or to allow Henry VIII to play real tennis, the courts and shops were dismantled and removed.

Westminster Hall provided a cacophonous, cavernous and magnificent theatre for the dramas that would take place there, including the state trials of William Wallace, Guy Fawkes, Charles I, and for seven long years, Warren Hastings. It was, however, bitterly cold in winter, and could lose some of its majesty when, at the spring tides, it was prone to such severe flooding by the river Thames that judges had to resort to rowing between courts.[3] Flooding threatened not only the participants but also the records of the proceedings themselves.

---

2   *OHLE*, VI, pp. 171–4.
3   Megarry, *A New Miscellany*, pp. 61f; J. H. Baker, *The Common Law Tradition: Lawyers, Books and the Law* (London, 2000), p. 256.

4. Westminster Hall c.1730, the heart of legal and regal England from the twelfth to the nineteenth centuries.

Plea rolls, written accounts of litigation in the central courts, and essential for their efficient running, can be dated back to the reign of Henry II, although the earliest surviving roll is from 1194. To provide the parchment to create a continuous and authoritative record of all that transpired in these courts over the succeeding seven centuries, some six million sheep were to give their lives.[4] Their sacrifice would allow the creation of a permanent reservoir of legal decisions (but not the reasoning behind them) upon which judges could begin to establish a doctrine of precedent that in its developed form remains a defining characteristic of the English system to this day.

With the law solidifying and cohering, pleading being rigidly formulaic, legal principles developing, judicial decisions in one case impacting on others, and judges enforcing more precise rules and more complicated procedures, it was not possible for most people to argue its more arcane features, in an increasingly formalised forum, and in 'law French'. In addition, the major growth of litigation in the courts at Westminster in the second half

4   *Ibid.*, p. 133.

of the thirteenth century made it increasingly difficult and expensive for those living outside London to plead their own cases: easier and cheaper to hire someone learned in the law to represent you and plead on your behalf. Enter the lawyer.

When Henry II ascended the throne there were no professionals trained in English law. None was needed. Courtiers and others could be co-opted to serve as judges when necessary. Such legal advice as was required was commonly sought from the clergy. Advocates were employed before 1200, but it was not until the thirteenth century that a lay literate profession emerges.[5] Counters or *narratores* – with right of audience in the Common Bench – were the first to appear, perhaps as early as the 1220s, practising at Westminster Hall, on general eyre, and in the City of London courts. During the fourteenth century they were organised into a fraternity known as serjeants-at-law, which was also a nursery for members of the judiciary. Legal expertise was increasingly essential.

By the end of the thirteenth century there far more long-serving justices than ever before, and their professional conduct was expected to be high: Edward I dismissed and fined large numbers of the judiciary for misbehaviour in office. There were also many attorneys-at-law, distant precursors of the modern solicitor, who were litigators, with different functions from those of advocates. Attorneys were representatives, dealing with formal aspects of litigation, managing cases, and acting on behalf of, and legally binding, their absent clients. Advocates or 'pleaders' accompanied their clients to court and argued the law and their case in their presence. The legal profession did not split to accommodate these different roles; the two branches grew simultaneously as a result of this division.[6] By 1300 there is evidence of formal instruction in the common law and statutes, the beginning of systematic legal education.[7] These law students were known as 'apprentices of the Bench'.

The reign of Edward I had been transformational for the common law. It had seen the rise of a legal profession with career judges subject to sanction, distinctions between lawyers, and even a degree of regulation: 'apprentices' no longer drifted into legal practice as the fancy took them, but were trained in the law and 'called to the Bar' in batches.[8]

---

5   J. H. Baker, *The Order of Serjeants at Law* (London, 1984), p. 9. Paul Brand, *Origins of the English Legal Profession* (Oxford, 1992), p. 3.
6   Baker, *Introduction to English Legal History*, p. 156.
7   Brand, *Making of the Common Law*, pp. 6–15, 57–75.
8   Baker, *Order of Sergeants at Law*, p. 15.

In the course of the following century as the royal courts took up permanent residence in Westminster, and litigation and the profession continued to mushroom, these common law lawyers, or students of the law, wanted and needed a convenient and convivial place in London where they could congregate, be accommodated, eat, drink and talk, and where they could study and learn. They migrated to the western edge of the medieval city where country fields and scattered villages began, beyond Temple Bar and Holborn Bar. There they were within easy reach of Westminster Hall. There the Inns of Court were established to lodge and educate the professionals needed in an increasingly specialised legal forum. In the fifteenth century Sir John Fortescue referred to them as an 'academy', constituting in effect the 'third university of England'.[9] They taught and transmitted the common law – whereas Oxford and Cambridge taught canon law and Roman civil law – and called their graduates 'to the Bar'. They were 'at once a legal university and an autonomous professional organisation unique in Christendom'. They ensured that English law would be isolated from the influence of continental and clerical jurisprudence, and retain its national character.[10]

The Inns of Court contained no serjeants-at-law, the most senior counsel with a monopoly of practising in the Common Pleas. Fortescue afforded them the same status as that of doctors of civil law or canon law. Usually numbering fewer than ten they formed the Order of the Coif, so named from the close-fitting skull-shaped white caps they wore. On appointment they had to sever their links with their Inns. Instead, most joined one of the two Serjeants' Inns, which by 1500 were situated, respectively, in Fleet Street and at the southern end of Chancery Lane. Here they would dine and discuss legal matters with judges of the King's Bench or the Common Pleas, all of whom – from the fourteenth until the nineteenth century – would come from their ranks. It was akin to a congregation of dons at high table in an Oxbridge college. Postprandial discussions between such luminaries of the law were instrumental in developing judicial consensus on tricky points of common and statute law. By this means was the common law organised, rationalised and refined. By this means were the justices able to give consid-

---

9   This very term was in use in Tudor times when the various Inns together formed a law school not much smaller than the University of Cambridge. It was later popularised by Coke and Blackstone, although the latter was looking back to a long-gone golden age: Baker, *The Common Law Tradition*, p. 3; Sir John Fortescue, *De Laudibus Legum Angliae*, (Cincinnati, 1874), pp. 187–95.

10 Francis Cowper, *A Prospect of Gray's Inn*, 2nd edn (London, 1985), p. 1; Baker, *Introduction to English Legal History*, p. 155.

ered and authoritative advice to the government. By this means was legal continuity preserved.[11]

All four of the Inns of Court claim roughly equal antiquity, and the precise date of their coming into being is not known. None was incorporated, nor endowed, nor 'founded'. They all evolved between roughly the second half of the fourteenth century and the first quarter of the fifteenth.[12] Their birth may have been induced by the return of the courts and legal profession to Westminster in 1339, after a lengthy sojourn in York. In addition nine or ten so-called 'inns of chancery' such as Barnard's, Staple, Clifford's, Clement's and Lyon's grew up to serve younger students seeking a grounding in legal procedure, and attorneys and clerks who could not get into one of the grander Inns. They had certainly begun their association with the Inns of Court by the end of the fifteenth century. By 1540 they had lost their independence completely and had become mere educational annexes. The study of the law began in an Inn of Chancery, before the eager and fortunate student progressed to an Inn of Court.[13] They are now all defunct, Clifford's alone limping into the twentieth century and succumbing in 1903.

Inner and Middle Temple were established on the land of the Knights Templar, who in 1185 had built the church that still dominates the heart of these two inns. With the papal suppression of the Templar order in 1312, their estate reverted to the Crown. Sometime later the 'gentlemen apprentices of the law' took up their quarters in this riverside sanctuary, and built around it. They were there for long enough to have accumulated legal papers and books, which were destroyed in the Peasants' Revolt of 1381. Whether they initially formed one society which split, or were always two separate bodies, is still uncertain, although lawyers had taken from the outset separate leases for the consecrated buildings near the centre of the Temple, and for the unconsecrated remainder. These affiliations soon became known as the Inner Temple and the Middle Temple, and were certainly distinct societies

---

[11] Fortescue, *De Laudibus Legum Angliae*, ch. L; *OHLE*, VI, p. 413; *EHD*, V, p. 532; Baker, *Order of Serjeants at Law*, pp. 72f; Baker, *Introduction to English Legal History*, pp. 155–8. In the seventeenth century the new rank of king's counsel took precedence over that of serjeant, and a silk gown became more desirable than a quaint coif. The old order was never abolished. It died with Lord Lindley, the last lonely serjeant, in 1921.

[12] There is slight evidence of the existence of Gray's and perhaps Lincoln's Inn in about 1340: Baker, *The Common Law Tradition*, pp.15–18.

[13] *OHLE*, VI, pp. 453–9.

5. The Inns of Court (in 1671): the Third University – in appearance, excellence and importance on a par with Cambridge and Oxford.

by 1388, when they are mentioned in a yearbook.[14] To this day the two Inns uneasily share the Temple church as a chapel.

Named after either the third earl of Lincoln or a fourteenth-century serjeant called Thomas de Lincoln, and based in the bishop of Chichester's old house off Chancellor's – or Chancery – Lane, was Lincoln's Inn. The earliest mention of it as a legal society is in 1417, and its own records, known as the Black Books, document a meeting of its governing council in 1422. There is no evidence of its existence in its present location prior to this date. It is probably of more recent foundation than the others.

Gray's Inn was established by the 1380s at the latest, and took its name from the de Grey family, whose patriarch, Baron Reginald de Grey, was Chief Justice of Chester under Edward I. Their home stood on the site of the Inn, and by this date had become a hostel for young lawyers. Some could also be young hotheads, prone to dissipation, and rivalry between the Inns would prove a catalyst for aggression. In 1457 seven students of Lincoln's Inn were expelled 'for lying in wait with swords and clubs in the middle of the night and having an affray with the Society of Gray's Inn'.[15] The early records of Gray's Inn were destroyed in a fire in 1684, and so its side of the story is not recorded. It was noted in 1655 that the junior members of Gray's Inn were observed 'throwing bread, knocking and breaking pots, refusing to mess together as they sit, not taking their meat in due course as it is brought up unto the several tables'. Their actions were prejudicial to 'the House, giving ill-example to new comers and to the dishonour of the government, being observed by strangers passing by the screen at meal times'.[16] The past had seen far worse, and the fourteenth century 'coroners' records taken alone might suggest dens of violent students, run by homicidal servants'.[17] In this respect, as in many others, the Inns of Court were not unlike the Oxbridge colleges upon which they were modelled.

Nonetheless, behind their walls the English legal profession was born, and the common law was nurtured, and to an extent made, by the 'oral systematic tradition', the 'common learning' and shared assumptions of a

14 J. H. Baker, *The Legal Profession and the Common Law* (London, 1986), pp. 3–6; Baker, *The Common Law Tradition*, pp. 31–4; Richard Havery, *History of the Middle Temple* (London, 2011), pp. 39–40. There was also an Outer Temple described in the plea rolls in 1448 as 'an inn of men of court'. It did not survive as a separate entity and was subsumed by its two neighbours.

15 The Black Books of Lincoln's Inn. There had been major outbreaks of violence between 'apprentices of the bench' on a number of occasions in the fourteenth century: Baker, *The Common Law Tradition*, pp. 12–16.

16 Gray's Inn Pension Books, I, p. 414.

17 Baker, *The Common Law Tradition*, p. 18.

learned profession. This continued until the rise of judicial positivism in the sixteenth century, when the law was no longer conceived as 'common learning' but as case law in a stricter sense. By the eighteenth century the Inns could no longer be compared to a university, but for three hundred years they had 'constituted one of the greatest law schools the world has ever known … and may fairly be said to have helped create the common law'.[18] These unique institutions, thoroughly entrenched in English social life, also helped preserve English law from Romanising influences, since the lawyers who dominated the Commons as well as the courts had received their legal education not in the universities where civil law was taught, but in the Inns where the common law was nourished.[19]

If the thirteenth century was when the law put down deep roots, its growth was largely beneath the surface. Not much of the law was enacted. The word 'statute' had hardly yet entered the lexicon; kings legislated by ordinance. First in the statute book is Magna Carta, but it is called a charter not a statute, and other measures such as those devised at Merton (1236), Oxford (1258), Westminster (1259) and Marlborough (1267) are called 'provisions'.[20] As of yet there were no statute rolls or rolls of parliament. It would not be until 1275 that 'statute-making as the essential and continuous activity of the king' began in England, when Edward I embarked on enthusiastic legislative activity producing such 'durable laws' in response to individual petitions for justice that he was later given the sobriquet 'the English Justinian'.[21]

As the thirteenth century drew to a close, rolls of the growing body of statutes began to be kept. Early in the next century the Commons were active in petitioning as a group, and by the end of the fourteenth century many petitions would be made directly to the 'Commonality of the Realm' instead of to the king.[22] Even so, the impact of statutory reforms of the law was moderate, and its aim modest: 'to perfect a common law system of procedure and thought which was in essence taken for granted'.[23] Even in the mid-fifteenth century, Fortescue, in his encomium of English law, would devote just one chapter of less than three hundred words to the making of

---

18 *Ibid.*, pp. 24–8.
19 *OHLE*, VI, pp. 12, 470ff.
20 *EHD*, III, pp. 351–4, 361–7, 370–6, 384–92.
21 Coke, *Institutes of the Laws of England*, II, p. 156.
22 Alan Harding, *Medieval Law and the Foundations of the Modern State* (Oxford, 2001), pp. 186–90.
23 *OHLE*, VI, p. 39.

statutes.[24] It was not until the sixteenth century that parliamentary legislation became extensive, far-reaching, sophisticated, and recorded in print.

Similarly the term 'common law' as referring to the law of the land, as distinct from custom, or special jurisdictions such as that of the Church or Admiralty, was not yet on the tip of every temporal lawyer's tongue, although it would be so by the end of the fourteenth century. Custom in fact was the great bulk of the law, the dominant custom being that developing in the king's court. This was the theatre of the royal justices, acting on the king's behalf, but enhancing their own significance.

With their experience growing and their collective memories accumulating, the need arose for a manual of far greater dimensions than *Glanvill*, and one specifically designed for the instruction of 'unwise' and 'unlearned' justices. Sometime before the mid-thirteenth century another treatise, also called *De Legibus et Consuetudinibus Angliae*, was composed largely by a judge called William of Raleigh, and supplemented and revised by Henry de Bracton, who had served as his clerk, and by whose name the whole work is known. Though unfinished, *Bracton* has been called 'the flower and crown of English jurisprudence ... Romanesque in form, English in substance'.[25] It was specifically pedagogic. It depicts the practice of the king's court as it was in the 1220s and 1230s, or sometimes as the author thought it should have been, and provides illustrations of how the common law operated, drawing on almost five hundred decisions evidenced in the plea rolls. But the author was trained in civil law, and it was Roman jurisprudence which supplied him with a number of concepts under which his English matter could be 'fashioned, for the first time, into an articulated system of principles, but with a precise technical vocabulary, infinitely more subtle than the language of the plea rolls, with which to describe and analyse it'.[26]

The inclusion in the *magnum opus* of many instances of case law and the reasoning behind the judgments was revolutionary, even though no one appears to have had access to the treatise prior to Bracton's death, and its influence was limited. It began a trend which resulted in the publishing of annual compilations of cases, called Year Books, which in turn allowed for

---

24 Fortescue, *De Laudibus Legum Angliae*, ch. XVIII.
25 P&M, I, pp. 206f. For a concise appraisal of views on the dating, authorship and purpose of this work, see *Bracton*, III, pp. xv–l; Paul Brand, 'The Age of Bracton', *The History of English Law: Centenary Essays on 'Pollack and Maitland'*, ed. John Hudson (Oxford, 1996), pp. 65–89.
26 *Bracton*, I, pp. xxxiiif.

comparisons to be made between decisions on similar issues in different courts, and was to end in a full-blown doctrine of binding precedent.

Romanism did not make the author an advocate of absolute monarchy. He expressed the English consensus that although 'the king has no equal within his realm' and is under no man, he is 'under God and under the law, because law makes the king ... for there is no king [*rex*] where will rules rather than law [*lex*]'. In short, a ruler should only be called 'king' if he exercised power in a lawful manner.[27] Later in the century, in the reign of Edward I, an abridgement of *Bracton* – in French rather than in Latin – known as *Britton* reiterated what was becoming the constitutional consensus. The higher law was statutory. Statute could change judge-made law. Statute proceeded out of the king's mouth. Even so, the mouth was muzzled. The king was not above the law. He could not by his mere word make or change the law, nor should he break it. He could issue writs that went beyond the law, but not against the law. His justices could improve, but not fundamentally alter, the law. Only by legislating could he make or change the law, and he could legislate only with the participation of parliament. This constitutional doctrine of powerful but limited monarchy was becoming ever more firmly established. By the same reign the term 'common law' had become commonplace, denoting the law of England. Constitutionalism and common law were siblings.

It did not take long for the students of the common law to become its champions and to proclaim abroad its intrinsic and essentially English merits. Many became high in government and took their view of the primacy of the law with them to its very heart. Sir John Fortescue was Chief Justice of the King's Bench from 1442 until 1461 when, as a result of the defeat and deposition of Henry VI during the Wars of the Roses, he was forced to flee first to Scotland and then to France. There, as part of a government in exile, he composed his *De Laudibus Legum Angliae* (*In Praise of the Laws of England*), in which he sought to demonstrate that 'the laws and customs of England are not only good, but the very best'. He also asserted the antiquity as well as the superiority of the English legal and constitutional inheritance over all others. Pre-dating the Roman invasion and planted in fertile English loam, it had slowly matured into near perfection. It was indigenous, not an alien import.

Fortescue distinguished between *dominium regale* (regal government), of which France was the exemplar and whereby kings ruled without the assent of their subjects, and *dominium politicum et regale* (political and regal government), which prevailed in England and required common assent to

---

[27] *Ibid.*, II, p. 33.

the laws. It was to protect their property and bodies that the English people 'submitted of their own will to the government of a king'. They had limited the powers of the rulers they chose. The latter held power subject to the will of the people and shared power with them. The king could not dispose of the lives and goods of the people arbitrarily, but was bound to protect them. The laws of England did not sanction the alien maxim that 'what pleases the prince has the force of law'.[28]

Judges, not kings, were the protectors and interpreters of the law. They exercised their discretion in a manner 'most beneficial to the common weal'. In England, because taxation and legislation required 'the assent of the whole realm' in parliament, the population of the kingdom was free and prosperous. Because they were involved in the government and in the evolution of the law, people were motivated to defend the country from foreign foes, and to take seriously civic responsibilities such as jury service. Juries were peculiar to England. Jurors, being stoutly independent farmers, could not easily be bribed nor suborned. Fortescue also first gave expression to what would later become known as 'Blackstone's formulation', stating that 'one would much rather that twenty guilty persons should escape the punishment of death, than that one innocent person should be condemned, and suffer capitally'. Unlike in France, no one in England could be lawfully condemned to death on the strength of confessions extracted by torture.[29] Unlike in France, ultimate power resided not in the king alone, but in the king-in-parliament. Fortescue's ideal England, secure in its self-satisfaction, was, as Shakespeare's, a 'precious stone set in the silver sea', isolated from the influence or 'envy of less happier lands'.

This England would soon become a 'less happier land', as it would be torn apart by the Reformation and yet another cataclysmic civil war. However, despite the turmoil at home and abroad, despite the triumph of Roman law on the Continent, and despite the rivalry sometimes posed by Chancery and the conciliar courts, the English common law survived and flourished.

[28] Fortescue, *De Laudibus Legum Angliae*, chs IX and XVII; *OHLE*, VI, p. 18.
[29] *Ibid.*, chs XXII, XXVII and XXXII.

PART II

CONFLICT OF LAWS
1500–1766

CHAPTER 10

The King's Conscience, the Lord Chancellor's Foot

> Reason to rule, but mercy to forgive;
> The first is law, the last prerogative.
> > Dryden, *The Hind and the Panther*

> If the parties will at my hands call for justice, then, all were it my father
> stood on the one side and the Devil on the other, his cause being good,
> the Devil should have right.
> > Sir Thomas More (Roper, *The Life of Sir Thomas More*)

THE social turmoil occasioned by the Wars of Roses, and the time it took for the new Tudor dynasty to assert its supremacy, unsettled the rule of law. To what extent is open to debate, but it was the perception at the time. Since the 1460s, maintained Richard III's parliament, the realm had been 'ruled by self-will and pleasure, fear and dread', and 'all manner of equity and laws [had been] laid apart and despised'.[1] For chaos to be banished and order imposed, for the law to be enforced, and for justice to be administered, a strong central authority was needed. The Tudor dynasty provided this, but the measures successive monarchs took to maintain law and order and the way they took them could also threaten the integrity of the common law. The exercise of the royal prerogative enabled effective and decisive government under the Tudors – who were adept at increasing the power of the Crown without seeming to endanger the constitutional balance or the rule of law – but under the less astute Stuarts engendered unease over the extent of arbitrary royal power.

The prerogative was exercised outwith parliament or the common law courts. It was necessary that the Crown retained some undefined executive power to deal with unforeseen and unforeseeable contingencies of administration and with political crises. But prerogative unrestrained smacked of the Roman imperial tradition and despotic theocratic monarchy, rather than the more contractual 'Germanic' kingship championed in England since Magna Carta or before. The relative power of the prerogative varied with

---

[1] *OHLE*, VI, p. 69.

the standing of the incumbent king. Under Edward I the prerogative was powerful indeed. Under his son it atrophied. During the century from the downfall of Richard II to the death of Richard III it lost ground to the more 'constitutional' view of kingship, but survived as a necessary adjunct to government, as it does to this day. Using the prerogative, in the Middle Ages kings had issued 'ordinances' which had the force of law. By Tudor times it was 'proclamations'. In 1539 parliament, perhaps a little overawed by the personality of the incumbent king, had even given statutory sanction to the deployment of this regal legislative fiat. The Statute of Proclamations was passed which empowered Henry VIII, in an emergency, to issue proclamations that would have the same force 'as though they were made by act of parliament'.[2] Whatever the overt purpose of the act, the fear was that it gave the king such powers to legislate as would undermine the constitution. But for its repeal in the reign of Henry's less intimidating son, Edward VI, an English king could 'have been as despotic as a French monarch'. Instead, repeal left 'to proclamations only such weight as they might possess at common law'.[3] That weight differed over time, and the assessment of it was never easy.

Even so powerful and forceful a monarch as Henry VIII, who could sway his judges, browbeat his parliament, and manipulate the legal process, nonetheless acted within legal forms and procedures, and accepted the general view of the Tudor age that even the king was bound by the law.[4] He could not use the prerogative to defeat lawful rights and long-held liberties. His officials could not use it as a shield for illegal acts they had committed at royal command. The king should be the very epitome of justice. Since a lawful resolution of an issue or dispute was not always a just one, equity (the expression of the king's conscience) and Star Chamber (another adjunct of the king's council) would remedy the inadequacies or injustices of an earlier royal creation, the common law.

In the fifteenth century, just as the land had grown increasingly lawless, so the law had become somewhat fossilised. Complacency accompanied conceit, and the prouder the practitioners of the common law were in their inheritance the less receptive to new or foreign ideas they became. The common law had developed quickly but had done so within a framework of certain recognised forms of action; outside these prescribed limits no action lay and no remedy could be given at law. The rule was 'no writ, no remedy'.

---

2   *EHD*, V, pp. 521ff.
3   Dicey, *Lectures Introductory to the Study of the Law*, pp. 48f; *OHLE*, VI, p. 64.
4   *OHLE*, VI, pp. 68f.

Restrictions were placed on the issuance of new writs. The law grew rigid, while injustice increased and circumstances changed. There were common and necessary practices in affairs of property – such as trusts – which the courts of common law did not recognise and so failed to protect. Mercantile cases, and those involving alien merchants, were outside the scope of common law. Procedure was slow, highly technical and very expensive, and a trivial mistake in pleading could lose a good case. The arrival of lawyers made the law more legalistic. Judges would often spend more time examining the validity of the writ than the merits of the claim. They often abandoned their undoubted discretionary powers, preferring certainty to justice. Injustice in individual cases was preferable to the inconvenience to the common law of admitting exceptions. This preference became law when in 1566 it became an indictable offence to claim that the King's Bench was a court of conscience. Judges palmed off responsibility for doing justice in particular cases onto the jury. The judicial oath was to act according to the law, whereas jurors swore to give a true verdict according to their conscience.[5] Judges also limited the role of juries in civil cases by single-issue pleading, admitting of no pleadings in the alternative and allowing only one contested issue of law to go to a jury, however complex the case. The jury's task was simplified, but at the cost of justice. The common law courts thus depreciated their own currency, and propelled litigants to look elsewhere for redress.

Litigants had long had recourse to the king, who was the 'fount of justice' with an almost sacred duty to right the wrongs of his people, and whose prerogative was as much a part of the law of the land as the common law. Equity and discretion were inherent in the royal person. Subjects could throw themselves on the king's mercy or conscience. Increasingly they did so, to an extent that the regal function of resolving petitions was eventually devolved to the chancellor, who could act in a way consistent with the moral basis, if not the strict letter, of the law. Successive chancellors developed a body of principles and rules called equity, which they applied in their new Court of Chancery. There procedure was heavily influenced by both Roman and canon law, in which the early chancellors, as clerics, were well versed, and involved the application of principles of fairness to particular circumstances. Equity, in a quest for truth alien to the common law, delved into the particular facts of a case and into the motives of the litigants. To so do, procedurally it had to rely not on juries but on the sworn answers of the parties, the interrogatory responses of witnesses, and the production and examination of documents. Where warranted, it distilled fairness out of the

5   *Ibid.*, pp. 46f.

dispute and instilled justice into the resolution. Where necessary, it even created new and important remedies such as injunctions, although these had the potential for conflict with the common law as they could be deployed to prohibit – under threat of imprisonment – the enforcement of a common law court order.

On the whole, equity was seen by most contemporaries as benevolent, an attempt to 'mitigate the rigour', or temper the rigidities, delays and unfairness, of the common law by allowing the courts discretion to find in accordance with natural justice in particular cases. One who believed he embodied the very spirit of equity, James I, expressed it thus: 'Laws are ordained as rules of virtuous and social living and not to be snares to trap good subjects; and therefore the law must be interpreted according to the meaning and not to the literal sense.'[6] Equity was not established as an alternative to the law, let alone as its rival. In accordance with the maxim 'equity follows the law', Chancery would defer to common law resolutions unless persuaded they were inequitable. Like his Heavenly Master, the chancellor came to fulfil the law, not destroy it. Equity stitched a tear in the fabric of justice. Along with the jury, this duality of law and equity is perhaps the most distinctive and important element of the English legal system.

Many common law lawyers also practised in Chancery, accepting its equitable jurisdiction as a necessary adjunct to the common law. Indeed, Chancery and the other conciliar courts in general 'did not threaten the common law system itself, because they had become in a sense an integral part of it, serviced by the same profession'. Chancery would survive, but its jurisprudence would be 'a gloss upon, not an alternative to, the common law'.[7] It enriched; it did not incapacitate. That was the future.

At the time some were less enamoured with what they considered to be the anarchic uncertainty engendered by the prerogative courts. In particular, the decisions the chancellors made were far from restricted and were often widely diverse, depending on the nature of the particular case or even on the conscience of the particular chancellor. John Selden, a prominent lawyer during the reigns of the first two Stuarts, peevishly sniped,

> Equity is a Roguish thing; for Law we have a measure, know what to trust to, Equity is according to the Conscience of him that is Chancellor, and as that is larger or narrower, so is Equity. 'Tis all one as if they should make the Standard for the measure we call a Foot, a Chancellor's Foot: what an

---

6   James I, *Basilikon Doron*, in *King James VI and I: Political Writings*, ed. Johann Sommerville (Cambridge 1994), p. 43.

7   *OHLE*, VI, p. 8.

uncertain Measure would this be? One Chancellor has a long Foot, another a short Foot, a Third an indifferent Foot: 'Tis the same thing in the Chancellor's Conscience.[8]

An equitable judgment could be an arbitrary one. Arbitration, the hallmark of equitable jurisdiction, and arbitrariness, its Achilles heel, could often be confused.

Such confusion was apparent no more so than when Cardinal Wolsey held the Great Seal of State, from 1515 to 1529. Under him the work of the courts of equity multiplied at the expense both of the common law courts and of the reputation of the conciliar. Wolsey dominated the equitable arena. As arbitration and negotiation in private suits were much in operation in all the conciliar courts, a non-lawyer such as he could exercise, untrammelled, his natural abilities and ideals of natural justice. Highly intelligent and with great self-confidence, Wolsey would hear suitors, and mediate or determine matters in both Chancery and Star Chamber. He had to heed the advice of other prominent councillors, but he kept consultation to a minimum.[9] His will was law. 'He spared neither high nor low, but judged every man, whatever his dignity, according to his merits and deserts', was one view of Wolsey in his judicial role.[10] Another is that he was an arrogant bully who abused his position and 'reinforced doubts about the justness of a one-man supreme court'. Whatever his merits as a judge, it was under Wolsey that relations between Chancery and the legal profession first soured. The development of *habeas corpus* by the King's Bench may have been a reaction to his arbitrary ways.[11]

Wolsey's successor, Sir Thomas More, was trained in the common law and attempted reconciliation with it. He denounced arbitrariness, but nonetheless still acted as an arbiter in giving awards, or as an umpire in deciding cases, and, despite the objections of the common law judges, continued to grant injunctions when it was 'just and convenient to do'. He even tried to persuade those judges to incorporate equity into their own courts 'to mitigate and reform the rigour of the law themselves', and so do away with any need for injunctions. Although they declined this offer, they concurred that More at least had acted justly in his deployment of the arsenal of equity.[12]

---

8   John Selden, *Table Talk* (London, 1689), p. 64.

9   John Guy, *The Cardinal's Court: The Impact of Thomas Wolsey in Star Chamber* (Hassocks, 1977), pp. 29, 35, 97.

10   George Cavendish, *Thomas Wolsey*, Folio Society edn (London, 1962), p. 52.

11   J. H. Baker, *The Reports of John Spelman*, Seldon Society 94 (1978), p. 80; *OHLE*, VI, pp. 175ff.

12   *OHLE*, VI, p. 178; William Roper, *The Life of Sir Thomas More*, Everyman edn (London, 1963). pp. 60ff; Guy, *The Cardinal's Court*, p. 98.

By their rejection of More's proposal for the equitable development of the common law, the judges ensured that Chancery would remain as a separate court of equity for centuries to come. Co-existence and cooperation between the two dispensations, the norm in the fourteenth and fifteenth centuries, persisted under the Tudors. By the seventeenth century, however, when an alien monarch from a civil law background increasingly tried to manipulate court processes for his own ends, conflict was inevitable.

CHAPTER II

Star Chamber: Keeping England in Quiet

> I hope the world will know that I am come hither this day to maintain
> the law, and do justice according to my oath.
>
> James I in Star Chamber (*EHD*, Vb)

CONFLICT coalesced in the Court of Star Chamber. The very name is now a byword for tyranny but this is a misnomer. In its inception, and throughout most of its history, it represented precisely the opposite. Its demise was tragic in the true sense that it was as a result of the corruption of the best. Star Chamber – *camera stellata* – consisted of two interconnected rooms in the Palace of Westminster. From the fourteenth century on the king's council met there, around a large table covered by a green carpet, to exercise its delegated powers, including judicial ones. It derived its authority directly from the king; it derived its name from the star-studded ceiling.[1] But fantasy also gilded it. 'Like as the stars do adorn the firmament and in the dark night do give their light unto the earth, so the lords of the nobility according to their calling do in this court shine forth by their virtues of piety, wisdom and good justice', gushed Richard Robinson in Elizabeth's reign.[2] Its first historian, William Hudson, writing under James I, went further in sycophancy, asserting that its starry decor demonstrated that the councillors sitting there in judgment were but a mere reflection of the grandeur of the monarch from whom all their powers flowed. Long before Louis XIV, James I was the Sun King:

> It is the seal of that court ... and it was so fitly called, because the stars have no light but what is cast upon them from the sun by reflection, being his representative body ... so in the presence of his great majesty, the which is the sun of honour and glory, the shining of those stars is put out, they not having any power to pronounce any sentence in this court, for the judgment is the king's only; but by way of advice they deliver their opinions, which his wisdom alloweth or disalloweth, encreaseth or moderateth, at his royal pleasure.[3]

---

[1] *EHD*, V(a), p. 375.
[2] *Ibid.*, p. 377.
[3] William Hudson, *A Treatise on the Court of Star Chamber* (London, 1792), p. 8.

Star Chamber came to greatest prominence under the Tudors and early Stuarts. Henry VII secured the throne in 1485 after the almost interminable Wars of the Roses. In such interesting times, powerful barons had fought, pillaged, and enhanced their power at the expense of the monarchy and of the people. With the undermining of royal authority, the administration of justice had been subverted and brought into disrepute. Bishop Latimer had condemned the propensity of judges to take what were euphemistically called 'gentle rewards' – bribes bestowed by the rich – 'either to give sentence against the poor, or to put off the poor man's cause'.⁴ The Act Pro Camera Stellata of 1487 did not affect, let alone create, the jurisdiction of the council in Star Chamber, but established a special tribunal in which the law enforcement function of the council was concentrated. This subcommittee had a fixed membership and the assured presence of lawyers. Its purpose was to enhance the administration of justice, to curb local magnates, and to deal with offences imperilling the safety of the realm.⁵

Under Henry VII Star Chamber became the scourge of the 'over mighty' subject. In its judicial role it was the very epitome of personal royal justice, speedy and resolute. It consisted of members of the king's inner circle, usually with the two Chief Justices included, acting as a court. Its power emanated from the throne. Miscreants standing before it were standing before the king himself. Sometimes this was quite literally the case, as the king upon occasion would preside over the proceedings sitting in 'a chair of state elevated above the table about which his lords sat'.⁶ Increasingly however, authority was delegated. Henry VII sat often in person, but when he went on progress around his kingdom he took some councillors with him and left the chancellor behind to preside over council meetings in Star Chamber.

His son, Henry VIII, attended Star Chamber regularly early in his reign, but then left it largely to Cardinal Wolsey. A strong chancellor could exercise great influence over the other councillors and even over the two Chief Justices who were wont to attend. Under Wolsey, Star Chamber's powers and prestige were enhanced to such an extent that it was thought by some at the time that it was his creation as a high court. Under Thomas Cromwell, Wolsey's former pupil, it gained its independence when in the 1530s the privy council was deliberately created out of the king's council, leaving the court of Star Chamber simply to continue where the old council had left off, but

---

4   *EHD*, V, pp. 532f; Alfred Denning, *Landmarks in the Law* (London, 1984), p. 49.
5   Guy, *The Cardinal's Court*, p. 19; *EHD*, V, pp. 537f.
6   Hudson, *Treatise on the Court of Star Chamber*, p. 9.

thereby giving it 'the professionalism and continuity that could only stem from a settled constitution'.[7]

Star Chamber was not a court of equity in the substantive sense but was analogous to Chancery, both in its Roman procedural model and in its equitable principles aimed at rectifying the inability of the common law courts to do full justice in some cases. Its jurisdiction was criminal and civil. Unsurprisingly much of its business overlapped with Chancery, though most of the civil cases coming before it alleged criminality as well. It also dealt with riot, fraud, forgery, perjury, criminal libel, conspiracy and malfeasance in public office. Many of these offences were the creation of Star Chamber. It could order the guilty party to undergo acts of public humiliation in the pillory, or to be whipped, or branded, or facially mutilated. It could also impose heavy fines and imprisonment. Treason was beyond its competence because, unlike the common law courts, it could not condemn to death. So too, for the same reason, were felonies, although to ensure a modicum of justice, in exceptional circumstances Star Chamber tried them but punished them as misdemeanours.[8]

As an adjunct of the king's council this prerogative court enjoyed a number of advantages over those of the common law. It did not have to rely on juries that could be bribed, or intimidated, or could show partiality. Indeed it could punish recalcitrant jurors, especially those deemed by trial judges to have found 'contrary to the evidence'. This usually denoted corruption. In later days, when the pressure on juries was not to come from overbearing sheriffs, or from the pockets or scabbards of scoundrels, but from central government itself, this would prove a dangerous precedent. Further, errant aristocrats could be interrogated and judged by members of the council. Star Chamber could not be intimidated by armed and riotous nobles. It could summon witnesses to establish the truth, or have enquiries made by local magistrates. Plaintiff and defendant were upon oath, and had to testify. It represented the king: it embodied the majesty of the law to a higher degree than the compromised common law courts. Councillors were the king's servants and amenable only to royal influence. Towards all subjects, regardless of rank, they could be and generally were fearlessly impartial. They could inflict penalties not available at common law, such as imprisonment or confiscation of property, which could hurt the nobility mightily.

Devised in part to protect humbler subjects from the unscrupulous but powerful, by Tudor times Star Chamber had become indispensable. As a

---

7   *EHD*, V, p. 524; Guy, *The Cardinal's Court*, pp. 131, 136ff.
8   *OHLE*, VI, p. 197; Guy, *The Cardinal's Court*, pp. 64f.

court supervising all other tribunals it upheld law and order in an age of social disruption, and tamed the manners of quasi-military barbarism. By the end of the sixteenth century it had become primarily a central criminal court responsible for enforcing common and statute law, supreme within, but integral to, the English judicial system. It became highly regarded in lay and legal circles, its prestige reaching its apogee in the reign of James I, when its authority to instruct and correct had penetrated to all levels of judicial practice.[9] Francis Bacon, who maintained that the integrity of the judges was their paramount virtue and that 'one foul sentence doth more to hurt than many foul examples, for these do but corrupt the stream; the other corrupteth the fountain', described it as 'one of the sagest and noblest institutions of this kingdom'.[10] He would, you may think, as he had been schooled in civil as well as common law and had been Clerk of the Star Chamber. His sentiments were shared, however, by his rival, the very embodiment of the common law, Edward Coke. He declared Star Chamber 'the most honourable Court (our Parliament excepted) that is in the Christian world, both in respect of the Judges of the Court, and of their honourable proceeding according to their just jurisdiction and the ancient and just orders of the Court'. 'This court', he asserted, 'the right institutions and ancient orders thereof being observed, doth keep all England in quiet.'[11]

By the time of Charles I society had changed, but Star Chamber had not. It was still useful but no longer indispensable, as ordinary tribunals were now strong enough to administer justice. Juries were no longer so overawed, or corrupted, by great lords, and judges no longer sat in fear of riot or resistance. It still did good work in non-political cases – which overwhelmingly dominated its work – but almost of all of these could have been heard in other courts.

More worryingly, a court created to check abuses developed abuses of its own. As its workload grew at the expense of the King's Bench and of the Common Pleas, so did delays. Due process meant slow progress, and most private cases seem to have taken a year to conclude.[12] But it was in its public jurisdiction that the real problems arose. The court sat in two capacities, prac-

---

9   *Ibid.*, p. 138.
10 Francis Bacon, 'Of Judicature', in *Bacon's Essays*, ed. Richard Whately (London, 1892). He was not to live up to his own standards, losing the office of Lord Chancellor in 1621, and being fined and imprisoned in the Tower for accepting bribes. It is a little disturbing that, while acknowledging this just censure, Bacon declared he was the 'justest judge that was in England these fifty years'.
11 Coke, *Institutes of the Laws of England*, IV, p. 65.
12 Guy, *The Cardinal's Court*, p. 113.

tically although not technically distinct: as a high-handed court of equity, and as the sword of political power. This had not been much of an issue under the Tudors, but under the less adept Stuarts its reputation plunged dramatically. Because it was controlled very largely by the Crown it could become, and be perceived as having become, an instrument of arbitrary rule, used to suppress political and religious dissent. Increasingly, Star Chamber was portrayed as an instrument of royal despotism, while the common law was seen as the protector of the rights and liberty of the subject. This came to a head under Charles I, and it is as a result of his actions that Star Chamber has suffered such ill repute. The fault did not lie with Star Chamber itself, but with Charles Stuart.

Rather than disbanding it as a great success that had achieved its ends, the king used it to silence critics of the court, Church or government, and, on one occasion, libellers of his friends and ministers. Intending to make his subjects fear his authority, he had in a few cases authorised heavy fines and humiliating punishments, which were imposed by judges, the creatures of the king, upon those who dared openly and publicly to oppose his arbitrary rule. Some had their noses slit or their ears cut off, some were pilloried or whipped – public examples of royal displeasure. The result was that the populace lost faith in Star Camber as a protector and saw it as an oppressor. One of the cases that most impacted on the popular imagination was that of the barrister, William Prynne. In 1633 he had his ears sliced off for publishing, shortly after the queen had acted in a masque, a polemic castigating actresses as whores. While in prison he wrote an attack on the bishops. In 1637 he was condemned again by Star Chamber (with Archbishop William Laud as a judge) to be put in the pillory, to have his ear-stumps removed, and to be imprisoned for life.[13] Punished along with him were two puritan divines, Henry Burton and John Bastwick, who had satirised the episcopacy.

The involvement of Laud, no friend of the common law, and, like his predecessor Becket, keen to free the Church from its trammels,[14] did little to enhance the reputation of the court. No one should be judge in his own cause. Yet here was the archbishop of Canterbury judging those who attacked bishops. He was hardly disinterested, being the deviser of the ecclesiastical policies that had led to the criticism in the first place. Laud was not prone to conciliate, but to persecute, those who defied him and his reforms. He used any weapon at hand. He already dominated the much disliked Court of High Commission, a secular court for church affairs established during

---

13 *ST*, III, pp. 711–69.
14 Hugh Trevor-Roper, *Archbishop Laud* (London, 1962), p. 173.

the Reformation. It now began to act in such close cooperation with Star Chamber that sometimes the two courts seemed to function as the spiritual and temporal arms of the same fierce justice. For example, when Dr Alexander Leighton wrote a virulent attack on the bishops, High Commission unfrocked him, but it was Star Chamber that had him flogged and imprisoned for life. Star Chamber was seen to have become the instrument of the bishops for the punishment of their detractors.

Despite the fact that the common law was even more savage in the sentences it could impose, it was the partisan and repressive action of the Star Chamber against honest and educated citizens that aroused fierce hostility, as well as the fact that it was seen to be stifling legitimate dissent rather than suppressing disorder and oppression. This beacon of justice in the time of the Tudors was being debased by their Stuart heirs. It also smelt of Rome. Those schooled in the common law pinched their noses.

CHAPTER 12

Torture

Trial by rack is utterly unknown to the laws of England; though once when the dukes of Exeter and Suffolk, and other ministers of Henry VI, had laid a design to introduce the civil law into this kingdom as the rule of government, for a beginning thereof they erected a rack of torture; which was called in derision the duke of Exeter's daughter, and still remains in the tower of London: where it was occasionally used as an engine of state, not of law, more than once in the time of Elizabeth.

Blackstone, Commentaries on the Laws of England

A NOTHER common myth is that Star Chamber resorted to torture. It did not. Torture was reserved for capital cases and was part of the royal prerogative, deriving from sovereign immunity from legal action. The king, or far more often his privy council, could warrant torture, and those so warranted could conduct torture, without fear of prosecution.[1] The exercise of this power became one of the important issues in the struggle between the Crown and the parliamentary common law lawyers, since to the latter torture was totally repugnant to the fundamental principles of English law as well as to reason, justice and humanity. Torture, it was said, had long been repudiated by the common law courts, which haughtily rejected it as cruel, as productive of unreliable evidence, and as degrading to all who had anything to do with it, including the courts. This stout rejection was hailed as a distinguishing feature of the common law, and was subject to proud claims by a long series of the greatest English jurists, from Fortescue in the fifteenth century to James Fitzjames Stephen in the nineteenth.[2]

Nonetheless, some eminent practitioners of the common law participated in torture. Edward Coke himself was, under Elizabeth, a commissioner for torture in at least nine cases. Once again it seems to have been the Stuarts' use of it – though they resorted to torture far less often and with more discrimination than their Tudor predecessors – that converted the common

---

[1] John Langbein, *Torture and the Law of Proof* (Chicago, 2006), pp. 129ff.

[2] Fortescue, *De Laudibus Legum Angliae*, devoted a whole chapter (xxii) to the subject; others merely reaffirmed his stance: Coke, *Institutes of the Laws of England*, III, p. 35; Blackstone, IV, p. 320; Stephen, *History of the Criminal* Law, I, p. 222.

law advocates to wholesale opposition, and induced them to trumpet the greater virtues of the torture-free common law. Torture was just not English, or so it was asserted, but some foreign import from less happy lands, a little like King Charles himself. In Charles's day Selden remarked:

> The Rack is used nowhere as in *England*. In other Countries 'tis used in *Judicature* [when, if there be insufficient proof,] they rack him if he will not confess. But here in England they take a Man and rack him, I do not know why, nor when; not in time of *Judicature*, but when somebody bids.[3]

The 'somebody' was one of the king's counsellors using the royal prerogative to apply torture.

Between 1540 and 1640 torture warrants were issued eighty-one times, and although there may have been some lost to the archives, the total is probably no more than one a year on average. Whatever the precise number, it is very small relative to the number of crimes. It was the Tudors, and Elizabeth in particular, who were the most prolific in their resort to torture, both for treason but also for a smattering of ordinary felonies such as murder, robbery and burglary.

The main torture centres were Bridewell and the Tower. The main methods were manacles and the rack. The latter was particularly feared. It was a frame with rollers at each end to which the wrists and ankles of the prisoner were fastened. The rollers were then ratchetted, the rope grew taught and limbs were stretched and dislocated. One rack-master boasted of racking a prisoner 'one foot longer than even god made him.'[4] The manacles, from which a prisoner was painfully suspended, avoided the dislocation and damage effected by the rack, and the opprobrium of public opinion that had been aroused against the barbarities of Elizabeth's rack-master, Thomas Norton. How often there was recourse to actual implementation of torture is hard to say. The commissioners for torture did not seem to relish their task, and the intended victim was first shown the devices in the hope that their sight alone would obviate their use.

By good fortune John Gerard managed to escape the Tower, and so was able to provide posterity with a detailed account of what he had endured. Gerard was a Jesuit priest who had stolen into England to minister to the Catholic faithful, or to undermine the state, depending on one's point of view. In 1594 he was betrayed, arrested and imprisoned, first for three years in the Clink – a holding prison for recusants – and then, after an escape

---

3   Selden, *Table Talk*, p. 216.
4   *Calendar of State Papers Domestic, Elizabeth, 1581–90*, ed. Robert Lemon (London, 1865), p. 48.

attempt, in the Tower itself.[5] In April 1597 the commissioners for torture, of whom one was Bacon, visited him in an attempt to get him to divulge the whereabouts of Henry Garnet, considered the most dangerous Catholic in England. They questioned Gerard at length about this 'enemy of the state'. When he refused to betray his fellow priest they produced a torture warrant authorising the use of 'manacles and such other torture as is used in [the Tower]'.[6] The commissioners begged him not to force them to resort to such measures, otherwise they would have to put him to the torture every day as long as he lived, or until he gave them the information they wanted. He was obdurate, and so was taken to the White Tower. Gerard described his macabre experience:

> We went to the torture-room in a kind of solemn procession, the attendants walking ahead with lighted candles. The chamber was underground and dark, particularly near the entrance. It was a vast place and every device and instrument of human torture was there. They pointed out some of them to me and said that I would try them all. Then they asked me again whether I would confess.[7]

His interrogators took him to one of the big wooden posts that held the roof, driven into the top of which were iron staples for supporting heavy weights.

> Then they put my wrists into iron gauntlets and ordered me to climb two or three wicker steps. My arms were then lifted up and an iron bar was passed through the rings of one gauntlet, then through the staple and rings of the second gauntlet. This done, they fastened the bar with a pin to prevent it slipping, and then, removing the wicker steps one by one from under my feet, they left me hanging by my hands and arms fastened above my head. The tips of my toes, however, still touched the ground, and they had to dig away the earth from under them. They had hung me up from the highest staple in the pillar and could not raise me any higher, without driving in another staple.

Gerard then went onto to describe the 'gripping pain' that came over him.

> It was worst in my chest and belly, my hands and my arms. All the blood in my body seemed to rush up into my arms and hands and I thought that blood was oozing out from the ends of my fingers and the pores of my skin. But it was only a sensation caused by my flesh swelling above the irons holding them. The pain was so intense that I thought I could not possibly endure it.[8]

---

5   John Gerard, *The Autobiography of a Hunted Priest*, trans. Philip Caraman (New York, 1952), pp. 104ff.

6   *Ibid.*, p. 107, n. 2.

7   *Ibid.*, p. 108.

8   *Ibid.*, p. 109.

Yet endure it he did. The commissioners left the warden and the torturers to it. The warden, 'out of kindness', would wipe the sweat from Gerard's brow, but as he soothed the pain he continued to implore the priest to give the information wanted. For four hours or more Gerard repeatedly fainted, was revived, and dropped 'eight or nine times that day'. When he was taken down his legs and feet were not damaged 'but it was a great effort to stand upright'. The following day he was put twice more to the torture, the manacles having to be fitted into the furrow between the swollen flesh. This time the pain was 'more severe in the hands' but 'less in the chest and belly'. To prevent suicide Gerard's knife, scissors and razor were taken away.[9]

After these sessions with the manacles the commissioners gave up on Gerard, and his torture ceased. He was not put to the rack nor does he mention it. Henry Garnet claimed that on one occasion Gerard was shown the rack but, as a result of his express resolve to reveal nothing, was spared it.[10] In October 1597 Gerard escaped the Tower and fled to the Continent.

Torture was seen as an instrument of necessity – to flush out conspirators – but not for the garnering of evidence. Francis Bacon put it succinctly: 'By the law of England no man is bound to accuse himself. In the highest cases of treason torture is used for discovery and not for evidence.'[11] Its selective use for this purpose ran parallel to the common law, but did not seem to threaten either it or English standards of justice. Indeed, given the intermittent but regular recourse to it in ordinary felony cases, at the end of Elizabeth's reign it could well have been incorporated into the English legal system.

The alien Stuarts, by contrast to their predecessors, confined its use to treason and sedition, terms which were largely coterminous. James warranted it only six times, notably on the most notorious traitor of them all, Guy Fawkes, who had conspired to blow up both parliament and the king. In an effort to extract information about the size and composition of this truly dangerous conspiracy – unparalleled in English history – he was racked, the effect of which is seen in his handwriting which was reduced to an erratic scribble.

Charles I, despite his reputation for savagery, was positively squeamish in using his prerogative to authorise torture. He did not use it even on John Felton, the assassin of his beloved duke of Buckingham. The story is that the king wanted to discover Felton's accomplices by putting him 'to the ques-

---

9   *Ibid.*, pp. 110–13.
10 *Ibid.*, p. 115.
11 'Of the Pacification of the Church', in *The Works of Lord Bacon*, 2 vols (London, 1838), I, p. 355.

tion', but wanted to do so by law and not by the use of his prerogative 'as it had been so often used in former reigns'. He consulted his judges on this matter, and they unanimously opined 'to their own honour and the honour of the English law, that no such proceeding was allowable by the laws of England'.[12] The king did not press the point, and Felton was not tortured. He was convicted and hanged.

Charles employed torture only twice, once at the beginning of his reign for treason, albeit on a man later proved innocent, and once at the end, on an inconsequential agitator and glover called John Archer. Archer had over-reacted to an admittedly incendiary tract written by one John Lilburne, a serving prisoner sentenced by Star Chamber, inciting the apprentices of London to demonstrate at Lambeth Palace to demand Lilburne's release, and to hunt 'William the Fox' – Archbishop Laud – who was blamed, unjustly it seems, both for the dissolution of the Short Parliament a few days before, and for the unpopular Irish policy adopted by the king. On the night of 11 May 11 1640 Archer, 'beating a drum in a warlike manner', led five or six hundred apprentices on Lambeth Palace, and from midnight until 2.00am. laid siege to it, demanding that 'the fox' be produced so that they could tear him to pieces. They were frustrated in their quest. Not only had Lambeth Palace been fortified, but the archbishop was not there, but across the river at Whitehall. Archer and some other rioters were arrested and imprisoned. To the consternation of the authorities, three days later a mob broke open the prison and liberated them. Two, including Archer, were recaptured. He was sent to the Tower on a charge of sedition. On Charles's express instructions, written in his own hand, Archer was interrogated on the rack by two of the king's serjeants-at-law to induce him to reveal the names of co-conspirators.[13] His torture was as useless as it was barbarous. He revealed nothing, and likely he had nothing to reveal. The king's deputy in Ireland, and leading adviser, Thomas Wentworth, earl of Strafford, told Charles 'unless you hang up some of them you will do no good with them'.[14] Archer was tried by special commission along with a sixteen-year-old sailor boy, Thomas Bensted, who had been shot during the riot and charged with treason. They were both hung, drawn and quartered.[15] Archer proved to be the last victim of author-

---

12 Blackstone, IV, p. 321; Langbein, *Torture and the Law of Proof*, pp. 94–123.
13 *EHD*, V(b), p. 1200.
14 Christopher Hibbert, *Charles I* (London, 1968), p. 150.
15 J. P. Lawson, *The Life and Times of Archbishop Laud*, 2 vols (London, 1829), II, p. 364; S. R. Gardiner, *History of England*, 18 vols (London, 1863–97), IX, pp. 348–59; Trevor-Roper, *Archbishop Laud*, p. 388f.

ised torture in England – though not of dismemberment. No warrant for torture would ever be issued in England again.

Despite its limited use, the rack has cast a long shadow over the reputation of Charles's exercise of his prerogative and, by unfair extension, over Star Chamber itself. As part of the assault on the prerogative powers, the Court of Star Chamber was abolished on 5 July 1641. The chamber itself was dismantled in 1806. Now all that is left is the name, the reputation, its door at Westminster School, and the infamous ceiling which now presides over a conference room of a hotel in the Wirral.[16] How are the mighty fallen!

---

[16] Leasowe Castle Hotel. In 1836 Sir Edward Cust, the then-owner of the castle, purchased the oak panelled ceiling of Star Chamber, thus saving it for the nation.

CHAPTER 13

The Writ and Charter of Liberty

Your Majesty's will is law.   W.S. Gilbert, *The Mikado*

STAR CHAMBER had increasingly excited the animosity and jealousy of the common law lawyers, particularly Edward Coke, its erstwhile defender, who now questioned the very legality of its jurisdiction. Chancery, and other equitable courts, were coming to be viewed as creating a separate system of justice rivalling the common law. Coke and others invoked and developed remedies to frustrate what they considered to be an abuse of the prerogative.

First among these remedies was *habeas corpus*, a judicial writ originating in the king's prerogative and having all the authority accorded a royal command. Its original purpose was to secure the presence in court of individuals in custody. This was transformed into a strong defence against authoritarianism. Already in the fifteenth century the writ of *Corpus cum Causa*, a species of *habeas corpus* originally pioneered by Chancery to secure review of inferior jurisdictions, had been used to challenge detention by 'special command of the king' or by the lord of the manor.[1] Under the Tudors the King's Bench developed the writ so that any free person was entitled, if detained other than after criminal conviction or for civil debt, to demand from the court a writ of *habeas corpus ad subjiciendum* directed to the keeper of the prison, hospital or place of private detention, commanding the keeper to bring up the body [*corpus*] of the detained person along with the cause of his incarceration. The judge would determine if the detention was justified. If it was, the court would remand the prisoner back to detention, but, if it was not, grant bail or release.

The writ came into general use to question detention, even if authorised by such powers in the land as Cardinal Wolsey or the king's council. In 1588 *Howell's Case* came before the King's Bench. Howell had been arrested on a warrant signed by the Secretary of State, Francis Walsingham. The court reluctantly accepted that the privy council had power to arrest without reason given. Three years later judicial disquiet resulted in a resolution to the

---

[1]   *OHLE*, VI, pp. 91f.

effect that, even in such a case, the gaoler must produce the prisoners when required by *habeas corpus*.[2] This resolution confirmed the authority of the King's Bench to intervene in the detention of anyone, no matter where in the realm they were held and no matter by whose authority they had been detained.[3]

At the beginning of the seventeenth century, in the hands of ingenious jurists, *habeas corpus* became a tool not just for freeing the unlawfully detained, but for exercising jurisdiction over the newer prerogative courts and in particular the Court of High Commission. From 1607 to 1612 Coke, by now Chief Justice of the Common Pleas, and his brother judges ruled in a series of cases that the Court was limited to ecclesiastical matters and had no authority to arrest laymen.[4] This was infuriating enough to the king whose prerogative was being impugned, but worse could befall. If extended, this deployment of *habeas corpus* would give common law courts indirect control over Chancery itself. Under the writ, the decision of the chancellor to imprison a person who had disobeyed his decree could be reviewed by the common law court, and if found wanting, the person imprisoned under that defective order would go free. This would shackle the chancellor. Moreover *habeas corpus* was only one of several legal weapons that Coke would wield with impertinent effect.

The first climactic case of Charles I's reign, and one where *habeas corpus* was frustrated, was that of the *Five Knights* in 1627. The king had sidestepped parliament, and used his prerogative to raise money. In 1626 he instructed the privy council to levy a 'forced loan', in effect to tax without parliamentary approval. Some MPs refused to pay, and were imprisoned without trial by royal command. Five of them, including Thomas Darnell (after whom the case is sometimes known), obtained a writ of *habeas corpus*. It came before the Chief Justice of the King's Bench, Edward Hyde (later, under Charles II, Lord Clarendon). John Selden MP, according to Milton 'the chief of learned men reputed in this land', acted as counsel for one of the defendants, Sir Edmund Hampden. Selden argued on the grounds of Magna Carta that without due process of law no one could lose his liberty and that the king's 'special command' was not law. The Attorney-General argued that the king's command was just that, and that the courts could not inquire into an act

2   *EHD*, V(a), pp. 391f.
3   *OHLE*, VI, pp. 93.
4   Coke, *Institutes of the Laws of England*, I, pp. 461–77.

of prerogative. The pliant Hyde concurred, and the King's Bench remanded the five to the Fleet Prison.[5]

As a result, in March 1628 parliament met in a state of high indignation and ready for a confrontation. Both sides claimed that history was on their side – the Commons led by Coke invoking Magna Carta and later precedents, the king declaring his allegiance to the laws and customs of the realm. The parliamentarians could respond with the definition of the relationship between the king and the law enunciated by Chief Baron Fray in 1441 and generally accepted outside royal circles: 'the law is the highest inheritance the king has, for by the law he himself and all his subjects are ruled. And if the law were not, there would be no king and no inheritance.' The law was the king's inheritance; it was not his instrument, even less his plaything. The laws would not be mute even though the king spoke. Coke in particular condemned the decision in the *Five Knights' Case* as undermining the liberties enshrined in Magna Carta, 'such a fellow as will have no sovereign'. His oratory rallied and united the House, 'as when one good hound recovers the scent the rest come with full cry'. Sir Benjamin Rudyard declared that he would 'be very glad to see that old, decrepit Law Magna Charta which hath been kept so long, and lien bed-rid as it were … walk abroad again with new vigour and lustre, attended and followed with the other six statutes [of Edward III]; questionless it will be a great heartening to all the people'.[6] Coke expedited the convalescence by devising a parliamentary riposte – the Petition of Right – which, amidst unctuous protestations of loyalty and deference, clearly declared arbitrary detention by royal fiat, taxation without parliamentary approval, and billeting troops in houses without the owner's consent, unlawful. The Petition 'put the final touch' to the earlier incremental development of the meaning and compass of Magna Carta.[7] It was the final gloss on the sacred text.

Charles, as weak as he was unwise, and too poor to reject parliament's terms, yielded with ill grace, asserting that 'the king's prerogative is to defend the people's liberties', and stipulating that he 'would not have his prerogative straitened by any new explanation of Magna Carta'. But yield he did. The Commons stood and cheered, while church bells rang and bonfires were lit throughout the land.[8] Such celebration would have done little to quench the

---

5   *ST*, III, pp. 1–233.
6   Faith Thompson, *Magna Carta, its Role in the Making of the English Constitution, 1300–1629* (Minneapolis, 1948), p. 86.
7   Holt, *Magna Carta*, pp. 13, 15.
8   Hibbert, *Charles I*, p. 102.

king's anger. This was more than just the first statutory restriction on the powers of the Crown since the accession of the Tudors. It was the culmination of the centuries-old development of Magna Carta itself. It was Magna Carta reaffirmed. A recent Lord Chief Justice has written that the Petition of Right was as significant to the rule of law as the Great Charter or *habeas corpus*, and its acceptance by the king was when the common law 'came of age'.[9] In 1640, parliament, now on collision course with the king who had tried to govern without it, passed the Habeas Corpus Act, putting on a statutory footing the common law principle that every person imprisoned by prerogative authority was entitled as of right to *habeas corpus*.

The major figure in this titanic struggle with the king, culminating in the Petition, was the septuagenarian MP, Sir Edward Coke, a former Chief Justice of the King's Bench. How did this come about? How did a judge appointed by a king become the champion of the law over kings? Who was Edward Coke and how significant in the history of the English common law was he?

9 Thomas Bingham, *The Rule of Law* (London, 2010), pp. 17, 20.

CHAPTER 14

Rex Lex *v.* Lex Rex[1]: *Sir Edward Coke*

We have a national law appropriate to this kingdom. If you tell me of other laws, you are gone. I will only speak of the laws of England.
                    Edward Coke in parliament, 1628

The appeal to precedent is in the law courts merely a useful fiction by which judicial decision conceals its transformation into judicial legislation; and a fiction is nonetheless a fiction because it has emerged from the Courts into the field of politics or of history.
                    A. V. Dicey, *Lectures Introductory to the Study of the Law*

EDWARD COKE was born in the reign of Edward VI to Robert Coke, himself a lawyer of Lincoln's Inn. After a period at Trinity College, Cambridge, Edward became a student at the Inner Temple, being called to the Bar in 1578. Living in turbulent times, Coke honed his views of the law into a weapon not merely by learned disquisition, but by excavation, and irrigation. 'Out of the old fields must spring and grow the new corne', he was to write.[2] His learning was prodigious, his industry untiring. As a practising barrister he kept copious notes of his own cases and those of others living and dead, a treasure trove from which he would later draw immense riches. All that he said would have the veneer of precedent and antiquity. A legal titan, he is considered to have done more than any other to create the modern notion of the rule of law.[3] One recent biographer has written, 'what Shakespeare is to those who write in English, Sir Edward Coke has been to lawyers of the English-speaking world'.[4] To an American judge he was 'the oracle and ornament of the common law'.[5] He was not, however, a nice man. He was disagreeable, irascible, arrogant, and a bully. Most notoriously he whipped his own daughter into submission when she had the temerity to demur at marrying the duke of Buckingham's brother, a match made not in

---

[1] 'The King is the Law' versus 'the Law is King'.
[2] Pref. 1 Rep., in *SWEC*, I, p. 6.
[3] *Ibid.*, p. xxiii.
[4] Allen Boyer, *Sir Edward Coke and the Elizabethan Age* (Stanford, 2003), p. 3.
[5] John Gest, *The Lawyer in Literature* (Boston, 1913), p. 158.

heaven but to further her father's frustrated ambitions. 'We shall never see his like again', his grieving widow was to write, 'praises be to God!'⁶

He was also capable of monstrous injustice. A great lawyer with tremendous skills, devoted without reservation to his client, can become a tool of tyrannical power if that client is a monarch. As both Solicitor-General and then Attorney-General to Elizabeth, making an enemy of Bacon, his rival for the post, who quipped that 'the less you speak of your own greatness, the more I will think of it',⁷ Coke was hardly immune from exercising what he would later condemn as arbitrary power. He was a commissioner for torture, legitimising the racking of prisoners of state. He extolled Star Chamber. But it was in 1603 at the beginning of the reign of James I, during the trial of Sir Walter Raleigh for treason, that Coke, as Attorney-General leading for the prosecution, showed himself at his worst. He disported himself more as if bear-baiting than prosecuting. He resorted entirely to bullying, hectoring and sneering at the fallen giant whom he castigated as a 'viper' and 'rankest traitor in all England'. By his contrasting display of dignity, Raleigh merely grew in stature, while Coke was reduced.⁸

When, however, those same skills were turned to the protection of his final client – the common law itself – Coke became the incarnation of that which he defended. He would do all he could to champion the supremacy of parliament and the Bench, the twins that he considered to be 'the fount and the vessel of the law';⁹ the twins that, under the Stuarts, he came to believe were under threat. Since Elizabeth's reign, Coke had been upholding the primacy of the law, and asserting the continuing importance of Magna Carta. Elizabeth was a monarch whom he adored. She was, after all, the 'gracious soveraigne who governeth her people by God's goodnesse in peace and prosperity *by these Laws*'.¹⁰ He had no lesser hopes for her successor James, and acclaimed the new king as 'the fountain of justice' – though significantly not as the fount of law.

6   S. E. Thorne, *Sir Edward Coke 1552–1952*, Seldon Society (1952), p. 4.

7   Lisa Jardine and Alan Stewart, *Hostage to Fortune: The Troubled Life of Francis Bacon* (London, 1998), p. 254. They were also rivals in love, or at least marriage. Both had set their eyes on Burghley's granddaughter, a wealthy widow, Lady Hatton. Coke won her.

8   *ST*, II, pp. 1–62. Gardiner (*History of England*, I, p. 138) considered that the trial itself marked 'a landmark in English constitutional history. The harsh principles then in repute among lawyers were enunciated by the judges with unprecedented distinctness, and as a consequence a reaction steadily set in from that moment in favour of the rights of individuals against the state.'

9   *SWEC*, I, p. xxv.

10 *Ibid.*, p. 39. My emphasis.

1725 —Sir Edward Coke.

6. Sir Edward Coke, the intemperate champion of the independence of the common law from royal control.

The king had ideas of a status more exalted than that accorded him by Coke, and the ability to articulate them. These ideas stemmed from his belief in the divine right of kings, from the example of Solomon as the epitome of a wise and just king sitting in judgment, and from his experience in Scotland. God made kings. Kings made the law. What they made they could interpret, and what they made they could change. The law did not instil justice into monarchs – they were the source of justice, and had an acute divinely inspired sense of justice. James asserted that 'the king, being the author of the law, is the interpreter of the law'.[11] Under the prerogative, the Crown possessed a reserve of wide and indefinite rights and powers, and asserted that this prerogative or residue of sovereign power was superior to

[11] *Trew Law of Free Monarchies*, *EHD*, V(b), pp. 397ff.

the ordinary law of the land, superior also to parliament. The king could suspend the operation of statutes, or grant dispensation from obedience to them. He could delegate to 'inferior judges', who were 'his shadows and ministers', the interpretative but not the creative part of his role. James agreed with the sentiments of the great champion of his prerogative, Francis Bacon, that judges ought to remember that their office is '*jus dicere*, and not *jus dare* – to interpret law and not to make law'.[12] Judges were to defend the prerogative, not to encroach upon it; to obey the king, not defy him. These views, which may or may not have passed muster in Scotland, would be viewed by many as alien to, and subversive of, English traditions. Opposition was inevitable, as was royal irritation with, and anger at, such presumption on behalf of mere subjects, all the more so if those subjects were lawyers or judges. However much he may genuinely have valued the common law itself, James had little regard for lawyers, whom he once likened to wind instruments.

The constitution was in flux. Change hung acrid in the air. Increasingly the courts had to adjudicate in disputes between the state and the subject and between the constituent parts of the state. The law was amorphous, unsure of itself, adrift on a shifting constitutional sea whose waters were made choppy by the bluster of entities jockeying for position, or vying for supremacy. In Bacon's words, the law at this time was 'almost like a ship without ballast'.[13] Legal authorities and precedents which could provide that ballast were contradictory, or ill reported. Someone who could collate, collect, and even distort past rulings, would not calm the coming tempest but could stabilise the legal vessel, and enable it to battle out the storm. Such a man was Edward Coke.

James came from a civil law background in Scotland, and civilian lawyers in England largely shared his views on royal absolutism, as was exemplified in John Cowell's law dictionary, *The Interpreter*, published in 1607.[14] The king also saw no incompatibility between the common law and his divinely ordained office. He had no need to. Hitherto judges had largely upheld the prerogative of the Crown. When Coke became Chief Justice of the Common Pleas in 1606, things were to change. By issuing writs of *habeas corpus* and 'prohibition' against the ecclesiastical courts, the latter preventing them from

---

12 'Of Judicature', in *Bacon's Essays*, ed. Whatley; David Willson, *King James VI and I* (London, 1956), pp. 257f.

13 Jardine and Stewart, *Hostage to Fortune*, p. 389.

14 *EHD*, V(b), pp. 406f. In 1610 parliamentary uproar over this publication, instigated by common law lawyers, led to it being suppressed by royal proclamation.

proceeding with particular causes, Coke came into conflict with James over the extent of the jurisdiction of the common law courts.

The king viewed Coke's stance as a brazen attempt to rob him of his prerogative. The following year they again vehemently disagreed over the use of prohibitions. During one confrontation, James asserted that he was the supreme judge, and could override the decisions of other judges, all of whom he had appointed and could dismiss at will. They might be lions under the throne, but they were under it and tethered. They should be 'circumspect that they do not check or oppose any points of sovereignty'. The king was the source of the temporal jurisdiction of the common law and of the spiritual jurisdiction of the Church courts, and it was for him to decide between rival jurisdictions; yet he would defend the common law. On the contrary, said Coke, the law defended the king, and quoted Bracton at him that the king was 'under God and the law'. At this, James made to punch his Chief Justice who, having made his daring point, prostrated himself before the monarch.[15]

At the same time, Coke maintained the primacy of the law over parliament. Coke believed that 'reason is the life of the law, nay the common law itself is nothing else but reason … the perfection of reason'. Unreasonableness, which would render custom of 'no force in law', could even invalidate legislation.[16] In 1610 he asserted that 'in many Cases, the Common Law doth controll Acts of Parliament, and sometimes shall adjudge them to be void: for when an Act of Parliament is against Common right and reason, or repugnant, or impossible to be performed, the Common Law will controll it, and adjudge such Act to be void'.[17] No power however great, no authority however absolute, no institution however venerable, could match the majesty of the law. This seed, planted by Coke, may have failed to take root in England, but it was destined to grow and flourish in the United States.[18]

Despite having almost coming to blows with Coke, James promoted him in 1613 to be Chief Justice of the King's Bench. This office carried more

---

[15] *SWEC,* I, pp. 478ff; Willson, *King James,* p. 259. The date was Sunday 10 November 1607, not 1608 as is often stated.

[16] *SWEC,* II, pp. 684, 701.

[17] *Dr Bonham's Case* (1610) in *SWEC,* I, pp. 264–83, at p. 275. Repugnant to whom? Sir Thomas More had denounced the Act of Supremacy as 'repugnant to the laws of God' and so void. Years later Gilbert Burnet (*History of His Own Time,* 6 vols (Oxford, 1823), II, p. 205) recorded what he deemed to be the 'sottish maxim' held among lawyers, 'that even an act of parliament against Magna Carta was null of itself'.

[18] Alfred Denning, *What Next in the Law* (London, 1982), pp. 319f. In the twentieth century Lord Denning, another legal colossus and maverick, thought that British judges should have powers similar to those of their American counterparts to review and, if necessary, to repudiate legislation.

kudos but was less well remunerated. It was also an attempt to neuter Coke by removing him from the Common Pleas where he had constantly to adjudicate in civil disputes between the king and his subjects. In the King's Bench, which dealt with offences against the Crown, there was less opportunity to clash with the prerogative. Coke was furious about his 'elevation', and blamed Bacon for it since, in the legal carousel, the latter had at last secured the attorney-generalship. Bacon won their joust with the retort, 'Your Lordship all this while hath grown in breadth; you must needs now grow in height, or you will be a monster.'[19] To salve the blow, the king made Coke a member of his council. Coke, James once quipped, in exasperation as much as amusement, was like a cat: 'throw her which way you would, she will light upon her feet'.[20] If he hoped by this tactical munificence to tame his feral 'cat' he signally failed. The judicial feline escaped the leash, and disputed the king's right to make or change the law by proclamation, or to delay or stop proceedings in the common law courts. Coke issued writs of *praemunire* – designed to protect royal rights of jurisdiction – against Chancery. That court was a special favourite of James's, who viewed it highly as the very embodiment of the king's conscience, tempering law with equity, and justice with mercy. Things came to a head in a series of cases made all the more rancorous by the personal animosity between Coke and his rivals: Bacon, the Attorney-General who had his eye on the chancellorship, and Lord Ellesmere, the current holder of that office.[21]

The first case came in 1615. Edmund Peacham, an elderly Puritan parson from Somerset, was arrested when notes for a sermon slandering the king and predicting his early death were found. James was not amused. All his life he had been berated by narrow-minded and fanatical clerics. He was determined on the utmost severity. Peacham was put in the Tower, and in a vain effort to get him to reveal the names of non-existent fellow conspirators he was put to the manacles, under the supervision of the Attorney-General himself.[22] To no avail. In frustration Bacon told the king that Peachum's 'raging devil seemeth to be turned into a dumb devil'.[23] Bacon decided that the only recourse was to try Peacham alone for high treason. But were Peacham's unspoken words treasonable? Coke had already publicly stated his opinion that they were not.

---

19 Jardine and Stewart, *Hostage to Fortune*, p. 340.

20 Frequently quoted, including in Cuthbert Johnson, *Life of Sir Edward Coke*, 2 vols (London, 1837), II, p. 380. He attributed it to Hammond Lestrange.

21 Bacon thought personal animosity played a large part: Jardine and Stewart, *Hostage to Fortune*, p. 365.

22 Langbein, *Torture and the Law of Proof*, p. 120.

23 *ST*, II, p. 871.

7. Sir Francis Bacon, Coke's legal rival and *bête noir*.

Bacon counselled the king to circumvent Coke's dominant – and in Bacon's view, malign – influence, by consulting the judges individually before the trial. Coke denounced what he considered to be an unconstitutional innovation. Although he finally yielded after all the other judges had succumbed, he still gave his opinion against the Crown. Peacham was convicted but died in Taunton Prison before he could be executed.

Conflict between the King's Bench and Chancery, inevitable as they vied for supremacy, broke out later the same year in two cases where judgment in the King's Bench had been in favour of fraudsters. The issue at stake was not the utility of equity itself, but the finality of common law judgments, and the expansion of Chancery jurisdiction at the expense of the common law courts.

The earlier case involved the imprisonment by Lord Ellesmere of a dishonest litigant named Glanvill who had succeeded in his action in the King's Bench but fallen foul of Chancery. Coke freed him and tried unsuccessfully to indict for *praemunire* – in effect contempt – those involved in the Chancery suit. In the later case, a land dispute between Magdalene College, Cambridge, and the earl of Oxford, it was alleged that Coke's ruling had been obtained by fraud. Ellesmere issued a common injunction out of Chancery prohibiting its enforcement. Coke retaliated by resorting to the point he had asserted in *Glanvill's Case*, declaring that this action infringed the Statute of Praemunire of 1353 – which treated recourse to 'any other court to defeat or impeach the judgments given in the king's court', as contempt – even though this provision had originally been intended to prevent appeals to Rome. Coke also deployed an act of 1403 that dealt with *res judicata*, the principle of finality in litigation. He contended that both these acts applied to Chancery. Ellesmere, whom James considered to be, in Bacon's words, 'an instrument of monarchy, of immediate dependence upon the king, and therefore like to be a safe and tender guardian of the regal rights',[24] disputed that this was the case, as equity had not come into play in the common law court, and Chancery only meddled with a common law judgment when corruptly obtained. Morality ensured legality:

> The office of Chancellor is to correct men's consciences for frauds, breach of trusts, wrongs and oppressions, of what nature soever they be, and to soften and mollify the extremity of the law … Law and equity are distinct, both in their courts, their judges, and the rules of justice; and yet they both aim at one and the same end, which is to do right … when a judgment is obtained by oppression, wrong and a hard conscience, the Chancellor will frustrate

---

[24] Jardine and Stewart, *Hostage to Fortune*, p. 363.

and set it aside, not for any error or defect in the judgments, but for the hard conscience of the party.[25]

James was determined to preserve the relief that equity provided from the rigour and extremity of the laws. He was equally determined to protect the position and status of Chancery, which he viewed as the court of his absolute power. He decreed that the *Res Judicata* Act did not apply to Chancery proceedings after common law judgment, and that *praemunires* were not to be used against it. In cases of conflict between common law and equity, equity should prevail. The broader constitutional claim that the king made that he could judge over all judges, and determine any jurisdictional differences between his courts, would not survive the civil war, being specifically repudiated in the same statute that abolished Star Chamber.

More friction followed. On 20 April 1616 the *Case of Commendams* came before the Exchequer Chamber. The king, by special licence, had granted to the bishop of Lichfield a rich sinecure held alongside his existing see *in commendam*, exempting the holder of the benefice from laws against holding other positions in the Church. James's ability to do this was questioned by those who had a right to present this living. Attacks were made on the prerogative, and in particular on the king's general right to grant *commendams*. The matter was adjourned until the 27 April for consideration by the barons of the Exchequer and judges of the King's Bench and the Common Pleas.

James could not endure having his prerogative wounded by being made subject to public dispute. He demanded that the judges consult with him before they reached a decision. He instructed Bacon to write to them to arrange a meeting and postpone the hearing. Coke denounced Bacon's letter and prevailed upon his fellow judges to reply to the king that to comply with his request would involve a delay of justice, and be contrary to law and their oath. James riled at the patronising tone of their missive, denied he was delaying justice, and commanded them to 'forbear to meddle any further in this plea till our coming to town, and that out of our own mouth you may hear our pleasure in this business'.[26] The matter was again adjourned, this time to 8 June. Two days before the resumption James, well briefed by a memorial written by Bacon, confronted his judges in front of the privy council. He lectured them on the prerogative, as his 'supreme and imperial

---

[25] [1615] 1 Chancery Reports, 1. A full and recent discussion of this case by David Ibbetson is to be found in *Landmark Cases in Equity*, ed. Charles Mitchell and Paul Mitchell (Oxford, 2012), pp. 1–32.

[26] Jardine and Stewart, *Hostage to Fortune*, p. 373.

power and sovereignty, which ought not to be disputed or handled in vulgar argument'. The common law courts had 'grown so vast and transcendent, as they did both meddle with the king's prerogative and had encroached upon all other courts of justice'. It was 'very undecent and unfit' for subjects to disobey royal command. All but Coke fell to their knees, begged forgiveness, and agreed to delay action in other cases involving the prerogative until they had consulted the king. Coke alone defended their erstwhile stance, and said that should such a case arise he would do what should be fit for a judge to do. James thought his arguments mere sophistry.[27]

The king and his chief judge were at loggerheads, but the former had the upper hand. Coke had been isolated, and had no choice but to capitulate. A few weeks after this encounter James addressed the Star Chamber, something he had never done before. He reviewed his whole case against judicial meddling and presumption. He re-emphasised that the limits of Chancery were for the king to determine, not for the judges to restrict. They were to keep to their own benches and not invade other jurisdictions. In conclusion, 'sitting here in a seat of judgment', James forbade any recourse to *praemunire* against Chancery.[28] He was triumphant.

Coke's reluctant acquiescence did him no good. At the end of June he was told he was allowed neither to sit on the privy council nor ride on circuit. He was effectively put on sabbatical leave to revise his *Reports* to make them more palatable. He merely tinkered. Although Bacon was impressed by his rival's jurisprudential endeavours he recognised that there were in his work 'errors and some peremptory and extra-judicial resolutions'. Ellesmere was more critical, accusing Coke of 'scattering and sowing his own conceits'. He was not mending his ways. In November, Coke was dismissed as Chief Justice. The 'four P's have overthrown and put him down, that is Pride, Prohibitions, *Praemunire* and Prerogative'.[29]

It has been said that 'no measure that James took to strengthen his authority succeeded half so well' as Coke's removal from the Bench.[30] Certainly the surviving judges reverted to knowing their place, as lambs – not lions – under the throne. As late as 1638, in the ship money case, Mr Justice Berkeley said that 'The law is of itself an old and trusty servant of the king's; it is his instrument ... it is common and most true, that *Rex is Lex*, for he is *lex loquens*, a

---

[27] Robert Aston, *James I and his Contemporaries* (London, 1969), pp. 80–5.
[28] Jardine and Stewart, *Hostage to Fortune*, p. 387.
[29] *Ibid.*, p. 389.
[30] G. M. Trevelyan, *England Under the Stuarts* (London, 1946), p. 106.

living, a speaking, an acting law ... the king cannot do wrong.'[31] However, the only legal lion remaining was not lying under the throne but roaring against it. Indeed, he did more than roar: he bit back. The old lion – Coke was sixty-five – still had sharp teeth. After further attempts to ingratiate himself with the king, and thwarted in the arena of the courts, Coke sought allies and another battleground. As a result of his 'martyrdom' his failings were forgotten, his foibles forgiven, and he became a living symbol of defiance of the king in defence of ancient liberties. He became an MP in 1620, and was quick to forge a compact between parliament and the common law against the royal prerogative. He proposed the Protestation of December 1621, claiming that 'the liberties, franchises, privileges and jurisdictions of parliament are the ancient and undoubted birthright and inheritance of the subjects of England', and that parliament had of right freedom of speech to discuss, *inter alia*, the defence of the realm and the Church.[32] It was not only the common law that was hallowed by history, but parliamentary privileges as well. Both were coming into increasing conflict with the king and his prerogative powers.

James was astute enough to circumvent any serious constitutional rift during his reign. Despite his understandable inability to appreciate the nuances of the English legal tradition, so different from that to which he was accustomed in Scotland, and for all his derision and irascibility when confronted with uppity lawyers, James was always careful to operate within the framework of the common law. The king lived up to his coronation oath to uphold the laws and customs of England. He never imprisoned anyone without trial, he never levied money from his subjects without the authorisation of parliament, and he never legislated of his own accord even though he believed that he could. He was 'more constitutional than Elizabeth had ever been'.[33] He had been largely victorious in his defence of the prerogative and of Chancery. James's son, who came to the throne in 1625, would not fare so well. Charles I had not been brought up to reign, but had become heir apparent only in 1612 after his older brother, Henry, died unexpectedly. Charles was relatively young, inexperienced, insecure, and a lot less canny than his father had been.

We have already seen Coke's role in drafting the Petition of Right in 1628 that the humiliated King Charles was compelled to accept. Between that year and the eve of civil war, Coke was not idle. Charles had offended against

[31] *EHD*, V(b), p. 391.
[32] *EHD*, V(b), p. 195.
[33] J. P. Kenyon, *The Stuart Constitution* (Cambridge, 1966), p. 8.

another basic tenet of the common law practitioners by altering the formula by which judges held office: not *quamdiu se bene gesserint*, or as long as they conducted themselves well, but *durante bene placito*, or during the king's pleasure. Drawing on his enormous learning, Coke wrote his magisterial *Institutes of the Laws of England*, justifying the claim that parliament and the common law were supreme in the state. This work, all of which (other than the first part, which came out in 1628) was published posthumously, was immediately recognised as authoritative, and was to become the basis of much modern British constitutional law. Coke had enlisted the professional pride of the students of common law against the rival systems favoured by the Crown in Star Chamber and in the admiralty and the ecclesiastical courts. Young men in the Inns of Court were being subverted and inspired to do more than plead cases in the courts – they could now envisage a grand constitutional function for their profession.

Realising that the pen was at least as mighty as the sword, Charles discouraged all studies likely to produce a wayward attitude in lawyers and others. The antiquary Robert Cotton, who had found warrant in Anglo-Saxon institutions and in the baronial wars of Henry III for doctrines of government unfavourable to the king, had his library impounded, while the further publication of that part of Coke's *Institutes* known as *Commentaries on Magna Carta* was prohibited and his papers seized.

At the height of his career Coke stood as a barrier against overweening regal power. He repeatedly cited his great predecessor, Bracton: 'The king is under no man but only God and the law, for the law makes the king.'[34] This assertion was without historical validity, but it was telling, courageous, and enduring. Concomitantly, Coke argued for the untrammelled discretion of the judge to 'do as a judge ought to do' without royal command or assent. He argued for a single set of laws, common throughout the realm, according to which liberty and property would be reliably regulated, without the recurrent loss of liberty that accompanied courts held by local lords, Crown administrators, and Church officials. The law, as Coke articulated it, protected the individual from tyrannical abuse. Coke read ancient precedents as if they had been newly written. This anachronistic tendency fanned the flames of his imaginative reinterpretations of ancient sources of law, making possible his wholesale translation of Magna Carta from a contract devised to protect the nobility, into a shield protecting all of the king's subjects.

Whether this was fair or justified is beside the point. Once Coke said something was the law, almost everyone agreed, although his great legal rival

---

34 *SWEC*, I, p. 102.

decried him as a 'legal tyrant' for making 'the law to lean too much' to his own opinion.[35] Coke, and his interpretation of the law, triumphed. In 1824 Chief Justice Best said, 'Lord Coke often had no authority for what he states, but I am afraid we should get rid of a great deal of what is considered law in Westminster Hall, if what Lord Coke says without authority is not law. He was one of the most eminent lawyers that ever presided as a judge in any court of justice.'[36] Thomas Carlyle best summed up the dextrous methods by which Coke achieved his legacy:

> The cause of Liberty, I have heard, is much indebted to Coke. If that be synonymous with the cause of Parliament, as for the moment it doubtless was, the debt is probable. In the stretching of Precedents, which he has of all sorts and ages, dug up from beyond Pluto and the deepest charnel-houses, and extinct lumber-rooms of Nature, which he produces and can apply and cause to fit by shrinking, or expanding, and on the whole, to suit any foot, he never had a rival.[37]

Dicey agreed. He considered that 'the fictions of the courts have in the hands of lawyers such as Coke served the cause both of justice and of freedom, and served it when it could have been defended by no other weapons'.[38] Notions of a legally limited monarch and subjects who held inalienable rights, were, thanks to Coke, now deemed to have existed since Magna Carta and before. Thus, 'one of the most disagreeable figures in our history is one of the most important champions of our liberties'.[39] At a dangerous period in the constitutional struggle it was he who first revived the theory that the law was not the instrument, but the boundary, of royal prerogative, and that the judges were not Bacon's 'lions under the throne', but umpires between king and subject. Coke believed that the 'ancient constitution of England', its origins lost in the remote mists of time but already established by the time of the Anglo-Saxon kingdoms and embedded in the very marrow of Englishness, had been embodied in a common law that was prior to, and took precedence over, the person of the individual sovereign. Preserved in custom, it merely waited its opportunity to assert itself, most obviously in Magna Carta. Coke,

---

35 Bacon not only had the greater intellect but a far greater gift for oratory. Ben Jonson (*Timber, or Discoveries Made Upon Men and Matter*) said of him that 'his hearers could not cough or look aside without loss ... the fear of every man that heard him was lest he should make an end'. William Townsend (*Modern State Trials*, 2 vols (London, 1850), II, p. 357) deplored Coke's debasing style, which 'exercised a pernicious influence over all pleadings at the bar' and 'thrust forth the art [of rhetoric] from our courts of law'.

36 *SWEC*, I, p. xxviii.

37 Thomas Carlyle, *Historical Sketches* (London, 1898), p. 176.

38 *Dicey, Lectures Introductory to the Study of the Law*, p. 18.

39 Trevelyan, *England Under the Stuarts*, p. 105.

in short, in his rulings as in his writings, had resurrected and enthroned Magna Carta, had undermined the royal prerogative, had enshrined – with caveats – the supremacy of parliament, and had ensured that the rule of law would persist. For a bad tempered old curmudgeon, not a bad legacy.

CHAPTER 15

Oedipus Lex: *The Trial of Charles I*

The King can do no wrong, that is, no Process can be granted against him.   John Selden, *Table Talk*

If ever a lawless act was defensible on the principle of self-preservation, the murder of Charles might be defended.
Samuel Taylor Coleridge, Notes on English Divines

CHARLES, when he felt financially secure enough, ignored the Petition of Right and dissolved parliament. He would rule alone, enforcing his will through the Court of Star Chamber. He resorted to an alternative form of taxation, raising finance by levying Ship Money – to pay for a navy – and by fining those who opposed his demands. For over a decade parliament's doors were locked and the king ruled on his own meagre wits and resources. After a costly military fiasco against the Scottish Covenanters, provoked into opposition by Charles's attempts to impose episcopacy in Scotland, the king, in 1640, was forced to recall parliament to raise money. Parliament and king remained at loggerheads.

One head had to fall: Thomas Wentworth, earl of Strafford would be for the chop. He was put on trial at Westminster Hall for high treason, but defended himself so ably that the Commons, fearing that he would be acquitted, was reduced to deploying a parliamentary device to bypass the proceedings.[1] The House preferred a Bill of Attainder against Strafford. This would ensure the required end simply by declaring that his death was necessary for the safety of the realm. The same device would do for Laud in due course. Charles cravenly gave way and assented to Strafford's attainder and beheading, a fate which he had promised 'upon the word of a king' would never befall his loyal servant, a betrayal for which he never forgave himself, and a humiliation which forever rankled. Charles had broken his royal oath, and sacrificed his own minister. His lesser subjects were more than justified in not trusting in their king's word.

In 1642 the clash between king and parliament exploded into a lengthy and bloody civil war. Many soldiers died on the battlefield and many more

---

[1]   *ST*, III, pp. 1382–1535.

civilians on the streets, in all a tenth of the population. Families were torn asunder, homes destroyed, and towns sacked. There were numerous reasons for the war, but a major factor was Charles's refusal to accept that he did not have the divine right to ignore or abjure the law of the land. *Rex* was not *Lex*. The assertion that the laws and customs of England were the possession of the people and a mainstay of the commonwealth provided 'a basis of legitimacy' to those who opposed the king.[2]

In the end, Charles I was defeated, and he surrendered himself in 1646. He had lost his freedom, much of his power, but not his throne and not his life. He was to forfeit both for subverting the Scots, and fomenting a second civil war on his unwilling and weary subjects. This lasted from May to August 1648, when again it resulted in defeat for the royalist forces. The king's hopes were crushed and his reputation further trashed. Even then negotiations continued, but royal intransigence scuppered them. Despite being in checkmate, Charles had no intention, in any circumstances, of conceding defeat and yielding to the victors' demands. Thus he sealed his fate. His enemies could depict him as a viper in the body politic, malign, treacherous and poisonous. He had been inadequate as a king, indeed he was inadequate as a man: petulant at times, easily led towards disaster, imperious without being assertive, arrogant with little to be arrogant about. Charles was a small man in great days, more a knave than a king. His political acumen was reduced, at the last, to mere casuistry and silly cunning. As Thomas Macaulay wrote, 'in every promise which he made there was an implied reservation that such promise might be broken in case of necessity, and that of the necessity he was the sole judge'.[3] Charles was prepared to betray his own supporters when pressed, and, many thought, his own country by dalliances with the Irish, French and Scots. He was responsible for two civil wars and the pointless deaths of thousands of his subjects. He was to die for the perception that he was a 'Man of Blood', a perception he had done so much to create and sustain.

Oliver Cromwell, among others, decided Charles had to be brought to account. Failed kings had died before, being killed in battle or murdered in captivity. During wartime the king could even have been court-martialled as an enemy commander bent on further aggression. But in Charles's case this peremptory justice was not done. His captors were convinced that he was subject to the law, and the law should try him, and, if found guilty,

---

2   Harding, *Medieval Law and the Foundations*, p. 334.
3   Thomas Babington Macaulay, *History of England*, 12th edn, 5 vols (London, 1856), I, p. 83.

condemn him like any other man. He was not to be done away secretly by means of any subterfuge. Charles's fate would be decided in the public gaze and by a court of law. The army decided to act decisively, and their 'Remonstrance' in November 1648 called for a purge of parliament and the trial of the discredited king.

So how was the law forged into an axe which beheaded a king? There was no precedent, as no king had ever been put on trial before, let alone on trial for his life. Certainly in Tudor times three queens had met their end at the block: Anne Boleyn in 1536, Katherine Howard in 1542, and Charles's own grandmother, Mary Queen of Scots in 1587, but all three were off point. Anne and Katherine were merely the wives of a king, not queens regnant. Mary was a foreign monarch, and Catholic claimant to the throne, who had been granted sanctuary in England and had undoubtedly plotted to overthrow the English queen. Even then Elizabeth was exceedingly reluctant to take the unprecedented step of, or to set a precedent by, having her rival judicially executed.

However sacrosanct a just king may have been, a king turned tyrant was a different matter. Tyrannicide had long been justified in political treatises, and James I, no mean writer on monarchy himself, had warned his son of the danger. Charles ignored the warning. Moreover, the myth of the 'Norman Yoke', imposed by brutal kings on an Anglo-Saxon people hitherto free, was coming into bud in the seventeenth century. According to that idealised interpretation of history, while ancient freedoms had been snatched away and repressed under successive rulers, the spirit of liberty had survived in the very marrow of the people. To overthrow a tyrant in the name of law and liberty, therefore, was not a recourse to treason but a reversion to tradition.[4]

During the two decades prior to 1649 there were some parliamentary moves made which, while not inevitably leading to a regicidal destination, certainly provided signposts along that way. In 1629 the House of Commons passed three resolutions aimed at the king's 'evil' counsellors and condemning as 'capital enemies of the commonwealth' any ministers who advocated extra-parliamentary taxation or innovations in religion. This resulted in the execution for treason of the two pillars of Charles's personal rule: Strafford in 1641 and Archbishop Laud in 1644. There was nothing unusual about the trial or

---

4   Such ideas persisted and crossed continents. They blossomed in succeeding centuries. Thomas Jefferson proposed that the legendary founders of the Anglo-Saxon polity, the brothers Hengist and Horsa, should be on the Great Seal of the United States as the embodiment of the freedoms of the Americans' 'Saxon' ancestors, who were unsullied by association with Norman monarchical despotism. Sir Walter Scott in *Ivanhoe* (1819) contrasted the dispossessed 'Saxons' with the covetous and oppressive Normans.

attainder of royal minions, but in these cases parliament widened the legal definition of treason to include attacks on the realm by subverting the laws or abusing delegated powers. This extended definition would leave open the possibility that treason might be committed by a king who attacked another sovereign institution integral to the state – parliament.

Two other measures brought the axe nearer the neck of the king. In 1642 parliament, without royal assent, passed the Militia Ordinance, which entrusted local defence forces to parliament's nominees.[5] In this act (in all but name), a distinction was made between the king-in-parliament, disobedience to whom was treason, and the king-outwith-parliament, whether acting by prerogative or arbitrary whim, who might be resisted by force. The doctrine of the king's two bodies was used to legitimate the Ordinance. This doctrine, which fully flowered in Tudor times, posited a distinction between the 'body natural' and the 'body politic', in the instant case, between Charles Stuart the man and Charles I the monarch:

> acts of justice and protection are not exercised in [the king's] own person, nor depend upon his pleasure, but by his courts and by his ministers, who must do their duty therein, though the King in his own person should forbid them: and therefore if judgements should be given by them against the King's will and personal command, yet they are the King's judgements.[6]

The particular individual was only king if he acted in a kingly way as defined by his parliament. Charles in his own eyes was emasculated. In the eyes of his enemies, he was no king but a petulant tyrant.

Ironically, the concept of royal duality had royal precedents. Both the king's prerogative and his conscience could be split in two. James I had told his judges that he

> had a double prerogative, whereof the one was ordinary and had relation to his private interest, which might be, and was every day, disputed in Westminster Hall; the other was of an higher nature, referring to his supreme and imperial power and sovereignty, which ought not to be disputed or handled in vulgar argument.[7]

How they could be distinguished was not clear. Before he assented to the execution of Strafford, Charles had been convinced by John Williams, the bishop of Lincoln, that the king had 'two consciences: a public and a private one'. While his private conscience would revolt against the condemnation of

---

5   During this period the legislative enactments of the two Houses were termed 'ordinances' because they lacked the king's assent.

6   Ernst Kantorowicz, *The King's Two Bodies* (Princeton, 1997), p. 9; *EHD*, V(b), pp. 684f.

7   Aston, *James I*, p. 81.

his loyal servant, his public conscience must be concerned to avert further bloodshed.[8] Strafford was sacrificed but bloodshed was not averted, as civil war ensued in which, in a Puritan slogan of the time, parliament was 'fighting the king to defend the King'.[9]

In 1648, six years after the Militia Ordinance, the so-called Long Parliament passed the Vote of No Addresses in response to news that Charles was entering into an 'engagement with the Scots'. This measure specifically referred to 'this unnatural war' which had been 'raised *by him* against his parliament and kingdom'. It prohibited all unauthorised negotiations with the king and deemed such contact high treason. Parliament would endeavour, despite the king, to 'bring the greatest security to this kingdom in the enjoyment of the laws and liberties thereof'.[10] No mention was made of evil counsellors causing the misconduct. This time war guilt was imputed to Charles Stuart himself. Political kingship was retained by, and embodied in, parliament. Charles was left – at present – only his physical body, flesh and blood.

Demands that, for his sins, 'the man of blood' be punished in the flesh grew in number and volume. Crucially, Cromwell was now convinced that Charles must be brought to book. But there were a whole host of problems if a king were to be held to account. The trial of the monarch was a constitutional conundrum. What was the charge to be? Treason was an offence against the king, and so how could it be committed by a king? There was a common law proposition adhered to by many judges that *Rex* is *Lex*, and so how could the common law be utilised to give authority and legitimacy to *Rex* v. *Rex*? Where would the king be tried and by whom? If he were tried at common law what of a jury? Charles had no peers to try him. In any case there were no privy councillors left, even were they competent to sit in judgment on their own king. As for attainder, the procedure successfully used against Strafford and Laud depended on members of the House of Lords siting as judges, and the dozen or so remaining members of the upper chamber were utterly opposed to any trial. It would have been so much simpler if Charles had succumbed to 'illness' or 'accident'.

Cromwell, however, was determined on something unprecedented, some form of trial. It had to be open, public and ostensibly if not overtly fair; not a 'show trial', dependent on fabricated confessions or suborned witnesses or forged documents. The world was to have displayed before it the hard

---

8   Hibbert, *Charles I*, p. 156.
9   Kantorowicz, *King's Two Bodies*, p. 23.
10   *EHD*, V(b), p. 735. My emphasis.

evidence of the king's manifest crimes. His perfidy would stand in stark contrast to the righteousness of the parliamentary cause. So it was hoped. Most importantly for Cromwell and his associates, all staunch Puritans, was the fact that this was God's work, and God's work should not be 'done in a corner'.[11] Divine judgment had already been demonstrated, and reiterated, in a despot's defeat in two civil wars. Cromwell was God's Englishman, not Charles Stuart. A king who had betrayed his divine trust and his own subjects should be brought to account before God and his people, in a public trial, and – if necessary – in a public execution. A treason trial in Westminster Hall would both calibrate human justice with divine judgment, and clothe the proceedings in a cloak of legality.

The cloak, however, had holes. As Charles was to ask, 'by what power, by what *lawful* authority' was he to be tried? Might rather than right was in the ascendancy. To try a king was unprecedented, and those determined on such a course were forced to resort to improvisation and expediency. What happened was not justice as the English knew it with a judge, a jury and in accordance with long-established law, but an *ad hoc* creation to deal with an otherwise insuperable problem: the fate of a king whose very existence posed a threat to the state.

Parliament did not pass legislation authorising the trial. It did not, and it could not, because it no longer existed, except in name. In a military coup on 6 December 1648, carried out by the aptly named Colonel Pride, the House of Commons had been 'purged' of the members who supported continuing negotiations with the king and who would oppose any measures to indict him. Many were expelled; others, including lawyers such as John Selden, refused to attend a parliament thus truncated. The eighty or so MPs – the 'Rump' – that remained passed an 'Ordinance in the name of the people of England', establishing a special tribunal called the High Court of Justice for the purpose of trying the king for treason. They did so by drawing not on the common law but on the Roman law conception of treason as the unlawful appropriation of sovereign power, while relocating the locus of that power from the king to the people. The king's public authority was uncoupled from his person. He was reduced to the status of a chief magistrate who had 'treasonably overstepped the jurisdiction of his office in derogation of the people's sovereignty'.[12] Under the Ordinance there were to be one hundred and fifty commissioners, as jurors, with twenty constituting a quorum, and

---

11 Colonel Harrison's phrase from his own trial as a regicide.
12 D. Alan Orr, 'The Juristic Foundation of Regicide', in *The Regicides and the Execution of Charles* I, ed. Jason Peacey (Basingstoke, 2001), pp. 117–37.

the two Chief Justices and the Chief Baron of the Exchequer were to be the judges. All three judges, however, although they were opponents of the king and had been recently appointed, denounced the proceedings as manifestly illegal. None of them would deign to participate in such a legal farce. The Lords rejected the measure unanimously. A king could not be a traitor.

Denied assent in the Lords, and deprived of judicial support, the handful of members left in the mutilated House of Commons decided to be a parliament unto themselves and on 6 January 1649 passed another enactment, this time styled an 'Act', establishing the High Court of Justice to try 'Charles Stuart' for 'high and treasonable offences'. Even in a 'purged' parliament the measure squeezed through by a narrow majority of twenty-six votes to twenty. This rump of the Rump purported to represent the will of the people of England. The royalist lawyer Sir Orlando Bridgeman observed, 'he that doth command by such an authority, it is his guilt'.[13]

To get their way, the residue of the House had arrogated to themselves the 'Supreme power of this Nation' with full authority to enact and declare law, 'although the consent and concurrence of the King and House of Peers be not had thereunto'.[14] This in itself could be categorised as a tyrannical usurpation by the Commons, or by Cromwell and his military might. Many did so call it, and not just ardent monarchists. One radical demagogue, the Leveller John Lilburne who thought the king evil, denounced the trial as a plot by the 'Grandees' and the 'silent independent' – Oliver Cromwell – to use the proceedings as a distraction from the more urgent problems of social and political reform. He feared above all that with the king removed by a process decreed by a military junta and 'mock parliament', and held outside the common law courts, a far worse tyranny would result.[15] His was the loudest voice, but it was not alone.

By this 'Act' the commissioners, now reduced to one hundred and thirty-five by the elimination of the names of all the peers and others opposed to the proceedings, assumed the function of both judge and jury. They were to be presided over by a barrister of Gray's Inn, the little-known and undistinguished John Bradshaw. He was no eminent member of the judiciary or

---

[13] J. G. Muddiman, *The Trial of King Charles the First* (Edinburgh and London, 1928), p. 64, note 9.

[14] *EHD*, V(b), pp. 749ff.

[15] Pauling Gregg, *Free-born John: A Biography of John Lilburne* (London, 1961), pp. 259ff; Andrew Sharp, 'The Levellers and the End of Charles I', in *Regicides and the Execution of Charles I*, ed. Peacey, pp. 181–201.

leading jurist, and was not much known in Westminster Hall.[16] He had, however, three credentials for such a role: he had held a minor judicial office in Cheshire, had publicly compared Charles to Nero, and had remained in London. The man chosen to prosecute was, like the president of the court, yet another barrister of Gray's Inn, called John Cook. He was not the first choice, and was nominated not because of his legal reputation but because he too was available at short notice when so many other lawyers had absented themselves from the capital, and the Attorney-General had conveniently fallen ill.

As perhaps the most extraordinary exemplar of the 'cab rank' rule, by which a barrister is bound to accept any case that comes his way, Cook took the brief 'to prepare and prosecute the charge against the king'. Cook was a man of testy principle. He was willing to take on the task. Earlier he had offered to give evidence on behalf of Strafford, by whom he had once been employed, and, as Cook well knew and surely resented, had been sacrificed and betrayed by the very man Cook was now asked to prosecute. His task may have been all the sweeter for that. Sweet or not, it was brave thing to do. This black brief would be the death not just of the defendant but of his prosecutor.

Cook was made Solicitor-General and given ten days to prepare. His initial task was that of all prosecutors: to devise the charge. Cook, in what has been called the 'Tyrannicide Brief', in effect indicted the king for war crimes. Charles Stuart was responsible for *both* the terrible wars that had wracked the nation, as well as for the atrocities committed by his forces during them.

On 20 January 1649, Charles was taken incognito from St James's Palace, up the Thames on a barge to Sir Robert Cotton's House, and thence on foot to Westminster Hall.[17] Oliver Cromwell, watching Charles's voyage into these legally uncharted waters, turned 'white as the wall'. Addressing his companions he said,

> My masters he is come, he is come, and now we are doing that great work that the nation will be full of. Therefore I desire you to let us resolve here what answer we shall give the king when he comes before us, for the first question he will ask us will be by what authority and commission we do try him.

16 Earl of Clarendon (Edward Hyde), *The History of the Rebellion and Civil Wars in England*, 6 vols (Oxford, 1721), V, p. 245.
17 C. V. Wedgewood, *The Trial of Charles I*, Folio edn (London, 1981), pp. 103f.

All were silent until one answered: 'In the name of the Commons in Parliament assembled and all the good people of England.'[18]

Charles I was duly put on trial at the south end of Westminster Hall, where a sufficient space could be made by removing the partitions between the courts of the King's Bench and Chancery. An armchair covered in red velvet was placed for him opposite the table behind which Bradshaw would sit. To accommodate the public, the rest of the Hall was shorn of all its booths and shops and obstructions. For rich spectators there were galleries built overlooking the place of trial itself.

For so extraordinary a trial security was a necessity to prevent any attempt to free the king or to assassinate the members of the tribunal. The most vulnerable, Lord President Bradshaw, had his beaver hat lined with steel plates to deflect any musket ball fired at his head.[19] For better security the public part of the building was divided from the judges and king by two parallel barriers – a wooden partition running from wall to wall and a few feet behind it a strong railing. The main body of the Hall had another railing set up down its entire length, along which soldiers were stationed. So that no one could forget the reasons why this trial was taking place, the colours taken from the king at Naseby hung round the Hall. By trying him at the southern end rather than in the centre, as was usual in treason trials, Charles could be brought into court, not through the main door and past the crowds, but through the network of buildings that lay beyond the Hall, between it and the river. He would be brought along corridors lined with soldiers. Although the public would hear little of what was going on as the acoustics were so poor, the judges ensured that twelve shorthand reporters were permitted to form a press gallery. Charles, king of England, accustomed to deference and bowed heads, was now a small isolated figure exposed to scrutiny from all sides and from all manner of persons. Not all, however, were hostile.

Out of fear or disgust, only sixty-eight of the one hundred and thirty-five commissioners were prepared to attend on the first day. Cromwell was one, accompanied by several other army officers including Harrison, and Pride. The most venerable, however, Thomas Fairfax, the parliamentary commander, had 'too much wit' to be there, as his wife shouted when his name was called.[20] Later in the proceedings when Bradshaw asserted that the court acted on behalf of the people of England, 'the parent or author of the law', this indomitable lady would again cry out that it was not a quarter

---

18 Muddiman, *Trial of King Charles*, p. 72.
19 A hat purporting to be Bradshaw's can be seen in the Ashmolean Museum, Oxford.
20 Clarendon, *History of the Rebellion and Civil Wars*, V, p. 255.

8. The Trial of Charles I was 'not a thing done in a corner'. In the vast public arena
of Westminster Hall the king sits alone facing Bradshaw and the other commissioners,
who occupy the area where the King's Bench and Chancery normally sat. To his right
is John Cook.

of the people of England who approved the proceedings, and it was Oliver Cromwell who was the traitor.[21]

Under armed guard the king was escorted into the Hall. 'After a stern looking upon the Court and the people in the galleries on each side of him', Charles took his seat, 'not at all moving his hat or otherwise showing the least respect to the Court.'[22] Bradshaw in turn addressed him as Charles Stuart, and told him he would hear the charge 'upon which the Court will proceed according to justice'. As Cook asked that the charge be read he was tapped on the shoulder by the king wielding his cane, and commanding him to give way. Charles poked him again and rose to speak. Cook ignored him and continued addressing the bench. Charles levelled a third blow and with such force that this time the silver tip fell off. Charles nodded to Cook to retrieve it, but his request was again ignored. As Cook went on, the king himself had to stoop to pick up the tip. The people were astonished at so ill an omen. The king, in his own eyes a divine majesty, had bowed before the majesty of his erstwhile law. The king was no longer above the law but beneath it, the source of law now the subject of law. It was a telling moment, seen as such by those who witnessed it.[23]

Cook's charge accused Charles of being guilty of 'high treason and other high crimes'. He was 'a tyrant, traitor and murderer, and a public and implacable enemy to the Commonwealth of England.' This charge began with a fundamental proposition: the king of England was not a person but an office, whose every occupant held in trust, and which could be exercised only in the defence of liberties. Charles Stuart had been 'entrusted with a limited power to govern by, and according to the laws of the land, and not otherwise, and by his trust, oath and office being obliged to use the power committed to him for the good and benefit of the people and for the preservation of their rights and liberties'. He had 'conceived a wicked design to erect and uphold in himself an unlimited and tyrannical power to rule according to his will and to overthrow the rights and liberties of the people'. In pursuit of this end he had 'traitorously and maliciously levied war against the present parliament and the people therein represented ... and had tried to procure invasions from foreign parts'. He had fomented a second war and was brewing a third. Thus Charles was responsible for all the murder, rapine and despoliation carried out in the civil wars. Cook in a very short time and under extreme pressure, had made tyranny a crime capable of commission

[21]　Muddiman, *Trial of King Charles*, p. 106.
[22]　*ST*, IV, p. 994.
[23]　*Ibid.*, p. 997; Geoffrey Robertson, *The Tyrannicide Brief* (London, 2005), p. 155.

by a head of state.[24] Many of the charges were true, but, if committed by a monarch, were they crimes? Even those who thought it a 'just thing' did not know 'how it may justly be done'. Charles's accusers were in danger of throwing 'their case away by forsaking the political ground on which they were strong for the legal ground on which they were weak'.[25] The king would exploit this to great effect.

Charles was to answer the charge, said Bradshaw, 'in the name of the people of England, of which you are elected king'. The king was not represented by counsel, but had likely been advised by another seventeenth-century legal titan, Sir Matthew Hale. If so it was a good choice. Hale was a Puritan, but with a reputation for integrity and impartiality. He had helped Strafford over his attainder, and Laud during his impeachment, articulating the argument on behalf of the latter that none of his offences constituted treason, not even when they were all put together, since 'two hundred couple of black rabbits' could not 'make a black horse'.[26] Hale was the obvious choice to counsel a king facing an unprecedented charge of treason, and Charles proved an apt pupil. As Cromwell had foreseen, he challenged the competency of the tribunal. He responded to Bradshaw's constitutional assertions by pointing out that England was 'never an elective kingdom; it was a hereditary kingdom for near this thousand years'. Charles was right of course. He was also arguably right in later contending that a king cannot be impeached since he is the source of law. When Bradshaw reminded him he sat before a court of justice, Charles rejoined, 'I find myself before a *power*', the power of the sword and not the sword of justice. Charles repeatedly enquired by what lawful authority they tried him. If they satisfied him of that he would answer the charge. The problem was that they could not answer what Bradshaw called a 'scruple against the authority of this court'.[27]

Consequently Charles denied their authority to try him, and over the next three days repeatedly refused to plead. He cleverly asserted that he did so as the champion of the common law, which was traduced. He did so not for himself alone but for 'the freedom and liberty of the people of England'. He must stand for their liberties more than ever his accusers did, 'for if power

24   Muddiman, *Trial of King Charles*, pp. 78ff.
25   Gardiner, *History of England*, XIII, pp. 300ff.
26   Gilbert Burnet, *Death and Life of Sir Matthew Hale* (London, 1682), p. 13. Counsel were allowed to argue the law, but not to represent their clients by cross-examination or making speeches. The argument was delivered by his senior, John Herne, ST, IV, pp. 577, 586, 599, 917 note.
27   Muddiman, *Trial of King Charles*, p. 90.

without law may make law, may alter the fundamental laws of the kingdom', no one was safe and secure in life or in property.[28] His own cavalier approach towards legality during his absolute rule was overshadowed by the patent illegality of his trial.

Charles's eloquent obduracy, or 'contumacious contempt', posed a dilemma. The charge was treason and, as Cook pointed out, at common law a refusal to plead to a charge of high treason, exceptionally, was taken as *pro confesso*, as an admission of guilt.[29] The Court should proceed straight to judgment. By accepting Cook's first proposition, it was spared the appalling prospect of subjecting a king to *peine forte et dure*. But if the king were deemed to be confessing, there could be no evidence adduced of his warmongering, of his double-dealing, and of his disregard for the lives of his subjects, no denunciatory prosecution speech, and no winning over a dubious public. It was a public relations disaster.

The Court rejected Cook's other demand for 'speedy judgment'. This was no ordinary traitor. This was no ordinary trial. A trial of sorts, albeit with a foregone conclusion, would continue, and continue it did for a further four days, no longer in the Hall but sequestered in the nearby Painted Chamber. Charles had to be shown to the eyes and ears of all to be convicted by over-whelming evidence, and not just by his own obstructive obduracy. By hearing in private the testimony of thirty or more eyewitnesses, the commissioners sought to further satisfy themselves 'of the truth of the facts laid down in the charge'. None of the military commissioners saw need to attend.[30] The other pressing issue was the punishment. Should the king die? It was the only penalty for treason, but to execute a king was unprecedented and fraught with risk. In these unique circumstances ways might have been found miti-gate the penalty. It was not to be.

Charles may have sealed his own fate. He may have wanted to. In the first winter of the civil war he had written that he meant to be either 'a glorious king or a patient martyr'.[31] In any case, on one fatal occasion, on being escorted from the Court, he was heard to mutter that he felt guilty only for his betrayal of Strafford, whose condemnation and execution he had allowed. He expressed no contrition, or even sorrow, for the many hundreds

---

[28] *ST*, IV, p. 998.

[29] *Ibid.*, pp. 998, 1000, 1002; Matthew Hale, *Pleas of the Crown*, 2 vols (London, 1736), II, p. 317; William Hawkins, *A Treatise of the Pleas of the Crown*, 3rd edn, 2 vols (London, 1739), II, p. 329; Blackstone, IV, p. 320.

[30] Muddiman, *Trial of King Charles*, pp. 211–23.

[31] Roger Lockyer, ed., *The Trial of Charles I*, Folio edn (London, 1959), p. 7.

of thousands who had died as a result of the wars he had inflicted on his country. Along with his aloof intransigence it may have been this callousness – brought to the attention of his judges – that consigned him to the block. More likely, his fate was already sealed. Cromwell had determined to cut off his head with the crown on it. Cook had stated bluntly that the king 'must die and the monarchy must die with him'.[32] The commissioners, with their military members returned, concurred.

When the Court reconvened, the king was no more pliant. Bradshaw gave a lengthy justificatory judgment before passing the sentence of death on this 'public enemy'. Fifty-nine of the commissioners – the 'regicides' – signed his death warrant, some more eagerly than others. It is perhaps significant that the first signature, that of Bradshaw, is small and faint, as though reflecting the writer's misgivings or fears, while the third, that of one 'O. Cromwell', is big and bold and reveals no hesitancy. Cromwell may well have considered the execution a 'cruel necessity', but necessity exonerated cruelty.[33]

As a result the one and only king of England ever to be judicially executed, was beheaded on a scaffold outside the Banqueting House on 30 January 1649. Security again was a major factor for the location: Whitehall in those days was narrow enough to thwart any royalist cavalry attempt to rescue the prey. So too was openness vital: this was not some grubby act carried out furtively, but the public execution of an erstwhile monarch in the presence of his people whom he had so grievously wronged. Charles, having walked through rooms where hung the Rubens paintings celebrating the divine rights of kings which he had commissioned, stepped onto the scaffold. Before the axe fell he, remembering his betrayal of Strafford, was heard to say, 'an unjust sentence that I suffered to take effect, is punished now by an unjust sentence on me'.[34] Seconds later the head of King Charles I was severed from his body. His killers were aghast that some spectators dipped their handkerchiefs in the royal blood, which was believed to work miracles of healing.[35] 'He nothing common did or mean/ Upon that memorable scene', was Marvell's immortalising encomium. Nothing became Charles's life like the leaving of it.

In the space of a thousand years English law had evolved from a rough code to settle disputes, constrain feuds, and keep the peace, into an institu-

---

32 Wedgwood, *Trial of Charles I*, p. 116.
33 Joseph Spence, *Anecdotes* (London, 1820), p. 275.
34 Hibbert, *Charles I*, p. 157.
35 Later, the *Eikon Basilike*, likely written by his chaplain, portrayed Charles as a Christ figure.

tion used to bring even a king to justice. Or so many thought and asserted. Bradshaw refused to be shaken, and though legality was not on his side, resolutely behaved as though it were in his attempt to establish the principle that even kings were answerable to law. Cook was unrepentant, later stating is his pamphlet, *King Charls* [*sic*], *His Case* – the speech he would have given had Charles not refused to plead – that the Court had been erected for 'the most Comprehensive, Impartial and Glorious piece of Justice that ever was acted and Executed upon the Theatre of England', and that 'the execution of the late king was one of the fattest sacrifices that ever Queen Justice had'.[36] Others condemned the whole charade as a travesty of justice.

However one views the strict legality of the proceedings, and they were irregular at best, to put a king on trial at all was a remarkable and daring achievement. It sent shudders down the spines of autocrats everywhere, providing a precedent of how they might be brought to account. The modern human rights lawyer and biographer of Cook, Geoffrey Robertson, goes so far as to claim that this first political trial of a head of state for crimes against the people became an international icon and progenitor of international criminal law.[37] An imperfect device, necessity's child, it has had an impact far greater than an axe on one royal neck.

Small wonder that Cook would be a marked man should the political situation change, as soon it did. With the Restoration in 1660 no mercy would be shown the surviving regicides – Cromwell, Bradshaw and thirteen others of the fifty-nine who signed the death warrant were already dead – and Cook, although not a signatory to the warrant, was prominent among the targets. He, along with others, was put on trial, inevitably found guilty, and suffered a traitor's death – hanging, drawing and quartering.[38] He had sacrificed everything for his convictions, for his profession, and, he thought, for constitutional law.

For some, however, England had displaced one tyrant to replace him with a tyranny as bad or worse. Cromwell's regime had the aura of a military dictatorship. It had gutted parliament, it had put a king on trial with only the vestiges of legality, and it repressed Dissenters: religious groups such as the Ranters, and political ones such as the Levellers. Would the law which had been manipulated to restrain monarchical tyranny prove the last bastion protecting the individual who dissented under a republic? The life and liber-

---

36 Muddiman, *Trial of King Charles*, p. 234.
37 Robertson, *The Tyrannicide Brief*, pp. 3, 364.
38 *ST*, V, pp. 947–1362.

ties of one man would force the issue. Though he had fought against the king, he had condemned the trial of Charles I as an illegal farce. He too would face trial for treason in 1649, but unlike the king, he would have a jury and he would be acquitted.

CHAPTER 16

Free-born John

The Laws of England, and the Privileges thereof, are my Inheritance and Birth-right.   Col. John Lilburne, 1649

JOHN LILBURNE was the most public and persistent *habeas corpus* litigant of any age. He was also a constant irritant in the side of every government, royal or republican, under which he lived. He was imprisoned by each in turn. A leading member of the radical sect known as Levellers, a passionate and idealistic rabble-rouser, an inveterate pamphleteer, and a self-taught lawyer, he was unstoppable and unquenchable. It was one of his friends who said of him: 'if the world were emptied of all but John Lilburne, Lilburne would quarrel with John and John with Lilburne'.[1]

He had been inspired into – rather than deterred from – spirited opposition to the government of Charles I by witnessing the savage treatment meted out to William Prynne and the others in 1637. The following year Lilburne was arrested for smuggling their proscribed books into the country. He refused to answer his Star Chamber interrogators, standing on *habeas corpus* and claiming that as a free-born Englishman he had a right against self-incrimination. The Court found him in contempt and ordered him to a public whipping followed by imprisonment.[2] This placed Lilburne centre stage, the position he loved. He became a celebrity, the crowds cheering the youth they indelibly dubbed 'Free-born John'. So much for the power of deterrent punishments. Two years later a member of parliament called Oliver Cromwell demanded and secured his release. It was, however, out of the frying pan, as at the outbreak of the civil war Lilburne enlisted as an officer in the parliamentary army, survived the battle of Edgehill, only to be taken prisoner by his old enemies. He was tried on a charge of high treason in the royalist headquarters of Oxford and condemned to death. Parliament again intervened on his behalf. When the House of Commons declared they would treat royalist prisoners in the same way, Lilburne was reprieved and later exchanged.

---

[1]   David Jenkins, *Notes and Queries* (London, 1852), IV, p. 134.
[2]   *ST*, III, pp. 1315–69.

He remained an icon of the parliamentary cause. After the war, in 1646 two little-known barristers, John Cook and John Bradshaw, were assigned by the House of Lords to argue that Lilburne's Star Chamber conviction was wrong in law. The House agreed that no man should be compelled to be his own accuser. Lilburne's sentence was quashed 'as illegal, and most unjust, against the liberty of the Subject, and the Law of the Land, and Magna Carta'. He was awarded £2,000 compensation.[3]

Without something or someone to oppose, Lilburne was lost. Not for long. In the years succeeding the civil war there was much for a radical to agitate about. Whoever was in power would be the target of his attack. He could be as nasty about erstwhile friends as about erstwhile enemies. Lilburne exploited the power of the printing press to disseminate his views and criticise the authorities in rousing, witty, and, some would say, seditious pamphlets. He infuriated every regime, monarchical or republican, and during the Commonwealth fell foul of the Lords, the Commons and Cromwell, the Lord Protector. Each imprisoned him in their turn. But they could not silence him. He shouted through cell windows; he smuggled tracts out of prison. Lilburne could not keep quiet or be kept quiet. He believed that the time had now come for all Englishmen to claim their rights and to do so loudly. Liberties such as freedom of worship and universal male suffrage, he maintained, were not bestowed by government, monarchical or republican, but by birthright confirmed by Magna Carta. Republican government could be as arbitrary and tyrannical as monarchical. Both could use and abuse the law. Magna Carta was a shield against both.

Lilburne repeatedly deployed the common law remedy of *habeas corpus*, by this time enshrined by parliament in the statute book itself. But what would become of a writ whose effectiveness derived from the king's prerogative, when the king was no more? On 8 May 1648 Lilburne stood before Justice Bacon and Chief Justice Rolle in the King's Bench. He had been fined and imprisoned for 'High Crimes and Misdemeanours', on the order of the House of Lords. This 'pearl in a dunghill' demanded, and secured, the right to argue his own case for release by means of *habeas corpus*. He put on his spectacles, held his plea before him 'as the lawyers do their briefs', and stated his case. His argument, however, failed on the grounds that the House of Lords was a court higher than the King's Bench. The judges remanded him back to the Tower.[4] He was later released, and his sentence remitted, after a weighty petition on his behalf by the Levellers and a speech by Sir

3   Gregg, *Free-born John*, p. 135.
4   *Ibid.*, p. 244.

John Maynard, who had been imprisoned with him and who reminded the Commons of 'what this brave invincible Spirit hath suffered and done for you'.[5]

In March 1649 Lilburne was again arrested for publishing another tract attacking the government. While he was in prison, parliament passed a new act that made words or deeds subverting the government or inciting mutiny in the army treasonable offences. A mutiny in Oxfordshire was attributed to Lilburne's pamphleteering, and he was charged with high treason. On 24 October 1649 Lilburne was put on trial for his life at the Guildhall.[6] This was to be one of the most significant trials in legal history. Lilburne was again to defend himself. Lawyers like to say, 'he who represents himself has a fool for a client', but John Lilburne was no fool. He was the greatest amateur advocate ever to set foot in an English court. In the course of a three-day disputation with the judges, this brilliant if irritating autodidact did more to establish the principles of due process and a fair trial than all the learned lawyers had managed in centuries. Previous treason trials had been conducted in a day, had been inquisitorial in nature, and had largely involved the public vilification of the accused. Such trials were not to establish guilt or innocence – guilt was assumed – but indelibly to impress on the public mind the vileness of the act, the vindication of the state, and the determination of the authorities to extirpate evil incarnate. Lilburne would not stand mute, nor would he acquiesce in the usual procedures. The court was not for him to be a cage but a stage, and he was a master of stage management.

Anticipating that his judges would expect him to challenge the authority of the court he surprised them by not so doing. Instead he picked at every aspect of court procedure. 'I went beyond their expectations and gave them such a cuff under the other ear as I believe they will never thoroughly shake soft the smart and pain of it.' He refused to plead without seeing the indictment and without legal advice, neither of which were at this time allowed. He refused to answer incriminating questions. He demanded public justice, until the judges gently pointed out that the doors were in fact open. He criticised plain 'Mr' Bradshaw, for hypocrisy for trying to interrogate him in the Council of State after the manner of Star Chamber, a practice that Bradshaw had himself condemned when acting for Lilburne in 1646. He took issue with the court when the Attorney-General spoke *sotto voce* to one of the judges. He decried the rule denying counsel to defendants on matters of fact, although he needed no advocate other than himself. Lilburne's trial

---

5   *Ibid.*, p. 245.
6   *ST*, IV, pp. 1269–470.

9. No fool for a client: John Lilburne on trial for his life in 1649 and in characteristic full flow.

achieved the consolidation of such defence rights as could be extrapolated from the recent proceedings against the king who had been treated with courtesy and indulgence, supplemented with further rights drawn from the republican values for which parliament had fought, viz. fairness and equality before the law. He repeatedly cited Coke's *Institutes* and Cook's *King Charls, His Case* as proof that governments that influenced judges were guilty of tyranny. After five gruelling hours an exhausted Lilburne demanded a pause in the proceedings. He bellowed: 'I appeal to the righteous God of heaven and earth against you!' God heard, and the scaffolding supporting the court collapsed. Despite this divine intervention his demand was refused, but he was granted 'a piss pot' to relieve himself in court, a receptacle he then offered to the jurors.

Finally he invited the jury to usurp the role of legislators and judges by deciding what the law should be, rather than what facts had been proved.[7] In the presence of his precious jury he told the judges that 'the jury by law are not only judges of fact, but of law also: and you that call yourselves judges of the law are no more but Norman intruders; and in deed and in truth, if the jury please, are no more but ciphers, to pronounce their verdict'.[8] The jury in an hour acquitted him against overwhelming evidence. This occasioned an eruption of cheering 'such as was believed was never heard in the Guildhall which lasted for about half an hour without intermission: which made the judges for fear turn pale and hang down their heads'. Bonfires were lit throughout England.

Lilburne's travails were not over yet. In 1651, for a libellous attack on the MP Sir Arthur Haselrig, he was found in contempt of parliament, which passed an act fining and exiling him on pain of death. When parliament was dissolved he came back to England. He was arrested for his illegal return, and put on trial on 13 July 1653 at the Old Bailey.[9] After many intemperate outbursts which delighted the crowds, the case was adjourned until 13 August. The prosecution, to secure a death sentence, had the seemingly simple task of proving merely that Lilburne had returned from exile.

But they had not reckoned with his power of persuasion. He invited the jury to pass judgment not just on the factual question of whether he had breached the sentence of banishment, but on the morality and legality of the

---

7   For a detailed account of Lilburne and 'jury law-finding' see Thomas Green, *Verdict According to Conscience: Perspectives on the English Criminal Trial by Jury, 1200–1800* (Chicago, 1985), pp. 158–99.

8   *Ibid.*, p. 173.

9   *ST*, V, pp. 407–61.

statute itself. They had the right to judge a statute on the basis of English fundamental law and acquit if they found it to be void and the sentence unlawful. It was, he said 'a lie and a falsehood, an Act that has no reason in it, no law for it'.[10] The jury agreed, and their verdict was a condemnation of the intemperate legislators: 'John Lilburne is not guilty of any crime worthy of death.'

The Council of State turned itself into a Star Chamber and called each juror before it to demand an explanation. The jurors were prepared for this – possibly by Lilburne – and each in turn gave the same: 'I gave the verdict with a clear conscience and I refuse to answer any questions about it.' The jury, inflamed by Lilburne's charismatic defiance, made itself an independent protector of the citizen against the state.

Lilburne, however, was still being held in custody. On 27 August he was transferred to the Tower whose Lieutenant was ordered to ignore any application for *habeas corpus* that Lilburne should make. Sure enough he soon sued for a writ, but Cromwell intervened personally and forced the court to adjourn. Power, not law, had won. For Lilburne the new dispensation was worse than the old. It proved more ruthless and more effective in silencing him.

An opportunity for Lilburne to escape detention arose in January 1654 when a Captain Streeter, imprisoned by the Council of State for publishing seditious pamphlets, obtained a *habeas corpus* on the grounds that an order of parliament ceased to be in force after a dissolution. On 11 February Streeter won his freedom. Lilburne would certainly try the same course. Cromwell decided to remove him to where the writ would not in practice run, even if it could in theory.

On 16 March 1654 the Council of State ordered Lilburne's removal to Jersey, from the legal island of the Tower to a real island far away. Nothing in law prevented the sending of a writ of *habeas corpus* to the Channel Isles, or so it was thought. It could certainly go to the Scilly Isles, although those islands as part of Cornwall were within the realm of England. Jersey was not, being merely one of the king's dominions by his Norman inheritance. It did not matter. Geography and the tight military control of the island, if not law itself, had put Lilburne beyond judicial oversight: out of sight, out of mind, out of earshot.

The governor of the island was ordered to ignore any writ of *habeas corpus*, in the unlikely event of one arriving, and to keep Lilburne close prisoner within the compass of Mont Orgueil – or Gorey castle as it is often

---

[10] Green, *Verdict According to Conscience*, p. 195.

called – overlooking the harbour of Gorey on the eastern end of the island. Built following the Norman invasion in 1204, by the seventeenth century the castle had been transformed into a prison. It was a most convenient and isolated spot to imprison someone such as Lilburne, who breathed the oxygen of publicity.

He was imprisoned in a cold if airy room, with *en suite* facilities, but he had no means of communicating with the Norman-French speaking locals, and no means of getting pamphlets out of the castle let alone off the island. The soldiers escorting him when he exercised were forbidden to speak to him. Lilburne refused exercise with 'a dogg at his heeles'.[11] When he infringed the rules, as he often did, he was put in solitary confinement. He would not buckle. A year in such conditions, however, seem to have left him a largely broken man and the damage to his health proved mortal. As a result he was released in 1655, to die just two years later in Eltham, aged forty-two. His epitaph is in an epigram:

> Is John departed? and is Lilburne gone?
> Farewell to both, to Lilburne and to John.
> Yet being dead, take this advice from me
> Let them not both in one grave buried be.
> But lay John here, lay Lilburne hereabout.
> For if they ever meet they will fall out.[12]

Silenced at last or not, Lilburne in his tempestuous life had succeeded in turning *habeas corpus* from a mundane legal device into a powerful instrument of civil liberty. It was the 'free-born right' of all to know and challenge the reason for their detention. Although his radical invitation to the jury to become lawmakers as well as fact-finders failed to take traction in England, it nonetheless has contemporary resonance in what the Americans call jury nullification and the British term perverse verdicts. The people, in the form of a jury, can refuse to convict those they consider are motivated by conscience, or that have been indicted under what the jury feel to be immoral laws.

In 1658 the Lord Protector died and two years later so did the dynasty he had begotten. Despite the odium in which Oliver Cromwell was held by the Restoration government, his success in silencing dissent had not escaped their notice. Lord Clarendon, the former Edward Hyde, Charles II's chief minister, proved happy to imitate his old enemy, and continued this republican device of sending prisoners to Jersey or Scotland, outside

---

[11] Gregg, *Free-born John*, p. 337.
[12] *Ibid.*, p. 355.

the jurisdiction, or at least the reach, of *habeas corpus*. Clarendon was later impeached for his time in office, and one charge he faced was that he had sent persons to 'remote islands, garrisons, and other places to prevent them from the benefit of the law'.[13]

---

[13] Paul Halliday, *Habeas Corpus from England to Empire* (Cambridge, MA, 2010), p. 232.

CHAPTER 17

From Restoration to Revolution and Reaction

If Not Guilty be not a verdict, then you make of the Jury and Magna Charta but a mere nose of wax.   William Penn (*ST*, II)

The Habeas Corpus Acts declare no principle and define no rights, but they are for practical purposes worth a hundred constitutional articles guaranteeing individual liberty.… These Acts are of really more importance not only than the general proclamations of the Rights of Man which have often been put forward in foreign countries, but even than such very lawyer-like documents as the Petition of Right or the Bill of Rights.   A. V. Dicey, *Lecture Introductory to the Study of the Law*

ONE major legacy of Lilburne's forensic forays was confirmed and reinforced in the Restoration period. In 1670 the principle of the independence of the jury came once more to the fore in *Bushell's Case*.[1] Jury independence had never been sacrosanct. Star Chamber had punished recalcitrant juries for a century and a half, and even after its demise in 1641 common law judges continued penalising jurors, particularly during the 1660s. But had they such power? John Kelyng, Chief Justice of the King's Bench from 1665 to 1671, thought so. He was 'an unbending representative of public power, who showed little patience for supposed English traditions of liberty that interfered with the administration of criminal justice'.[2] Once he was denounced in parliament for quoting Cromwell in calling Magna Carta 'Magna Farta', words he initially denied but later admitted he might have said. He favoured compelling jurors to convict not only in cases involving religious dissent but in cases of homicide – although in this he may have been trying to protect apprentices from being beaten to death by their masters. Recalcitrant jurors he would fine or imprison.

The issue came to a head when the 'Cavalier Parliament' determined to exact revenge on religious dissent. Amongst the other discriminatory measures of the so-called Clarendon Code, it passed in 1664 the first of two Conventicle Acts – that 'quintessence of arbitrary malice', as Marvell put

---

[1]   *ST*, VI, pp. 951–98. The best analysis is in Green, *Verdict According to Conscience*, pp. 200–64. A shorter account is given in Denning, *Landmarks in the Law*, pp. 134–52.

[2]   Whitman, *Origins of Reasonable Doubt*, pp. 174f.

it[3] – banning any religious assembly or 'conventicle' of five persons or more, other than Anglicans worshipping according to the *Book of Common Prayer*.[4] Catholics, Presbyterians and Quakers were the targets of this law. Two leading Quakers, William Penn and William Mead, were arrested while preaching to a crowd of 300 or 400 people on Sunday 14 August 1670 in Gracechurch Street in the City. They were put on trial in the Old Bailey. Their judges included the Mayor and the Recorder of London. A jury was empanelled. After their demand for a copy of the indictment was acceded to, both Penn and Mead pleaded 'not guilty in manner and form'. The misdemeanour charge facing the Quakers was that they did 'unlawfully and tumultuously assemble and congregate themselves together, to the disturbance of the peace … to the great terror and disturbance' of many of the king's subjects. The latter words were to prove fatal to the prosecution. It was somewhat hard to imagine peaceable Quakers having that effect on even the most fragile of his majesty's flock, nor did the evidence of the arresting officers suggest that they had.

Furthermore, when the prisoners were allowed to speak, Penn, a member of Lincoln's Inn, demanded to know what law they were alleged to have broken. The first Conventicle Act had expired in 1668 and was not yet renewed. What had been done in Gracechurch Street in August 1670 could not fall foul of it. In answer to Penn's question, all the Recorder could answer was 'upon the common law'. Penn then asked, 'where is that common law?' The Recorder, flummoxed, prevaricated: 'you must not think that I am able to run up so many years, and over so many adjudged cases, which we call common law, to answer your curiosity'. In mock bewilderment Penn asked if he were to plead to an 'indictment that hath no foundation in law?' The Recorder, unable to answer, retorted, 'you a saucy fellow, speak to the indictment'. Penn, knowing he was on firm ground, asserted that the proceedings were arbitrary and that the prime 'question is not whether I am guilty of this indictment, but whether this indictment is legal'. The Mayor and Recorder ordered that the recalcitrant prisoner be placed in the 'bale-dock' – a remand enclosure some yards away. Mead, who had also studied law, made the same point, and quoted Coke's *Institutes* to show that under common law an unlawful assembly was when three or more assembled together to do an

3   *The Poems and Letters of Andrew Marvell*, ed. H. M. Margoliouth, 3rd edn, 2 vols (Oxford, 1971), II, p. 314.
4   *EHD*, VIII, pp. 384ff.

unlawful act.⁵ Here there was no evidence of any unlawful act. He too was removed from the court.

In the absence of the accused the Recorder summed up the case as 'preaching to the people and drawing a tumultuous company after them'. The witnesses proved the preaching. Penn shouted from the bale-dock: 'I appeal to the jury who are my judges, and this great assembly, whether the proceedings of the court are not most arbitrary, and void of all law.'

The jury retired upstairs to deliberate. After an hour and a half, eight returned, but four, including the foreman, Edward Bushell, remained in their room. Unanimity was needed for a verdict. The judges ordered that the recalcitrant jurors be brought down to the court. The Recorder rounded on them and especially on Bushell, whom he considered to be the 'cause of this disturbance' and 'an abettor of faction'. He threatened to put his mark on him. The twelve jurors were then sent off to reconsider. After some considerable time they returned to the court. They said that they had agreed on a verdict. When the question was put as to whether Penn was guilty or not, Bushell replied 'guilty of speaking in Gracechurch Street'. He would not say that this was an unlawful assembly. The judge refused to accept this verdict and ordered them out again to 'make an end to this troublesome business'. This time, after half an hour the jury found Penn guilty of preaching to an assembly and Mead not guilty of anything.

The judge, furious at this refusal to follow his directions, interjected, 'you shall not be dismissed till we have a verdict that the court will accept'. The Recorder confined the jury overnight 'without meat, drink, fire and tobacco', to reconsider. 'We will have a verdict', he told them, 'by the help of God, or you shall starve for it.' Perhaps just as well, as even a chamber-pot was to be denied them. Penn interjected once more. 'Looking upon the jury', he said, 'You are *Englishmen*, mind your privilege, give not away your right.' Bushel replied, 'Nor will we ever do it.'

The next day they brought in the same verdict. Again they were confined to reconsider. To no avail. Penn was guilty of speaking in Gracechurch Street, but not more. Bushell, who had done as his conscience dictated, was denounced as 'a factious fellow' who had suborned the other jurors. Even the 'not guilty' verdict on Mead was rejected by the court. Once again the jury were sent off to reconsider. Once again they returned the same verdict. Bushell was directly threatened by the Recorder. It did not help the jurors' cause when Penn himself interjected on their behalf, invoking Magna Carta and expressing outrage that 'the jury should be thus menaced'. 'Is this

---

⁵ Coke, *Institutes of the Laws of England*, III, Ch. lxxix; Blackstone, IV, p. 146.

according to the fundamental laws? Are they not my proper judges by the Great Charter of England? What hope is there of ever having justice done when juries are threatened and their verdicts rejected.' The judge, unmoved, dismissed the Charter in the same term as his predecessors, as 'Magna Farta', and ordered the jury to come to another verdict. Again they refused to budge from their original words.

They were again sequestered overnight without sustenance, to reconsider or starve. This time they decided to comply with the demand to bring in a true verdict. The unanimous verdict on both defendants was not guilty. This, the irate Recorder believed, was 'contrary to the full and manifest evidence and contrary to the direction of the court on a matter of law ... and in contempt of the Lord King and his laws, and to the great impeding of justice, and the bad example for all other jurors who default in similar cases.' As a result he fined them forty marks each and, pending payment, imprisoned them in the notorious Newgate Prison, next door to the Old Bailey. From there Bushel and three others who had refused to pay claimed *habeas corpus* on the basis that the fine had no legal validity and so their detention was unlawful. The case was by no means certain to be resolved in their favour, as five years earlier in *Wagstaffe's Case*[6] the fining of the jury in another Quaker prosecution in the King's Bench was not overturned, and a parliamentary attempt in 1668 to declare illegal the fining and imprisonment of jurors had died in committee.

The Old Bailey jurors were, however, brought before Sir John Vaughan, Chief Justice of the Common Pleas.[7] In a decisive judgment that overturned *Wagstaffe*, Vaughan held that a jury had an absolute right to find a verdict independently of the views of the trial judge. He fixed on the premise that a juror still retained the right to use private knowledge in coming to a verdict, and private knowledge was by definition beyond the ken of the judge. If a juror betrayed his private knowledge he endangered his soul. As any juror could have private knowledge, no juror could be fined for his verdict.

Bushell's case, which conclusively established this fundamental principle of English justice that no jury can be fined nor imprisoned for any verdict they may give, is commemorated with a plaque set in the wall inside the Central Criminal Court, as the Old Bailey is now called. Its effects continue to this day, and juries, however perverse their decision may seem, are free to be perverse.

*

---

6   *R* v. *Wagstaffe* [1665] 1 Keble 934, 83 Eng. Rep. 1328.

7   *ST*, VI, pp. 999–1025; *EHD*, VIII, pp. 86–9.

In May 1679 parliament, increasingly concerned about the means by which the executive was evading the reach of the law, passed the Habeas Corpus Amendment Act for 'the prevention of imprisonment beyond the seas'. It gave all citizens the absolute right to have the validity of their imprisonment considered by a superior court, and improved the machinery by which the right might be enforced. *Habeas corpus* could be sought from Chancery and the Exchequer as well as from the King's Bench or the Common Pleas. Any judge refusing an application for a writ would be heavily fined. A writ once issued, the prisoner had to be produced within twenty days; no person released under a writ could be recommitted for the same offence; and none, in an attempt to subvert the long arm of the law, could be sent as prisoner beyond the seas, let alone to Scotland! This act has been lauded as 'the most effective remedy against executive lawlessness that the world has ever seen', and the 'chief guarantor of English liberty'.[8] It barely scraped into law.

A lovely but unlikely tale has it that the bill, having got through the Commons but being repeatedly blocked in the Lords, secured its passage there by a sleight of hand. The opposing sides each appointed a teller to count the vote, Lord Norris for the Nos and Lord Grey for the Ayes. The story goes that Lord Norris, 'being a man subject to the vapours', was distracted just as a particularly fat member was about to vote. Lord Grey, discerning that this voter carried more weight than others, counted him as ten. Thanks to one obese aristocrat the bill passed with a majority of two.[9] Just as well it did, given that James II would soon be on the throne.

With the accession of James II in 1685 the absolute authority of kings to make and unmake laws was again a live issue, and the judiciary were largely supine. James asserted a power to dispense individual Catholics from the effects of the Test Acts of 1673 and 1678, which prevented them from holding public office. To gain compliance he eroded the independence of the judiciary and subverted the rule of law. He removed recalcitrant judges and replaced them with those who would serve his ends. He handpicked the youthful – and pliant – Edward Herbert to replace the infamous George Jeffreys – whom James had promoted to Lord Chancellor – as Chief Justice. He chose well. When Herbert was invested as a serjeant he gave away rings on which were inscribed the motto *Jacobus vincit, triumphat lex* – 'where James conquers the law triumphs'. The king then sought to contrive a test case to provide a

---

8   Dicey, *Lectures Introductory to the Study of the Law*, p. 236; Bingham, *The Rule of Law*, p. 14.

9   Burnet, *History of His Own Time*, II, pp. 250f.

judicial ruling on the legality of his dispensing power. *Godden* v. *Hales* was a collusive action brought for this purpose. Sir Edward Hales was a Catholic who had taken up an army commission without fulfilling the requirements of the Test Acts. Godden was his coachman who brought an action against his master in the King's Bench. Hales pleaded a royal dispensation. In June 1686 the new Chief Justice and ten out of eleven justices, invoking a divine analogy, held that 'there is no law whatsoever but may be dispensed with by the supreme lawgiver, as the laws of God may be dispensed with by God himself, as it appears by God's command to Abraham to offer up his son Isaac'. They declared that as the kings of England are sovereign princes, and the laws of England are the king's laws, 'it is an inseparable prerogative in the kings of England to dispense with penal laws in particular cases and upon particular necessary reasons', of which 'the king himself is sole judge'. A feigned case, and a rigged bench, had ensured this result. Critics likened this ruling to Judas's betrayal of Christ.[10]

Fears about the James's increasingly absolutist tendencies were aggravated by his maintenance of a standing army of just under 20,000 men, quartered on reluctant citizens and corporations, and officered to some extent by Catholics such as Hales, all beneficiaries of the dispensing power. This was anathema in peacetime, when it was feared that the only thing for such a force to subdue was Magna Carta.[11] Catholics were also admitted to the privy council and imposed as heads on reluctant Oxbridge colleges. Flouting legality, James established an Ecclesiastical Commission, the Court of High Commission in another guise, to police and control the Anglican Church. Finally, and most egregiously, he intended not merely to dispense Catholics from the Test Acts, but, pending repeal, to suspend the very operation of those laws enforcing conformity to the Church of England and requiring the taking of religious oaths before gaining employment in government office. He did so by a Declaration of Indulgence, first issued in 1687. His erstwhile promises to preserve 'the government both in church and state as ... by law established', rang hollow.[12] Where would it all lead? Continental comparisons were discomfiting. James II was increasingly perceived as being the dark shadow cast across England by that ultimate anti-Protestant and absolutist despot, the 'Sun King', Louis XIV of France. The birth of a son and heir

---

10 *EHD*, VIII, p. 83; Tim Harris, *Revolution: The Great Crisis of the British Monarchy, 1685–1720* (London, 2006), pp. 192ff.

11 William Gibson, *James II and the Trial of the Seven Bishops*, (London, 2009), p. 54; Harris, *Revolution*, pp. 185–95.

12 *Ibid.*, p. 41.

to James in June 1688 meant that the shadow of Catholic despotism might never lift.

In the same month opposition to the king was galvanised by the trial of seven bishops led by the learned and saintly archbishop of Canterbury, William Sancroft, on a charge of seditious libel.[13] These were no revolutionaries, but conformist Tory ecclesiastics schooled in obedience to the temporal power, but alarmed by James's 'papist' proclivities and cavalier attitude to the law. They had been appalled by the reissue of the Declaration of Indulgence in April, and by the royal demand that it be read in churches. In a written protest, the seven bishops refused to order their clergy to propagate the Declaration from the pulpit, and questioned the legality of the dispensing and suspending power. For this they were prosecuted, turning them into national heroes. They were saved from becoming martyrs by a jury who found them not guilty.

Erstwhile loyal and quiescent Anglicans had been affronted. A predominantly Tory parliament had been alienated. Dissenters who, despite James's overt blandishments, had never trusted his motives, yearned for the security of Protestantism that only his departure would ensure. Opposition thus unified, appalled and affrighted, led to an invitation, sent on the day of the bishops' acquittal, to James's son-in-law, William of Orange, to invade England. Burnet justified this act of treason by arguing in print that whereas non-resistance to the king applied only 'to the Executive Power', it did not extend 'to an invasion of the Legislative Power or to a total Subversion of the Government', for the law 'did not design to lodge that Power in the King'.[14] The invitation was enthusiastically accepted by William, and his triumphant appearance with an impressive force culminated in the hasty 'desertion', long-term disgrace and, under the reassuring guise that he had abdicated, permanent deposition of James II. He had un-kinged himself.

The ensuing Revolution settlement, negotiated compromise though it was, ensured that the rule of law and parliamentary privilege conclusively triumphed over royal prerogative. The Bill of Rights, passed on 16 December 1689, gave statutory force to the Declaration of Rights that had accompanied the offer of the crown to William and Mary. Parliament was taking no chances. The preamble denounced the 'late' king's 'endeavour to subvert and extirpate the Protestant religion and the laws and liberties of this kingdom'. To 'vindicate and assert … the true, ancient and indubitable rights of the

---

[13] *ST*, XII, pp. 183–422.
[14] Quoted in Harris, *Revolution*, pp. 287f.

people of this kingdom', fundamental limitations were placed on the 'the pretense of prerogative'. The 'pretended power' of suspending, or dispensing with, laws was declared illegal. The Ecclesiastical Commission was 'illegal and pernicious'. Jury trial was protected. Personal liberty and security were safeguarded by prohibiting the requirement of excessive bail, the imposition of excessive fines, and the infliction of cruel and unusual punishments. The keeping of a peacetime standing army without parliamentary consent was 'against law'. Parliaments were to be held frequently and by free election, and none could impeach nor question what was said or done therein. In a crucial addition to the Declaration, Catholics and those married to Catholics were excluded from the succession to the throne.[15]

The exigencies of the time, and its own ambiguities enhanced the settlement's appeal to both sides of the political spectrum. Whigs such as John Locke, who published his *Two Treatises of Government* in 1689, were intent that James had been deposed for breaching trust by violating the constitution. It was for the people to decide when a breach of trust has taken place, and to the people that power reverted. The people, through their representatives convened for the purpose, had then bestowed it on William and Mary. Tories salved their consciences by asserting that James had not been deposed but had abdicated or — better — 'deserted' the throne. His line continued through more or less hereditary succession. The fabric of monarchy had been torn but was mended. As Edmund Burke expressed it a hundred years later when referring to what he considered to be the 'cornerstone of our constitution', William's accession had been an act of unique necessity and a 'small and temporary deviation from the strict order of a regular hereditary succession'.[16] In 1689 both sides had conferred and compromised. The dual monarchy was the resultant fudge.

Despite the Bill's assertion that it was vindicating ancient rights, and the arguments that what resulted was an essentially conservative coup, it is now widely accepted that, along with the Act of Settlement, it was more radical, completing unfinished business from the civil wars, changing not only the king — radical enough — but the kingship, and making 'new law under guise of declaring the old'. The reality was that it marked a fundamental shift in the balance of power in favour of an elected parliament, and against the arbi-

15 *EHD*, VIII, pp. 122–8.
16 Edmund Burke, *Reflections on the Revolution in France* (1791), Folio Society edn (London, 2010), pp. 13ff.

trary rule of an individual. An hereditary but constitutional and Protestant monarchy had been established.[17] The sovereignty of parliament was ensured.

In contrast, no restraints were placed upon the new sovereign – the king-in-parliament. Unlike the American Constitution, the Bill of Rights did not protect the citizen from the 'tyranny of the majority'.[18] Congress cannot infringe the written constitution. Parliament, constrained merely by convention, can alter the unwritten constitution at will. The final buttress of the new dispensation came in 1701 when, as a result of the inability of Mary or her sister Anne to provide an heir, 'An Act for the further limitation of the Crown, and better securing the rights and Liberties of the Subject', was passed. In a tacit tribute to John Lilburne, this Act of Settlement declared that 'the laws of England are the birthright of the people'. It put more restrictions on the powers of future monarchs, insisted they be Anglicans, and passed over the Jacobites in favour of the Hanoverians.

It also ensured another prerequisite of the fair trial: the independence of the judiciary. Judges were never again to be 'lions under the throne', the big beasts of a royal menagerie. Thenceforth they held office *quamdiu se bene gesserint* ('during good behaviour'), not under the sufferance of the king. Judicial independence was subject to a single caveat: errant judges could still be removed, but only by joint address of both houses of parliament. The 'independency and uprightness of judges' were trumpeted as 'essential to the impartial administration of justice'.[19] However, while they could not be deposed from office by, they still owed their appointment to, royal command. Political patronage in judicial appointments was to remain powerful for generations to come. 'The great object of every government, in electing the judges of the land', should have been 'to obtain the most skilful and learned men in their profession, and at the same time, men whose character [gave] the best security for the pure and impartial administration of justice.' The system of judicial promotion sinned 'in both these particulars'.[20] The gratitude and loyalty of the new incumbent could play the same role as servility and insecurity.

Testing times would test the judges. Were they truly independent and prepared to do justice though the heavens might fall? Cromwell and Clarendon, on

---

[17] Julian Hoppitt, *A Land of Liberty? England 1689–1727* (Oxford, 2000), p. 23; Harris, *Revolution*, p. 494.

[18] Vernon Bogdanor, *The New British Constitution*, (Oxford, 2009), p. 54.

[19] *EHD*, VIII, pp. 129–35, at p. 134. In 1760 another act ensured that judges would retain office even on the demise of the monarch: *EHD*, X, p. 247.

[20] Brougham's Speech, 7 February 1828, *EHD*, XI, p. 364.

grounds of state necessity, had both managed to render the reach of *habeas corpus* ineffectual. Later governments in times of national crisis, such as the Jacobite Rebellion of 1745, resorted to total suspension. The danger was that governments, once accustomed to suspending the operation of *habeas corpus*, could further attempt to curtail the liberty of citizens in circumstances less dangerous to the life of the nation than to that of the government. The second half of the eighteenth century would provide the battleground upon which government and the law would contest the liberty of the subject. In this the statutory independence of the judiciary would be crucial, an independence exemplified in the decisions it made in a number of cases featuring John Wilkes.

'That damned fellow Wilkes' was an unlikely champion of liberty. To some he was little more than 'an unprincipled adventurer'.[21] He was very much a libertine, an enthusiastic member of the notorious Hell-Fire Club, and the author of a lewd and licentious parody of Pope's *Essay on Man*. He was also an able polemicist, an instinctive demagogue, a champion of the freedom of the press, and a radical MP. He was the most 'wicked and agreeable fellow' that William Pitt the Elder had ever met.

On 23 April 1763, Wilkes anonymously published issue 45 of *The North Briton*, a satirical periodical of his own creation. It ridiculed George III's speech at the opening of parliament and exploded the fiction that it was the king's own doing rather than the composition of his ministers. The royal address had extolled the Treaty of Paris, which had ended the Seven Years War. By this treaty, Wilkes rightly thought, the government had thrown away many of the fruits of victory, and had 'saved England from the certain ruin of success'. He had cheekily observed that this 'was certainly the peace of God for it passeth all understanding'. He contrasted the prerogative of the Crown with the prerogative of the people – freedom. Resistance to arbitrary government was enshrined in the English Constitution. The king – or 'first magistrate' as Wilkes called him – was mightily offended by what he deemed to be scurrilous and treasonable words. He demanded action.[22]

The government, on the positive advice of the law officers, misguidedly decided to prosecute Wilkes for seditious libel. They did so by employing a 'general warrant' – an executive device of dubious legality. It was not founded on common law or statute, but stemmed in some way from the royal prerog-

---

[21] Henry Brougham, *Historical Sketches of Statesmen*, 6 vols (London, 1845), V, p. 220.

[22] *EHD*, X, pp. 252–6; John Wilkes, *The North Briton, XLVI Numbers Complete*, 4 vols (London, 1772), III, pp. 247–60; Arthur Cash, *John Wilkes, The Scandalous Father of Civil Liberty* (New Haven, 2006), p. 100.

ative. Such a warrant named crimes but not the criminals, and authorised royal messengers to break into any house to seize what they would, and to arrest anyone and everyone of whom they had the slightest suspicion. It was under such a warrant, authorising the arrest 'of the authors, printers and publishers' of the 'seditious and treasonable' issue 45, that Wilkes, despite his assertion of parliamentary immunity, was detained and his papers were seized.

His lawyer wisely declined to take the normal route of seeking a writ of *habeas corpus* from the King's Bench, dominated as it was by the hostile Chief Justice, Lord Mansfield, and instead resorted to the Common Pleas. Chief Justice Pratt presided there. He declared this 'a most extraordinary warrant' and issued 'an *habeas corpus*, returnable forthwith'. In a vain attempt to try to circumvent this device, Wilkes was transferred to the Tower of London. There, as the popularly proclaimed 'jewel', he awaited his fate. On application by the brilliant and brave Sergeant John Glynn, Pratt granted a writ against the Constable of the Tower. The matter again came before the Chief Justice, who, despite his earlier remarks casting doubt on the legality of general warrants, did not decide that issue but, on 6 May, discharged Wilkes from custody since his arrest breached parliamentary privilege. Nonetheless, Wilkes, never one to stand on a narrow technicality when a broad principle would do, turned a personal vindication into universal condemnation of warrants. He claimed his success as a triumph for freedom in general and not just for parliamentarians.[23] General warrants, with their sweeping powers to extinguish individual rights at the behest of the executive, were perceived as all but illegal. The expectant crowds agreed, the vast space of Westminster Hall resounding to the cries of 'Wilkes and Liberty'. This novel slogan was to be a clarion call in London for years to come.

The next few years saw a spate of legal actions on the issue of the legality of general warrants themselves. A major victory came in December 1763 when Wilkes's case against Under-Secretary Wood for trespass and seizure of papers was heard at Westminster Hall.[24] During the course of the trial the government provided evidence that general warrants had been used many times since 1662 without legal challenge. Pratt, in directing the jury, dismissed this as irrelevant, and did so in trenchant terms: 'precedents are ... no justification of a practice in itself illegal' and against the constitution. The judge was openly appalled at the assertion that royal messengers had a discretionary power 'to search wherever their suspicions may chance to fall':

---

[23] George Rude, *Wilkes and Liberty* (Oxford, 1962), p. 27.
[24] *ST*, XIX, pp. 1154–77; *EHD*, X, pp. 256f.

If such a power is truly invested in a Secretary of State, and he can delegate this power, it certainly may affect the person and property of every man in this kingdom, and is totally subversive of the liberty of the subject.

The jury found for Wilkes and awarded him £1,000 in damages. This decision was not yet a universal condemnation of general warrants as it related not to the arrest of individuals, but to the entry into private houses by agents of the Crown who could 'break open their desks and seize their papers contrary to the fundamental principles of the constitution'. The right of privacy was established in law, a right that 'rendered a man's house his castle'.[25]

The first pronouncement on the legality of warrants as instruments of arrest was to be made not by Pratt, but by none other than the pre-eminent legal authority in the land, Lord Mansfield himself. Despite his hostility to Wilkes and despite his earlier reservations about Pratt's decisions on this issue, in two cases in 1764 and 1765 he condemned the arrest of persons under general warrants. He too dismissed the argument from 'usage'. Usage had great weight, but would 'not hold against clear and solid principles of law.… The form of the warrant probably took its rise from a law for licencing the press (13 & 14 Charles II, ch. 33) which is law no more: it arose from a law, which is now expired.' Mansfield's brother judges agreed that such warrants were 'void and illegal'.[26]

The *coup de grace* was to be delivered in November of 1765, when the issue again went before Pratt, by then Lord Camden and soon to be Lord Chancellor, in the case of *Entick* v. *Carrington*.[27] Carrington, a king's messenger, had been dispatched under a general warrant to seize the papers of the Revd John Entick, a leading contributor to the *Monitor*, a weekly periodical and persistent critic of the government. Lord Camden confirmed the illegality of such warrants and made the famous pronouncement that 'with respect to the argument of State necessity, or a distinction which had been aimed at between State offences and others, the common law does not understand that kind of reasoning, nor do our books take notice of any such distinction'. In his judgment he referred to and denounced the intrusion into Wilkes' property as a contravention of Magna Carta.

Belatedly the craven politicians caught up with the judges, when in April 1766 a resolution of the House of Commons finally condemned as illegal and obnoxious the whole practice of deploying general warrants. But it was

---

[25] Cash, *John Wilkes*, p. 160.
[26] *Leach v. Money* (1765): *EHD*, X, pp. 257f.
[27] *ST*, XIX, pp. 1030–74, the fullest account as the writer had access to Camden's full judgment from his notebook; *EHD*, X, pp. 258–63.

the decisions of the common law courts that had 'erased the last vestige of absolute monarchical power, the last loophole in the constitution wherein the will of the monarch' – or of his ministers – 'constituted the law'.[28]

The seventeenth century had seen seismic changes, not least to the law of the land and the constitution of the country. The king reigned on sufferance and only in accordance with law. Judges had escaped their royal leash. Juries were free to say as their conscience or qualms dictated. And *habeas corpus* had become 'the Great Writ of Liberty', having vanquished every device sent to stifle it. In the following century it too would further enhance its reputation. No longer was it merely the free-born English that it would protect, but their slaves as well.

---

[28] Cash, *John Wilkes*, p. 162.

PART III

THE TRANSFORMATION OF THE LAW
1766–1907

CHAPTER 18

The Purity of England's Air

Legum denique ... omnes servi sumus ut liberi esse possimus
('In the end we are all slaves to the law that we may be free')
Cicero *Pro Cluentio* LIII.146

The constitution is pervaded by the rule of law on the ground that the general principles of the constitution (as for example the right to personal liberty, or the right of public meeting) are with us the result of judicial decisions determining the rights of private persons in particular cases brought before the courts.

A. V. Dicey, *Lectures introductory to the Study of the Law*

O N Thursday 28 November 1771, a ship called the *Ann and Mary* was moored in the Thames ready to leave for the West Indies with its cargo. That cargo had a name that would reverberate in English legal history for the case that bore it and for the ruling that concluded that case, known simply to posterity as the Mansfield Judgment.

The cargo had been a domestic slave and had been given the name James Somerset by his white owner, a Virginia trader aptly called Charles Stuart. Stuart came over to England and of course, along with a lot of other items of domestic property, brought his slave with him. He was a valuable piece of property worth some £50. Somerset managed to escape and lose himself among the several thousand blacks who already lived in London. Slave catchers, however, were put on his track and he was captured, shackled and put on board the *Ann and Mary* to be taken to Jamaica and sold into plantation work. This was not done in secret, the law was not being evaded. An owner had lost his property, given a reward for it being found, and now wanted to dispose of it at his will, as he would have done of a lost ring or a pig that had escaped its enclosure.

Enter the veteran anti-slavery activist and autodidact, Granville Sharp. Sharp may have been a lowly ordnance clerk at the Tower, living modestly in Old Jewry, but he was no ordinary one. He had taught himself, among other things, Hebrew, and was an accomplished polemicist against what he considered the outrageous, unchristian commerce in slaves. Many years before he had first got involved in anti-slavery activities when he was asked by his brother William, to bring a 'nearly blind and doubly lame' escaped slave called Jonathan Strong to St Bartholomew's Hospital. Strong had been hit so hard around the head with a pistol that the butt had separated from the stock. Sharp was outraged that any man could be so treated with legal impunity. Over the subsequent years he had taken on several cases involving slaves, but none proved quite the one to challenge their legal status in England. This matter of Somerset might just fit the bill and answer the question: though Britons might never be slaves, could slaves exist in Britain?

Sharp knew he had no time to lose. He secured a writ of *habeas corpus* from the King's Bench and rushed it aboard the *Ann and Mary*. The captain, confronted by the writ, could not disobey and Somerset, at least temporarily, was handed over to the court. The matter came before William Murray, Lord Mansfield himself, the premier judge of England. Mansfield was more than that. He is, alongside Coke, the most important and transformative jurist in English legal history. He was, of course, Scottish. Sharp, however, had reservations about this pillar of the establishment and seriously underestimated the man he thought 'deplorable of heart'. Mansfield had been Attorney-General in the Commons and Speaker in the Lords, disapproved of Wilkes and his liberties, and, despite coming from a Jacobite family, was an ardent unionist.[1] He was also the founder of modern English commercial law and a prime advocate of free trade. Was he the judge to endanger this, the very life blood of England?

Mansfield, however, had an extraordinary and independent mind. He had courage, was fair, had an instinct for justice and also a staunch Enlightenment belief that positive laws should derive from natural law and be based on common sense, morality and reason. He had a high regard for equitable principles, which he had imbibed from observing Lord Hardwicke, and in his own judgments he had introduced them into the common law. Precedents should be signposts, not manacles. Convenience, neither personal nor national, should ever be the sole determinative of judicial findings. He had previously declared on the issue of Wilkes's outlawry that the Constitution did not permit reasons of state to influence the judgment of the courts:

> God forbid it should! We must not regard political consequences, howsoever formidable they might be: if rebellion was the certain consequence, we are bound to say '*fiat justicia, ruat coelum*' [let justice be done though the heavens fall].[2]

---

1   Norman Poser, *Lord Mansfield: Justice in the Age of Reason* (Montreal and Kingston, 2013), pp. 111, 121.

2   *ST*, XIX, pp. 1103–37.

He also had a most unusual domestic set up. His nephew John Lindsay, a naval captain, had had an affair with a woman, probably a slave, found aboard a Spanish vessel he had captured. The product of this liaison was an illegitimate daughter, Dido Belle. She became like a daughter to her great-uncle, Lord Mansfield. He adored her. She lived with him, was a beneficiary of his will, and is seen in a portrait alongside his legitimate grand-niece. This was surprising enough in eighteenth-century England, but what was even more surprising was that Dido was black. To what extent this personal circumstance affected the great man's thinking we can never know, but it must have had some impact.

Both sides were well represented. Serjeant Glynn, the learned libertarian and Wilkes's old champion, was one of those chosen by Sharp. Somerset's barristers argued that as there was no law legalising slavery in this country, it must be illegal. The slaver's counsel countered by submitting that as contracts for the sale of slaves were valid under English law, that must validate slavery in England.

Somerset's case was not the first on the question of whether slaves were property, and as such could be bought and sold and conveyed anywhere the owner wished, just as cattle could, or whether blacks in England had the same legal rights as the native born. There was another argument based not on contracts for sale but on confession of faith. In 1609 Edward Coke himself had said that as perpetual enemies of Christians, infidels could be perpetually imprisoned. But what if the infidel converted? No longer an alien infidel, but a fellow Christian?

The first recorded slavery case was that of *Butts* v. *Penny* heard in the Court of the King's Bench in 1677.[3] The judges allowed a master to sue in *trover* for the loss of a black slave. *Trover* was a common law form of action to recover the value of goods or chattels by reason of an alleged unlawful interference with possessory rights. Consequently the judges thought a black slave was his master's property. The reason for this was that commercial custom permitted the buying and selling of blacks as 'merchandise'. However, the Attorney-General asked the court to postpone final judgment to the following term. It was never resurrected. There the issue rested until 1694, when in *Gelly* v. *Cleve* compensation was granted for the loss of a slave. It was 'adjudged that *trover* will lie for a negro boy; for they are heathens, and therefore a man may have property in them'.

---

3   83 Eng Rep. 518 (KB 1677).

Three years later *Chamberline* v. *Harvey*[4] came before Chief Justice Holt. A black litigant argued that slavery could not exist in England because it violated the law of nature, the common law had a presumption in favour of liberty, and a slave 'being baptised according to the rite of the Church, is thereby made Christian, and Christianity is inconsistent with slavery'. His master, citing *Butts* v. *Penny*, argued that it could not be denied that '*trover* would lie for the negro', Christian or no. 'Who would squeeze the sugar from the cane once all slaves had been sprinkled with holy water?' Holt, however, denied that *trover* would lie for 'the taking of a negro', no matter what *Butts* said, nor would an action for trespass, because both actions were available only to owners of chattels and blacks were not ownable. The black was not a slave but a 'slavish servant', akin to an apprentice. The master might recover the servant's lost services but not the servant himself.

The matter came before Holt again in 1701 in the case of *Smith* v. *Brown and Cooper*.[5] Smith sued for non-payment for a slave sold in Cheapside, but the Chief Justice held that 'As soon as a negro comes into England, he becomes free. One may be a villein in England but not a slave.' Under the law of Virginia blacks may be saleable, but not in English law. His fellow judge, Mr Justice Powell, went further in distinguishing a negro from a villein: 'the law takes no notice of a negro' and 'a black was to be treated as an Englishman'.

Holt returned to the matter in 1705 in *Smith* v. *Gould*.[6] Smith (who may have been the litigant in 1701) sued Gould from whom he had bought a 'singing Ethiopian negro' and 'other goods'. Gould argued that Smith could not sue in *trover* as one man could not own another. Smith countered that on the authority of English and Mosaic law, 'negroes were merchandise', like monkeys. Holt, overruling the mere opinion in *Butts* v. *Penny*, declared that 'the common law takes no notice of negroes being different from other men. By common law no man can have a property in another ... there is no such thing as a slave by the law of England.'

On the authority of the highest judge in England the matter seemed settled. The planters were worried, and so in 1729 in Lincoln's Inn they wined and dined the law officers of the Crown, the Attorney-General, Sir Philip Yorke, and the Solicitor-General, Charles Talbot. These two legal notables, both to become Lord Chancellors, obliged their hosts with a 'Joint Opinion'. The planters wanted them to negate the two principal arguments against

4   87 Eng Rep 598ff, 830 (KB 1697).
5   91 Eng Rep 566 (KB 1701).
6   91 Eng Rep 567 (KB 1705); 92 Eng Rep 338 (KB 1706).

black slavery: baptism – though no slave had ever been freed because of that – and breathing England's air. Yorke and Talbot expressed their view that slavery was legal, and they did so 'to correct a mistake, that slaves became free by their being in England, or by their being baptised'. A slave entering England does not become free and remains the property of his master. This was just an opinion, albeit from weighty authorities. Twenty years later in *Pearne* v. *Lisle*,[7] Yorke, now Lord Chancellor Hardwicke, tried to make the joint opinion law. He did not quite succeed in this, but his august opinion still held considerable sway. Black slaves were 'as much property as any other thing'.

Nonetheless the argument continued, and Lord Chancellor Henley in 1762 reverted to Holt's judgment. In *Shanley* v. *Harvey* it was held that 'as soon as a man sets foot on English ground he is free: a negro may maintain an action against his master for ill usage, and may have a *habeas corpus* if restrained of his liberty'.[8]

When William Blackstone published the first volume of his vastly influential *Commentaries on the Laws of England* in 1765, and the amended second edition the following year, he generally supported Holt's position, but nonetheless reflected the still not-quite certain state of the law. Blackstone in his own time was seen, alongside Coke, and Hale, as one of the paladins of the law.[9] Since 1758 he had been the first Vinerian professor of English law at the University of Oxford – a chair that Mansfield had helped create on his behalf – and before that had been a renowned lecturer on, and apologist for, the common law, which he considered to be 'the best birthright, the noblest inheritance of mankind'.[10] His four-volume work based on those lectures and constituting a masterly exposition of the whole of the law would consolidate, but did not create, his authoritative status.

In the chapter 'Of the Absolute Rights of Individuals', he cited Holt for the proposition that 'this spirit of liberty is so deeply implanted in our constitution, and rooted in our very soil, that a slave or a negro, the moment he lands in England, falls under the protection of the laws, [and so far becomes a free man, though the master's right to service may probably still continue,] and with regard to all natural rights becomes *eo instanti* a freeman'.[11] It is often said that the addition (in square brackets) in the second edition amounted to

7   27 Eng Rep 47 (Ch 1749).
8   2 Eden 125 (Ch 1762).
9   His influence persists to this day, not just in England but especially in the United States, an irony since he staunchly opposed the American rebellion.
10 Blackstone, IV, p. 436.
11 *Ibid.*, I, p. 123.

HONORABLE
Mᴿ JUSTICE BLACKSTONE.

10. Sir William Blackstone, an erudite and influential academic from the second university. He tried to give shape and system to the morass of the common law.

a severe retraction from the unequivocal statement made in the first. This is not so. It merely transposes for the sake of clarity and consistency that which Blackstone had already stated in the fourteenth chapter of the first edition, entitled 'Of Master and Servant'. There he reiterated that

> pure and proper slavery does not, nay cannot, subsist in England ... [whose law] abhors, and will not endure the existence of, slavery within this nation ... And now it is laid down that a slave or negro, the instant he lands in England, becomes a freeman; that is the law will protect him in the enjoyment of his person, his liberty, and his property. Yet with regard to any right which the master may have acquired, by contract or the like, to the perpetual service of John or Thomas, this will remain exactly in the same state as before: for this is no more than the same state of subjection for life, which every apprentice submits to for the space of seven years, or sometimes for a longer term.

The less than precise phrase 'by contract or the like', may provide a clue as to what Blackstone meant. He seemed to be saying that just as a free man could voluntarily contract to serve another for many years or even for life and yet still be protected 'in the enjoyment of his person, his liberty, and his property', so a former slave, now a free man, was no different. He would remain a servant or apprentice, if he contracted, but not a chattel. He still retained rights under the law. This may merely have been intended to reflect Holt's judgment in *Butts* v. *Penny* that 'the black was not a slave but a "slavish servant", akin to an apprentice'. For Holt, the distinction was of substance; with Blackstone it is far from clear if that was the case.

Further confusing the issue, Blackstone got into semantic difficulty. When considering the effect of baptism on the issue, he asserted that while it could not dissolve a civil contract, baptism was irrelevant, since English law 'gives liberty, rightly understood, that is, protection, to a Jew, a Turk, or a heathen, as well as to those who profess the true religion of Christ ... The slave is entitled to the same liberty in England before, as after, baptism; and, whatever service the heathen negro owed to his English master, the same is he bound to render when a Christian.'[12] What did liberty under the law mean? The law protects a freed slave 'in the enjoyment of his liberty', he says at one point, and then defines liberty as 'protection' in another. How can the law protect protection?

The assertion first made in an early nineteenth-century biography of Sharp, and lazily repeated thereafter, that Blackstone capitulated to pro-

---

[12] *Ibid.*, I, pp. 411ff.

slavery pressure from Mansfield is without any historical foundation.[13] In a letter to Sharp, Blackstone told the abolitionist that he had

> only desired not to have a passage cited from my first Edition as decisive in favour of Your Doctrine (Book I, Chap. 1) which I thought had been sufficiently explained in Chap. 14; but when I found it had been misunderstood both by yourself and others, I found it necessary to explain it more fully in my subsequent Editions.

He concluded that 'it did not become me to pronounce decisively, on a Matter which is *adhuc sub judice*,[14] whatever the inclination of my own Opinions may be'.[15] His own explanation is the most convincing. Blackstone had not capitulated nor been compromised, but may have been guilty of a certain lack of clarity and circularity in argument. In that, he accurately reflected the current state of the law. It was to be *sub judice* for some time, until it fell to Mansfield to clarify what the law was.

Mansfield had a lot to ponder: common law precedents; local laws in colonial America; a treatise which temporised; and differing legal opinions from the highest authorities. Of the latter, one of the most significant had emanated from Hardwicke, whom Mansfield revered and of whom he said 'when his Lordship pronounced his decrees, wisdom himself might be supposed to speak'.[16] The case was adjourned pending judgment. This judgment would prove decisive. It was not made lightly. In the past in cases that had come before him as Chief Justice, Mansfield had managed to avoid ruling on the legality of slavery or the slave trade. He agonised over this decision, sitting in his library at his Hampstead home of Kenwood House with a bust of Homer, bequeathed to him by Pope, by his shoulder, and a representation of the pillar of Solomon behind. He recalled the words that began Locke's *First Treatise of Government*: 'Slavery is so vile and miserable an Estate of Man, and so directly opposite the generous Temper and Courage of our Nation; that 'tis hardly to be conceived, that an *Englishman*, much less a *Gentleman*, should plead for't.' He scoured the common law for legal precedents. He examined the statute law of England and further afield. He considered whether the law of colonial Virginia had any bearing on English

---

13 P. Hoare, (*Memoirs of Granville Sharp*, 2 vols (London, 1828), I, p. 59; F. O. Shyllon, *Black Slaves in Britain* (London, 1974), pp. 55, 63f., 67f; James Walvin, *England, Slaves and Freedom* (Mississippi, 1986), p. 35; Simon Schama, *Rough Crossings* (London, 2005), p. 40.

14 Still under judicial determination.

15 Letter of 20 February 1769, in Wilfred Prest, *William Blackstone* (Oxford, 2008), p. 252.

16 Poser, *Lord Mansfield*, pp. 48, 119.

law. He fretted that if slaves in England were suddenly set free they would starve.

Finally, on Monday 22 June 1772 he delivered a judgment that not only freed an indigent slave but fixed the common law as the great guarantor of liberty. His exact words are unknown, as court reporting at that time was primitive and no copy of his text, if ever one existed, has come to light. If Mansfield had one in his library it went up in flames eight years later during the Gordon Riots. From the records we have, a reasonable attempt may be made to reconstruct the thrust of what he said or did not say. In effect, he ignored the joint opinion. He returned to first principles. The words he most likely used were strong stuff:

> The state of slavery is of such a nature that it is incapable of being introduced on any reasons, moral or political, but only positive law, which preserves its force long after the reasons, occasion, and time itself from whence it was created, is erased from memory. It is so odious that nothing can be suffered to support it but positive law. Whatever inconveniences, therefore, may follow from the decision, I cannot say this case is allowed or approved by the law of England; and therefore the black must be discharged.[17]

The import of his words was clear: without the specific sanction of common law or statute, slavery could not be legally sanctioned or condoned. Most of the accounts accord in one essential: the great judge described black chattel slavery as 'odious'. The famous words often attributed to him – *Fiat Justicia Ruat Coelum* – on this occasion were probably said by one of the barristers during legal argument. Similarly, 'the air of England is too pure for any slave to breathe: Let the black go free', was probably an elaboration of the more prosaic, 'the black must be discharged'.[18] However, these majestic phrases, whether or not they reflect Mansfield's intent, certainly reflected the impact of his judgment.[19]

Like Magna Carta, the Mansfield Judgment has taken on a historical significance well beyond what its framer could have anticipated. It was

---

[17] *ST*, XX, pp. 1–82, 136; *EHD*, X, pp. 263f, as recorded by the shorthand writer Capel Lofft. Mansfield never demurred from this report of what he said: Steven Wise, *Though the Heavens May Fall* (Cambridge, MA, 2005), pp. 181–4.

[18] Five days after the judgment, the *Morning Chronicle* and *London Advertiser* published a poem celebrating the fact that 'Tyrants no more the servile yoke prepare,/ For breath of Slaves too pure in English air': Shyllon, *Black Slaves*, p. 165.

[19] Its benefits were not restricted to slaves. In 1854 a group of Russian naval deserters were detained by one of their officers in Guildford. With the assistance of the local police they were transported back to Portsmouth in order to be re-embarked on their ship. Their detention was declared illegal and they were set free: Dicey, *Lectures Introductory to the Study of the Law*, pp. 239f.

THE EARL OF MANSFIELD.

11. Lord Mansfield, the pillar of the legal establishment, whose word was law and whose influence persists, in all his grandeur. A Scot who was the greatest judge in England.

buttressed a few years later in 1778 when the Court of Session in Scotland in the case of *Knight* v. *Wedderburn* reached the same conclusion in a judgment that was both erudite and independent, since it did not consider *Somerset* a conclusive authority. Although his ruling decided the relatively narrow issue of whether a slave could be forcibly removed from England, Mansfield knew or suspected that it would have wider import. He knew it broke new ground; he knew it would be used to attack slavery itself; and he knew many feared it would damage British trade and commerce: these were the 'inconveniences' he was mindful of. But neither he nor anyone else could have anticipated the immediate and far-reaching impact it did in fact have: that it would forge the hammer that would break the chains of slavery, initially in England, where some fifteen thousand slaves were in effect declared free, then in its Empire. The first to celebrate what they considered a pivotal moment in the history of enslavement were London's black inhabitants. A few nights after the judgment had been given, two hundred of the better off held a party near Westminster Hall at five shillings a head to toast Lord Mansfield. His name was not just to resound to the accompaniment of drinking and laughter at a London party, but around the entire English-speaking world. Like his name, his judgment took on a life of its own, was soon adorned with sonorous phrases, and sped across the Atlantic to the West Indies and the American colonies.

There it was seen as one of the causes of the Revolutionary War, a war fought by freedom-loving Americans partly to preserve their right to own slaves, a right that Mansfield and the common law were endangering. The Constitution of the United States came into effect in 1789 after several years of debate. Many of the Founding Fathers were prominent common law practitioners. They relied on Magna Carta, treating it as a higher law that the Crown could not defy. The law expressed in the Constitution was made supreme, binding not only the executive and judges but the legislature as well. Tom Paine was right to say that in the United States 'the law is king'. For king read tyrant, for the law adopted there still allowed slavery. Had the Americans lost the War of Independence, or had they never fought it, the American colonies would have remained within the British Empire and slavery would have been abolished there as it was in the rest of the Empire in 1834. Instead, slavery was maintained for another thirty years and a cataclysmic civil war had to be fought before its abolition was achieved. The victory of America in 1789 was freedom's defeat.

Thus, as in the later case of a snail in a bottle of ginger beer in Paisley,[20]

---

[20] *Donoghue* v. *Stevenson* [1932] AC 562.

can a seemingly insignificant case, one involving a penniless slave, change or clarify forever the law of England and beyond. *Habeas corpus* – Lilburne's sword and Somerset's shield – remains to this day part of the law of the land, but it is hardly ever employed. That is not because it has become weak and useless, but because it has triumphed. Imprisonment without charge is anathema; for those who are remanded in custody there is a presumption of bail. Only in recent years with the legislation attendant on the 'war against terror' has resort to *habeas corpus* been necessary again.

Mansfield, despite his seminal judgment ensuring freedom, was still a pillar of the establishment. In 1780 his London house with its priceless law library was burnt down, not by pro-slavers, but by anti-Catholic bigots during the course of the Gordon Riots. Neither he nor his library deserved this unlucky fate. He was not the only one to suffer. England had been plagued by riots for centuries and the eighteenth century witnessed recurring fears of rampant criminality, civil disorder, and even bloody revolution. These fears would have a deleterious effect on the law and its punishments.

CHAPTER 19

The Menace of the Mob

There ever were and ever will be mobs in England, while we remain a
free people.   'HS' in the *Gazetteer*, 1768

IN AUGUST 2011 rioting swept England, and the mob, for a time, seemed
to rule the streets. The police initially held back, although they had the
power to intervene in public disturbances without any other interposition.
They had legal sanction vested in them by the 1986 Public Order Act. Before
the eighteenth century, governments would have relied on the common law
to suppress disorder – under common law riot was a misdemeanour unless it
was politically inspired, in which case it was deemed treason. After 1715 reliance was placed on the reading of the Riot Act, which had been enacted the
previous year. The Riot Act was to stay on the statute book for two hundred
and sixty years, and survives to this day in the armoury of angry parents.[1]
The act deemed all riots 'heinous offences', not mere misdemeanours. The
preamble referred to 'many rebellious riots and tumults [that] have been
taking place of late in divers parts of this kingdom' – a reference to the Tory
mobs of 1710 and persisting Jacobite agitation culminating in the insurrection of 1715 – and stated that those involved 'presume to do so, for that the
punishments provided by the laws now in being are not adequate'. Twelve
or more engaged in riotous assembly were to be ordered by the mayor, a
magistrate or other official to disperse within the hour. If a group failed to
do so, the members would be guilty of a felony without benefit of clergy,
punishable by death. Force could be used against them and anyone assisting
in their dispersal was exempt from any legal consequences should injury or

---

[1]   It was last used in 1919 in Glasgow's 'Battle of George Square' on 31 January, when
the sheriff had the act ripped from his hands as he tried to read it, and in Liverpool
and Birkenhead on 3 August, during a police strike. In events strikingly reminiscent of
2011, shops were smashed and looted, and goods strewn across the streets. *The Times*
described the area as 'the Ypres of Liverpool', an image of carnage fresh in people's
minds. Soldiers were called out with fixed bayonets. They charged the crowd several
times and fired a volley over their heads. Even a battleship and two destroyers were
dispatched to the Wirral. The Riot Act was repealed in 1967, and in 1986 the Public
Order Act abolished the common law offence of riot and replaced it with a statutory
one, with a maximum penalty of ten years' imprisonment.

death occur. The use of force to suppress disorder would have to come from the army. There was disquiet at the threat that soldiers could pose to English liberties, but ultimately there was no one else.

The unforeseen corollary was the belief that without this procedure and without the specific instruction of the civil power, no such military action could be taken with impunity. An overzealous magistrate or soldier, if he were not careful in the authorisation or implementation of the act, could find himself being charged with murder. Despite the fact that the common law powers to deal with riots were not abrogated, statutory powers being merely added to the arsenal, many of those in authority, including ministers, magistrates and the militia, thought and feared otherwise.

The original impetus and rationale for the Riot Act was anxiety engendered by the supporters of the deposed Stuarts, but riots over all sorts of issues were a commonplace in the eighteenth century. Alongside political agitation, when crowds were often manipulated and deployed as instruments of pressure, were more mundane eruptions of public violence over prices and wages, turnpikes and enclosures, cider taxes and surgeons. They were reactionary rather than revolutionary. Apprentices and other young men were often involved in large numbers, and window-smashing and looting routinely accompanied the violent and drunken expression of grievances or prejudices. A few prominent examples will suffice to give the flavour, including one illuminating instance from London at the start of the eighteenth century – before the act – and culminating in the most notorious of them all, again in London, towards the end.

In 1705, in the wake of an abortive Jacobite invasion, the Whigs had won a majority over the Tories, at a time when the country was war-weary and overtaxed, and feelings against foreigners and Dissenters were running high. Into this cauldron stepped an irascible High Church clergyman and staunch Tory from Oxford, Dr Henry Sacheverell. Like others of his ilk he was nostalgic for the good old days – the last few years of the reign of Charles II, when the Church of England was exalted and Whigs and Dissenters were kept in their place. The Toleration Act brought in under William III had elevated these factious groups at the expense of the Established Church. In the reign of Queen Anne, the 'phanatick' Whigs were in the ascendant, buoyed up by the brilliant victories of Marlborough against Louis XIV. Anglicanism was under threat as non-conformity was increasingly unshackled.

On 5 November 1709 in St Paul's Cathedral, Sacheverell preached the annual sermon commemorating two great Protestant triumphs: the detection of the Gunpowder Plot in 1605 and William of Orange's landing in

England in 1689. The sermon he delivered was appropriately inflammatory. It was an outright attack on the government, on toleration and on Dissenters, and a rallying cry to the Church of England both to stand firm in its exclusivity and stand up for itself by excommunicating its enemies. Sacheverell's overt repudiation of the right of active resistance to the secular power challenged the legitimacy of the Glorious Revolution itself. This was no minor matter. After Queen Anne – the last Protestant Stuart – would the Tories accept the Hanoverians as her successors, or would they look to 'the king over the water', James, the Catholic pretender, exiled in France? The Whig government reacted by having the preacher impeached, in effect for seditiously asserting Jacobitism.

The House of Commons brought a prosecution for 'high crimes and misdemeanours'; Sacheverell would be tried by the House of Lords who would vote for guilt or innocence. It was intended to demonstrate that 'every seditious, discontented, hot-headed, ungifted, unedifying preacher ... who had hopes of distinguishing himself in the world by a matchless indiscretion, may not advance, with impunity, doctrines destructive of the peace and quiet of her Majesty's government'.[2] The doctrine was non-resistance, something governments usually welcomed rather than found threatening. But these were strange times.

Sacheverell's trial[3] did not take place until February of the following year, by which time the populace had been whipped up by Tory agitators and Anglican divines into a frenzy of rabid support for a reactionary Tory. During the course of the proceedings in Westminster Hall, rioters, crying 'High Church and Sacheverell', but curiously armed with crowbars, eschewed their icon's insistence on non-resistance, demolishing Dissenters' meeting-houses and burning the contents. For hours the government seemed paralysed, until the queen herself urged and agreed that her guards should be deployed to restore order. Unaided, or unencumbered, by the yet unenacted Riot Act, the guards fought off an attack on the Bank of England, considered to be the Dissenters' Temple of Mammon and the depository of the Whigs' profits from the war, and quickly quelled the disturbances. They did all this, in the face of a carefully orchestrated rampage involving very large numbers of participants including several in the professions, without firing a single shot or occasioning a single fatality. This was rebellion but not revolution.

---

2   Robert Walpole presenting the charge against Dr Henry Sacheverell to the Lords on the second day of the trial.
3   *ST*, XV, pp. 1–522.

Although Sacheverell was convicted it was by a narrow majority, and his sentence was the mildest possible, a three-year suspension from preaching. London and the provinces celebrated what almost amounted to an acquittal with the ringing of church bells, the lighting of bonfires and two days of heavy drinking. Violence had won. The Whigs had lost and, in the ensuing election to parliament, were trounced by the Tories.

The Wilkite riots of the 1760s and 1770s were overtly political and were inspired by a unifying slogan of 'Wilkes and Liberty'. The most substantial was that of March 1768. John Wilkes, the self-styled martyr to the cause of liberty, despite his triumph over general warrants, had at last in 1764 been expelled from the Commons and outlawed after a conviction in his absence, not just for seditious libel (his reprinting of No. 45), but for an obscene libel (his 'publication' of *An Essay on Woman*, an erotic parody of Pope).[4] Finally in 1768 he returned to England, stood for parliament, and in March was duly elected as member for Middlesex. For two days, notwithstanding Wilkes's appeal for order, his supporters of 'the inferior set celebrated too riotously'.[5]

A little later they took their adulation even further. Wilkes had finally surrendered to custody over his outlawry, and on 27 April was imprisoned on Mansfield's direction in the King's Bench Prison in Southwark. For a fortnight there were more or less continuous riots. On 10 May, the day parliament convened, a crowd of many thousands descended onto St George's Fields outside their hero's place of incarceration, hoping in vain that he would be taken in triumph to the Commons. They pinned a piece of doggerel on the prison wall which began: 'Venal judges and Minister combine/ Wilkes and Liberty to confine.' Two Southwark magistrates were summoned by the prison marshal, and a troop of horse and a hundred men of a Scottish regiment were deployed by the government in their support. The hasty magistrates ordered the offending verses torn down, an action that enraged the hitherto peaceful assembly. The protesters began shouting 'Wilkes and Liberty! Liberty, No King! Damn the King. Damn the Govern-

---

4   *ST*, XIX, pp. 1075–1137. Wilkes had ordered his publishers to print thirteen copies exclusively for the Hell-Fire Club. Ironically, the actual 'publication' was done by the House of Lords to facilitate their prosecution of Wilkes. For a reconstruction and analysis of this notorious parody see Arthur Cash, *An Essay on Woman* (New York, 2000).

5   This 'inferior set', often dismissed as a 'mob' or 'rabble', included voters, shopkeepers, craftsmen and tradesmen, as well as apprentices, servants and labourers: Rude, *Wilkes and Liberty*, pp. 43ff, and George Rude, *The Crowd in History, 1730–1848* (London, 1981), p. 61. Cash calls the 'Wilkes mob' 'one of the best behaved of the century': *Essay on Woman*, p. 12.

ment!' Defending liberty had become sedition. The reading of the Riot Act by Justice Samuel Gillam was met with derision, and stones were flung at his head. More outraged than injured, he ordered the soldiers to fire into the crowd surrounding the prison, and when they did so they 'fired at random … and seemed to enjoy their fire', as a constable later testified in the Old Bailey.[6] During the 'massacre' they killed seven or so on the spot and wounded a dozen more. In all, eleven lives were lost that day, including a William Allen whom troops mistook for the stone-thrower, and 'shot to death in his father's cow-house'.[7] Rioting exploded all over London. The king threatened to abdicate.

Captain Murray and two of the Scottish grenadiers were charged with Allen's murder, and, although the officer and one of his men were discharged before trial and the remaining defendant was acquitted when the prosecution could not prove he was responsible for the killing, the message had gone out that troops could not act disproportionately with impunity, even if authorised. Gillam himself was put on trial at the Old Bailey for murder but was acquitted.[8]

In June, in a remarkable volte-face, Mansfield reversed Wilkes's outlawry. Wilkes was, however, fined and imprisoned for his libel convictions. Languishing in gaol he became an even greater martyr for liberty, all the more so when the Commons not only expelled him as an MP but declared that he was incapable of election. Thrice Middlesex re-elected him; thrice the will of the voters was thwarted. Indeed, the will of the voters was subverted, as the Commons admitted as a member the candidate who had lost to Wilkes. The grave danger was that if the majority in the Commons – not parliament – could declare one candidate incapable, and install his losing opponent, they could do so likewise to others, and the House would become a self-appointed clique rather than a freely elected assembly representing the will of the people. This was a fundamental attack on the constitution launched by the Commons itself. The streets seethed. The country convulsed. In America the worst fears of the colonists seemed realised.[9] The City elected Wilkes an alderman. As such he would sit as a judge at the Old Bailey, alongside

---

6   Rude, *Wilkes and Liberty*, p. 52.

7   *Ibid.*, p. 51.

8   *Ibid.*, pp. 49–56; Rude, *The Crowd in History*, pp. 55ff; Peter Thomas, *John Wilkes: A Friend to Liberty* (Oxford, 1996), pp. 82f; Ian Gilmour, *Riot, Risings and Revolution: Governance and Violence in Eighteenth-Century England* (London, 1992), pp. 315ff.

9   Cash, *John Wilkes*, pp. 260f.

Mansfield himself,[10] and at the Guildhall. As such he would thwart the will of the Commons, humiliate its agents, and successfully agitate to allow the press to report proceedings in parliament by threatening to arrest Black Rod himself should he try to arrest printers within the precincts of the City. Wilkes would become lord mayor. But still he could not take his seat in parliament.

That would have to wait until 1774, and another parliamentary election. This time the victor was admitted. Once seated, Wilkes lost no time in advocating radical reforms, startling the Commons by trying to introduce a bill for universal male suffrage. But his incapacitation from the earlier parliament still rankled, and still threatened democratic integrity. It was not until 1782, after the government had been comprehensively discredited by the fiasco of the American Revolution, that Wilkes would finally achieve his end of expunging the resolution of 1769 which had rendered him incapable of being elected.

Wilkes had singularly triumphed in all his public endeavours: general warrants were a thing of the past, privacy was recognised at common law, press freedom was expanded, electors were free to elect anyone of their choosing, the Commons could not legislate unilaterally, and the iniquities of the electoral system had been exposed. His influence on the new American constitution was profound. In the disdainful opinion of Edmund Burke, 'there had been no hero of the mob but Wilkes'.[11] If that is so, then 'the mob' chose their hero wisely.

Politics was not the only issue to stir up popular passion in the eighteenth century. So too did the price of food and the level of remuneration. If the former rose or the latter fell, riots often ensued. Every county was affected, but urban areas saw the worst. Take Nottingham, for instance. On Thursday 2 October 1766 riots broke out at the Goose Fair, held annually in the old market square. Large quantities of high-priced cheeses had been put on sale, but were beyond the means of most of the locals. Some 'rude lads' told the traders they could not remove their produce until the town was fed. A growing crowd descended on the stalls, and people 'liberated' the

---

10 Wilkes and Mansfield were to become friends and mutual admirers: Poser, *Lord Mansfield*, p. 256.

11 Burke had always harboured serious reservations about the rabble-rousing means Wilkes deployed and thought him unprincipled, if effective: Edmund Burke, *Correspondence*, ed. Thomas Copeland, 10 vols (Cambridge, 1958–78), I, p. 349. Burke would reflect further on these events in *Thoughts on the Cause of the Present Discontents*, published in 1770.

produce they could not afford to buy. Smaller cheeses were carried away, while larger ones were rolled down the street. The mayor, trying to intervene, was knocked over by a cheddar. Things got uproariously out of hand, and the civil authorities could do little to calm them. Later that night troops were ordered in from Derby and order was temporarily restored. The following day saw a resurgence of violence, and the soldiers opened fire occasioning one fatality, that of a farmer, although he was not trying to expropriate, but to guard, the cheeses. Nottingham was not just the scene of further rioting over food prices – wheat in 1788, and bread in 1795 – but of wage riots. In 1779 textile workers responded with arson and machine-smashing to the defeat in the Commons of a bill that should have regulated minimum standards for their wages. Property belonging to every hosier known to have opposed the bill was attacked, and the house of a Samuel Need, who had led opposition to popular grievances, was burned to the ground. Every window of Arkwright's mill was smashed and rioters attempted to set fire to it. More than 300 cotton frames were flung into the streets. Order was not restored for three days.

Such riots were routine, and as nothing compared to the Gordon Riots of 1780. In the course of six days more damage was done to London than to Paris during the French Revolution. The literati depicted the scene in apocalyptic terms. William Cowper, who lived through the conflagration, compared 'blazing London [to] a second Troy'. Later Charles Dickens gave the most vivid depiction of untrammelled violence and destruction occasioned by the riots in his novel, *Barnaby Rudge*.

The rioting was triggered by attempts in parliament to meliorate the disabilities under which Catholics laboured. Vehement passions were aroused, nursed by a fanatical and unhinged Scottish nobleman, Lord George Gordon, President of the Protestant Association. He summoned a huge demonstration to present a petition to parliament. His address to them was so inflammatory that mass disorder broke out, although many of the troublemakers were not members of the Protestant Association, but disparate groups who exploited the opportunity to run amok, looting and robbing. Many of the rioters did not know whether Popery 'was a man or a horse and did not care'.[12] Rioting was infectious and fun. Apprentices and prostitutes alike took part. So too did children. Even some of the better off got carried away in the excitement of the moment. Gordon seems to have been genuinely shocked by what transpired, and later traversed London urging his supposed supporters to

---

12 Christopher Hibbert, *King Mob: The London Riots of 1780* (London, 1958), p. 81.

disperse. The authorities shared the same surprise, and had taken virtually no precautions despite forewarning of the huge numbers Gordon intended to bring to Westminster. The six constables and two magistrates that could be found were somewhat impotent in face of a crowd estimated at 14,000.

There were only a few troops stationed in London, but, under the direction of the Lord Mayor and his council, they could be utilised. The respective conduct of the soldiers and authorities on the first day was typical of their behaviour throughout. The troops behaved well and were very restrained under extreme provocation, but were hamstrung by lack of orders from the civil power. In particular, the 'Wilkite' Lord Mayor, Brachley Kennett, abdicated all responsibility, and dismissed all attempts to get him to intervene. He later claimed, self-servingly, that the riots had taken him so much by surprise that he was seized with a 'fit of temerity which made him not know what he was about'.[13] Suspicions lingered that the Lord Mayor may have been complicit in the riots, conniving at disorder that would strengthen his hand against the king and government.

Without civil sanction the troops were uncertain about their legal position, and feared being prosecuted, as had happened in 1768, if they took action. Although soldiers were often present at the scene of a riot, they would watch what was going on, sometimes limply appeal for order, and then march away. The Commander-in-Chief, Lord Amherst, was enraged by the supineness or indifference of the magistracy since, in his view, 'it was the duty of the troops to act only under the authority and by direction of the civil magistrate'. This view of their supposed legal disability which prevailed among the military was not fanciful. It rested on the widely known opinions of the Attorney-General, Sir Philip Yorke, and of Lord Raymond, another legal authority. In 1741 Mansfield himself had gone much further, and argued that civil magistrates had no power to call in the army to suppress a riot even if the civil authorities were powerless to do so. After his own bitter experience of the disturbances he repudiated this argument and again asserted his judicial dominance, justifying the use of the military. He did so by making the obvious, if unusual, observation that the Riot Act did not take away pre-existing powers to use force to stop a riot; it only created the additional offence of failing to disperse after the reading of the Act. Deferring – yet again – to Yorke had been a 'fatal error', as the archbishop of York commented to his son.[14]

[13] *Ibid.*, pp. 58–60.
[14] *Ibid.*, pp. 91, 122.

The principle bastions of law and order were targeted as symbols of oppression. Newgate Prison was badly damaged and its inmates liberated. Painted on the wall of the prison was the proclamation that the inmates had been freed by the authority of 'His Majesty, King Mob'. Then King Mob turned its eye on other targets. Most of the other London prisons were burnt down, and forcible collections made 'for the poor prisoners'. The Bow Street Runners' office was destroyed. People were burnt to death or died under falling buildings. On one occasion, rioters were making a bonfire of the possessions of a Catholic businessman and placed on top several caged canaries. They refused to free them as they were 'Popish birds and should burn with the rest of the Popish goods'.[15] Such fire engines as existed were prevented from extinguishing flames, and rioters at the Fleet Prison tried to push an engine belonging to the Royal Exchange Fire Insurance Office into the conflagration. Huge quantities of gin and rum were 'liberated' and, being imbibed, fanned the flames.

The Bloomsbury house of the Chief Justice was also attacked. Mansfield was particularly targeted as he had a longstanding reputation for religious tolerance and even indulgence. In his youth he had been a close friend of the Catholic satirist Alexander Pope. On the bench, he consistently sought to lighten the legal burdens placed upon Catholics, burdens he thought obsolete and unnecessary, and construed discriminatory statutes narrowly.[16] Mansfield was an obvious target as the epitome of liberal-minded elitism. Although forty guardsmen were deployed at his residence, they refused to intervene in the absence of a magistrate. Eventually one arrived with more troops and read the Riot Act, but was ignored by the crowd. The troops finally opened fire and killed six rioters. They then dispersed, thinking their task done. The mob returned and burnt Mansfield's house to the ground, along with his priceless library. The arsonists then walked around with iron bars wrenched from the railings or stolen from ironmongers, threatening to knock down anyone who did not contribute 'mob-money' to their 'Rioters' Fund'.[17]

It was not until Wednesday 7 June that the government finally took firm action and brought in 7,000 soldiers from the Home Counties. By royal proclamation the king empowered the military to use force without the permission of a magistrate. Amherst immediately issued orders to all his officers in London to use force 'for dispersing the illegal and tumultuous

[15] *Ibid.*, p. 61.
[16] Poser, *Lord Mansfield*, pp. 351ff.
[17] Hibbert, *King Mob*, p. 81.

assemblies of the people'.[18] When the City's Common Council, meeting in the Guildhall, heard of this, one of their members finally took a stand. John Wilkes, realising that he should distance himself from the culpable inactivity of the mayor and the other aldermen, persuaded Kennett to promise to call out a *posse comitatus* – able-bodied citizens of the county summoned on the authority of the magistrates to assist in maintaining public order. Wilkes returned to his ward to raise such a force to augment the regular troops. He would later boast of his men shooting two rioters attacking the Bank of England.

Throughout the day another 15,000 county militia from Canterbury to Coventry poured into the 'town at every avenue' to assist the regulars. Field artillery were also deployed. The Tower pulled up its drawbridge and flooded the moat. It was not officially martial law, but it felt very like it. Military camps, like mushrooms, emerged everywhere overnight. Barracks were established at Hyde Park, which 'resembled the field of Malplaquet before the battle'.[19] Some Londoners such as the father of Sir Joshua Reynolds wondered if they had awakened in Turkey and were to be dragooned out of their freedom.[20] Most however, rapturously welcomed the influx of soldiers and the restoration of order.

By the evening the royal palaces, the Bank of England, the Guildhall and Inns of Court were all defended by troops, and many communities had taken the law into their own hands by forming vigilante patrols. One comprising some four hundred gentlemen and their servants guarded Lincoln's Inn Fields, while the Inns themselves were defended by the lawyers who had chambers there. In Barnard's Inn twenty-two sets of chambers were burnt down before troops arrived to assist the beleaguered attorneys. The officer sent to the Temple declined the armed assistance of the motley collection of lawyers who had gathered there. As he marched his soldiers out through the gates he locked them behind him with all the members of the legal fraternity on the other side. To their howls of protest he addressed them: 'Gentlemen, I am much obliged for your intended assistance, but as I do not choose to allow my soldiers to be shot, so I have ordered you to be locked in.'[21] One determined but drunk young lawyer climbed the wall and ran after the soldiers until he and his efforts to assist were floored by a sergeant with the butt of his musket.

---

18 *Ibid.*, p. 92.
19 *The Morning Chronicle*, quoted in Hibbert, *King Mob*, p. 93.
20 *Ibid.*, p. 114.
21 *Ibid.*, p. 106.

By Thursday morning troops were also strategically positioned on all the bridges over the Thames, with large forces on both London and Blackfriars bridges. More and more Londoners were equally determined to defend themselves and their properties from any unruly elements. The authorities had seized the initiative and were finally back in control, although the rioting sporadically went on for the rest of the day. Throughout Friday and the following days the government took steps to tighten their grip and keep control. Troops were still coming in to supplement the sizeable force already gathered, and cavalry patrolled the streets.

London was a sad sight. It 'offered on every side the picture of a city sacked and abandoned by a ferocious enemy', as one observer noted while surveying the scene from a rooftop. Another wrote that the conflagration 'furnished a sight … which surpassed the appearance of Mount Vesuvius in all its fury'.[22] Perhaps over 500 people had lost their lives during the riots. According to very conservative government figures some 285 rioters were killed by troops and 173 wounded. Many more were arrested, some while dividing their plunder. They were a rather pathetic sight in the broad light of day and with their bravado gone. Many were impoverished, many were petty criminals, many were drunk. The ease with which, as Gibbon put it, 'the scum' had 'boiled up to the surface in *this* huge cauldron' was frightening.[23] Who could say it would not happen again?

Retribution was swift, but, apart from some lynchings, it was not extra-judicial. The government explicitly declined to try rioters under martial law. Even so, and even by eighteenth-century standards, the trials were rushed through at a remarkable pace. Within twelve days forty-four rioters received death sentences at the Old Bailey, and a further twenty-four were condemned in the Southwark Sessions which followed. Ultimately, twenty-one men, women and children were hanged, several of them being under eighteen. Thomas Taplin, who had been a Fagan character in charge of about fifty ragamuffins who had extorted 'mob-money' on his behalf, was the most notorious of the condemned.

But these were small fry. There must have been, it was thought, some guiding hand, some external and alien force directing the endeavours of this flotsam! Despite wild rumours that the whole catastrophe was insti-gated by members of the Opposition, or more likely by French or American

[22] *Ibid.*, p. 108.

[23] Letter of 10 June 1780 to Mrs Gibbon, in *Miscellaneous Works of Edward Gibbon, Illustrated from his Letters, with Occasional Notes and Narrative, Complete in One Volume*, ed. John, Lord Sheffield (London, 1787), p. 300.

agents provocateurs, none was apprehended. But George Gordon himself was. On the Friday he was arrested and conveyed to the Tower. In the absence of others he was to bear the brunt of responsibility, even though Horace Walpole believed that Gordon and religion were but godmothers to the 'shocking affair'. Unlike the lesser mortals tried and dispatched, Gordon was to wait for his fate to be decided.

In February 1781 he charged with high treason on the basis that although his individual actions were not treasonable, treason could be imputed to him from all the circumstances. The trial was held in Westminster Hall before Lord Mansfield himself. Gordon was defended by his own cousin, a young barrister of whom we shall hear more, Thomas Erskine.[24] Erskine was junior counsel to Lloyd Kenyon, another distinguished lawyer, but one who lacked criminal experience and was a poor jury speaker. Erskine, of just three years' call, had never appeared before a jury. Nonetheless he had a growing reputation, was given a key role, and delivered the address. The trial began at 9.00a.m. on 5 February and continued until 5.00a.m. the following day. The prosecution was vigorous and confident. The members of the jury would have seen with their own eyes the terrifying events of the preceding June. A verdict of guilty was inevitable. So it would have been but for one man. Erskine, in an early example of his electrifying speeches, persuaded the jury that Gordon, for all his folly, had not instigated nor incited the riot, nor countenanced the destruction of Mansfield's house and library. Erskine was not just eloquent: he was measured, reasonable, and learned in the law. Lord Gordon was acquitted in under half an hour. Dr Johnson rejoiced that he 'had escaped, rather than a precedent should be established for hanging a man for *constructive treason*', which would be a 'dangerous engine of arbitrary power'.[25]

Perhaps the most shocking consequence of the riots was the suggestion emanating from Lord Shelburne that a police force be established on the French model. Not even this orgy of destruction could warrant so radical a departure from our traditions and so grave a threat to our liberties. Better be 'governed by a mob than a standing army', as the radical Whig Charles James Fox contended. Better draconian deterrents than a police state.

---

[24] *ST*, XXII, pp. 175–237, 1253; Thomas Erskine, *Speeches*, 4 vols (Chicago, 1876), I, pp. 86–155.

[25] Lord Campbell, *Lives of the Lord Chancellors*, 7th edn, 10 vols (New York, 1878), VIII, p. 44.

CHAPTER 20

The Fear of the Felon

The hungry judges soon the sentence sign,
And wretches hang that jury-men may dine.
                    Alexander Pope, *The Rape of the Lock*

He saw a lawyer killing a viper
On a dunghill hard by his own stable;
And the Devil smiled, for it put him in mind
Of Cain and his brother, Abel.
                    Samuel Taylor Coleridge, 'The Devil's Thoughts'

I N A LAND OF increasing wealth, where freedom was paramount and police were absent, property crime was a perennial problem. As far back as 1690 John Locke had asserted that 'government has no other end but the preservation of property'. Blackstone in 1766 opined that 'nothing so generally strikes the imagination and engages the affection of mankind as the right of property'. It could equally be said that 'the greatest offence against property was to have none'.[1]

With no police force and no forensic science service, the only means of deterring crime was through exemplary punishment: whipping, transportation and hanging. In the eighteenth century an already sanguinary system was to get even bloodier. The solution to the problem of how to protect movable property – from handkerchiefs to stallions – propounded by such luminaries as Archdeacon Paley was to impose the death penalty for a myriad of offences, including such trivial ones as shoplifting or pickpocketing. In the late eighteenth century, Sir Francis Buller, when consoling a condemned felon at Maidstone assizes, did so with the words, 'you are to be hanged not for stealing horses but that horses be not stolen'.[2] They encapsulated the theory perfectly.

---

[1]   John Locke, *Second Treatise on Government* (1690), ss. 85 and 94; Blackstone, II, p. 2; E. P. Thompson, *The Making of the English Working Class* (London, 1963), p. 61.

[2]   Buller was reputedly 'more learned than humane', his learning being shown in this unattributed quotation from a seventeenth-century essay 'On Punishment', from the *Political, Moral and Miscellaneous Thoughts and Reflections* of George Savile, Marquis of Halifax.

The Waltham Black Act of 1723, the most draconian statute ever enacted by a British parliament, started the process whereby England was to have more capital statutes than any other country in Europe. Brought in to deal with the threat posed by forest poachers and robbers who blacked up their faces to carry out their depredations, the act created fifty separate capital offences, including wrecking fish ponds and damaging trees. Parliament caught the craze, cast aside any sense of proportion, and began enacting capital statutes almost on demand. Benefit of Clergy, which had been one of the means of reducing the death toll in earlier times, was reined in. Although in 1706 the reading test had been abolished, and the benefit had become available to all first-time petty offenders, parliament, soon realising the error of its lenity, began to exclude many minor property crimes from its scope. Eventually, housebreaking, the shoplifting of goods worth more than five shillings, and the theft of sheep and cattle all became felonies without benefit of clergy and earned their perpetrators automatic death sentences.

By the end of the century some two hundred and twenty offences were deemed by parliament to warrant death. All were equally subject to these laws, but those who offended against them were not those who had property but those who had not. In effect, the 'laws grind the poor and rich men rule the law'.[3] The rich men were in parliament; the poor whom their laws ground were everywhere, from impoverished rural labourers on farms to destitutes on city streets. Many of the capital crimes were minor property offences, and many put on trial for committing them were minors themselves. In 1825 one John Smith was tried at the Old Bailey for housebreaking. With no barrister to represent him, no witnesses to call on oath, all he could do was protest his innocence. In vain. He was found guilty and hanged. He was fifteen. This was no miscarriage of justice, in as much as his trial had followed the due process of the day, a jury had convicted him on the evidence, and parliament's laws had condemned him to die. This statutory system was aptly named the Bloody Code.

At its heart was London's hall of justice, the Old Bailey. Today it may look like a palace of justice, but in the eighteenth century it was a death trap in more ways than one. In Georgian times trials were held in a courtroom exposed to the elements in the hope of preventing jail fever – typhus, a disease caused by bacteria spreading through the bites of lice and fleas – from infecting others. In 1750, long after the building had been enclosed, an outbreak of jail fever promiscuously killed sixty people, including two judges and the Lord Mayor. In these rather fetid surroundings, coterminous with

---

3   Oliver Goldsmith, *The Traveller*, l. 386.

the Bloody Code, a revolution was taking place in English trial procedure: the rise of adversarial advocacy.

Up until this time the 'no counsel rule' had prevented lawyers from championing those accused of serious crime. The rule possibly stemmed from a rape case in Edward I's time, when judges held that counsel could not appear for those charged with treason or felony as it was *lèse majesté* for counsel to speak against the king. They could appear for the Crown, however. As a result of the Glorious Revolution, the victorious Whigs enacted the Treason Trials Act of 1696.[4] They had first-hand experience of the misuse of treason charges, and were determined to prevent a repetition. The act relaxed the 'no counsel rule' by giving a right to representation, but in treason trials alone.

This was the acorn from which the oak grew. But the next stage of growth was to be by judicial practice and not by legislation. Judges sought ways to mitigate the severity of the law. They would be sticklers over procedure and would dismiss many a case on a technical infraction of the rules. They went further, ceding some of their centrality in the trial process. From the 1730s, judges at the Old Bailey and the Surrey assizes were allowing counsel to appear and cross-examine in felony cases, a concession possibly prompted by the increasing use of 'thief catchers' and other witnesses for reward, in whose interests it was to manipulate evidence and even manufacture crimes.[5] Accomplices hoping to save their own necks by becoming 'Crown witnesses' had every incentive to give perjured testimony. Miscarriages of justice had to be averted. The judge being the prisoner's protector was no longer deemed adequate. This concession was entirely new and welcome. Hitherto many defendants charged with capital offences, exposed to the alien environment of the courtroom with its strange and unfamiliar procedures and terminology, and with their lives hanging in the balance, would have been terrified into incoherence when compelled to defend themselves. It is no surprise that erudite and experienced advocates began to be increasingly in demand by those who had the means to pay for them. Many did not.

One right that all defendants did have was to trial by jury. Jurors could be open to persuasion, either by rational argument or by emotional appeals. Juries could be induced to act according to their sense of morality or Christian charity rather than by the evidence, and were increasingly wont to show mercy or pity, either by acquitting the guilty, or by 'a kind of pious perjury'[6] reducing the amount stolen to beneath the threshold for hanging. In cases

---

4   *EHD*, VIII, pp. 89ff.
5   Langbein, Lerner and Smith, *History of the Common Law*, pp. 690ff.
6   Blackstone coined the phrase, IV, p. 239.

where the law quarrelled with conscience they often had no wish to be 'guilty of blood'.[7] Juries as well as judges had considerable power – and often used it – to recommend a pardon. A high proportion of the condemned would be reprieved. There was a strong religious tradition exemplified in Jeremy Taylor's 1660 *Ductor Dubitantium* ('The Doubters' Guide'), which placed acting according to conscience above acting according to office. The great jurist, Sir Matthew Hale, concurred: 'the best rule is *in dubiis* [when in doubt] rather to incline to acquittal than conviction'. In matters of blood he 'would always choose the safer side'.[8] So too would many a juror. Archdeacon Paley, writing in 1785, complained that jurors hesitated to convict because they wanted to preserve a 'safe' conscience. In addition, barristers, by their ability at cross-examination or powers of persuasion, could influence juries, and although still not allowed to address them directly on the evidence,[9] could so construct their questioning, so insert asides, or so address the judge in the presence of the jury as to get round this prohibition by indirect insinuation.

Lawyers up until then had not had a very good press. They dealt mainly with civil matters, land, debts, property disputes, all of which were lucrative. They could prosecute but not defend. They were seen to be venal and partisan. They were not the defenders of the poor and oppressed. During the civil war period one writer referred to 'that general and inbred hatred which still dwells in our common people against both our laws and lawyers.'[10] Mr Peachum, in Act I of *The Beggar's Opera* of 1728, opined: 'It ever was decreed, sir/ If lawyer's hand is fee'd sir,/ He steals your whole estate.' Most savagely William Manning, in the eighteenth century, castigated them: 'from their professions and interests lawyers are the most dangerous to liberty and the least to be trusted of any profession whatsoever'.[11] The rise of trial advocacy, as well as the dark days at the turn of that century, were to change all that. The lawyer as hero was about to arise.

---

7   On the moral dilemma facing judges and juries see Whitman, *Origins of Reasonable Doubt*, passim.

8   Burnet, *Death and Life of Sir Matthew Hale*, p. 25.

9   Though Erskine managed to get away with it at the Sussex assizes in 1786: Campbell, *Lives of the Lord Chancellors*, VIII, p. 68. Did others?

10   Christopher Hill, *Liberty Against the Law* (London, 1997), p. 265.

11   *The Key of Liberty: The Life and Democratic Writings of William Manning, 'A Laborer,' 1747–1814*, ed. Michael Merrill and Sean Wilentz (Cambridge, MA, 1993), p. 141.

CHAPTER 21

Garrow's Law?

A lawyer is to do for his client all that his client might fairly do for himself, if he could.   Dr Johnson (James Boswell, *Journal*)

The art of cross-examination is not the art of examining crossly. It's the art of leading the witness through a line of propositions he agrees to until he's forced to agree to the *one fatal question*.
                              John Mortimer, *Clinging to the Wreckage*

ONE of the beneficiaries and main instigators of these changes was a barrister who was largely lost to history until he was recently resuscitated by academic historians, and latterly by the BBC: William Garrow.[1] His fall into rapid obscurity is due to the fact that unlike his great contemporaries he was no defender of civil liberties and no great orator. In his later years he became a Tory MP and Attorney-General who opposed both political and penal reform, and, in cases of criminal libel, defended the use of special juries selected by the Crown. Perhaps paradoxically, Garrow's early years as a barrister – mainly for the defence – mark him out as one of the pioneers of the art of advocacy and of the adversarial system. He helped effect a revolution in the conduct of court proceedings and greatly improved the lot of the accused.

Born in Middlesex, the son of a Scottish clergyman and schoolmaster, Garrow was apprenticed to Thomas Southouse, an attorney in Cheapside, who encouraged his young protégé to strive for the Bar. After completing his articles, Garrow enrolled in Lincoln's Inn in 1778, and was called five years later. For the eight years he had lived in London he had been fascinated by the criminal law, and regularly attended the Old Bailey. He now stepped out with wig and gown onto the familiar stage on which he would perform wonderfully for the next two decades.[2]

---

[1]   Notably John Langbein, *The Origins of Adversary Criminal Trial* (Oxford, 2003), and John Hostettler and Richard Braby, *Sir William Garrow* (Hook, 2009). Between 2009 and 2011 the BBC produced a drama series called *Garrow's Law* based on the Old Bailey Online.

[2]   Other than both of us being of Scottish ancestry, I have another connection with this extraordinary man. His house in London was at 25 Bedford Row, now a barristers' chambers with a complement of over sixty members, of whom I am one.

Prior to Garrow's day the judge was the main focus of any trial. He directed on the law, he was to ensure the trial was fair, and if any cross-examination of prosecution witnesses was to be done it was the judge who did it. How much such assistance aided the defendant is an open question. Judges were not always seen to be the apogee of impartiality, and some could find the court day a little enervating. No felony trial could be adjourned, and although many were over in minutes, some lasted long into the night. In 1699 Spencer Cowper, a barrister and the grandfather of the poet, was tried for murder before Baron Hatsell. Cowper defended himself ably although the judge, behaving 'with languid indifference', tried to hurry him along. Towards the end of a relatively lengthy day, an exhausted judge admitted he was struggling to sum up the case. 'I am sensible I have omitted many things', he told an equally tired jury, 'but I am a little faint and cannot repeat any more of the evidence.'[3] Cowper was the unintended beneficiary of this omission. He was acquitted. In 1727 he was made a judge.

If this depiction of the judicial role seems rather surprising to us, it is because of a remarkable transformation that has taken place in the common law system over the last three centuries, one that went beyond due process to enshrine in English court procedure the principle of the equality of arms, of simple fairness. It is a transformation that reflected seismic shifts in society, from the ideas of the Enlightenment to the demands of the Industrial Revolution, and from political reform to the rise of the popular press.

Garrow was to the fore in the transformation of trial procedure. By his audacious interventions in over a thousand cases at the Old Bailey, he helped both to ensure a general right in any felony trial to advance a defence using a trained lawyer, and to alter the relationship between judge and defendant and judge and jury. He shifted the focus onto the case presented by the prosecution. A trial conducted by Garrow became a test not of the accused's endurance, but of the prosecutor's evidence against him. Being unable to address the jury directly, Garrow could not rely on rhetoric. Instead he became a wonderful exponent of the forensic art of cross-examination, which in his hands could upon occasion become very cross indeed. Cross-examination and confrontation were to Garrow synonyms.[4] But there was more to his art than that. Sometimes he had more the manner of a surgeon dissecting evidence than of a ruffian bludgeoning witnesses. A neat incision with a forensic scalpel could be most effective, and even as deadly, especially when coupled with psychological acumen. In one cross-examination, which lasted

3   Stephen, *History of the Criminal Law*, I, pp. 419–22.
4   For examples see Hostettler and Braby, *Sir William Garrow*, pp. 33–62.

three hours during which the court was in dead silence, 'Mr Garrow's eyes were scarcely once off the witness; they seemed to penetrate into her very soul, and lay open the inmost workings of her mind ... he broke in at last upon the truth of the story, and finally made her so palpably confute herself, that his victory was complete.'[5] But it was the victory of a chess master not a rugby player.

A great practitioner himself, he was well aware of the dangers of being exposed to public scrutiny. He often advised his clients to stay silent, not to make unsworn statements as they were allowed, not to open themselves up to questioning and comment, but to let him attack the witnesses against them. On one occasion he told three prisoners 'to leave the case where it is. It is in perfect good hands.'[6] He was right in his advice. His clients were acquitted.

An almost inevitable consequence of the presence of trial advocates such as Garrow and their forensic skills was that the quality of evidence would be challenged, and the standards by which it should be judged were made overt. Garrow was to the fore in discriminating between strong and weak evidence, in demanding the exclusion of some sorts of evidence, and in formulating, through assertion, such fundamental articles of criminal proceedings as the burden and standard of proof. Garrow reinforced these rules and standards by endless repetition in front of juries. He expanded them but did not invent them.

They had a slow gestation, and were brought in by judges, primarily to salve the consciences of jurors. The standard of proof – 'beyond reasonable doubt' – emerged in Westminster Hall and the Old Bailey at the end of the eighteenth century as a formula intended to ease the qualms of those jurors who might otherwise refuse to convict of capital crimes for fear of endangering their souls. The Bloody Code made this dilemma worse by divorcing punishment from justice. It was no accident that the concept crystallised precisely in the years when the alternative to the noose – transportation – temporarily collapsed as a result of the American Revolution. The uncertainty of the fate of the accused brought a real crisis to English justice, and it cannot be a coincidence that the rise of defence counsel and the formulation of the standard of proof came in at the same time.[7] The earliest example of the latter that I can find is in 1781, and comes from no lesser authority than Mansfield himself. Directing the jury in the case of Lord George Gordon,

5 *Ibid.*, p. 67.
6 John Hostettler, *A History of Criminal Justice* (Hook, 2009), p. 241.
7 Whitman, *Origins of Reasonable Doubt*, p. 200.

the Chief Justice told them that 'if the scale should hang doubtful, and you are not fully satisfied he is guilty, you ought to lean on the favourable side and acquit him'. Similarly, in a 1784 trial the judge told the jury that 'if any doubt at all hangs upon your minds, if you feel the least suspicions, any balance at all, you know it is much the safest way, and it must be most pleasant to you, to lean to the merciful side and acquit him'.[8] There are many other like cases in the Old Bailey records of the 1780s, some of which specifically use the phrase 'reasonable doubt'.[9]

The key nostrum of the presumption of innocence has also been attributed to Garrow. In 1791, by addressing the judge on the law he indirectly told a jury that 'it should be recollected by all the bystanders that every man is presumed to be innocent until proved guilty'. Of course he wanted the jury to think that this was established law, but it was the first time we have a record of it being said in court. Whether or not he actually formulated the proposition, the fact that it has been attributed to him is a tribute to his impact on the trial process and on the rights of the accused.

One result, bemoaned by detractors, of the shift of emphasis onto defence counsel and the extensive cross-examination of hostile witnesses was that the trial became less of a quest for truth (if in reality it ever had been), and more a duel between the contesting advocates who increasingly dominated the trial process. Their aim was not to ascertain the truth of the matter (though truths could be incidentally disinterred), as was supposedly so in a more inquisitorial system, but to determine whether the case against a particular defendant stood up.

The rise of advocacy was ultimately to transform another important and obvious aspect of court proceedings: their duration. In the eighteenth century, trials were routinely dealt with in a matter of minutes. Today jury trials rarely conclude in one day, while many last weeks or months, or more. This too is, in part, the legacy of Garrow and his ilk. By their creative approach to the rules of evidence and by their aggressive questioning, defence barristers became the star turns of the courtroom, and in so doing forced prosecutors to take up similar techniques and tactics. The adversarial system had been born.

Of course it took more than one man's ingenuity to change fundamentally the way in which criminal trials were conducted. The mystery is what those other factors might have been. In 1883 Sir James Fitzjames Stephen noted that the most remarkable change in the character of criminal trials,

---

8   Quoted in Whitman, *Origins of Reasonable Doubt*, p. 186.
9   *Ibid.*, pp. 195–9; Langbein, *Origins of Adversary Criminal Trial*, pp. 261–6.

the gradual relaxation of the rule against defence counsel in felony trials, was also the most mysterious.[10] How the adversarial system gained traction is still unclear, although being clarified. It was not the result of parliamentary intervention, nor of some magisterial work of jurisprudence. Judges opened the door. Barristers, and in particular those practising at the Old Bailey, 'where advocates have always used a licence of tongue unknown in Westminster Hall',[11] pushed their way in. It may be no coincidence that this development happened in England in the middle of the eighteenth century, the high point of the Enlightenment, and at the same time as the Industrial Revolution was transforming much more than just the economy.

In eighteenth-century Britain the prevailing intellectual climate was one of rigour, even of scepticism. Leading thinkers, such as the Scottish philosopher David Hume, emphasised the importance of direct experience in the acquisition of knowledge. Learned institutions, such as the Royal Society, championed and popularised the scientific method. The instinct of the educated person of Garrow's generation would be to take nothing for granted, but to question received wisdom and to test the evidence.

Rights were no longer the preserve of monarchs and aristocrats. Lawyers during the Industrial Revolution who had been working in commercial litigation were accustomed to talk about patent rights or mineral rights, and these accrued to ordinary citizens. These concepts filtered into the criminal law. Their colleagues in the criminal courts took this a stage further and introduced a bolder concept, that defendants had rights – the right to silence, and the presumption of innocence, for example. The criminal defendant was no longer a passive object of procedure but an active participant with rights.[12] Such a person required a barrister to uphold those rights. Garrow triumphed because the time was ripe.

Yet for all his flair in court, and his importance in the development of the adversarial trial, Garrow is overshadowed by an even greater contemporary, his old 'chum', colleague and rival, Thomas Erskine. Unlike Garrow, Erskine was able to address juries directly and at length, and was a master of the twin arts of cross-examination and oratory.[13]

---

[10] Stephen, *History of the Criminal Law*, I, p. 424.

[11] Macaulay, *History of England*, I, p. 447.

[12] R. Vogler, *A World View of Criminal Justice, passim.*

[13] *The Times*, 5 January 1790 referred to him as Erskine's chum. Even today they remain rivals: *Garrow's Law* has provided a remarkably accurate depiction of the conduct of Old Bailey cases in the eighteenth century, although the name is a bit of a misnomer as several of the principal cases attributed to Garrow by the BBC were in fact those of Erskine.

CHAPTER 22

The Tongue of Cicero: Thomas Erskine

It was reserved for the genius of Erskine to pour a new light upon the courts, to refine, elevate, and electrify his audience. He coerced the sympathies of jurors by some potent spell, and in answer to his impassioned appeal, 'Give me your hearts!' they surrendered them at discretion to the great magician.

William Townsend, *Modern State Trials*

BOTH Garrow and Thomas Erskine were of Scottish origin, both were called to the Bar by Lincoln's Inn, and both rose to prominence in London in the period in between the American and French Revolutions. Charismatic and with a superb analytical mind, the latter was in tune with the new chords of political thought of the eighteenth century. Whereas Garrow appears to have been driven largely by ambition, and to have been deeply conservative by nature if not always in action, Erskine throughout his long career deployed his considerable talents selflessly in the defence of wider Enlightenment values and of liberty. His younger contemporary, Henry Brougham, wrote an adulatory essay on him.[1] Lord John Russell was no less effusive, attributing to Erskine 'the tongue of Cicero and the soul of Hampden'.[2] To a modern jurist, he was 'the very greatest advocate who ever practised at the English Bar',[3] and could hold his own with the titans of antiquity. Even Lord Campbell, parsimonious of magnanimity, who in his biographies of the Lord Chancellors was held to have 'added a new terror to death', repeatedly extolled his virtues: 'many generations may pass away before his equal is presented to the admiration of mankind.... As an advocate in the forum, I hold him to be without an equal in ancient or modern

---

[1]   Brougham, *Historical Sketches*, II, pp. 55–66.

[2]   *Dictionary of National Biography* (1885).

[3]   Norman Birkett, *Six Great Advoates* (London, 1961), p. 82. This opinion is definitive, especially given the source: Norman Birkett was himself a very great advocate and was personally acquainted with the finest advocates of his own time. His little book on great advocates is the transcript of a series of talks that he gave for the BBC in 1961. As well as Erskine, he chose Charles Russell, Edward Clarke, Edward Marshall Hall, Patrick Hastings and Rufus Isaacs. The last three of these Birkett knew well and had heard in action.

times.'[4] Those generations have passed and have thrown up many a fine advocate, but none that has surpassed him. If English law has a hero it is the Scot, Tom Erskine.

Born in Edinburgh in 1750, Erskine was sent to school in St Andrews, before entering both the navy and army in turn. In 1774 a chance encounter with a judge led to Erskine deciding to read for the Bar. One day, dressed in his lieutenant's uniform he had strolled into the assizes taking place in the garrison town where he was stationed. Presiding over the court was the Chief Justice. Mansfield noticed the dapper young soldier and invited him to join him on the bench better to observe and absorb the proceedings. The more he witnessed, the more Erskine became convinced that he could better the barristers in front of him. Before the day was out his course was set. The following year he entered as a student at Lincoln's Inn. He secured pupillage in the chambers of one of the luminaries of the Bar, Sir Francis Buller of the Middle Temple, soon to become King's Counsel and, in 1778 at the age of thirty-two, a judge of the King's Bench.[5] Erskine, after a short interlude when he studied at Trinity College, Cambridge, was called to the Bar by the Honourable Society of Lincoln's Inn in July 1778.

As a result of another chance encounter, Erskine blazed his way onto the forensic stage. Taking shelter from the rain in the house of man named Ellis, Erskine was invited to dine. He was not the only guest. One of the subjects discussed around the table was that of abuses in the administration of Greenwich Hospital. These fraudulent goings-on had lately been brought to light, and the conduct of Lord Sandwich, the First Lord of the Admiralty, criticised, by the Lieutenant Governor, Captain Baillie. For exposing this scandal Baillie was suspended, and prosecuted for criminal libel. Sandwich himself kept very much in the background, but instigated others who had also been defamed to take legal action. Erskine spoke vehemently against the corrupt and tyrannical behaviour of Sandwich. What he did not know was that Baillie was one of the guests. Liking his fervour and discovering that Erskine had been in the navy, Baillie would have him as one of those to represent him at Westminster Hall.[6]

4   Campbell, *Lives of the Lord Chancellors*, VIII, pp. 291f.
5   Affection and appreciation did not prevent Erskine standing up to his old pupil-master, which, in the face of being consigned to the cells for contempt, he did in the *Dean of St Asaph's Case* in 1784: Lloyd Stryker, *For the Defence* (New York, 1947), pp. 130ff.
6   *Ibid.*, pp. 49–64.

In November 1778 the case came before Mansfield and two other judges to decide whether the facts justified the matter going for trial.[7] Erskine was the last to speak for the defence. His seniors had addressed the court at length and tediously the day before. Now this young novice would have to rise to the occasion to draw the attention of the judges. He was inspired. Had the matter not touched on such high principles, Erskine began, he should have left the case entirely to others, but 'upon an occasion of this serious and dangerous complexion when a British subject is brought before a court of justice only for having ventured to attack abuses, which owe their continuance to the danger of attacking them, I cannot relinquish the high privilege of trying to do justice to such merit, and I will not give up even my small share of the honour of repelling and of exposing so odious a prosecution'.[8] Erskine then tore into the government of the hospital, and named Sandwich the prime villain. Mansfield at this point interjected, and rebuked the young advocate for attacking Lord Sandwich when he was not before the court, but Erskine would not back down and silenced even Mansfield with the words that followed:

> I know that he is not formally before the court ... but I will bring him before the court. I will drag him to light who is the dark mover behind this scene of iniquity. If [Lord Sandwich] keeps this injured man suspended, or dares to turn that suspension into a removal, I shall then not scruple to declare him an accomplice in their guilt, a shameless oppressor, a disgrace to his rank, and a traitor to his trust.

Erskine knew that Mansfield would 'determine according to law'. Erskine would bow to the sentence. He would even consider that Captain Baillie's 'meritorious publication' was 'an offence against the laws of this country'.

> But then I shall not scruple to say that it is high time for every honest man to remove himself from a country in which he can no longer do his duty to the public with safety; where cruelty and inhumanity are suffered to impeach virtue, and where vice passes through a court of justice unpunished and unreproved.[9]

As Erskine spoke, 'every look was fixed upon him ... every syllable he uttered was eagerly caught up ... breathing was almost suspended, and, as often he paused, if a flake of snow had fallen it would have been heard to fall'. Erskine's faith in British justice was not to be crushed: Baillie was discharged, and Erskine lionised. When asked how he had the temerity to stand up to

7   *ST*, XXI, pp. 1–485.
8   Erskine, *Speeches*, I, pp. 27f.
9   *Ibid.*, pp.52, 55.

Mansfield, he simply replied, 'I thought I heard my little children plucking at my robe and crying out to me, "Now, Father, is the time to get us bread".'[10] His children would never want for bread again.

Erskine did not court popularity, nor did he put preferment before probity. Otherwise he would not have taken on the defence of Lord Gordon after the 1780 riots. This was no aberration, more of a habit. Over a decade later he was to represent his most notorious client, the first of a long line of radicals and republicans: Thomas Paine.

A Quaker with a wonderful facility with words and a compelling simplicity of expression, Paine was the most influential and feared pamphleteer of his day. He had been a propagandist for the American Revolution. Now he was an apologist for the French. His *Rights of Man*, published in two parts in 1791 and 1792, had been penned as riposte to Edmund Burke's minatory *Reflections on the Revolution in France*, which the previous year had exploded like a grenade on the political scene. Fearful of what was happening just across the Channel, and foreseeing the horrors to come, Burke had seemingly moved well away from the opinions he had expressed on what had happened across the Atlantic. Paine turned on the man he once revered as 'a friend of mankind'.[11] Worse of course, he turned on his own country. Her hereditary monarchy was tyranny, her unwritten constitution illusory, and her laws tyrannical. Even the sacred Bill of Rights was 'a Bill of Wrongs'. He demanded a new constitution for Britain, based not on property and precedent but on first principles. It was what Burke abhorred. With his gift of prophecy, Burke declared that the only refutation such a book deserved was 'that of criminal justice'.[12] That is what it got.

Events in France had been changing British attitudes to the revolution there, and sympathisers were becoming suspect. The time had at last come for the government to act against this treacherous gadfly, Tom Paine, who by the phenomenal success of his book was more responsible than anyone else for the 'Jacobin' ideas being widely disseminated among the lower classes, Burke's 'swinish multitude'. French victories were celebrated in the streets of Sheffield, and a tableau of Britannia displayed that depicted Burke riding on a pig.[13] Charged in May 1792 with seditious libel, Paine went to Paris to await his trial in December. There he became a member of the National Conven-

---

10 Campbell, *Lives of the Chancellors*, VIII, p. 30.
11 Thomas Paine, Preface to the English Edition of the *Rights of Man*, in *Political Writings*, ed. Moncure Conway (Pennsylvania, 1978), pp. 331–4.
12 John Keane, *Tom Paine: A Political Life* (London, 1995), p. 323.
13 Thompson, *Making of the English Working Class*, pp. 74, 94, 104.

tion. Treason became synonymous with his name. He took the safer part, and declined to attend his trial – it would take place without him. He could, however, still be represented, if any barrister would risk the public opprobrium of being Satan's mouthpiece, and attempt to defend the indefensible.

Erskine was asked to take this role on. He was warned against it and had much to lose, yet he agreed. He had been retained and would take Paine's brief 'by God'.[14] The trial took place in the King's Bench sitting at the Guildhall.[15] As a result of Fox's recently passed, and still contentious, Libel Act of 1792, juries were now empowered to determine what constituted libel, a reform that owed much to Erskine's conduct of the Dean of St Asaph's case six years earlier. Paine's was, however, a special jury, whose members were restricted to the better off and better educated, predisposed to convict. Undaunted, Erskine deployed a tactic he would use repeatedly of implicating his opponents in the very 'crimes' they were now prosecuting. To defend Paine he must tackle Burke. He would mine Burke's earlier writings to undermine his later. Erskine quoted at length from these works to show that he had shared similar views about the American Revolution to those of the defendant. What had changed? Not Paine. He was no less a republican when he penned his earlier polemic, *Common Sense*, which had done so much to inspire the Americans in their revolt against the Crown.[16] That volume had contained the same principles and criticisms as *The Rights of Man*. That volume had been sold freely in every bookshop in London. Burke had not decried its contents, nor feared its publication. Paine, in short, had stayed true to his beliefs; Burke had not.

This was a good trial tactic but a little unfair on Burke, who was adamant that he remained consistent to his principles. He firmly believed that there existed in England civil liberties, such as trial by jury, and freedom from arbitrary arrest and unlawful detention, which were honed over centuries, and which constituted the hallmarks of a good and just society. Tangible civil liberties were what he cherished, not intangible human rights. He detested the abuse of power from wherever it came, king or mob. He revolted against the untrammelled tyranny of the majority. He loved 'a manly, moral, regulated liberty', secured by 'the equality of restraint', in which the liberty of one could not trespass on the liberty of another. Liberty was 'but another name for justice, ascertained by wise laws and secured by well constructed institutions.' Indeed the 'most sacred rights and franchises' the English cherished

[14] Donald Thomas, *A Long Time Burning* (London, 1969), p. 133.

[15] *ST*, XXII, pp. 357–471.

[16] Erskine, *Speeches*, I, pp. 497–506.

derived not from some abstract principle, but from 'an inheritance'. From Coke to Blackstone, the great oracles of the law were 'industrious to prove the pedigree of our liberties'. He had heretofore championed the traditional liberties of British colonists pushed into insurrection by an overweening British government. It was not the assertion of 'truths', such as those that later prefaced the Declaration of Independence, that Burke had lauded, but the threat to American liberties that he had deprecated. There was nothing contrary in denouncing a French revolution which sought to destroy everything and everyone on the basis of 'metaphysical abstraction' in all its 'nakedness and solitude ... stripped of every relation'. The concept of 'the rights of man', in the abstract and divorced from the necessary constraints of an ordered society and its laws, said Burke, could be – and was – deployed to justify tyranny and terror.[17] Many of these sentiments Erskine would have affirmed, as he too considered that the fundamental right inherent in the English constitution was the right to live under an equitable system of law, a right to justice. Law protected liberty from the oppression of the autocrat or of the revolutionary. Without justice there could be no liberty.

Despite another stellar performance, his efforts were in vain. The jury members had made up their minds before Erskine began. They required no reply. Paine was convicted and outlawed. Erskine did not just lose the case, and lose it badly – for taking it at all he lost his sinecure as Attorney-General to the Prince of Wales. Many a lesser man would have kept the post and refused the client. Not Erskine. It was his duty to defend even those – or particularly those – whom others would desert. It was in his speech to the jury in Paine's case that Erskine gave his ringing encomium of English advocacy and law:

> I will forever, at all hazards, assert the dignity, independence, and integrity of the English Bar, without which impartial justice, the most valuable part of the English constitution, can have no existence. From the moment that any advocate can be permitted to say that he will or will not stand between the Crown and the subject arraigned in court where he daily sits to practice, from that moment the liberties of England are at an end. If the advocate refuses to defend from what he may think of the charge or of the defence, he assumes the character of the judge; nay he assumes it before the hour of judgment; and in proportion to his rank and reputation, puts the heavy influence of perhaps a mistaken opinion into the scale against the accused, in whose favour the benevolent principle of English law makes all presumptions, and which commands even the very judge to be his counsel.[18]

---

[17] Burke, *Reflections on the Revolution*, pp. 6, 26f; Burke, *Correspondence*, VI, pp. 41ff; Connor Cruise O'Brien, *The Great Melody* (London, 1993).

[18] Erskine, *Speeches*, I, pp. 474f.

12. Thomas Erskine, the form of Apollo and the tongue of Cicero. A Scot who was the greatest advocate in England.

Fortunately for liberty and the rule of law, Erskine was at the pinnacle of his powers in this last decade of the eighteenth century when England's rulers were at their most paranoid. They had increasing reason to be worried. Burke's prophecies were coming true: the Revolution had given birth to the Terror. On 21 January 1793 France beheaded its own monarch and ten days later declared war on Great Britain, inviting insurrection. That which was sown might find fertile ground. There remained in England many vocal sympathisers with revolutionary ideals, a potential Fifth Column. There were others who worried that, should the French and their friends prevail, they too would be dragged to the guillotine or gallows by a baying home-grown

Jacobin mob. The Prime Minister, William Pitt, tried his best to scotch sedition and allay those fears, but in so doing risked eviscerating the long-won
liberties of Englishmen by resorting to the methods of those he feared. In
what was described severally as a 'sanguinary plot', or 'the English Terror',
the government unleashed the gravest attack on freedom of speech and association in the whole of British history.

From early 1793 a witch-hunt ensued. Up and down the country radicals were arrested, and preachers, printers and booksellers were imprisoned.
Individuals were dangerous enough, but conspiracies were deemed far more
insidious. Popular associations had been springing up where radical parliamentary reform and constitutional change were advocated. Their members
openly aligned themselves with the French revolutionaries, and applauded
events across the channel. These were the enemy within, those who would
countenance revolution in Britain. These dens of the disaffected were infil-
trated by government spies whose exaggerated reports – which increased
their reward – encouraged the government to overestimate both the republican sympathies and the influence of the societies.[19]

On 22 May 1794 the Habeas Corpus Act was suspended for the first
time in half a century. Six days before, weapons had been found secreted in
Edinburgh intended to be used in a genuine but feckless plot at insurrection
devised by a merchant called Robert Watt. The justification for suspension was
set out in the preamble. It referred to 'a traitorous and detestable conspiracy'
that had been formed 'for subverting the existing laws and constitution, and
for introducing the system of anarchy and confusion which has so lately
prevailed in France'. Parliament, fearing the example of the French Convention, decided to copy it. Despite, or because of, the 'Jacobin' Fox's attempts
to prevent this measure passing, he could muster only twenty-eight MPs to
vote against suspension. One of this small minority was Thomas Erskine.
Burke in his last act in parliament voted in favour, despite recognising that
it was 'certainly a suspension of our liberties'.[20]

The government moved even before the act was passed. On 12 May Thomas
Hardy, a shoemaker and the secretary of the London Corresponding Society,
a relatively harmless body of largely artisan agitators who campaigned for
parliamentary reform and a wider franchise, was arrested. This was soon
followed by the arrest of others, including a colleague, John Thelwall, and
John Horne Tooke of the like-minded Society of Constitutional Information. They were held in the Tower without charge and without recourse

19 Thompson, *Making of the English Working Class*, pp. 488ff.
20 Burke, *Correspondence*, VII, p. 544.

to *habeas corpus*. Meanwhile, in Edinburgh Watt was convicted of treason and condemned to death. In September the London radicals were indicted for high treason, the definition of which had been expanded by government lawyers, not by legislation. Those who dared to suggest that democratic rights should be extended and parliament reformed were now to be deemed traitors. Though their ostensible aims were merely for reform, and though no single act of theirs was treasonable, taken together these would amount to a 'traitorous conspiracy' for subverting the laws and constitution. It was this extraordinary doctrine of 'constructive treason' – deployed against Gordon – that was again to be tested in the courts. Many thought the charge too severe, but there were ways round public squeamishness. Special juries were to be deployed to ensure the right resolution. They were expected to be pliant in finding outspoken radicals guilty of 'compassing the death of the king'. It was a special jury that had convicted Paine.

It was to be Paine's counsel who was to defend those indicted in 1794. Had they been convicted, not only would their lives have been forfeit but the government would have put into effect a further eight hundred arrest warrants. Erskine and his eloquence alone stood between England and this fate. He was to eviscerate Pitt's attempts to prosecute dissent and thwart reform.

The first trial, that of Thomas Hardy, began at the Old Bailey on Tuesday 28 October 1794 before Sir James Eyre, Chief Justice of the Common Pleas and other justices including Sir Francis Buller.[21] Garrow was one of the prosecutors. It lasted an unprecedented nine days, with only the Sunday as a day of respite from this forensic marathon. Hitherto all felony cases had to be concluded within one day. In excoriating style Erskine demolished witness after witness for the Crown. One of them – Henry Alexander – was obviously a spy and an informer. He claimed to be speaking from contemporaneous notes but frequently gazed at the ceiling as if seeking inspiration. With heavy sarcasm Erskine thundered: 'Good God almighty! Recollection mixing itself with notes in a case of high treason – oh excellent evidence!' The value of defence counsel is revealed in this. Had Erskine not been there to cross-examine and comment, would anyone have noticed the weakness of contaminated or confabulated evidence? So it went on for five days. Despite having previously directed the grand jury to find a true bill against Hardy and the others, Eyre was conspicuously fair, and may well have changed his mind on the merits of the prosecution during the course of the trial, especially after hearing Erskine's opening speech.

---

[21] *ST*, XXIV, pp. 199–1407.

Erskine had the power to persuade judges as well as juries. He fused eloquence with logic, and passion with persuasion. He turned the prosecution case on its head. Disarmingly he began by agreeing with the Attorney-General in praising the British constitution and bemoaning the state of anarchy into which Revolutionary France had fallen. The prosecution had been commenced ostensibly to save Great Britain from 'the calamities incident to civil confusion' evident in France. But to convict Hardy would not save Britain from, but would plunge it under, 'the dominion of a barbarous state' where 'every protection of law is abrogated and destroyed', where no man can say 'under such a system of alarm and terror that his life, his liberty, his reputation, or any other human blessing, is secure to him for a moment'.[22] To find for the prosecution was to inflict on Britain the very harm the Crown sought to forestall. The thrust of his argument was that the radical organisations were advocating a revolution in ideas, not a violent revolution. He quoted at length from Burke's earlier criticisms of a parliament opposed to the people, to warn the jury 'against considering hard words against the House of Commons as decisive evidence of treason against the king'. Erskine declared that 'men may assert the right of every people to choose their government without seeking to destroy their own'. His peroration, urging his audience not to conjure up a spirit of self-destruction, nor to 'set the example here of what in another country we deplore' but to cherish 'the old and venerable laws of our forefathers', was said in little more than a hoarse whisper.[23] He had been speaking non-stop for seven hours. His final words were greeted with thunderous applause, whether for their content or the fact of their ending is not clear.

They had their effect, however. After another three days of defence evidence, of speeches and of summing up, on Wednesday 5 November the jury acquitted, the foreman fainting after he had delivered the verdict. Hardy and Erskine were taken in triumph through the streets. The crowds had not celebrated like this since Wilkes's day.

The second trial in the series began on Monday 17 November. Once more Eyre was the presiding judge.[24] The defendant was John Horne Tooke, a former clergyman radicalised by Wilkes. He was a very English sort of radical. He had compared George III to Nero but remained a constitutional monarchist. While admiring the French he condemned Robespierre and the Terror. He thought the British way better and that change could be effected

---

[22] Erskine, *Speeches*, II, p. 404.
[23] *Ibid.*, p. 589.
[24] *ST*, XXV, pp. 1–748.

peacefully. Tooke had a history of acerbic conflict with the authorities, and in 1765 had written 'The Petition of an Englishman', a scathing pamphlet attack on Lord Mansfield himself. It was not promising. Unabashed, Erskine quoted again from Burke. He even summoned him to give evidence but in the event did not call him: wiser and safer to quote the younger Burke than question the older one. Burke complained that 'Tooke and his advisors had the impudence to summon me as a witness for them, the ill nature to keep me waiting for several days, the prudence to discharge me.'[25] Erskine did, however, call William Pitt to give evidence, and many asked 'in what other country could a humble prisoner have forced the chief of state to lay aside his conduct of a foreign war and step into the witness box like any other man'.[26] Through clenched teeth Pitt was forced to admit that he in his earlier years had been 'guilty' of advocating the same reforms he had now pilloried as constituting treason. Pitt conceded he had attended meetings and shared the views of Tooke in the 1780s. It was a devastating admission. Eyre summed up for another acquittal, and the jury obliged him after only eight minutes deliberation.

The third case of the year, that of the agitator John Thelwell, had the same result, thanks again to Erskine's eloquence and self-confidence. When his intrepid but rash client showed an inclination to harangue the jury himself, on the ground that he would be hanged if he did not, Erskine bluntly told him: 'you'll be hanged if you do'.[27] Thelwell thought better of it. This third acquittal sealed the fate of hundreds of other prosecutions waiting to be heard. The government backed down, disdaining further humiliation.

Thanks to the heroic efforts of Erskine, the evenhandedness of Eyre, and the independence of juries, the common law and liberty under the law had been vindicated and the lives of reformers preserved. Erskine had struck 'a blow for liberty whose echoes have not ceased to ring'.[28] He had gained a series of victories unequalled in their importance to the cause of constitutional law. Lord Holland said of him:

> His wonderful exertions in the trials of 1794 stemmed the torrent of political violence which was rapidly rising.... Had Horne Tooke and his associates

---

[25] Burke, *Correspondence*, VIII, pp. 66, 79. Erskine and Burke had been MPs together. There was no one Erskine admired more. He revered Burke as 'a prodigy', while disagreeing with many of his views. Although Burke, in a letter of 26 May 1795, savaged Erskine for invoking him in the treason trials, remarkably they remained on friendly terms throughout their acquaintance.

[26] Stryker, *For the Defence*, p. 330.

[27] Campbell, *Lives of the Lord Chancellors*, VIII, p. 118, note 2.

[28] *Ibid.*, p. 342.

fallen victims to a charge of constructive treason, it would not have been long ere the first men in the country … would have suffered their fate; for a system of political vengeance and persecution as merciless though in the opposite direction from Robespierre's, would have been inevitably established. From such scene I believe we were protected chiefly by the successful genius of Erskine.[29]

Erskine went on to many more forensic triumphs and ultimately rose to become Lord Chancellor of England. He was not only a great orator but a fine and creative lawyer. When elevated to the peerage he took the simple but striking motto, 'Trial by Jury'. A man whose name is now sadly half-forgotten even within legal circles – though his statue dominates the library of Lincoln's Inn to this day – he was not only the greatest barrister ever to practise at the English Bar, and a 'master of forensic eloquence',[30] but the most tenacious champion of liberty the courts have ever seen. Lawyers tend to begrudge excellence in others. Not so with Erskine. His peers, hardly the most modest of souls, thought him peerless, and so set him in stone in the very heart of legal London, an exemplar to all. England owes as much to him as to Magna Carta.

This new fairer adversarial trial procedure, pioneered to such effect by Garrow and Erskine, would colonise half the world. Not all its practitioners could match the former's surgical precision in cross-examination, while the latter's high rhetoric could descend into bathos when deployed by less polished practitioners. Despite its critics then and now, it was adopted by many of the British colonies and the new-born United States of America, and has reached far beyond imperial shores. It is still expanding. In the last two decades alone, Taiwan and several Latin American countries have adopted an adversarial approach. It is one of England's best and most benevolent exports.

---

29 Stryker, *For the Defence*, pp. 487f.
30 William Townsend, *The Lives of Twelve Eminent Judges*, 2 vols (London, 1846), I, p. 398.

CHAPTER 23

The Drum Major of Liberty: Henry Brougham

> I stand engaged to bring before you the whole state of the common law
> … with the view of pointing out those defects which may have existed
> in its original construction, or which time may have engendered, as well
> as considering those remedies appropriate to correct them.
>
> Henry Brougham in the House of Commons,
> 7 February 1828 (*EHD*, XI)

BORN the year Garrow entered, and Erskine left, Lincoln's Inn, the third member of the Scottish trinity of great common law lawyers is Henry Brougham. Although his father was English, his mother was Scottish, and Henry was born and brought up in the intellectual centre of the Enlightenment world, Edinburgh. He was educated at both the Royal High School there and at its university, studying natural sciences and mathematics as well as law. Admitted to the Faculty of Advocates in 1800, he practised little in Scotland before he too, in 1803, enrolled in Lincoln's Inn. Five years later he was called to the English Bar.

A founder of, and leading contributor to, the radical publication *The Edinburgh Review*, and an ardent opponent of slavery, he was guaranteed a warm reception by the leading London Whigs, Lord Grey and Fox in particular. He enthusiastically engaged with Wilberforce in his anti-slave trade campaign and wrote several tracts in support.

He also successfully represented John and Leigh Hunt in their trial for seditious libel, the supposed libel being an exposure of the extent and severity of flogging in the British Army. In February 1811 the trial took place in the King's Bench before Chief Justice Ellenborough, and was prosecuted by a future Chief Justice, Vicary Gibbs.[1] Addressing the jury, Brougham told them that they were trying a more general question than whether the article was written for a wicked purpose: 'You are now to determine whether an Englishman still enjoys the privilege of freely discussing public measures.' Lord Ellenborough was impressed by Brougham's 'ability, manliness and eloquence', but not convinced. He told the jury that he himself had 'no doubt that the libel had been published with the intention imputed

---

[1] *ST*, XXI, pp. 367–414.

to it'. The jury disagreed and acquitted both defendants, to the surprise of Brougham himself. One of his Scottish friends, John Murray, exulted: 'the prosecution of libels is carried too far and it is a great object that it should be checked. You are the first person since Erskine who has done so and you have a much higher situation than any ministry could give you.'[2]

There is a coda to this story: in December 1812 Brougham again represented the Hunts, who were being prosecuted by the Solicitor-General – William Garrow – for libelling the Prince Regent. Brougham complained that 'Garrow reserved himself in a way quite new, and very cowardly, saying ten words and waiting for me, so that all he said was in reply.' Garrow's tactics, however, worked, as this time Brougham, despite firing 'very close and hard into the prince', lost the case.[3] The Hunts were sentenced to two years in prison.

A glittering political career also beckoned Brougham, with a ministry a distinct possibility. In 1810 he had been elected member for Camelford, a rotten borough controlled by the duke of Bedford. In the House he shone, and his powers of oratory took off. In 1811 he successfully introduced a Slave Trade Felony Bill which, when enacted, gave teeth to the earlier abolition of the trade by making it a felony punishable by imprisonment or transportation to participate in it. His devotion to, and exertions on behalf of, the anti-slavery cause would never abate. His ability to sustain an argument and hold an audience in parliament by the power of his oratory was eclipsed only by Erskine's ability in the courts. Brougham still boasts the record for speaking without pause: he did so for six hours. He was tipped as a future Whig leader. Yet he could be abrasive, arrogant and dismissive of less able members, not attributes designed to ensure success. His power of invective made more enemies than friends. He could also be very outspoken when others would yield or temporise. When the Prime Minister, Spencer Percival, was murdered in the lobby of the House of Commons by a deranged merchant called Bellingham, Brougham not only refused to allow a vital debate to be adjourned, but condemned the summary trial and speedy execution of the assassin as 'the greatest disgrace to English justice'.[4]

Unlike Erskine, he was too cerebral and too condescending to be an exemplary jury advocate. It was only in cases where some large principle of individual or political liberty was involved that he was at his extraordinary

2   Chester New, *The Life of Henry Brougham to 1830* (Oxford, 1961), pp. 53ff; Francis Hawes, *Henry Brougham* (Edinburgh, 1957), p. 70.

3   Henry Brougham, *Life and Times*, 3 vols (New York, 1871), II, pp. 59f.

4   New, *The Life of Henry Brougham*, p. 64.

best. Where he did excel was in the more august arena of the House of Lords. Here in 1820 he defended Queen Caroline, the ill-used but foolish and ridiculously indiscreet consort – 'pure in-no-sense', as it was said – against charges of adultery levelled against her so that George IV could both divorce her and strip her of her titles. The procedure for so doing was under the Pains and Penalties Bill. which was brought before the House of Lords by the Tory government of Lord Liverpool. First there had to be a 'trial' before the peers. In reality it was a part of the parliamentary debate.

The defence was hampered by the intrinsic unfairness of the proceedings. Brougham's requests for the particulars of the time and place of the allegations and the names of the witnesses were refused. His attempt to put before the peers evidence of the king's own adultery and disreputable conduct was stymied. The Lords, however, could not prevent the cross-examination of those witnesses called against Queen Caroline. It was devastating. The prosecution's crucial eyewitness to the supposed adultery was Teodoro Majocchi, a former servant of the queen. His evidence was so extensive and damaging that unless it could be discredited her cause was lost. Early in the cross-examination Brougham 'seemed to grow taller and looked just as Wellington had when he saw an opening in [his enemy's] line'. An early answer to one of his questions was *non mi ricordo* ('I do not remember'), and this answer was repeated several times even to questions about matters that, were Majocchi telling the truth, he must have been able to recall. Brougham scented blood and had the face, figure and tone to intimidate when he chose. Majocchi fell into confusion and contradiction, and was reduced to repeating time and time again, *non mi recordo*, in all eighty-seven times. The Italian phrase passed into popular usage for those who had been paid to lie. As the prosecution progressed the queen soared in popularity.[5]

Then it was the turn of Brougham to speak for the defence, and he did so with 'one of the most powerful orations that ever proceeded from human lips'.[6] Reading the speech now this professional assessment is hard to understand as it has not worn very well as oratory, but its impact at the time was overwhelming. Lord Minto wrote to his wife the next day, apologising for an earlier note that was barely comprehensible. He had not recovered the full use of his senses 'from the most extraordinary display of oratory ever exhibited at the Bar by any one man, for he really seemed to possess the varied powers and excellencies of all the best speakers' he had heard. Erskine

5   New, *The Life of Henry Brougham*, pp. 250f; Brougham, *Life and Times*, II, pp. 289–95.
6   The words of Brougham's co-counsel, Thomas Denman, who would end up as Lord Chief Justice, quoted in New, *The Life of Henry Brougham*, p. 253.

himself, who had begged the Lords for a fair trial for Caroline, rushed out of the House during the peroration, tears rolling down his cheeks, hands before his face, and exclaiming that he could not stand another second of it.[7] Such was Brougham's eloquence that although the bill passed, it did so by a meagre nine votes, and was withdrawn before suffering an anticipated defeat in the Commons. The queen and her counsel had triumphed.

The outcome of the trial made Brougham one of the most celebrated men in the country. His legal practice rapidly increased, although, as a marked man, he had to wait until 1827 to become King's Counsel. It did not take him long to give counsel to the king, whose prestige would be enhanced by reform of the law. In 1828 Brougham, in the House of Commons, delivered a six-hour speech ranging over the whole field of jurisprudence. He pointed out defects in the common law and criticised failings in the administration of justice. He called for radical reform. His peroration defined the very essence of a great legal system based on simplicity, accessibility and fairness, a system which his speech helped to forge. He asserted that the king would have a prouder boast than Augustus who had found Rome built of brick and left it marble, 'when he shall have it to say that he found law dear, and left it cheap; found it a sealed book – left it a living letter; found it the patrimony of the rich – left it the inheritance of the poor; found it a two-edged sword of craft and oppression – left it the staff of honesty and the shield of innocence'.[8]

Brougham could exhort and implore, but as yet he could not implement. His time, however, would soon come, and he would leave a lasting mark. When the Whigs took office in 1830 the new premier, Lord Grey, made him Lord Chancellor, becoming Baron Brougham and Vaux. In this role he could institute major legal reforms, most enduringly when he 'smuggled the bill' through parliament creating the judicial committee of the privy council to adjudicate on cases of legal significance throughout the Empire, when he established the Central Criminal Court, and when he began the slow cleansing of the Augean stable that was Chancery.

In addition, Brougham made a considerable contribution to liberty by giving what contemporaries described as a 'superhuman' speech in favour of the Reform Act of 1832 and by the staunch advocacy of his long-cherished Slavery Abolition Act of 1833. In 1834 the Whigs resigned office, and Brougham with them. He lost the chancellorship, but from his seat in the Lords Brougham remained an inveterate champion of freedom and fairness.

7   New, *The Life of Henry Brougham*, pp. 253ff; Stryker, *For the Defense*, p. 562.
8   *EHD*, XI, pp. 364–8.

13 The Trial of Queen Caroline, Brougham's forensic triumph, in all its sumptuous splendour.

In 1836 he saw his Prisoners' Counsel Act become law, giving defendants the right to be represented and authorising defence barristers to address the jury.[9] In 1838, after news came of British colonists obstructing the emancipation of slaves or of ill-treating former slaves, he spoke with passionate conviction in the House:

> The slave ... is as fit for his freedom as any English peasant, ay, or any Lord whom I now address. I demand his rights; I demand his liberty without stint ... I demand that your brother be no longer trampled upon as your slave.[10]

Equating the worth of a slave with members of the aristocracy took some guts. It is hardly surprising that on his passing thirty years later, he was mourned as 'The Old Drum-Major of the Army of Liberty'.[11]

---

[9] The act is sometimes known as the Defendants' Counsel Act, as in *OHLE*, XIII, pp. 77ff. Oddly, Volume XI, p. 642 has the more common form.

[10] Henry, Lord Brougham, *Speeches on Social and Political Subjects*, 2 vols (London, 1857), II, p. 279.

[11] *The Daily Telegraph* commenting after his death on 7 May 1868.

CHAPTER 24

The Bonfire of the Inanities: Peel, Public Protection and the Police

> I want to teach people that liberty does not consist in having your house
> robbed by organised gangs of thieves and in leaving the principal streets
> of London in nightly possession of drunken women and vagabonds.
> Robert Peel to the duke of Wellington, 5 November 1829 (*EHD*, XI)

IN THE early nineteenth century a campaign began to restrict the scope of the noose. Members of parliament, such as Sir Samuel Romilly and Sir James Mackintosh, led the way. In 1819 a House of Commons Select Committee on Criminal Law chaired by the latter, advocated means of increasing the efficiency of the criminal laws by abating their undue rigour. It proposed the repeal or amendment of obsolete statutes, the revision of the forgery laws, and the abolition of capital punishment for larceny in shops, houses and ships, and for stealing horses, cattle and sheep. Instead, the alternatives of transportation and imprisonment should be made more effectual.

Without an agency capable of preventing and detecting crime, however, a mitigation in the deterrent effect of exemplary punishments was unlikely. But a police force was anathema to many of the Whig legal reformers, who feared that it could become an instrument of executive tyranny. It would be akin to a standing army. The last time England was subjected to such was under the ill-omened James II. He paid for this affront to liberty with his throne. In London, policing, such as it then was, was confused and inefficient, relying on constables, beadles, churchwardens, unpaid constables, and nightwatchmen equipped with lanterns and rattles. The Bow Street Runners patrolled the main highways. There was a Thames Police and fifty City police. All were rivals.

In 1822 Robert Peel entered the Cabinet as Home Secretary. The criminal justice system was a muddle, with a plethora of acts, some antique, some overlapping, all confusing. Attempts had been made to impose order on chaos. Blackstone, in his Oxford lectures, had sought to show undergraduates – laymen – a system of law which reached reasonable results behind institutions and procedures of quite unreasonable artificiality. Not all were convinced. So horrified by this approach was Jeremy Bentham, that it inspired him a few years later to publish his *Fragment on Government*, a vitriolic attack on Blackstone and his *Commentaries*. It also led Bentham to develop his own radical ideas on legislative and penal reform and codification, and to campaign for them tirelessly throughout his long life. Finally, in Peel, a politician of eminence and weight came into the Home Office who had a similar instinct for ordered reform. Although Bentham criticised him – Bentham criticised everyone always – for what the philosopher thought was the politician's failure to act from first principles and for timidity in the handling of law reform, the 'weak and feeble' Peel eventually charmed and won Bentham over, not so much by his personality but by the practical successes he achieved. In 1832 Bentham, in a mixed metaphor, congratulated Peel on crossing the Rubicon and falling 'into the same pit with me'.[1]

The task of making the law clearer and simpler was bound to lead to some melioration in penalties. Peel saw the gradual mitigation in punishment as the consequence of modernising the criminal justice system, rather than as an end in itself. He also recognised that the fuller implementation of the reformers' aims would take time, and believed that they would be best secured by specific measures and not by general propositions. Peel had three objectives: simplification, consolidation and mitigation, and probably saw them in that order of priority, though recognising that they all went together. In 1822 he wrote that he did not think that there was 'any irreconcilable difference upon points of real importance between the reasonable advocates for the mitigation of the criminal law and the reasonable defenders of it'.[2] Peel admitted that some would say he was too cautious and slow, but he thought it unwise to force too many changes in rapid succession on the existing framework of the law without adequate deliberation and perhaps without the necessary concurrence of the judicial authorities. Peel's preference for a steady but cautious relaxation of the law rather than a sudden and sweeping change was based not on a desire to enforce the death penalty rigidly, but on his view of the expediency of retaining discretionary powers in the hands of the judiciary, to be used as circumstances required until the effects of the various legal reforms were fully apparent. In 1827 in a speech in the Commons advocating amelioration of the law, he said 'if parliament were to proceed too rapidly to overthrow the existing enactments, a strong prejudice might arise in the country against measures that were intended for the public good; and thus the great object of justice and humanity might be

---

[1] Norman Gash, *Mr Secretary Peel* (London, 1961), p. 333; Douglas Hurd, *Robert Peel* (London, 2007), p. 16.

[2] Gash, *Mr Secretary Peel*, p. 319.

defeated'.[3] Steeply rising crime figures reinforced his view. Crime rose from about 50,000 criminal commitments in the years 1809–16, to almost 100,000 in the years 1818–25. Convictions rose from under 30,000 to over 60,000, and capital sentences rose from 4,000 to almost 8,000 (although only 536 were carried out in the first period and 579 in the second). The main rise was in property offences.

Peel reassured parliament and the public by asserting that he was not proposing fundamental changes in the law, but was proceeding gradually with improvement. To Peel's mind, cautious and sure, it was of greater consequence to create an agreed maximum of consent over a wide field of legal reform than to risk obstruction and defeat by pressing forward immediately to the furthest visible objective. Thus he meliorated the effect of the law by modifying rather than abolishing statutes. With Peel proposing changes, changes were made almost without opposition. His measures managed to pass even in the Lords, who were more prepared to raise the minimum limit of goods stolen from a dwelling from 40s to £5 rather than abolish capital punishment for larceny completely. He consulted with judges and won over potential opponents. Above all, he inspired trust.

As a result, he could introduce consolidated legislation to govern three-quarters of all criminal offences on the statute books. Between 1825 and 1828 a total of 278 statutes were repealed or consolidated. Ninety-two statutes on theft – by far and away the most prevalent crime – were reduced to thirty pages. Benefit of clergy, the artificial device that had mitigated the Bloody Code, was finally abolished in 1827: it was no longer necessary. He got agreement to the proposal that except where a felony had been specifically made a capital crime, it was in future to carry a punishment of seven years' transportation or two years' imprisonment. He repealed the Waltham Black Act, and abolished capital punishment for a large number of offences, including arson and malicious shooting.

The death penalty remained for forgery under an Act passed in 1830. Forgery had long been considered a particularly heinous offence, undermining as it did the paper currency that was becoming the lifeblood of commerce. Britain's war with revolutionary France had triggered a series of runs on the Bank of England, draining its gold reserves. Fearing it would run out, it increased the use of bank notes, but their level of sophistication was inadequate and counterfeiters saw a lucrative niche. For many a small tradesman the fear of being incarcerated in a debtor's prison proved a greater incentive to commit forgery than the death penalty a deterrent.

---

3 *Ibid.*, pp. 340f.

14. Robert Peel, radical creator of the police force and conservative consolidator of the law.

Between 1797 and 1821 the Bank of England brought more than two thousand offenders to trial, a tenth of whom went to the gallows.[4] As time went on juries became more squeamish and were less prone to convict. Even the Bank wanted the law made less draconian to ensure a higher conviction rate. The Lords defeated a Commons attempt to remove the punishment, but at least Peel managed to regularise and mitigate the law. One hundred and twenty statutes dealing with forgery, with sixty of them imposing capital punishment, were reduced to one, a mere six pages long. To forge a note was

4 The Mint was equally keen to prosecute coiners.

death; to forge a receipt for the same amount was no longer capital. In short, he made the laws more practicable but hardly more just. It was, however, a significant first step, and one the more ardent reformers would have been unlikely to achieve. By 1830 the consolidation was almost complete, but Peel was happy to think that law reform and mitigation would come up again. Between the law books of George III and those of William IV there was now a great divide. Peel wanted more effective law and order; the reformers wanted justice and mercy. Both eventually got their way.

Peel was not finished by far. He revised the scale of lesser punishments. Any considerable reduction in the scale of capital punishment would necessitate an effective system of secondary punishment. In April 1823 he opposed the abolition of whipping, saying it was 'incumbent upon those who advocated the necessity of mitigating the severity of the penal code, in respect of capital punishments, to beware of rendering such an experiment impracticable by narrowing too much the scale of minor punishments'. Whipping was less severe than solitary confinement. The 'enlightened severity' of Sidney Smith appealed to Peel. In 1826 he wrote to Smith that when prisoners were given a normal diet, their lot in winter was 'thought by people outside to be rather an enviable one'.[5] The present prison population were living more comfortably than was consonant with strict penitence.

Most prisons, however, were locally run, provision was haphazard, and standards varied wildly. To a mind such as Peel's this disarray was offensive and would not do. A wrongdoer's lot should not be determined by the geographical accident of whether he or she lived in Shropshire or Surrey. He set about standardising the conditions of imprisonment. The Gaol Act of 1823 provided for a common gaol or house of correction in every county and in London and other towns, administered by local magistrates, financed by local rates. It proposed a system of prisoner classification, forbade alcohol, called for the appointment of a surgeon and a chaplain, for the provision of education and inspection, and it introduced payment for gaolers and education for inmates.

Legal procedure was also improved. The Jury Act of 1825 reduced eighty-five statutes dealing with juries to one. The number of judges was increased. Quakers and Moravians were allowed to give evidence on affirmation in criminal courts. Unless they had been convicted of perjury, criminals who had served their sentence could give evidence in criminal courts. The level at which many cases were heard was lowered, moving from the assizes to the quarter sessions, and from there to the magistrates' courts. Peel even

---

5   Gash, *Mr Secretary Peel*, pp. 316ff.

embarked on reforms of the Scottish legal system. Clarity and simplicity were the hallmarks of all his endeavours as Home Secretary.

With the decline in sanguinary punishments and with informants increasingly discredited in courts, the detection of crime and an increase in the conviction rate would have to compensate for the diminution of deterrence. In addition, public order was very important in the emerging economy, as the Home Office's 'disturbance file' showed. To counter the threat of crime and disorder in the whole of London, a city of over a million inhabitants, Peel had a patchwork police force of a few hundred inadequately trained, poorly motivated, and easily tempted men. He researched into ways of improving this situation by enquiring at home and abroad and by amassing statistics. He advocated the creation of a civilian police force.

In March 1822 he moved for a Select Committee on Policing in London to gain 'as perfect a system of police as was consistent with the character of a free country'. It reported on 17 June 1822, concluding that it was 'difficult to reconcile an effective system of police with that perfect freedom of action and exemption from interference which are the great privileges and blessings of society in this country'. The language may have been more restrained but the sentiments expressed were the same as those of the Select Committee four years earlier, when such a proposal had been called 'odious and repulsive', one which would be rejected with abhorrence by a free people.[6] Deep in the marrow of most Englishmen, not just radicals such as Brougham, was the long-cherished belief that lawlessness was preferable to intrusion or oppression by the state. A centralised professional police force smacked of despotism.

While parliament pursed its lips, Peel persisted. He had caught the tide. Industrialisation and urbanisation had increased both the fear and the reality of crime and disorder. The embers left by the Gordon riots were still smouldering, and burst into life in the many sporadic bouts of violence that broke out in the 1820s. In 1828, again Home Secretary, Peel agitated for a change to the rudimentary police establishment that in his view the country had 'entirely outgrown'. It lacked uniformity. It was uncoordinated. It was fragmented. He managed to get another parliamentary committee, mainly composed of those sympathetic to such change, to examine the problem. He deluged it with statistics about the rise of property crime in London. In July it duly reported, recommending a police force for the capital.[7]

---

6 *OHLE*, XIII, pp. 23f.
7 Gash, *Mr Secretary Peel*, pp. 493f.

The result was the 1829 Metropolitan Police Act, which established a police force, under the control of the Home Office, for a ten-mile radius from the centre of London (excluding the City, which got a similar but separate police force in 1839). It was left to the Home Secretary to establish its character. He had a lot of discretion over size, structure, recruitment and deployment. At the same time he had to convince the public that he was not creating a police state, nor was he intending to curtail liberty. He tried to ensure that 'the Met' would not be regarded as a sanctuary for the incompetent and the genteel. There was to be no officer caste. It was to be professional and homogenous. It was also to be civilian in character, not military, an important distinction and one needed to win support for a permanent uniformed body operating in the streets of the capital. 'The police are the public, and the public are the police', wrote Peel in his remarkable *Principles of Law Enforcement*, which prefaced the 'General Instructions' issued to every new recruit. In it, constables were enjoined 'to preserve public favour' by 'ready offering of individual service and friendship to all members of society without regard to their race or social standing, by ready exercise of courtesy and friendly good humour'. The Met was divided into police divisions, and one thousand 'peelers', or 'bobbies' as they affectionately became known, were to be appointed on merit alone, under two supervising magistrates – soon styled 'commissioners' – accountable to the Home Secretary. The force was financed by a special police rate which replaced the amount spent on parochial watchmen and constables. Its headquarters was in Scotland Yard.[8]

Although Peel's ambitions were restricted to London, his measures, in fits and starts, were emulated elsewhere until in 1856, under the County and Borough Police Act, all counties and cities were obliged to form their own police forces, centrally supervised but locally administered. There was still a place for diversity amidst uniformity. The fears of a police force being an agent of oppression were largely allayed.

These developments in the nature of policing in turn brought in a big change in the way in which crime was prosecuted. With the police increasingly responsible for the detection of crime – the Met appointed its first detectives in 1842 – as well as for its prevention and the apprehension of criminals, the prosecution of offences naturally devolved onto them. The long era of private prosecutions was coming to an end, and, in the course of Victoria's reign, the practice largely ceased. Most welcomed the change, as the pre-existing system had been under attack for years from senior members of the judiciary, parliament and the press. The state would at last be respon-

8   Gash, *Mr Secretary Peel*, pp. 497–503.

sible not just for the trial and punishment of offenders as it always had been, but for prosecuting them as well.[9]

Peel was proud of reforms most of his predecessors would have resisted. He believed that his party had lagged behind public opinion which was more liberal than its policies. He said in 1827, 'Tory as I am I have the satisfaction of knowing that there is not a single law connected with my name, which has not had for its object some mitigation in the severity of criminal law, some prevention of abuse in the exercise of it, or some security for its impartial administration.'[10] Though he rejected a criminal code, what he did accomplish represented, in its scope and thoroughness, a fresh point of departure in the history of English criminal law. In his most innovative measure, the creation of a police force, he was well ahead of both public and parliamentary opinion. It was to be his greatest legacy.

His work in mitigation of the law's severity was more hesitant and more temporary, but he abolished or restricted capital punishment in many cases. He still adhered to the efficacy of the deterrent effect of the noose. Peel temporarily left office in 1830, and the Whigs took over. His cautious approach, perhaps necessary at first, was soon being outpaced by public opinion. The succeeding Whig government allowed measures to go through that abolished the death penalty for many offences, including forgery. Within three years Peel's trickle of reform had become a flood threatening to overwhelm the dam Peel had maintained.[11] By 1841 almost all capital offences were reserved for major acts of violence and for sodomy.

The formation of a police force was the product of legislation. So too had been the Bloody Code, transportation, the creation of the penitentiaries, and the expansion and later restriction of the death penalty. By contrast, the developments in the substantive criminal law during the nineteenth century were largely the result of judicial decision-making in response to specific cases, issues or concerns, of which the law relating to insanity and to necessity provide excellent and interesting examples.

---

9   *OHLE*, XIII, pp. 63–7.
10 *Parliamentary Debates*,1827, xii, cols 393–411.
11 Gash, *Mr Secretary Peel*, p. 485.

CHAPTER 25

Lunacy and the Law

Ye people of England rejoice and be glad
For ye're now at the will of the merciless mad.
So if a dog or man bite you beware being nettled
For a crime is no crime – when the mind is unsettled.
'On a Late Acquittal', *The Times*, 1843

THERE IS A rule of law still extant that can be indirectly attributed to Robert Peel. In 1843 he was enjoying a second term as Prime Minister. On Friday 20 January a young Glaswegian woodturner called Daniel M'Naghten (variously spelt McNaughton or McNaghten) shot Edward Drummond, the Prime Minister's secretary, at point-blank range in the back of the head. The wound was mortal, ensuring Drummond a lingering death. Had it not been for the intervention of one of Peel's new police constables – James Silver of A Division – M'Naghten would have fired again and finished off his victim on the spot. A clearer case of premeditated murder could hardly be found, the intended victim was no less than the Prime Minister. Yet the jury, with the active encouragement of the judge, acquitted M'Naghten on the basis that he was insane and so not guilty of the offence.

The issue of insanity as a defence to felony had always been left to the discretion of the trial judge and to the good sense of the jury. No statute had been enacted laying down the law; no considered judgment of senior members of the judiciary sitting *in banc*[1] had determined it; no binding precedent had been established. The formula usually applied was that of the trial judge in *Edward Arnold's Case* of 1724.[2] 'Crazy Ned' had shot and wounded Lord Onslow. The judge directed the jury on the test for insanity in the following terms: 'whether the accused is totally deprived of his understanding and memory and knew that he was doing no more than a wild beast or a brute, or an infant'. This became known as 'the wild beast test'.

---

[1] 'As a bench', a multi-judge sitting of one of the old common law courts (the King's Bench, the Common Pleas or the Exchequer) to decide questions of law: Stephen, *History of the Criminal Law*, II, p. 152.

[2] *ST*, XVI, pp. 695–725.

Apart from this, the foremost authority to discourse on the subject of criminal insanity was Hale in his *Pleas of the Crown*, published posthumously in 1736. Although only an opinion, coming from such a source, and echoing the views of Coke, it long carried weight. Hale had written that to protect a man from criminal responsibility there must be 'total deprivation of memory and understanding'. He went on to assert that

> there is a partial insanity of mind, and a total insanity.... It is very difficult to define the invisible line that divides perfect and partial insanity; but it must rest upon the circumstances duly to be weighed and considered both by the judge and jury, lest on the one side there be a kind of inhumanity towards the defects of human nature; or on the other side too great an indulgence given to great crimes.[3]

Hale's dictum put the onus on the jury, but precluded 'partial insanity' from affording a defence. Only 'perfect madness' would suffice.

Once again it was Thomas Erskine, in *Hadfield's Case*, his last state trial, who made an indelible mark in the development of law in relation to insanity and criminal liability. It provides an excellent example of a trial court determining not just the facts of the behaviour but the legal definition of insanity itself, a definition not decided by the judge after legal argument but acceded to after a jury speech by defence counsel. In 1800 James Hadfield, a former soldier with a distinguished service record, fired a gun at King George III, who was sitting in the royal box at Drury Lane Theatre. The shot missed, as Hadfield probably intended it should. The would-be assassin was apprehended with ease. The play went on. The king remained to the end. Six weeks later Hadfield was put on trial for treason in the King's Bench before Chief Justice Kenyon, three justices and a jury.[4] The prisoner had a right to choose his own counsel and his choice was Erskine, who was assigned to him at public expense.

The facts were not in dispute. The legal implication of the mental state of Hadfield was. The Attorney-General, prosecuting with Garrow to assist,[5] accepted Hale's test that if a man were 'completely deranged so that he knows not what he does [and] is incapable of distinguishing between good and evil', then 'the mercy of our law says that he cannot be guilty of a crime'.[6] The Crown, however, were confident in their ability to show that

3 Hale, *Pleas of the Crown*, I, p. 30.
4 *ST*, XXVII, pp. 1281–1356.
5 With considerable licence, the BBC series *Garrow's Law* removed Erskine from the scene entirely and replaced him, as defence counsel, with Garrow!
6 Stryker, *For the Defence*, p. 372.

the prisoner was far from fitting this category. Witnesses testified to the fact that throughout the day Hadfield had acted and spoken as a sane man would act and speak. He had purchased 'super-fine gunpowder', had displayed two pistols he had bought at a bargain price, and had told his barber that he was going to a play.

The only witness Erskine bothered to question was none other than the duke of York. He had been one of the first to apprehend the felon, and had recognised Hadfield as a soldier who had once served under him in Flanders as an orderly. Erskine asked but three questions of him, eliciting the answers that orderlies were chosen from only the most tried and trusted men, that Hadfield had told the duke that he was 'a man tired of life' who had meant no harm to the king, and that Hadfield had thought his actions would lead to his own death. Erskine then addressed the jury in an opening speech of astounding audacity.[7] He began with a panegyric to English justice. The fact that the potential assassin of the king had been unmolested on arrest and had been afforded a fair trial 'covered all over with the armour of the law … provided with counsel by the king's own judges' but not of their choosing, 'exhibits to the whole civilized world a perpetual monument of our national justice'. He then went on to discourse on the law – its determination was not yet the sole preserve of the trial judge. He quoted that revered authority Hale, whose dicta seemed to exclude Hadfield from a defence.

Like Icarus, Erskine took flight, embarking on one of the most unusual and hazardous of all legal undertakings: to find the rationale behind the law and persuade the judge and jury to accept his conclusions in the face of generally accepted assumptions, hallowed by antiquity, usage and authority. He had to convince the jury not only 'that the unhappy prisoner was a lunatic, within my own definition of lunacy, but that the act in question was the immediate, unqualified offspring of the disease'. Would the wax in his wings melt?

First he dealt with the authorities, Coke and Hale. 'The true interpretation of [total deprivation of memory and understanding] deserves the utmost attention and consideration of the court. If a total deprivation of memory was intended in the literal sense of the words' it would apply only to idiots and not to madmen. With a psychiatric penetration – before psychiatry existed[8] – he propounded the best formulation of what would later be called the defence of 'irresistible impulse'. He distinguished those cases that were easy for the law to deal with – the idiot who from birth knows not his own

---

7   Erskine, *Speeches*, IV, pp. 165–211.
8   The first recorded use of this term is in 1846.

age nor the name of his father, and the manic or lunatic, periodically 'laid prostrate under the state of frenzy where all the ideas are overwhelmed – for reason is not merely disturbed but driven wholly from her seat'. Erskine then propounded a third novel and more legally troublesome category, 'where the delusions are not of that frightful character … yet where imagination … still holds the most uncontrollable dominion over reality and fact'. Such cases, he argued, mocked the wisdom of the wisest because persons so afflicted could recall facts, and reason rationally, but were labouring under 'a delusive image, the inseparable companion of real insanity', which was 'thrust upon the subjugated understanding, incapable of resistance, because unconscious of attack'. Erskine concluded that 'delusion where there is no frenzy or raving madness is the true character of insanity'.

Erskine had his own *coup de theatre*. He had instructed Henry Cline, a pre-eminent surgeon, to examine the prisoner in Newgate. Cline discovered two deep sword wounds in the prisoner's skull, battle injuries in the service of king and country, which had penetrated the brain and caused insanity. Hadfield had almost lost his life. He had irrecoverably lost his senses. His behaviour subsequent to his discharge had been bizarre and dreadful, attacking his own infant son.

Cline and other witnesses confirmed all that Erskine had said. Dr Alexander Crichton, a specialist in dealing with madness, then gave his opinion that Hadfield was insane. With some twenty more witnesses to call, Lord Kenyon interrupted and asked the Attorney-General if he could call witnesses to contradict the facts established by Erskine. He could not, and accepted the circumstances entirely. The judges and prosecution counsel accepted Erskine's definition of insanity, and accepted that Hadfield was indeed insane. Garrow suggested that the jury bring in a verdict of not guilty by reason of insanity, thus providing a legal basis for Hadfield's future confinement in Bedlam (Bethlem Hospital). The jury so did, and the prisoner became a patient. King George, touched by intermittent madness himself, would not have been displeased. Erskine had performed an extraordinary and lasting service to the law governing insanity. 'From obscurity, so far as the law is concerned' the proper test for insane delusion 'was brought into the limelight by Erskine … and as a result of his oratory became for a time the sole test of insanity for the courts.'[9] He had overthrown and replaced the dicta of Hale.

Or had he? In 1812 two cases – that of Bowler and Bellingham – threw considerable doubt on this. Thomas Bowler was a farmer who had harboured a grudge against another farmer whom he shot and injured. John Bellingham

9 Stryker, *For the Defence*, p. 385.

was far more notorious, a notoriety achieved from killing Spencer Percival, the only British Prime Minister ever to be assassinated. Bellingham said he would rather have killed the British ambassador to Russia. Any representative of what he considered to be oppressors was a legitimate target. Despite calling medical evidence of madness, both Bowler and Bellingham had been found guilty and hanged. They had both been tried according to the older conception of insanity. Chief Justice Sir James Mansfield, presiding over Bellingham's trial, directed that the 'law was extremely clear: if a man were deprived of all power of reasoning, so as not to be able to distinguish ... right or wrong', he would not be criminally responsible. Erskine's third category of a man obsessed with a perceived injury and who reeks revenge, but who can distinguish right from wrong, could not, according to Mansfield, avail himself of the defence of insanity.

The conduct and conclusions of both these cases were heavily criticised by the medical and legal professions, and the judiciary as a whole preferred Erskine's approach. More benign and more consistent with contemporary medical thinking, it was to be confirmed in 1840 in another case of attempted royal assassination. Edward Oxford had shot at the young Queen Victoria while she was riding in a coach up Constitution Hill. He too missed. He too was tried for treason.[10] He too called witnesses to testify to his odd behaviour and of his father's and grandfather's madness – although the Crown had witnesses aplenty to testify of his normality. He too called doctors to give expert evidence of his mental state. They opined that he was insane or imbecile or both. Despite the suspicion that 'the medical men went to Newgate predisposed and predetermined to see a madman', he too was acquitted on the grounds of insanity. The judge specifically criticised *Bowler's Case* for its 'barbarous' outcome, while the Attorney-General, who was prosecuting, declined to refer to *Bellingham's Case* 'as there are some doubts as to the correctness of the mode in which that case was conducted'.

M'Naghten's Case was to follow the same course as *Oxford's*. But it was its aftermath which resulted in the M'Naghten Rules that finalised and fossilised the legal definition of insanity. Although the Rules were founded on dubious authority, backtracked on Erskine's definition, and have been criticised many times by lawyers and doctors, they have persisted to this day. In March 1843 the trial took place at the Old Bailey before the Chief Justice of the Common Pleas, Sir Nicholas Tindal, flanked by two other justices – Williams and Coleridge.[11] Money, the provenance of which is unknown but

10 Townsend, *Modern State Trials*, I, pp. 102–50.
11 *Ibid.*, I, pp. 314–411.

which may have come from a medical profession interested in the criminal law revisiting its attitude to insanity, provided this obscure Scotsman a lavish defence. He was represented by an impressive array of barristers, led by Alexander Cockburn QC, a future Chief Justice.

In his opening speech Cockburn quoted his predecessor Erskine's definition of lunacy and told the jury that 'in this doctrine is the true interpretation of the law to be found'. M'Naghten had been under a double delusion that 'the Tories' were persecuting and pursuing him wherever he would go in this country or abroad, and that Drummond was in fact the Prime Minister. Several witnesses gave impressive testimony as to the duration and severity of his delusional beliefs. Eight doctors were called to give evidence on the issue of his sanity. Their unanimous medical testimony was that the prisoner was acting under a delusion of such latent potency as to deprive him of all self-control. He himself had told one of them that even if he took 'a ton of drugs it would be of no service to him'. The doctors diagnosed partial insanity or 'monomania' – probably paranoid schizophrenia of a particularly malignant kind – such that 'a ton of drugs' would be of little use.[12]

The Chief Justice asked the Solicitor-General if he had any evidence to combat this medical consensus and warned him that if he had not the judges would have to stop the case. The prosecution conceded. The jury were briefly directed by Tindal that to convict they would have to be satisfied that at the time of the shooting M'Naghten had 'the competent use of his understanding so as to know that he was doing a wicked and wrong thing', and was 'sensible ... that it was a violation of the law of God or of man'. This was the old test. Then Tindal made a volte-face. He referred to the unanimous medical evidence, and asked if they really needed to be reminded of more. He emphasised that if they thought that 'the subject was involved in very great difficulty', they should probably acquit. They took the hint, declined the offer, and found the defendant not guilty on the ground of insanity. M'Naghten escaped punishment but suffered treatment. He would not be hanged as a murderer but detained as a patient under the Criminal Lunatics Act 1800 – enacted in the wake of the Hadfield case. He was sent first to Bethlem Hospital, and then in 1864 to the newly built Broadmoor. He died there in 1865, aged 52.

The whole of the legal proceedings had more than a hint of contrivance and the aroma of fish. To those wishing to mitigate the severity of the law in these cases it must have seemed that they had achieved their aim and

12 Donald West and Alexander Walk, eds, *Daniel McNaughton: His Trial and the Aftermath* (Ashford, 1977), pp. 91–9.

that the law on insanity had finally caught up with medical advances. This evolutionary process, however, was soon brought to an abrupt end. Ossification would set in.

The 'not guilty' verdict occasioned much outrage in parliament and the press. M'Naghten had not missed. Drummond had died. The spectre loomed large of dangerous lunatics stalking the land who could kill with impunity. Public protection was being sacrificed on the altar of insanity. Sympathy for the victim was being perverted into sympathy for the 'poor unfortunate' felon. Even the radical medical periodical *The Lancet* protested, while Queen Victoria, echoing public disquiet, wrote to her Prime Minister, Robert Peel, in trenchant terms and with much emphasis:

> We have seen the trials of Oxford and M'Naughton [*sic*] conducted by the ablest lawyers of the day ... and *they allow and advise* the jury to pronounce a verdict of *Not Guilty* on account of *Insanity* when *everybody* is morally *convinced* that both malefactors were perfectly conscious and aware of what they did! It appears from this that the force of the law is entirely put into the judge's hands, and that it depends merely upon his charge whether the law is to be applied or not. Could not the Legislature lay down the rule which ... Chief Justice Mansfield did in the case of Bellingham, and why could not the judges be *bound* to interpret the law in *this* and in *no other* sense in their charges to the juries?[13]

It was Henry Brougham who first raised the 'state of the law relating to crimes of persons alleged to be labouring under partial insanity', and invited the Lord Chancellor or Lord Chief Justice to 'take the matter in hand'.[14] The ensuing angry debate in the Lords propelled Lord Lyndhurst, the Lord Chancellor, to revive an obsolete piece of constitutional machinery which enabled the House to gauge the view of the judges as to a particular point of law in the form of answers to specific questions. Five hypothetical questions were formulated and put to a panel of judges, presided over by none other than Tindal himself. On 19 June 1843 all but one of the judges replied. Their answers do not, however, form a judicial ruling on a specific case which had come before them. They merely constitute judicial opinions on questions that the Lords had a dubious right to ask, and that the judges were not obliged to answer.[15] Dissenting, Mr Justice Maule took exactly this line, vigorously objecting to being asked to answer questions in the abstract and without hearing argument on the subject. He feared that such answers

---

13 A. C. Benson, *The Letter of Queen Victoria*, 3 vols (London, 1907), I, p. 587.
14 West and Walk, eds, *Daniel McNaughton*, p. 10.
15 Stephen, *History of the Criminal Law*, II, pp. 154f.

might 'embarrass the administration of justice when they are cited in criminal trials.'

Nonetheless these answers were to hold sway as authoritative, and, as the M'Naughten Rules, have repeatedly been accepted in common law jurisdictions as the standard test for criminal liability in relation to mentally disordered defendants. In short, the jury is to be directed that

> to establish a defence on the ground of insanity, it must clearly be proved that, at the time of the commission of the act, the party accused was labouring under such a defect of reason, from disease of the mind, as not to know the nature and quality of the act he was doing, or if he did know it, that he did not know he was doing what was wrong.

If the accused passed the test a special verdict of 'not guilty by reason of insanity' is to be delivered and the disposal is a medical one.[16]

The Rules represented a major retreat from the position taken in M'Naghten's case. Had his jury been directed in the terms of the Rules, it would have inevitably brought in a 'guilty' verdict. He was acting out of grievance, wanted revenge, and so he knew what he was doing and he knew that his action was both unlawful and wrong. The common law in relation to insanity, which had been sensibly evolving, ossified. The Rules were too narrow a test of criminal responsibility. They made no allowance for the phenomenon of 'irresistible impulse' – ineffective volitional control. Attempts were made to circumvent their restrictive nature. James Fitzjames Stephen, writing in 1883, expressed his reservations about the wording which he too, as a judge, felt obliged to adopt in cases where the defence of insanity arose.[17] He wanted to allow for irresistible impulse to negative criminal responsibility, and in a case he had presided over in 1881 he reformulated the direction in a way more favourable to the accused.

However, such was the authority given to the Rules both in their origin and in their reiteration, that subsequent judicial modification to fit new developments or even novel circumstances became impossible. In 1922 in *True's Case*, the Court of Criminal Appeal finally took its chance to state its authoritative view. Ronald True had boasted that he would commit a murder and then did so, killing a prostitute in a spectacularly violent manner. Four doctors gave evidence that he was insane, but the jury, having been directed on the law by the trial judge, convicted him. The Court of Criminal Appeal

---

16 The Trial of Lunatics Act 1883, s.2(1).
17 Stephen, *History of the Criminal Law*, II, pp. 153f.

upheld the verdict. Indeed they thought that the judge had been overgenerous in his direction. The M'Naughten Rules were 'sufficient and salutary'.[18]

Among other problems they occasioned, the survival of the Rules prevented the formulation within common law jurisdictions of the concept of diminished responsibility. By contrast, in Scotland this took place as early as 1867.[19] English law had to wait a long time for parliamentary intervention. This belatedly arrived in the Homicide Act of 1957, brought in to help maintain public support for capital punishment by curtailing the noose for the episodically insane or moderately mad. Even then diminished responsibility merely reduced murder to manslaughter. It did not provide a complete defence, but mitigated the consequences, and was exclusive to murder charges. The test for insanity in murder and all other cases remains that devised in 1843. The M'Naughten Rules, as their name suggests, were the result of an arcane and suspect procedure. They provide a very clear example of 'judge-made' law, a law that has lasted a very long time and many think is in dire need of review.[20]

It was not the only lasting legal development to be spawned in this way during the reign of Queen Victoria. Another judicial ruling of equal importance and longevity was also formulated in an irregular manner. It came out of a most curious case on the vulnerability of edible cabin boys when faced with the exigencies of the sea. M'Naughten insanity was mentioned as a possible defence, but not relied upon. The live issue in this case was not insanity but necessity.

[18] 16 Criminal Appeal Reports, p. 164; West and Walk, eds, *Daniel McNaughton*, p. 133.
[19] Lord Deas in *R. v. Dingwall*. West and Walk, eds, *Daniel McNaughton*, pp. 10–11.
[20] Jeremy Dein and Jo Sidhu, 'Legal Insanity', in *Cases that Changed Our Lives*, ed. Ian McDougall (London, 2010), pp. 103–12.

CHAPTER 26

Necessity Knows No Law

Tried by a jury and five judges as well
What they have suffered it is hard to tell,
They have been condemned and sent back to gaol,
And quickly respited they need not bewail,
The Queen in her mercy can soon set them free
And so end this terrible tale of the sea.
Anon, 'The Terrible Tale of the Sea'

But to stand an' be still to the Birken'ead drill is a damn' tough bullet
to chew,
An' they done it, the Jollies – 'Er Majesty's Jollies – soldier an' sailor too!
Rudyard Kipling, 'Soldier An' Sailor Too'

A s the nineteenth century progressed, and despite the proliferation
of legislation as the source of law, leading cases and precedent had not
disappeared from the legal scene. When important legal issues arose, the
judges did not have to wait on parliament to act or ask a question: they could
establish or develop the law themselves. They rather enjoyed it.

Before 1848 the procedure had been an informal one. Criminal cases
in which a legal difficulty arose were 'reserved' for consideration by the
judiciary in London. The question of law was 'argued before the judges
by counsel, not in a court of justice but at Serjeants' Inn of which all the
judges were members'.[1] They could recommend a free pardon if they thought
the prisoner wrongly convicted in law. If not, the sentence was executed or
judgment was passed. Reasons for their decision were not given. In 1848 a
statutory body replaced this informal tribunal. It was called the Court for
Crown Cases Reserved, a quorum of which consisted of five judges. The
Lord Chief Justice had to be one, and the others were usually the most senior
judges of the Queen's Bench available. Should one of these judges insist,
the case would be referred to the whole body of fifteen. The court, having
heard argument, would reverse or confirm any judgment of the lower court,
or direct that court to give judgment. In short, it could give authoritative
rulings on the law where the law was thought uncertain. Any assize judge

---

[1] Stephen, *History of the Criminal Law*, I, p. 311.

or even the chairman of the quarter sessions could 'reserve' a point of law for determination by this august panel. But to do so there had first to be a conviction.

No more celebrated a case was to come before this tribunal – or rather before the five judges, as a result of jurisdictional gymnastics, reconstituting themselves as the new Queen's Bench Division – than that of *R. v. Dudley and Stephens* in 1884. The issue here was an important one: 'when hunger dictates, why not eat the cabin boy?' Was the 'custom of the sea' consonant with the precepts of the common law? Should necessity know no law?

On 5 July an elderly sea-going yacht, the aptly named *Mignonette*, en route to Australia had sunk off the coast of Africa. The three adult crewmen and Richard Parker, the seventeen-year-old ordinary seaman (often referred to as the 'cabin boy'), were adrift in a lifeboat for many days. Apart from two tins of turnips they had neither food nor fresh water, and were reliant on whatever rain fell or sustenance could be snatched from the sea. One turtle was all they could catch and it lasted them seven days. Eventually the three men were rescued and got back to Falmouth sixty-four days after their ordeal began. The boy, alas, did not. On being asked how they had survived so long in such conditions, Captain Tom Dudley and Mate Edwin Stephens freely admitted that they had killed, bled, and eaten the cabin boy, of course. They even provided written depositions to the shipping master in the customs house. Honesty was not to prove the best policy. Along with Edmund (or Ned) Brooks, the third adult member of the crew, they were duly arrested and charged with murder. They were bewildered by this turn of events and expressed amazement that they had no right to eat the boy, since survival cannibalism was an age-old 'custom of the sea'. Killing the boy first, however, rather than devouring him after he had died a natural death, was to prove the sticking point.

Maritime tradition was well established: in dire necessity occasioned by shipwreck, the survivors would draw lots and kill and devour the loser, although there is suspicion that the draw was often rigged as the lot had a tendency to fall on the obvious candidate: the youngest, the passenger, the black. W. S. Gilbert had even satirised it in his 'Yarn of the "Nancy Bell"', published in 1869, in which an old salt willingly told his tale:

> 'Twas in the good ship *Nancy Bell*
> That we sailed in the Indian sea,
> And there on a reef we come to grief
> Which has often occurred to me....
>
> For a month we'd neither wittles nor drink,
> Till a-hungry we did feel,

So we drawed a lot, and accordin' shot
The captain for our meal.

Either the lot thus described was very fair or the captain was unpopular.

In 1837 Edgar Allan Poe had published a prescient work in which art mirrored a later reality: 'The Narrative of Arthur Gordon Pym'. In that dark tale the shipwrecked castaways also catch a turtle, and most eerily the member of the crew finally killed and eaten was called none other than Richard Parker. Where the tale diverges from that of the *Mignonette* is that this Richard Parker was sacrificed after lots were drawn, a proposal which he himself had made.[2]

Contentiously in the case of the *Mignonette*, although Dudley had suggested such a course, lots had not been drawn, since Brooks refused to participate (although he did not decline to partake in the provender provided). Parker, they thought, was inevitably going to die, having imbibed sea-water which in those days was believed to be fatal. In a sense he had drawn his own lot. He was not, however, consulted, nor did he assent to his demise. On either 24 or 25 July Tom Dudley, with a small knife, put the boy out of his misery by cutting his throat. By killing Parker rather than letting him die naturally, Dudley secured his blood and so ensured his own survival and that of his crew. Rescue came a few days later in the shape of a German sailing barque, the *Moctezuma*, which came upon the three survivors as they were having their 'breakfast'. As the anxious castaways prayed that the barque had seen them, 'in a peculiarly unhappy expression, Dudley said that during this period, "their hearts were in their mouths"'.[3] When they were spotted and taken aboard, it was obvious to their rescuers that the men were in very poor shape, and would not have survived much longer. The sailor boy had served his purpose well.

Interest in the *Mignonette* was international. It was the fourth cannibal case to hit the news in 1884. The others were of Americans: William Owens who had consumed a dead companion; Alferd Packer, the Colorado Man-Eater,

---

2 Donald McCormick, *Blood on the Sea* (London, 1962), pp. 11 and 19, takes coincidence one step further when he states as a fact that during the voyage of the *Mignonette* Dudley was reading this very novel. For this we have only the author's word as he cites no source, but he invents dialogue and so mixes fantasy with reality that it may very well be a coincidence too far. In ironic homage, Yann Martel in his shipwreck narrative *Life of Pi*, names the tiger Richard Parker: the consumed becomes the carnivore.

3 Dudley's account, quoted in A. W. Brian Simpson, *Cannibalism and the Common Law* (Chicago, 1984), p. 69.

who had murdered his employers before eating them;[4] and Adolphus Washington Greely, whose heroic expedition to the Arctic had ended in disaster and 'survival cannibalism'. This grisly aftermath, having been covered up, was exposed by the *New York Times* in August.[5] On both sides of the Atlantic the public appetite for such forbidden flesh was being deliciously whetted.

Reaction in England to what occurred on the *Mignonette* was mixed. Initially there was distaste that Englishmen should resort to the cannibalism associated with savages, and unease over their failure to draw lots. As the facts emerged, and it became known that Dudley had proposed just such a procedure, the popular mood turned overwhelmingly in the survivors' favour. They were not the malevolent figures of the popular imagination, but upright and Christian men faced with a moral and physical dilemma of the most acute sort. Sympathy rather than revulsion was the instinct aroused. Richard Parker's own brother, another mariner, publicly shook their hands.

There was, however, official concern in the Home Office and among the judiciary about 'this very dreadful case'. If yielding to temptation were sanctioned, necessity might become 'the legal cloak for unbridled passion and atrocious crime'.[6] In addition, high Victorian moralism was outraged by the rather fluid morality of the high seas. What may have been permissible and even laudable in Classical times, such as Agamemnon sacrificing his daughter Iphigenia to ensure his fleet reached Troy, was seen in a different light under a Christian dispensation. Neither the amorality of Machiavelli nor the atheistic Utilitarianism of Bentham, would find succour within the common law. Nor would the most controversial and unsettling book of recent times, Darwin's *Origin of the Species*, published in 1859. It was already being expressly cited as authority for the proposition that the 'survival of the species' justified Parker's killing.[7] This case, tragic as all accepted it to be, provided the perfect opportunity for the custom of the sea to be regulated by the common law and for the sanctity of life to be exalted over the survival instinct.[8] Legality and Christian morality would be fused. Sympathy for the

---

4   F. Mazzulla and A. Muzzulla, *Al Packer: A Colorado Cannibal* (Denver, 1968), *passim*. Packer's first name was so spelt.

5   Simpson, *Cannibalism and the Common Law*, pp. 147–60.

6   *R. v. Dudley and Stephens*, 14 QBD (1884), 273.

7   Simpson, *Cannibalism and the Common Law*, pp. 81, 89.

8   An earlier instance of survival cannibalism, which had taken place after the sinking of the *Euxine* in 1874, had proved less expedient to prosecute. It would have been even more of a *cause celebre*: the crew of a ship owned by the Conservative MP for Plymouth, notorious for starving his men, had been reduced to eating each other. In another extraordinary coincidence Stephens had once served on the *Euxine*. *Ibid.*, pp. 31, 176–94.

plight of the mariners could be combined with an assertion of the rule of law. This could become a major leading case establishing an important legal principle, without the actors involved suffering unduly. Early on the Crown did not oppose bail, and, in an act virtually without precedent, men charged with a capital offence were set free.

The law had to decide whether necessity could be a defence. Did the old maxim 'necessity knows no law' hold?[9] By Victorian times legal opinion was divided. The law had largely followed the lead of Sir Matthew Hale, who held that, in peacetime, 'if a man be menaced with death, unless he will commit an act of treason, murder, or robbery, the fear of death doth not excuse him'.[10] But with law reform on the agenda, diverse views began to be heard. In 1839 the commissioners on Criminal Law advised that necessity might serve as an excuse or justification for homicide. Seven years later the Commissioners for Revising and Consolidating the Criminal Law decided not to support such a defence. They preferred to leave those who had acted under such circumstances 'to the mercy of the Crown'. In 1879 the Criminal Code Bill Commissioners were not prepared to suggest that necessity afforded a defence and left the question to be determined by 'applying the principles of law to the circumstances of the particular case'.[11] But there had been no English case.[12] The argument had been necessarily hypothetical. Could what had happened on the *Mignonette* be what the legal establishment had been waiting for?

There was a call to, and a blueprint for, action. In 1883, a year before the *Mignonette* went down, Sir James Fitzjames Stephen, a judge of the Queen's Bench Division, had published his magisterial and monumental three-volume *History of the Criminal Law in England*.[13] His analysis of the law was to have a fundamental impact on the course of events. He too noted

---

9   The English version of the Latin proverb *Necessitas non habet legem* has a long history, the phrase 'Neede hath no law' appearing in the fourteenth-century *Piers Plowman*. It still resonates among wags who nickname some judges 'Necessity', because they know no law.

10 Hale, *Pleas of the Crown*, I, p. 51.

11 David Perry, 'Death on the High Seas', in *Cases that Changed Our Lives*, ed. McDougall, p. 114.

12 In 1842 the American case of *US* v. *Holmes*, while providing no binding precedent, raised the same question: was necessity a defence to homicide? Sailors had jettisoned the surviving passengers from a badly leaking lifeboat. One was put on trial for manslaughter and convicted.

13 Coincidentally, when Stephen ruled in 1884 in *R.* v. *Price* that privately conducted cremation was not illegal, the Home Secretary, Sir William Harcourt, wryly observed that judges would soon approve of cannibalism as a means of disposing of the dead: Simpson, *Cannibalism and the Common Law*, p. 122.

that there was little authority on the subject of what he called compulsion by threats of injury or by necessity, and bemoaned the fact that – remarkably – it had seldom came before the courts and then only in the form of marital coercion. It was 'one of the curiosities of law', and a subject on which the law of England was 'so vague that if cases raising the question should ever occur the judges would practically be able to lay down any rule which they considered expedient'.[14] In his extensive researches he had found only two reported cases bearing on the issue, and they were both to do with duress, not necessity: one was of a man forced to fight for the Jacobites in 1745; the other of a man compelled to participate in machine-breaking. Stephen defended Hale's stance on this 'on the grounds of expediency', and applied it to *all* crimes without exception:

> Criminal law is itself a system of compulsion on the widest scale. It is a collection of threats of injury to life, liberty, and property if people do commit crimes. Are such threats to be withdrawn as soon as they are encountered by opposing threats? The law says to a man intending to commit murder, If you do it I will hang you. Is the law to withdraw its threat if someone else says, If you do not do it I will shoot you?

> Surely it is at the moment when temptation to crime is strongest that the law should speak most clearly and emphatically to the contrary. It is of course a misfortune that a man should be placed between two fires, but it would be a much greater misfortune for society at large if criminals could confer impunity upon their agents by threatening them with death or violence ... A wide door would be opened to collusion, and encouragement would be given to associations of malefactors ... No doubt the moral guilt of a person who commits a crime under compulsion is less than that of a person who commits it freely, but any effect which is thought proper may be given to this circumstance by a proportional mitigation of the offender's punishment.[15]

Here it was: legal expediency coupled with ameliorating clemency. It was a compelling conjunction, arguably equally applicable to compulsion by necessity, just waiting for the right case.

The judiciary decided that the matter of the *Mignonette* provided the perfect opportunity for them to act on Stephen's suggestion. They would rule on necessity. They would determine the legality of this 'law of the sea' – and it would apply to the land as well – with lots or without, and once and for all. To do so they needed a conviction, but would any jury convict these upright mariners who had faced such a dilemma? Public opinion as evidenced in Falmouth favoured the defendants. Even the family of this

---

[14] Stephen, *History of the Criminal Law*, II, p. 108.
[15] *Ibid.*, II, pp. 107f.

particular cabin boy had accepted his fate and cast no blame, other than expressing the caveat that they should not have killed him but let him die first. On a memorial tablet to the teenager, at the insistence of his elder brother, a telling verse from the Acts of the Apostles was to be inscribed: 'Lord, lay not this sin to their charge' (Acts 7. 60). Throughout England many people considered the accused to be little less than heroes who had endured and survived a terrible ordeal.

In the eyes of the law, guilt seemed clear since the facts were incontrovertible and had been admitted by the defendants. However, their depositions had not been made with a view to criminal proceedings. They could be challenged. An eyewitness was needed, and all three survivors had been charged. The Crown decided to offer no evidence against Brooks and make him instead a prosecution witness. The two remaining defendants, Dudley and Stephens, were sent to the Exeter assize where their trial would begin on Saturday 1 November 1884 before Baron Huddleston. Huddleston, the son of a merchant captain, was a mediocre judge, but tractable, and ideal for ensuring the right conclusion to the case: a conviction. That was not quite what he achieved.

The first legal hurdle for the prosecution to surmount was the grand jury, all local worthies, who would determine if there was sufficient evidence to put the defendants on trial. In principle the grand jury could exercise independent judgment and either throw out the indictment for murder completely, or reduce it to manslaughter. Either recourse would stymie the opportunity of making the *Mignonette* affair into a leading case. Huddleston was determined to ensure that that did not happen. Without brooking argument from the barristers present, in his charge – or lecture – to the jury, Huddleston surveyed the law on the matter and directed them that necessity was no defence to murder. He also indicated that no harm would ultimately befall the seamen. The grand jury found a true bill. The defendants could be indicted.[16] The trial proper could then begin on the following Monday, again before Huddleston, but this time with a 'petty' or trial jury deciding on guilt or innocence.

This gave rise to the second problem. The judiciary wanted a definitive judgment on necessity. As a result of section 3 of the Judicature Act of 1873, the Court of Queen's Bench had been abolished as of 1876. It, and all the assize courts, were fused into a single institution known as the High Court. By section 40 of the act, the High Court could exercise the powers of the

---

[16] The grand jury was abolished, with some exceptions, in 1933, the surviving instances disappearing in 1948. It persists in the United States to this day.

former Court for Crown Cases Reserved by sitting as a bench of five judges to determine difficult points of criminal law and to give binding rulings. For it to do so a conviction was necessary, but in this case it was anything but certain that the jury would oblige. Petty juries were socially less elevated, and could be less pliant, than grand juries. They might not play the game.

At the start of the trial, counsel for the Crown opened his case before the jury by rehearsing the same arguments as Huddleston had deployed before the grand jury two days previously. He also raised, swiftly to dismiss, another possible defence: that of temporary insanity under the M'Naughten Rules. Defence council, who disagreed with this analysis of the law, could not be prevented from arguing in due course before the jury, that necessity was a defence to murder. Huddleston, however, would then have to tell the jury that this defence riposte was nonsense and that it was their duty to convict. But that would not have been the end of the matter. Such a legal ruling could not have guaranteed a conviction. A judge could not order a jury to find as he wanted. Jurors could be persuaded to acquit even the manifestly guilty in a sympathetic case such as this. More likely they would compromise by finding the men guilty, not of murder, but of manslaughter. This too would be a forensic disaster.

Consequently, the trial judge proposed to circumvent what would have been very risky proceedings by reviving an obsolete procedure known as a 'special verdict'.[17] All moral responsibility would be taken out of the hands of the jurors. Their consciences would be unperturbed. They would be relieved of the invidious task of bringing in a verdict of guilt or innocence on these men. They would not have to endure hearing the dread words of the death sentence Huddlestone would have to pass. Instead, they could be told merely to determine the bare facts (which were not in dispute) and could leave it to the judiciary to determine, upon these facts, the legal consequences for the unhappy defendants. Huddlestone would then immediately refer the matter to a higher tribunal to decide if he had got the law on necessity right or wrong. This tribunal could rule authoritatively on the legality of the custom of the sea.

After the prosecution evidence had been called, the judge invited such a special verdict from the jury, the only viable alternative, he explained, being a verdict of guilty. For their convenience he had even produced a draft special

---

17   Stephen, *History of the Criminal Law*, I, p. 311, observed that by 1883 special verdicts had 'gone almost entirely out of use, having been superceded by the establishment of … the Court for Crown Cases Reserved'. The last time it had been used was almost a hundred years before.

verdict for them. The jury acquiesced, and duly delivered such a verdict, delineating the facts as they had been artfully construed by Huddlestone. They even recommended mercy for men who did not yet need it. Bizarrely the case was then adjourned until 4 December to the judge's rooms in the newly constructed Royal Courts of Justice. This gothic fantasy in the Strand had been built as the prime seat of justice to provide a suitably splendid and permanent home for the courts, which in 1826 had been displaced from the venerated but antiquated Westminster Hall and consigned to inadequate accommodation nearby.

But to which higher court could the *Mignonette Case* be sent for final resolution? Legal contortions over jurisdiction and procedure arose out of the use of the archaic special verdict. In days gone by, when a special verdict was recorded, the case could be moved from the assize court to the senior and distinct Court of the Queen's (or the King's) Bench for a determination of the law to be made. The Queen's Bench no longer existed. The new High Court, acting as the Court for Crown Cases Reserved, required a conviction. In this case there was none. Where was the matter to go for resolution? Finally it was decided that Baron Huddleston should call in four other senior judges to sit with him in the adjourned assizes, which would take place in London, not Exeter, where the judges were not sitting as commissioners of assize but as judges of the Queen's Bench Division, in a trial the first part of which neither they, nor the Lord Chief Justice, then presiding, had attended.[18] By this ingenious if convoluted device, it was hoped, the judges would have the authority to establish the law on necessity. Having done so they would then apply their findings to the facts of this case. This procedure too was questionable in the extreme. In effect, the judges were being called upon to be both jury and judge, to convict the men of murder and to sentence them to death. It was all very odd and confused, and the judges got themselves in a terrible twist in the course of what has rightly been described as an 'unsavoury manipulation of the procedures',[19] but in such manner was a fundamental point of law established.

On the 4 December the matter of the *Mignonette* was brought before the five judges sitting in the court of Lord Coleridge, Chief Justice of England, in the Royal Courts of Justice. Five days later, after legal argument and an adjournment, Coleridge gave what was more of a sermon on, and an encomium of, the English sense of good behaviour, than an authoritative judgment based on clear reasoning and expressed principle. It was raptur-

---

[18] Simpson, *Cannibalism and the Common Law*, pp. 219–23.

[19] *Ibid.*, p. 237.

ously received at the time as being 'a lucid exposition of the law and an eloquent statement of the code of morality' for those whose lives are imperilled. More recently it has been castigated as 'a miserable failure of judicial nerve'.[20] Coleridge's words, however, had resonance:

> To preserve one's own life is generally speaking a duty, but it may be the plainest and highest duty to sacrifice it. War is full of instances in which it is a man's duty not to live, but to die. The duty, in case of shipwreck, of a captain to his crew, of the crew to the passengers, of soldiers to woman and children, as in the noble case of the *Birkenhead*; these duties impose on men the moral necessity, not of the preservation, but of the sacrifice of their lives for others, from which in no country, least of all, it is to be hoped, in England, will men ever shrink.

The drawing of lots – the casting of responsibility onto providence – would not, and should not, avert guilt. In a Christian country – England especially – self-sacrifice should always come before the sacrifice of others. It was the epitome of Victorian moralism: women and children first. The exemplar of this was not the yacht *Mignonette* but the troopship *Birkenhead*. This early ironclad had struck a rock and gone down off Cape Town in 1852. There were not enough lifeboats for all aboard. The soldiers and sailors, far from pushing the more vulnerable into the sea, let alone eating them, had stood to attention as the woman and children took their places in the boats. Not a man had tried to join them, and most of the men had been lost to the sea or sharks. The band playing on as the *Titanic* went down epitomised the same noble spirit of 'the Birkenhead Drill'.[21]

This was the ideal, and the ideal was to be upheld. Lord Coleridge acknowledged that 'we are often compelled to set up standards we cannot reach ourselves, and to lay down rules which we could not ourselves satisfy'. If the court could not quite make self-sacrifice a legal duty, it could make sacrificing others a crime. The judges duly determined that the common law overrode the custom of the sea, and that the slaughtering, butchering, and eating of cabin boys, even when peckish, was murder. Dudley and Stephens were adjudged guilty of murder and were condemned to die. It is the only

---

20   *OHLE*, XIII, p. 277.

21   This was the British way, so different from that of the French and of the Americans! In 1816 the French frigate *Medusa* had been wrecked en route to Senegal. The captain and senior officers, far from sacrificing themselves, made off in the boats, abandoning one hundred and fifty other survivors to a near-certain fate adrift on a raft. Even with resorting to cannibalism only fifteen of those abandoned survived. Their desperate lot was immortalised by Gericault. As a shocking adjunct to *U.S.* v. *Holmes*, women and children had been abandoned on the sinking ship as the captain and crew took to the lifeboats.

time that a death sentence has been passed in the Royal Courts of Justice.[22] It was also a dread formality, as the judiciary knew full well that the defendants would be reprieved through an act of executive clemency.

So the law, fashioned in this contrived manner, remains to this day. Necessity is no defence to murder (though it might well be mitigation). The fundamental legal principle is that no one should be allowed to adjudge his own life better than that of another and then be the executioner as well. The end cannot justify the means.[23] Let British cabin boys rejoice! On 12 December the sentence imposed on Dudley and Stephens was, however, commuted to six months' imprisonment, so their rejoicing should be restrained. And in future, reticence rather than candour would be the custom of the sea.

---

[22] David Perry, 'Death on the High Seas', in *Cases that Changed Our Lives*, ed. McDougall, p. 116.

[23] *R. v. Howe* [1987] 1 AC 417; *Re A (Children) (Conjoined Twins: Surgical Separation)* [2001] 2 WLR 480.

CHAPTER 27

The Apollo of the Bar: Edward Marshall Hall

The great lesson he taught us throughout his long and arduous life at the Bar was the faculty of not appearing to believe in one's case, but of actually believing in it.   Sir Ernest Wild (Bowker, *Behind the Bar*)

The advocate must acquire the art of being passionate with detachment and persuasive without belief.... There is no lawyer so ineffectual as one who is passionately convinced of his client's innocence.... Nothing is left of Sir Edward but a list of 'Notable Trials' and a few anecdotes about his outrageous way with an air-cushion.
John Mortimer, *Clinging to the Wreckage*

PARLIAMENTARY legislation in the nineteenth century continued the reform of the criminal law. Today no courtroom drama is complete without the defence barrister vehemently addressing the jury on his client's behalf. It is the culminating point of the defence, cross-examination merely providing the material for the speech. Yet until 1836, except in treason trials, only the prosecution had this privilege, not the defence. In that year the Prisoners' Counsel Act specifically authorised defence barristers to address the jury. Defendants could not yet give evidence under oath in their own defence, and barristers, allowed at last to speak on their behalf, were in effect their mouthpieces. The adversarial system as we know it was fully formed.

This change allowed for the inexorable rise of defence barristers, who began to dominate the court room in all sorts of cases from the venial to the most vile. The defence speech was to be the highlight of the case, and required flamboyance and theatricality. Advocacy was an art, but it was also an act. The barrister as thespian was emerging. With the advent of the popular press such men would become celebrities. The role was tailor-made for a showman, and none mastered it better than the tall, handsome young Rugby and Cambridge man, Edward Marshall Hall, who in 1882 was called to the Bar at the Inner Temple. He benefited from a striking figure, classical features, an engaging demeanour, and a willingness to take lessons in stage-craft from none other than the leading actor of Victorian England, Henry Irving, himself. Marshall Hall looked, and would soon sound, the part. He had the gifts of both empathy and understanding. He also had an intimate knowledge of medicine and of firearms – invaluable attributes when cross-examining in many a murder case.

While Erskine and Brougham were fêted during their lifetimes, Marshall Hall was perhaps the first celebrity barrister, a beneficiary of the newspaper age, a careful manager, even manipulator, of the media. Although he courted publicity and was undoubtedly a show-off, his motives should not be misconstrued. Before the introduction of the first form of 'legal aid' provided by the 1903 Poor Prisoners' Defence Act, funding for the defence was non-existent. After the act it was still inadequate. If defendants could not fund their own defence personally, there were few means of recourse open to them. They had to rely on public donations, the amount of which would depend in large part on their personal attractiveness, or on doing a deal with a newspaper. Marshall Hall, who campaigned all his professional life for the appointment of public defenders, exploited the latter to the full. It was to be a symbiotic relationship. Marshall Hall was God's gift to the tabloids, newly sprung up and jostling each other for prime position. He got money out of them to pay for his cases and they got copy out of him, covering his trials in detail and making him famous.

He was an excellent cross-examiner, but his forte was the speech to the jury. Nowadays his manner and tactics would seem completely over the top, just as would the sort of melodramatic stage-acting his contemporaries adored. But in his day, Marshall Hall could draw the crowds and wow the jury as no other. He was entertaining, even captivating. He would sweep into court with his robes flowing and take his seat. A junior clerk always in attendance would lay out his 'armoury' before the great man, an armoury consisting of an adjustable footstool, an instrument case for compass, ruler and magnifying glass, an assortment of coloured pencils, an air cushion and a throat spray. The latter two were deployed with disruptive effect as Marshall Hall would inflate the cushion or noisily inhale from his spray always, it seemed, at critical moments.[1] All eyes would turn on him. His mesmeric qualities were well described by Norman Birkett, junior counsel for the Crown in what was known as the *Green Bicycle Case* of 1920:

> I shall always remember the moment when Marshall Hall came into court ... He brought with him a strange magnetic quality that made itself felt in every part of the court. The spectators stirred with excitement at the sight of the man whose name was at that time a household word, and a faint murmur ran from floor to gallery ... every eye was fixed upon him. He was a very handsome man, with noble head and a most expressive face.... When he addressed

---

[1]   *Ibid.*, p. 230.

the judge it was seen that to his great good looks and majestic bearing there
had been added perhaps the greatest gift of all in the armoury of an advocate
– a most beautiful speaking voice.[2]

While some of his clients may have got away with murder, Marshall Hall
could get away with more or less anything. 'He had the rare gift of using
true pathos in his advocacy', noted Birkett, and was the only advocate he
'ever saw who wept before the jury and allowed the tears to stream down
his cheeks as he spoke.'[3] His trademark during the course of a speech was to
stand tall and erect, extending his long arms to emulate the scales of justice,
slowly tipping them as he spoke, tipping them towards an acquittal.[4] To pull
that off without exciting mirth was some achievement. Even noisily inflating
an air-cushion during prosecution counsel's speech seemed in him unexcep-
tionable. Juries adored him, as did the press. His cases were lavishly covered
and eagerly devoured. As time went on he developed a reputation for being
invincible, so that he started every trial with the public expectation that he
would pull off the impossible. He usually did.

For the first part of his career Marshall Hall could make powerful speeches
on behalf of his clients, but he could not call them to give sworn evidence
nor expose them to cross-examination. The Criminal Evidence Act of 1898
changed all that, by bringing in another crucial reform. The accused were
for the first time allowed to give evidence on oath as part of their defence.
From now on barristers would have to advise their clients to maintain their
right of silence or expose themselves to the scrutiny of the court. In murder
cases such a decision was a matter of life or death. Many a barrister kept to
the old ways, the new being fraught with risk. Risks were something that
Marshall Hall was prepared to take.

Great thespian he may have been, but Marshall Hall could also be a great
impresario. His tactic was to set a scene in which his client could star. He did
so by a combination of incisive cross-examination of prosecution witnesses,
by making an opening speech outlining his case, by calling defence witnesses
before the defendant gave evidence, and by dramatic court room 'demonstra-
tions'. One of the most effective of these was in the 1908 *Yarmouth Murder
Case*, when he and his solicitor re-enacted before the jury how a revolver
could go off accidentally during a drunken struggle.[5] Having set the scene,

---

2   Birkett, *Six Great Advocates*, p. 12.
3   *Ibid.*, p. 14.
4   First performed in the *Yarmouth Murder Case*: Edward Marjoribanks, *The Life of
    Edward Marshall Hall* (London, 1929), p. 273.
5   Bowker, *Behind the Bar*, p. 32.

15. Edward Marshall Hall, dapper and debonair, the darling of the popular press.

he directed the acting, and under his direction many an accused gave the performances of their lives, so saving them. One nearly did not, because he could not resist ham acting.

His name was Robert Wood. In 1907 he was the accused in what became known as the *Camden Town Murder*, one of the great unsolved cases of the Edwardian era. Wood was charged with having murdered Emily Dimmock, a prostitute who went by the working name of Phyllis. Her body had been found in her lodgings: her throat had been cut. Wood, an associate of hers, was soon arrested and charged. Marshall Hall was briefed for the defence.

The trial began on 12 December in the newly constructed building housing the Central Criminal Court as the Old Bailey was officially known. It was a sensation, and was covered in enormous detail by the press. Marshall Hall was on his best form. He attacked the veracity and accuracy of the Crown's witnesses. He succeeded in casting serious doubt on those who had identified Wood as the man seen near the scene at the time of the murder. But now he had a crucial decision to make. Should his client give evidence, as now he could, or stay silent? Few prisoners had taken the stand in murder trials before, and none had done so successfully in the Old Bailey. All had gone to the gallows. The legal consensus was that silence was the better part of valour.

Not for Marshall Hall, at least not after reflection. Initially he was unequivocally opposed to Wood taking the stand. It was a young junior barrister called Wellesley Orr, who had done some work on the case, who persuaded him that if Wood did not take the stand he would hang. Marshall Hall was prepared to take good advice no matter whence it came. Nonetheless it was a daring move to call Wood, all the more so when his client's demeanour was taken into account. He was an effete artist, and an associate of the avant-garde painter Walter Sickert, who in turn was to capitalise on his friend's discomfiture by depicting the London *demi-monde* in a series of lurid paintings called 'The Camden Town Murder'. Wood was too flamboyant for his own good, and would come across as a poseur. Marshall Hall had observed in another case that 'vanity is an inherent disease in murderers and, thank God, it has hanged most of them.'[6] It almost hanged Wood.

During the trial he had sat languidly in the dock and hardly 'raised his chin from the long fingers on which it rested'. On the stand he was a very bad witness. He began disastrously. Marshall Hall started with a direct question that got to the heart of the matter – 'Did you kill Emily Dimmock?' This elicited not a determined 'No', but a smile. The question was repeated. So was the smile. Marshall Hall told him he must 'answer straight'. This at

6   Marjoribanks, *The Life of Edward Marshall Hall*, p. 48.

least got a reply: 'I mean it is ridiculous.' Wood refused to take Marshall Hall seriously, answering the most basic questions in a high-pitched tone of hauteur. To others he indulged in theatricality or broke into overblown prose. He was an amateur, a ham. He was also on trial for his life.

By contrast, Marshall Hall was a pro. He too was theatrical, he too could be dramatic, but he could modulate his tone, and hold his audience. He spoke directly to the jury, looking them in the eyes, convincing them of his sincerity:'I am confident as an advocate', he said 'that there is not one single one of you, much less all twelve of you, who dares to say this man in the dock murdered Emily Dimmock.' He then quietly expressed mild disapproval of the procedure in those days which gave the prosecution the first and last word. Then he burst out in dramatic fury: 'I say again I want a verdict of not guilty and nothing else, a verdict of not guilty, to kill this charge so that none of the lying witnesses can galvanise it hence into any semblance of life.' The *Daily Mail* reflected on what it termed the performance of his career: Marshall Hall had conducted the defence with 'strenuous and impetuous power … constructing his scheme of evidence with wonderful acuteness, building up his material in really faultless order, and with the cumulative effect of the most skilful dramatist.' It was a 'speech whose chief appeal was dignity.… He has appealed on dual grounds – to hearts, to intelligence. He has captured both.'[7] This is the essence of advocacy. More likely Marshall Hall's speech, but quite possibly his own demeanour, saved Wood from the gallows. The jury could not believe that such a prissy man could commit so savage a crime.

The 'not guilty' verdict was greeted by the expectant crowd gathered outside the Old Bailey with the sort of mawkish mania associated with the death of Princess Diana in our own day: 'Women shrieked and became hysterical. Several on the edge of the crowd fell to the ground, and were borne away fainting into neighbouring shops and houses, and then the crowd gave itself to an orgy of cheering.'[8] Cases such as the *Camden Town Murder* could guarantee a major circulation boost for the popular press. Victorians and Edwardians, reclining on their antimacassars, hungered for titillating excitement and racy tales. The genre of detective fiction had already taken off, supplementing the horror stories of an earlier generation. But this was real life detection and real life horror. The guilty pleasure!

Knighted in 1917, Sir Edward Marshall Hall continued in his role as a barrister almost until his death in 1927. In his honour the flag over the Inner

---

7　*Ibid.*, p. 262.
8　*Ibid.*, p. 259.

Temple was flown at half-mast. His chambers at No. 3 Temple Gardens 'felt strangely empty and stilled.... Everything appeared so subdued after the tempestuous presence of Marshall Hall had gone.'[9] His triumphs may have been ephemeral, his impact on the law non-existent. His legacy lies in the public perception of what a great barrister should be.

9   Bowker, *Behind the Bar*, p. 154.

PART IV

THE RULE OF LAW
1907–2014

CHAPTER 28

'The Martyrdom of Adolph Beck' and the Creation of the Court of Criminal Appeal

The Law is the true embodiment
Of everything that's excellent
It has no kind of fault or flaw.
And I, my Lords, embody the Law.

W. S. Gilbert, *Iolanthe*

THE MORE the newspapers covered trials, the more their reporters took an interest in the cases they covered and developed a degree of forensic expertise. Something was to happen that had never happened before. Trials, and the investigations behind them, were put under public scrutiny. Some of the latter seemed to show the hand of Inspector Lestrade more than that of Sherlock Holmes. The prurient and pugnacious upstarts of the press were straining at the leash to savage the system of justice. Doubts about it were creeping in. Perhaps it was not infallible; perhaps mistakes could be made; perhaps the innocent were sometimes convicted; perhaps executive review would prove inadequate; perhaps – perish the thought – an innocent could be hanged.

It was not just the plebeian police who were subjected to rough handling. The exalted legal process itself, and even the words and actions of the judiciary, fell under the spotlight of an investigative and demotic press, devoid of due deference. Judicial decisions were scrutinised and even criticised, and potential miscarriages of justice, thought virtually impossible in what was considered to be a near-perfect legal system, became front page news. These developments initially damaged, but ultimately sustained the reputation of the courts and of trial by jury. A legal system that believes itself perfect is doomed to disappoint, but one that is capable of admitting mistakes, and is willing to incorporate safeguards, ensures it has the flexibility to survive and flourish. One press campaign would prove decisive. Instigated by the recently created tabloid, The *Daily Mail*, it was encouraged by Sir Arthur Conan Doyle, the creator of the doyen of detectives, and an amateur sleuth himself. It was to prove so effective that it helped bring about the necessary change and create a judicial institution designed to rectify errors. The campaign centred on the case of Adolph Beck, a convicted fraudster.

In 1877 a rogue calling himself 'John Smith' – actually a Joseph Meyer – had been imprisoned for swindling women out of their money and jewellery. In a classic of the genre, the charming cad had done so by posing as an aristocrat, assuming the portentous but entirely fictitious title, Lord Wilton de Willoughby. The victorious prosecuting counsel had been one Forrest Fulton. Eighteen years later 'Lord Willoughby' was back in action, duping further victims out of their property. Ten of them identified a Norwegian called Adolph Beck as the miscreant, although several others were equally sure he was not. A handwriting expert called Gurin confirmed that the incriminating documents in 1895 were in Beck's disguised hand. He was also of the opinion that the same hand was responsible for the exhibits in 1877. This latter evidence was not to be adduced when Beck was tried at the Old Bailey in March 1896. 'Smith's' erstwhile prosecutor was to be Beck's judge: Sir Forrest Fulton, by then the Common Serjeant.[1] When defence council tried to elicit from Gurin the fact that the exhibits from 1877 (when Beck was demonstrably in Peru) were in the same hand as those written in 1895 (attributed to Beck), the judge ruled that no mention of this 'collateral matter' should be made to the jury. The mainstay of the defence was smashed. The prosecution witnesses were consistent and confident, and their evidence cumulative and conclusive. Beck was identified as the swindler by an overwhelming number of independent victims whose evidence had apparently been corroborated by expert handwriting evidence. Guilt could hardly have been clearer. Beck was convicted within a few minutes, and imprisoned for seven years.[2]

Desperate to prove his innocence, he tried to get his conviction reopened. Criminal appeals on points of law were permitted but not on points of fact. A verdict could not be reversed. All Beck's solicitor could do was to petition the Home Office repeatedly for a re-examination of the case in the hope of obtaining a royal pardon. This was known as executive review. In 1845 the House of Lords had appointed a committee to enquire into the desirability of broadening appellate review. All of the judges had echoed the views of Baron Parke when he had given evidence before it: errors in the administration of criminal law were very rare; for such as did occur a pardon was

---

[1]   The most senior judge, after the Recorder of London, in the Central Criminal Court. In 1900 Sir Forrest Fulton would be promoted to the senior post.

[2]   E. R. Watson, *Trial of Adolph Beck* (Edinburgh, 1924), pp. 115–56.

adequate; an appellate process would be expensive, and the delay occasioned would impair the deterrent effect of swift and decisive justice.[3] The irrationality of this irked some. Stephen observed that 'to pardon a man on the ground of his innocence is in itself, to say the least, an exceedingly clumsy mode of procedure'.[4]

Pardons were extremely hard to get and none was forthcoming for Beck. Despite the fact that it could be shown that he was in South America when 'Smith' was convicted in 1877, and that an assiduous government clerk, tasked with investigating these petitions, had discovered from prison records that 'Smith' was Jewish and circumcised and that Beck was neither, nothing was done to secure the latter's release. He served his sentence, was set free in 1901, only to be re-arrested for like offences in April 1904 when several other victims – encouraged by the police – identified him as 'Willoughby'. The same handwriting expert confirmed their evidence. Once again he was tried at the Old Bailey and convicted. The trial judge, Mr Justice Grantham, had misgivings and respited the sentence.

The *Daily Mail* campaigned on his behalf. One of its reporters, George Sims, having convinced himself of Beck's innocence, wrote many articles pointing out the obvious.[5] *The Daily Telegraph* followed suit, talking of a conspiracy, censuring the Home Office, and advocating the creation of a court for criminal appeals. Yet it was only when 'Smith' was caught red-handed in July 1904 while Beck was still in prison, and confessed to the other crimes, that the latter's innocence, despite the ostensible strength of the evidence, was undeniable. The handwriting expert retracted. The identifying witnesses had all been mistaken. A blatant miscarriage of justice had taken place. Beck was released on 19 July, and was later awarded £5000 in compensation.

Rarely has a miscarriage of justice case had greater impact. Twice Beck had been wrongfully convicted on seemingly unimpeachable evidence. Outrage grew into a demand for legal reform. It was little assuaged by the report of a committee of enquiry set up to investigate – or to camouflage. It largely exonerated Sir Forrest Fulton (who was, in fact, very much at fault), the prosecutor and the police (both of whom bore part of the blame). It attributed the fiasco to Home Office underlings and the prison department. The committee had considered that taking the evidence of judges and counsel was 'a very anxious and difficult part of our inquiry', as both the honour of

---

3 Langbein, Lerner and Smith, *History of the Common Law*, p. 704.
4 Stephen, *History of the Criminal Law*, I, p. 313.
5 Later reproduced in a pamphlet entitled 'The Martyrdom of Adolf Beck'.

the Bar and the Bench had been besmirched. They were anxious that a judge of the status of the Recorder of London should not be subject to questioning in the form of cross-examination. The Recorder glibly lied his way out of embarrassment, leaving lesser mortals to take the fall.[6] The enquiry nonetheless knew that 'the man in the street', after reading the strictures of Mr Sims, needed to be enlightened 'as to how the vaunted integrity of the profession had so contrived matters that an innocent man was twice convicted, without his real defence ever being put before a jury'. It was a Herculean task and one quite beyond their power.

Beck's was not the only notorious case to come to public attention. Conan Doyle, in articles in *The Daily Telegraph,* had also championed the Anglo-Indian solicitor, George Edalji, a Parsi clergyman's son. In 1903 Edalji was another victim of a manifest miscarriage of justice. Short-sighted and cerebral, he was supposed to have roamed the Staffordshire countryside at night maiming horses. He had no motive. He had an alibi. He was an improbable suspect. Yet, as an outsider in a close-knit community, and as a victim of racial stereotyping, he was first accused in an anonymous letter and later found guilty in court. Ten thousand people, including lawyers, petitioned for his exoneration, but they had no effect on the Home Office. The authorities dismissed the possibility that an innocent man had been convicted, preferring instead to sustain a travesty of justice. In the interests of justice, the heavens might have been allowed to fall, but the integrity of the English criminal justice system could never be called into question. It took until 1907 for Edalji to receive a pardon, a pardon bestowed grudgingly.[7]

Fuelled by cases such as these, brought to prominence by the press, public disquiet about the integrity of the criminal justice system grew, and calls for structural reform got louder. Executive review was plainly inadequate. An appellate court was needed. The judiciary on the whole did not agree, and Lord Alverstone, the Lord Chief Justice, was a staunch opponent of its creation. Finally, reluctantly, in 1907 parliament intervened and the Court of

---

6   Watson, *Trial of Adolph Beck*, pp. 45, 247–96. In 1924 Watson himself was refused access to Home Office files about the case.

7   Gordon Weaver, *Conan Doyle and the Parson's Son* (London, 2006); Rosemary Pattenden, *English Criminal Appeals 1844–1994* (Oxford, 1996), pp. 27–34. Conan Doyle was to champion yet another 'alien' who was the victim of a shocking miscarriage of justice. In 1909, in Glasgow, Oscar Slater, a German Jew, was convicted of murder, again on risible identification evidence. He was sentenced to death but reprieved. Conan Doyle led the campaign to clear him. Final vindication came in 1928, when the Scottish Court of Criminal Appeal quashed the conviction: William Roughead, *Trial of Oscar Slater*, 4th edn (Edinburgh, 1950).

Criminal Appeal was created to hear appeals against conviction and sentence, not just on the law but on fact and on evidence. It would sit in the Royal Courts of Justice, upon the roof of which stood those divinely inspired exemplars of law-giving and justice: Moses and Alfred.

The 1873 Judicature Act had abolished all the old central courts and created the Supreme Court of Judicature, consisting of the Court of Appeal for civil cases, and the High Court of Justice, organised initially into five divisions: the Queen's Bench, the Common Pleas, the Exchequer, the Chancery and Probate, and the Divorce and Admiralty. In 1881 the first three were merged into the Queen's Bench Division. Each of the Divisions exercised both legal and equitable jurisdiction, and where there was conflict between the common law and equity, equity prevailed. To them was now added a Court of Criminal Appeal (CCA) although technically it was not part of the Supreme Court of Judicature.[8]

Despite the opposition of the bulk of judiciary to the creation of a CCA, and despite their denial of the need for one, the legal system had been forced to admit, in deed if not in word, that it was, after all, fallible in criminal matters, and verdicts could be wrong, not just in law, but in fact. For the first time those convicted of criminal offences had a right of appeal. Far from being a sign of weakness, this new court showed English law was strong enough to acknowledge and deal with its mistakes. Judicial adherence to the belief in the infallibility of English justice, and distaste for gainsaying the verdicts of juries and for criticising the sentences passed by judges, persisted, however, and limited the effectiveness of the CCA for many years to come. Fears that the new court would be inundated with cases proved alarmist.[9]

Miscarriages, of course, could still take place, whatever the safeguards. This was particularly serious in capital cases, where the condemned prisoner would be dispatched within three weeks of conviction, beyond the reach of any terrestrial court. Medieval judges had looked to God for the final definitive word. In more modern times this infallibility was ascribed to the jury. But once police incompetence or impropriety, procedural imperfections, and jurors' fallibility were admitted, the imposition of the ultimate sanction was thrown into doubt. It was to be another sixty years, and partly as a result of being forced to face the possibility that the innocent had been hanged,

8   *OHLE*, XI, p. 805.
9   *Ibid.*, p. 808; XIII, pp. 136f; Pattenden, *English Criminal Appeals*, p. 22.

before parliament abolished the death penalty for good and all. Courts and juries can and do still make mistakes, but no longer fatal ones.

Appeals were not restricted to the CCA, or to criminal or civil matters. When liberty was at stake in wartime there was a right of appeal against detention, even if there was no right to representation.

CHAPTER 29

Liberty Sacrificed to Security

Bad laws are the worst sort of tyranny.
Edmund Burke, speech at Bristol, 1780

The legal system we have and the rule of law are far more responsible for our traditional liberties than any system of one man one vote. Any country or Government which wants to proceed towards tyranny starts to undermine legal rights and undermine the law.
Margaret Thatcher, speech at the Conservative Party conference, 1966

HISTORICALLY, as during the war with revolutionary France, parliament has suspended *habeas corpus* to allow for executive detention. More recently the preference has been to pass emergency powers explicitly authorising it. In 1915, Regulation 14B was brought in under powers delegated to the privy council under the Defence of the Realm Act 1914 (DORA), in response to the perceived threat of pro-German collaborators within the populace. Arthur Zadig, of German birth but a naturalised British subject, was one of those so detained. He sought *habeas corpus* and challenged the very validity of the regulation. DORA contained nothing about detention and those who voted for it could not have envisaged anything as exceptional as Regulation 14B being introduced. *R. v. Halliday ex parte Zadig* (Halliday being his detention-camp commandant) made its way to the highest court in the land, the judicial committee of the House of Lords, where it was argued in March 1917. The issue was simple: should major changes in the constitution be authorised solely by parliament, or should the executive be allowed to make such changes by delegated legislation? Zadig argued that 14B was *ultra vires* – in excess of executive power – and that to uphold the validity of the Order in Council which had introduced the regulation would be to undermine the sovereignty of parliament. Five judges in the King's Bench Division – including the recently appointed Mr Justice Atkin – and three in the Court of Appeal had rejected this argument. So too did four out of the five judges in the Lords. The lonely dissenter was the dour Scots Presbyterian, Lord Shaw of Dunfermline, who stated that parliament had never sanctioned 'such a violent exercise in arbitrary power'. The *Law Times*, in what might be described as an extraordinary tirade, described his speech as 'an extraordinary tirade on the subject of what he calls British Liberty'. Zadig remained imprisoned. Liberty remained fettered.[1]

During the Second World War nearly two thousand Nazi and Fascist sympathisers as well as 'enemy aliens', and even those with 'hostile associations', were interned under Regulation 18B issued in pursuance of the Emergency Powers (Defence) Acts of 1939 and 1940 which, unlike DORA, explicitly authorised the making of regulations for detention and otherwise restricting civil liberties. Regulation 18B empowered the Home Secretary to detain indefinitely anyone whom he had reasonable cause to believe to be 'of hostile origin or associations', and over whom control had to be exercised in the interests of national security. Herbert Morrison, as Home Secretary throughout most of the war, ruthlessly wielded what he himself considered to be a 'terrible power', while Churchill, initially an enthusiastic apologist for the large-scale incarceration of 'enemy aliens and suspect persons', came – even in the midst of war – to have severe misgivings about this gross violation of civil liberty.

> The power of the executive to cast a man into prison without formulating any charge known to the law, and particularly to deny him the judgment of his peers, is in the highest degree odious and the foundation of all totalitarian government, whether Nazi or Communist.[2]

Odious or not, it was deployed repeatedly, and more and more were drawn into its net.

Internees were not charged with any offence. They were not put on trial. They were, however, allowed an appeal to the Home Office Advisory Committee, under the chairmanship of Norman Birkett KC, the foremost trial advocate of his generation. He was appointed in September 1939 despite fears that he 'would be inclined to take too liberal a view and give the aliens, rather than the country, the benefit of the doubt in cases where nothing very definite can be proved'. The fears were misguided as Birkett assured Sir John Anderson, the then Home Secretary, that any remaining doubt would be 'resolved in favour of the country and against the individual'. He recognised the importance of the work but bemoaned in equal measure the lack of remuneration and, once mass internment came in, the increasing and 'grievous' delays as a result of which 'many people are in prison this Christmas [1940] who have been there since last May, without any trial or

---

[1]   A. W. Brian Simpson, *In the Highest Degree Odious: Detention without Trial in Wartime Britain* (Oxford, 1992), pp. 24f.
[2]   *Ibid.*, pp. iii, v, 1, 110.

reasons given for their detention'.[3] Despite 'suffering in spirit daily', and possibly detesting the whole system, he was prepared dutifully to continue with his arduous task until the end of the war.[4]

For the purpose of appeal, lawyers could assist detainees to prepare their case for the Committee but were not allowed to represent them there. The Committee not very helpfully provided the appellants with the regulatory reasons for their detention – they may have been of 'hostile origin or association', they may have been suspected of 'acts prejudicial to the public safety' – along with a few laconic details specific to the individual. Neither the evidence upon which the accusations were based nor its source was provided. The Committee itself was furnished with a much more substantial résumé called the 'Statement of the Case'. The hearings were little more than interrogations of the vulnerable detainees who had no prior warning of the questions that would be put to them, nor of the procedures of the Committee. Critics in the Commons likened it to Star Chamber.[5] Birkett, however, was invariably courteous, tried to be fair, and in the more flagrant cases was prepared to recommend suspension or revocation of the order so as to 'keep some small element of justice alive in a world in which we are supposed to be fighting for it'.[6] Anderson was also liberally inclined, and almost invariably agreed with the recommendations. As the 'Phoney War' subsided into a catalogue of military and naval defeats, and paranoid fears of a Fifth Column resurfaced, Birkett's 'liberal' approach became suspect. A witch-hunt was on. Mass internment began.

In the ensuing months, despite the paucity of evidence against them, Birkett rejected the appeals of the fascist leader Sir Oswald Mosley and his wife – and Churchill's cousin – Diana, against their internment for conspiring to organise a Fifth Column. However, convinced of egregious mistakes made by the security services, and convinced that the Fifth Column did not exist, Birkett became less tractable. More recommendations for release were made. To enhance his status, or to ensure his compliance, on 3 November 1941 Birkett was offered elevation to the High Court Bench. The same day, the case of *Liversidge* v. *Anderson* was decided by the Law Lords. It has resonated through legal history, not for its judgment, but for the dissenting speech of one of the judges.

---

3   *Ibid.*, pp. 82–6, 261–73; Montgomery Hyde, *Norman Birkett* (London, 1964), pp. 469, 472.
4   Simpson, *In the Highest Degree Odious*, p. 416.
5   *Ibid.*, p. 90.
6   Hyde, *Norman Birkett*, p. 470.

In May 1940 Anderson had ordered the incarceration in Brixton Prison of a Jack Perlzwieg, a Jew who went under the name Robert Liversidge. The Secretary of State had declared that he had reasonable cause to believe that Liversidge was hostile and had to be controlled. Birkett's Committee, troubled though it was by the case, had reluctantly recommended he remain in detention. In March 1941 Liversidge took out an action for false imprisonment, hoping for a jury trial and to force the Home Secretary to give evidence in court. He was frustrated in this, but the matter eventually ended up before the Law Lords.

The issue they had to decide was whether the court could investigate the objective basis for the Home Secretary's reasonable cause of belief, or whether his belief was merely subjective as the Home Secretary asserted. The majority of the judges, holding that national security was paramount, concluded that the judgment as to whether there was a reasonable suspicion was one entirely for the Home Secretary to make, and that as he held such a belief and had acted in good faith, he need not disclose the basis for his decision. His actions and the reasonableness of his beliefs were not justiciable in a court of law. One judge dissented. Lord Atkin – who in the First World War had ruled against Zadig in the Divisional Court – made what was to become the defining statement of the need for judicial independence, no matter the exigencies of the time. He reproached – and offended – his fellow judges. They had, he said, shown themselves 'more executive minded than the executive' when confronted with the issue of the liberty of the subject.

> In this country, amid the clash of arms, the laws are not silent ... they speak the same language in war as in peace. It has always been one of the pillars of freedom, one of the principles of liberty for which on recent authority we are now fighting, that the judges are no respecters of persons and stand between the subject and any attempted encroachments on his liberty by the executive, alert to see that any coercive action is justified in law.

In this case, he declared, he had 'listened to arguments which might have been addressed acceptably to the Court of the King's Bench in the time of Charles I'.[7]

Atkin's dissent – or denunciation more like – was ill received. The Lord Chancellor, Viscount Simon, pressured him to revise it before publication. He refused. Yet in a whole succession of cases (with the exception of one

---

7 *Liversidge* v. *Anderson* [1942] AC 206, at 244. Simpson, *In the Highest Degree Odious*, p. 363, cogently but perhaps a little parsimoniously argues that Atkin's 'passion was inspired not by any special commitment to liberty but by concern over the relative status ... of judges on the one hand, and officials and ministers on the other'.

presided over by Lord Denning who thought the majority in *Liversidge* right),[8] Atkin's stance, whatever its motivation, has been approved and the actual decision in the case denigrated, ignored or bypassed. The actions of the executive in curtailing the liberty of the subject are to be judged by an objective standard. Only in a few jurisdictions such as Singapore and Malaysia has the majority judgment been preferred.

As a result, in recent years the highest courts have been much more robust in the defence of the liberty of the subject. Lord Scarman in 1974 warned that precisely in times of national crisis – or perceived national crisis – when the law should be most vigilant, it was constrained by the doctrine of parliamentary sovereignty.

> When times are normal and fear is not stalking the land, English law sturdily protects the freedom of the individual and respects human personality. But when times are abnormally alive with fear and prejudice the common law is at a disadvantage: it cannot resist the will, however frightened and prejudiced it may be, of parliament.[9]

At the same time as Scarman was issuing his warning, Britain was joining the European Community, which exposed it to continental legal systems none of which relied on the doctrine of parliamentary sovereignty, and most of which afforded a greater legal protection to individual rights. The power of parliament was less untrammelled than in the past. In another major development the Human Rights Act of 1998, passed in tranquil times by Mr Blair's first Labour administration, gave courts the power to denounce, but not to invalidate, statutes. It was a major advance in the protection of individual rights and liberties. His later administrations, however, with their histrionic approach to national security, were prepared to jettison hard-won rights and basic civil liberties. There are now more than a thousand laws and regulations permitting officials to force entry into homes, cars and offices. Nearly half have been introduced since 1997, but the most serious incursions into British freedoms have taken place as a result of the 'war on terror'. Most particularly we have had several attempts to erode 'one of the most fundamental safeguards of personal liberty in this country: the limit on the time a [terrorist suspect] ... may be held in custody without being charged'.[10]

The justification for this erosion of liberty was the assertion that the life of the nation was in jeopardy. Mr Blair insisted that when facing a terrorist threat, it is 'a dangerous misjudgment to put civil liberties first'. To do so 'was

---

8   Denning, *Landmarks in the Law*, pp. 228–33.
9   Leslie Scarman, *English Law – The New Dimension* (London, 1974), p. 15.
10 Bingham, *The Rule of Law*, p. 150.

misguided and wrong'.[11] In this he agreed with the Bush administration in the United States, which showed much skill in circumventing the rule of law, and in avoiding the word 'torture' by deftly redefining it. Blair's successor, Mr Brown, in his foreword to the United Kingdom's 'Strategy for Countering International Terrorism', wrote: 'The first priority of any government is to ensure the security and safety of the nation and all members of the public.' The guiding principle of both premiers was Cicero's dictum: *salus populi suprema lex*, the safety of the people is the supreme law.[12]

That maybe so of Rome and Roman Law. It is not so of England and the common law. In this country the safety of the people resides in the rule of law and not in resiling from it. It is encapsulated in the dictum of Benjamin Franklin as inscribed on the pedestal of the Statue of Liberty: 'They that can give up essential liberty to obtain a little safety deserve neither liberty nor safety.' Turning away from long-cherished liberties would not be a victory over tyranny and terrorism, it would be a betrayal of all we hold dear, and wish that others could enjoy. A former Lord Chief Justice, Lord Bingham, stated this when he wrote: 'we cannot commend our society to others by departing from the fundamental standards which make it worthy of commendation'.[13]

Indeed, the threat of terrorist attack has galvanised both the British government and that of America to do just that, in actions that have undermined the very rule of law and natural justice that make Western society worth preserving. The motive of the United States in detaining terrorist suspects in Guantanamo Bay was similar to that of Clarendon when he removed detainees to Jersey or Scotland: to deny them the remedy of *habeas corpus* in domestic law.

In the United Kingdom, Part 4 of the Anti-Terrorism Crime and Security Act 2001 authorised the detention without charge or trial of foreign nationals suspected of involvement in terrorism but who, as a result of several strong rulings of the European Court of Human Rights, could not be deported from this country. Many of the suspects came from countries where it was likely they would be tortured or suffer degrading treatment if returned. The Court of Human Rights had held that the prohibition provided by Article 3 of the European Convention on Human Rights against ill-treatment applied equally absolutely in expulsion cases:

---

11 'Blair: Shackled in War on Terror', *Sunday Times*, 27 May 2007.
12 Cicero, *De Legibus*, III.iii.viii.
13 Bingham, *The Rule of Law*, p. 136.

Whenever substantial grounds have been shown for believing that an individual would face a real risk of being subjected to treatment contrary to Article 3 if removed to another state, the responsibility of the contracting state to safeguard him or her against such treatment is engaged in the event of expulsion.

In such circumstances, 'the activities of the individual in question, however undesirable or dangerous, cannot be a material consideration'.[14] Confronted with this problem, David Blunkett, the then Home Secretary, introduced indefinite detention for suspected international terrorists who could neither be prosecuted nor deported. To pass such a measure, the United Kingdom had to derogate from Article 5 of the Convention (the right to liberty), a derogation permitted 'in time of war or other public emergency threatening the life of the nation'. The provisions applied only to foreign nationals, presumably the result of a 'deliberate political decision' as Lord Bingham thought, since the government would have considered that it would be a very grave step to detain British citizens in this way. The act came into force in December 2001, only a month after the bill had first been introduced into parliament. Draconian legislation impinging on human rights and personal liberties was subjected to a mere sixteen hours of debate in the Commons and less in the Lords. Adequate scrutiny there was not.[15]

Under section 21(1) and (2) of the act, for detention to be authorised two conditions have to be satisfied. The Home Secretary has to have *a reasonable belief* that the person's presence in the United Kingdom is a risk to national security, and also a *reasonable suspicion* that the person is a terrorist concerned in 'the commission, preparation, or instigation of acts of international terrorism', or is a member of, belongs to, or has links with, an international terrorist group. Most of those Blunkett so deemed were accommodated within the maximum security conditions of Belmarsh Prison in south-east London. This was subject to much criticism. Perhaps the most humiliating observation was that made to Chris Mullin MP by the Zimbabwean ambassador, that 'we have the rule of law in Zimbabwe. We don't lock up people for years without trial, as you do in Belmarsh.'[16]

The detainees resorted to the courts, and finally in October 2004 their appeal came before the judicial committee of the House of Lords, in what became known as 'the Belmarsh Case'.[17] No fewer than eight out of nine judges of the highest court in the land declared Part 4 of the 2001 act to be

---

[14] *Chahal* v. *UK* [1997] 23 EHRR, 413, para 80.
[15] Bogdanor, *The New British Constitution*, p. 56.
[16] Christopher Mullin, *A View from the Foothills* (London, 2009), p. 537.
[17] *A* v. *SS for Home Department* [2005] 2AC 68.

incompatible with the United Kingdom's obligations under Article 5 of the European Convention on Human Rights. The detention provision, the Law Lords said, did not address rationally the threat to national security; it was disproportionate and not strictly required by the exigencies of the situation; and it unjustifiably discriminated against foreign nationals.

On this latter point, Lord Chief Justice Bingham asked if *habeas corpus* were really limited to British nationals as was suggested? He, following precedent, gave 'an emphatic "no" to the question', citing Mansfield's judgment in the Somerset case to establish the principle that 'every person within the jurisdiction enjoys equal protection of our laws'. Lord Hope held that it was an essential safeguard, 'if individual rights and freedoms are to be protected ... that minorities, however unpopular, have the same rights as the majority'.[18]

Lord Hoffman, who thought this the most important case in his lifetime, alone rejected the Government's submission that there was a public emergency threatening the life of the nation such as to justify derogation. He did not 'underestimate the ability of fanatical groups of terrorists to kill and destroy, but they do not threaten the life of the nation. Whether we would survive Hitler hung in the balance, but there is no doubt we shall survive Al-Qaeda.' He allowed the appeal on the ground that there was no such emergency. His words, like those of Lord Atkin before him, have a resonance for a country that survived both Stuart despotism and Pitt's Terror:

> Such [a power of detention] in any form is not compatible with our constitution ... It calls into question the very existence of an ancient liberty of which this country has until now been very proud: freedom from arbitrary arrest and detention. The power which the Home Secretary seeks to uphold is a power to detain people indefinitely without charge or trial. Nothing could be more antithetical to the instincts and traditions of the people of the United Kingdom. Freedom from arbitrary arrest and detention is a quintessentially British liberty, enjoyed by the inhabitants of this country when most of the population of Europe could be thrown into prison at the whim of their rulers. It was incorporated into the European Convention in order to entrench the same liberty in countries which had recently been under Nazi occupation. The United Kingdom subscribed to the Convention because it set out the rights which British subjects enjoyed under the common law ... The real threat to the life of a nation, in the sense of a people living in accordance with its traditional laws and political values, comes not from terrorism but from laws such as these. That is the true measure of what terrorism may achieve.[19]

Their Lordships went further. Even without considering the European

---

18 *Ibid.*, para. 108.
19 *Ibid.*, paras 86–8, 96–7.

Convention, they judged that the statute offended against the most basic principles of the common law.

In the United States the courts took a similar line. The Supreme Court case of *Boumediene* v. *Bush* held that detainees had a constitutional right to *habeas corpus*. Justice Kennedy cited Magna Carta, the *Five Knights' Case*, and that of James Somerset. He quoted Alexander Hamilton's observation that 'the practice of arbitrary imprisonment has been in all ages the favourite and most formidable instrument of tyranny'. He concluded that, 'The laws and Constitution are designed to survive and remain in force in extraordinary times. Liberty and security can be reconciled, and in our system they are reconciled within the law.'

CHAPTER 30

Nuremberg and Norman Birkett

One comes upon an all-important English trait: the respect for constitution-alism and legality, the belief in 'the law' as something above the state and above the individual, something which is cruel and stupid, but at any rate incorruptible ... The totalitarian idea that there is no such thing as law, there is only power, has never taken root.

George Orwell, 'The Lion and The Unicorn'

Let them have a trial, and let them have justice. That's one of the things me and my mates fought for.

A British guard at Nuremberg (Bowker, *Behind the Bar*)

PERHAPS the gravest threat to the rule of law came during the twentieth century, and in an international context, when brutal totalitarian regimes, in particular Hitler's and Stalin's, passed unconscionable laws, subverted legal safeguards, corrupted the independence of the judiciary, and instigated show trials. The law was made subject to naked evil. After the horrors of the Second World War, swift and brutal revenge could have been exacted on the beaten foe, Nazi Germany, especially by its equally vicious adversary, Soviet Russia. Churchill himself initially expressed a preference for summary execution with the use of an Act of Attainder to circumvent legal obstacles. Instead, post-war Europe oversaw two remarkable developments. The first was the creation, very much along common law principles, of the Nuremberg Tribunal to try the Nazi war criminals. The second was the drawing up of the European Convention on Human Rights, again largely devised by common law lawyers, led by Britain's main prosecutor at Nuremberg.[1]

The trial of the major war criminals, held between 20 November 1945 and 1 October 1946 at Nuremberg, the cradle of Nazism, was unique. For the first time the surviving leaders of a defeated nation were put on trial for Criminal Conspiracy (Count 1), with specific counts alleging Crimes against Peace (Count 2), War Crimes (Count 3), and Crimes against Humanity (Count 4). The indictment introduced a word new to international law into the lexicon: 'genocide'. That a court was established to try the alleged perpetrators of these offences was a remarkable achievement. The Americans, the British,

---

[1] See Chapter 31 below.

the French and the Russians all had to agree on its creation and conduct. It was an amalgam of different legal systems, the British and American being common law. Although the Americans led the prosecution and their chief prosecutor was no less than a Supreme Court Justice, Robert Jackson, it was the British who came to dominate both among the judges and among the advocates, and it was the British jurisprudential contribution more than that of any other that established the principles of international criminal law.

The British appellate judge, Lord Justice Lawrence, was chosen to be the President of what was called the International Military Tribunal. His appointment to the senior judicial role was quickly vindicated. By his emollience and integrity he maintained the cooperation of the panel of judges, no mean feat. He was considered exemplary in his conduct of the trial, and he ensured that the proceedings were deemed fair and just by almost every observer, including many of the defendants. He embodied the very essence of impartial justice.[2] Alongside him, as his alternate, was none other than Mr Justice Birkett.[3]

Perhaps unsurprisingly, schooled in the adversarial tradition, by far and away the best advocates were British. High expectations, however, were had of the leader of the American team, Mr Justice Jackson, who had made a masterly and memorable opening statement, and whose task it was to cross-examine the key defendant, Hermann Goering. The judges had the utmost confidence 'in his ability to achieve the desired end' of exposing and shattering the leader of the surviving Nazis and 'exposing the Nazi regime in all its horrible cruelty', and so demonstrating before the world that the 'trial had served its supreme purpose'.[4]

This confidence was soon shaken, as Goering exploited the shortcomings of the cross-examination to vindicate his conduct and expound and extol Nazi ideas and beliefs for future generations of Germans. The English observers, in particular, were aghast. Birkett, the master craftsman of the art of advocacy, was excoriating:

> Mr Justice Jackson, for all his great abilities … had never learnt the very first elements of cross-examination as it is understood in the English courts. He was overwhelmed by his documents, and there was no chance of the lightning question following upon some careless or damaging answer, no quick parry and thrust, no leading the witness on to the prepared pitfall, and above all

2   R. W. Cooper, *The Nuremberg Trial* (Harmondsworth, 1947), p. 27.
3   An alternate judge is a standby who can substitute for a judge who may be ill, absent, excused or otherwise unavailable to carry out judicial functions.
4   Hyde, *Norman Birkett*, p. 509.

no clear overriding conception of the great issues which could have been put with simplicity and power.[5]

After years as Attorney-General and justice of the Supreme Court, Jackson lacked – if he ever had – 'the sixth sense of the cross-examiner which subconsciously anticipates the working of a witness's mind'.[6] His three-day attempt at questioning the pompous Reichsmarshall was categorised as 'an intellectual mess'. His target was unscathed and held the stage. Goering was enjoying toying with his would-be tormentor. He was 'the master of Mr Justice Jackson'. With a fluency in German and a better understanding of the documentation Goering scored easy hits, humiliating his foe. There were many own goals. For instance a document which Jackson produced indicating that Goering had been planning 'the liberation of the Rhineland', the latter could point out was in fact about 'the cleaning of the Rhine'. He graciously admitted to that. Jackson produced another document purporting to be minutes of a meeting, but acknowledged that he did not know what it said. Goering did: he was not present. Lawrence curtailed one session with the telling verbal slip, 'Perhaps we had better adjourn now at this *state*.'[7]

The Tribunal too was criticised for letting the defendant use the witness box as a platform for speeches designed for an outside audience. Yet better to err on the side of indulgence to the accused than to muzzle him too readily, especially in a trial as momentous as this. A competent advocate should not need judicial assistance in controlling a witness, as the leading British prosecutor, Sir David Maxwell-Fyfe would observe.[8] Jackson's failure cast a shadow over the whole enterprise. It looked as though the Cassandras who had always warned that a trial would be a platform for Nazi propaganda, or that it would degenerate into protracted farce, might be vindicated. This was Birkett's view. He despaired and wrote, 'the great battle was lost, and once lost there may be partial but never complete recovery. The position may be improved, but never quite redeemed.'[9]

---

5   *Ibid.*, pp. 510f.

6   Earl of Kilmuir, *Political Adventure* (London, 1964), p. 112.

7   Ann Tusa and John Tusa, *The Nuremberg Trial* (London, 1983), pp. 281f; Hyde, *Norman Birkett*, p. 510. My emphasis.

8   Kilmuir, *Political Adventure*, p. 113. Maxwell-Fyfe, the future Viscount Kilmuir, was in fact the British deputy chief prosecutor, but Sir Hartley Shawcross, the Attorney-General, only attended the trial to make, albeit 'resounding', opening and closing speeches: Cooper, *The Nuremberg Trial*, p. 34.

9   Tusa and Tusa, *The Nuremberg Trial*, p. 291; Hyde, *Norman Birkett*, p. 510. Jackson failed to learn from his experience or master his brief, and did not improve when questioning another defendant, Schacht: Tusa and Tusa, pp. 344f.

16. Judgment at Nuremberg: Associate Justice Robert Jackson (left) and David Maxwell-Fyfe (right), the former an impassioned orator but no inquisitor, the latter an assassin well schooled in the adversarial system of the common law. In the centre is Robert Falco, the French representative.

Partial, perhaps complete, redemption was achieved (as was further humiliation for Jackson) by Maxwell-Fyfe, who expertly demolished this apologist for the Third Reich. He did so by a formidable command of the voluminous documentation and a considerable understanding of the structure of the Nazi state. Although few would claim that Maxwell-Fyfe was a brilliant practitioner – Birkett did not rate him highly – his questioning of Goering was a masterclass in how to do it: courteous, succinct, and utterly devastating. His manner was calm, his questions were short and precise and based on a detailed mastery of the facts. Maxwell-Fyfe had no need of the Tribunal's assistance. The moment Goering tried to expand on an answer, he would cut him short: 'I have put my question … I pass on to another point.' For five hours it went on. The approach was deceptively simple, as it was intended to be. Maxwell-Fyfe 'held on like a bulldog; held on without ever noticing the witness's impertinence, his sallies, his wit, and sneers which gradually died down', noted the American judge, Francis Biddle, impressed. Goering was impotent with rage, 'defending himself with clenched fists, his face flushed and angry'. Under this relentless but incisive interrogation Goering crumbled. He was revealed as a bully and a bluster.[10]

Maxwell-Fyfe would go on to cross-examine other defendants. When they were in the witness box, a journalist noted,

> you could see them brace themselves when [Maxwell-Fyfe] rose to cross-examine – and what drama, what intellectual satisfaction, there were in the form and texture of his questioning: what hidden menace in his disarming approach ... 'I want to be perfectly fair' ... – he would begin, and then go on to make what amounted to an accusation of murder.[11]

This approach seemed to be a revelation to the Americans, the French, and above all the Russians.

Even more important than effective cross-examination was the legal undergirding of this exceptional trial, and the legal bases of the determinations reached. Despite his secondary status, all the major public statements and legal rulings – which very much helped to redeem the proceedings – were drafted by Norman Birkett, the supreme British legal all-rounder of the twentieth century, and one of the greatest criminal advocates of all time. Originally destined for the Methodist Ministry, Birkett read history, theology and finally law at Emmanuel College, Cambridge, and opted for the last. He was called to the Bar at the Inner Temple in 1913. He began his legal career in Birmingham, but was later taken on by none other than Marshall Hall at his chambers in Temple Gardens. Birkett became a Liberal MP in 1923, and was made QC in 1924. He was described by his 'old friend and opponent', Maxwell-Fyfe, as

> one of the greatest forensic orators of the twentieth century ... the last great example of the "biblical tradition" which is a strong strand in English advocacy. Whoever his client, his cross-examination was possessed of a moral earnestness which hushed many a crowded court, and his speeches always had a flavour of the Authorised Version.[12]

A lowly clerk was transfixed by a 'voice full of music' when he happened upon Birkett in the High Court: 'it was the sound that entranced me, the perfect enunciation, the spellbinding pitch. I stood rooted.'[13] After one

10 Kilmuir, *Political Adventure*, pp. 114f; Tusa and Tusa, *The Nuremberg Trial*, p. 286.

11 Cooper, *The Nuremberg Trial*, p. 33.

12 Hyde, *Norman Birkett*, p. 583; Kilmuir, *Political Adventure*, p. 100.

13 A. E. Bowker, *A Lifetime with the Law* (London, 1961), p. 60.

17. Norman Birkett KC, as great a jurist as he was an advocate, and 'a positive menace to the administration of justice!' Here, *Punch*: 'if yet again he strays/ Back to his homicidal ways,/ Will do his level best to work it/ So that his counsel may be BIRKETT.'

brilliant speech in a difficult case, Birkett was championed by the *Daily Mail* as 'the greatest legal discovery of the year'.

His forensic triumphs famously included the 'Brighton Trunk Murder' case of 1934 in which, against overwhelming evidence, he secured an acquittal for Toni Mancini, who on his deathbed admitted to being the murderer. Another leading barrister and contemporary, Sir Patrick Hastings, remarked that

If it had ever been my lot to decide to cut up a lady in small pieces and put her in an unwanted suitcase (as Mancini had done) I should without hesitation have placed my future in Norman Birkett's hands. He would have satisfied the jury (a) that I was not there; (b) that I had not cut up the lady; and (c) that if I had she thoroughly deserved it anyway.

One judge said of Birkett that his powers of persuasion were 'a positive menace to the administration of justice!' Such arduous cases, Birkett once complained, took 'years off a man's life'. His junior sagely replied: 'Maybe – but they add years to his client's.'[14]

Nonetheless his greatest contribution to the law was not in the ephemeral arena of jury trials, nor in his more recent role on the internment Advisory Committee, but as a judge who helped craft the most significant legal development of the twentieth century. The Nuremberg proceedings were of fundamental importance in establishing that nations were subject to international law, and that the defeated tyrants would be held to account, not by a firing squad but by a court of law. Mr Justice Birkett, as he had then become, was at the forefront of this. Despite being offered and then denied the principal British role in Nuremberg, his impact there was profound. It began early when the Americans wished to indict Alfred Krupp, the son of the industrialist Gustav, in place of the father who was too ill to stand trial. Birkett was aghast at the proposal and pointed out that 'this was not a game of football in which a reserve could be fielded without more ado'. Although Birkett as an alternate had no vote, his view prevailed. He well understood the larger significance of the protracted proceedings:

> This trial can be a very great landmark in the history of international law. There will be a precedent of the highest standing for all successive generations, and aggressor nations great and small will embark on war with the certain knowledge that if they fail they will be called to grim account. To make the trial secure against all criticism it must be shown to be fair, convincing and built on evidence that cannot be shaken as the years go past.... The world must be patient (and so must I!) for what is being done now assuredly belongs to history.

Nonetheless, he firmly believed, and confided to his diary, that 'if all the matters had been rigorously excluded which were repetitive or cumulative ... this trial would certainly have been of shorter duration, the issues more clearly and lucidly defined, tempers would have been more equitable, and general benefits would have resulted.'[15]

When the judges adjourned to deliberate and to compose their judgment, Birkett came into his own. He displayed 'a greater and swifter command of

---

14 Hyde, *Norman Birkett*, p. 1; Bowker, *Behind the Bar*, p. 238.
15 Hyde, *Norman Birkett*, pp. 496, 503ff.

the documents than anyone on the Bench', and, perhaps as important, maintained a cordial relationship with the other judges, the Russians in particular. He took part in all the debates, and he was asked to write the first draft of what was considered to be 'perhaps the most far-reaching legal judgment of all time', an international Magna Carta.[16] The capacity for expression matched the clarity of his mind and his command of the evidence. He concentrated on the law against which each defendant would ultimately be assessed. The result of this crystallisation of the legal principles upon which their judgment was to be based was to generate disagreements and debate among the judges, hardly surprising since they represented four legal systems and eight personalities. Most controversial was the charge of conspiracy, alien to French law, but which Birkett considered vital if the Nazi regime were to condemned for planning aggression and murder. In the event, large sections of the 50,000 words ultimately delivered were by Birkett, including the passage on conspiracy, concluding that 'continued planning, with aggressive war as the objective has been established beyond doubt'.[17]

The Tribunal convicted nineteen of the defendants and acquitted three. Of the nineteen, Goering committed suicide before the sentence of death could be executed, eleven were hanged, and the remaining seven served varying terms of imprisonment. This had not been a political 'show trial' in the Soviet sense. It had shown to the world that victorious nations, acting in concert, could administer stern justice, and not savage revenge, on the vanquished, and that war crimes and genocide would not go unpunished. Nuremberg had completed what the trial of Charles I began.

Contemporaries were quick to recognise the signal jurisprudential contribution made by the British judges, and in particular by Birkett. It was small consolation for being passed over for a peerage that Jowitt, the Lord Chancellor, wrote to him of 'the great debt which this country owes you for your work in 1946'.[18] A greater consolation, and an assurance that his name would go down in history, came from two sources: Lord Simon, a former Lord Chancellor, and John Parker, the American alternate judge at Nuremberg.

Simon wrote that 'Birkett was an admirable choice.... Justice with him is not divorced from mercy, but when he tries the bully he does not forget the victim. The country owes much to him … for vindicating our conceptions of an impartial trial under the rule of law.'[19] An even more generous – but justi-

---

[16] Cooper, *The Nuremberg Trial*, pp. 31f.

[17] Tusa and Tusa, *The Nuremberg Trial*, pp. 447–50.

[18] Hyde, *Norman Birkett*, p. 530.

[19] *Ibid.*, p. 527.

fied – encomium was delivered by Parker, who made plain the fundamental importance of Birkett's contribution:

> He realised thoroughly the importance of the business in which we were engaged. He was tireless in his efforts to draft a judgment which would not only do justice to those on trial, but would also commend itself to the wisdom of mankind and the dispassionate judgment of history. Although only an alternate member of the Tribunal ... his voice was heard in all its deliberations, his hand drafted a large and most important part of its judgment, and no one ... had a greater part than he in shaping the final result. If, as I confidently believe, the work of the Tribunal will constitute a landmark in the development of world order based on law, to Norman Birkett must go a large share of the credit for the success of the undertaking. To few men does the opportunity come to labour so mightily for the welfare of their kind.[20]

---

[20] Parker's Foreword to Bowker, *Behind the Bar*.

CHAPTER 31

Wrongs and Rights

There is in the English constitution an absence of those declarations or
definitions of rights so dear to foreign constitutionalists ... Most foreign
constitution-makers have begun with declarations of rights.
A. V. Dicey, *Lectures Introductory to the Study of the Law*

THE European Convention on Human Rights, formerly known as the
Convention for the Protection of Human Rights and Fundamental
Freedoms, was drafted in 1950 by the Council of Europe . This body had
been founded on 5 May 1949 by the Treaty of London, the United Kingdom
being one of the initial ten signatories. The Council pre-dated the European
Union and remains a completely separate entity. It is a purely an intergov-
ernmental and consultative body with no power to bind individual member
states, of which there are now forty-seven. These include serial human rights
offenders such as Russia, but not Belarus or the Vatican. Its purpose is to
promote cooperation in the areas of the rule of law, the enforcement of
human rights, and the preservation or development of democracy. The
Convention was the first offspring of the Council.

In the light of the manifest and terrible abuses of human rights in the
Second World War, the Convention was intended to prevent any recurrence
of such evils. By the time of its drafting, however, it was also seen to be a
bulwark against the insidious growth of Communism in Eastern Europe,
and 'a beacon to the peoples behind the iron curtain', thus explaining the
many references to values and principles that are 'necessary in a democratic
society',[1] and the refusal of the Soviet Union to join the Council of Europe
or apply the Convention.

Sir David Maxwell-Fyfe was appointed chairman of the legal and administrative committee that drafted the Convention. He wanted to get international sanction behind the maintenance of the democratic freedoms and
rights that the British had taken for granted for generations, what he called
the 'basic decencies of life'. He could also draw on the example and inspiration
of the 1948 Universal Declaration of Human Rights of the United Nations

---

[1] Kilmuir, *Political Adventure*, p. 183.

itself, drafted by John Humphrey, a Canadian legal scholar in the common law tradition. If the common law is not the parent of the Convention, it is at least its wet-nurse. There is nothing alien to British traditions about the contents of the Convention, although that is not so true of its implementation. Civil liberties – perhaps a better, and certainly a less contentious term – are at the heart of any democratic society. Liberties, however, are granted. Rights are inherent. A grant can be rescinded; a right cannot.

In view of the curtailment of liberties by the two most murderous dictators of all time, Hitler and Stalin, it is not surprising that the term 'rights' was preferred. The British did not object. Indeed it was Maxwell-Fyfe who argued for them, albeit in Burkean terms, insisting that they be stated not as 'vague generalities, but in terms that could be enforced by a court of law'. He was proud of the fact that the Council of Europe had 'succeeded in doing what the United Nations had failed to do, namely, to create an enforceable convention guaranteeing democratic rights'.[2] To enforce these rights, the European Court of Human Rights was established in Strasbourg.[3] Thus, in the creation and development of the two main legal bastions against the resumption of tyranny in Europe – the establishment of the international criminal court and the European Convention on Human Rights – common law lawyers played a signal part.

The latter appealed more to lawyers of a conservative bent than to those of socialist tendencies. In 1951 Great Britain, with Churchill's enthusiastic support, was one of the first countries to ratify the Convention, although alone of all the member states apart from Ireland, it did not incorporate the provisions of the Convention into domestic law. Britain feared that to do so would compromise the doctrine of the sovereignty of parliament and flattered itself that there was no need, assuming that the rights and freedoms guaranteed by the Convention could be delivered under the common law. Aggrieved parties would have to exhaust domestic remedies before they could resort to Strasbourg. It was a typical British muddle. Britain had agreed to comply with Convention rights, but would not allow for them to be secured in her own courts.[4] Since the national courts rarely paid more than a passing nod at Strasbourg's jurisprudence, Britain faced the regular humiliation of losing more cases in Strasbourg than any other member. When it lost, it

---

2   *Ibid.*, pp. 176–84.
3   Just as the Convention pre-dates and has nothing to do with the European Community or Union, so the Strasbourg court has nothing to do with the Court of Justice of the European Union, established in Luxembourg.
4   The White Paper *Rights Brought Home: The Human Rights Bill.* Cm 1997, 3782.

reluctantly complied with the ruling, but comply it did. It was expensive, embarrassing and unnecessary.

It was not until 1998 and the Human Rights Act that this anomaly was substantially resolved by obliging British courts, if at all possible, to interpret all domestic legislation in a way that is compatible with the European Convention. Where this is not possible, the courts cannot overturn legislation but may issue a 'declaration of incompatibility'. This is not a concept entirely novel to the judiciary. There is the obvious precedent that judges, when attempting to ascertain the meaning of a parliamentary statute, will presume that 'parliament did not intend to violate the ordinary rules of morality or the principles of international law, and will therefore, *whenever possible*, give such an interpretation of statute as may be consistent with the doctrines both of private and of international morality'.[5]

British courts can embarrass parliament; they cannot usurp it. They can criticise and even condemn legislation, but they cannot overrule it. Section 3(2)(b) of the act specifies that any attempt to render domestic legislation compatible with the Convention 'does not affect the validity, continuing operation or enforcement of any incompatible primary legislation'. Whereas delegated or subordinate legislation such as Orders in Counsel, regulations and by-laws, may be struck down by the courts, primary legislation is protected. Article 13 of the Convention – providing for an effective judicial remedy for violations – was not included in the Human Rights Act, and so, despite what is often asserted, the Convention has not been incorporated into British law. Judges can, however, set aside any legislation of the Scottish parliament or Welsh assembly which is incompatible, since they are non-sovereign legislatures. Thus the European Convention is fundamental law for those bodies but not for Westminster.[6] Parliament still has the upper hand, sovereignty is preserved, if only just. As one eminent commentator has recently put it, for good or ill, judges will 'come to play a much more important role in determining the scope of our rights than they have done hitherto'.[7]

The Human Rights Act has been seen as a defining moment in the life of the British constitution and in revolutionising the understanding of rights. The traditional view, as espoused by Dicey in particular, was that the common law protected liberties by providing remedies rather than by enforcing rights. Liberties were dependent on parliament. Parliament not only *could* do no

---

5 Dicey, *Lectures Introductory to the Study of the Law*, pp. 58f. My emphasis.
6 Bogadnor, *The New British Constitution*, pp. 60ff.
7 *Ibid.*, p. 43.

wrong, but *would* do no wrong. The law was a check on the executive and on the abuse of power. Parliament would not abuse its power. The sovereignty of parliament and the rule of law were opposite sides of the same coin. So it was believed. Parliamentary sovereignty was predicated on the assumption that parliament would never infringe fundamental rights. Consequently those holding this view thought that there was no need of a Human Rights Act, and declarations of incompatibility would never be made.

How wrong they were. A 'Human Rights culture' was to develop, and the understanding of the rule of law was to evolve until it incorporated the protection of those basic human rights which every liberal society should uphold. If rights exist which are intrinsic to humanity, rather than being merely the hard-won fruits of political and social struggle, no legislative body however supreme has the right to infringe them, though it may have the power. As a result, especially in fraught times, there could well be real conflict between parliamentary sovereignty and this view of rights protected by the rule of law.

It has not always been so. In Victorian times and for much of the twentieth century the judiciary and the legislature had been willing allies not in the protection of rights, but in the enforcement of morality or moral conformity.

CHAPTER 32

Deprave and Corrupt: Blasphemy,
Obscenity and Oscar Wilde

The individuals of the state, like members of a well-governed family,
are bound to conform their general behaviour to the rules of propriety,
good neighbourhood, and good manners; and to be decent, industrious
and inoffensive in their respective stations.
> Blackstone, *Commentaries on the Laws of England*

Obscenity if not a term capable of exact legal definition; in the practice
of the courts it means 'anything that shocks the magistrate'.
> Bertrand Russell, 'The Recrudescence of Puritanism'

LAW, by regulating behaviour, constrains freedom. Liberty has rarely
meant licence: not only are actions that harm others – such as assaults
and thefts – prohibited, but also, at varying times in English and British
history, behaviour that, if it harms at all, harms only the individual. For
instance, suicide until 1961 was a criminal offence in England, and homosexual acts were punishable until 1967. Conversely, drug-taking, which once
was legal, is now an offence. In contrast, the consumption of alcohol, the
intoxicant directly related to much violent crime, has never been prohibited
by law in the western world, other than in a disastrous experiment in the
United States.

Such activities as the physical expression of homosexual love, or the taking
of drugs, are made into crimes, not because they are intrinsically evil, but
because the mores of a particular society at a particular time deem them to be
so.[1] Such criminalisation is an expression of the coercive morality – or tyranny
– of the majority. Victorian moralists, in particular Evangelicals who were
'at the core of God's self-appointed law enforcement agency', were ardent in
their campaigns to protect women and children from sexual predation, and
chimney sweeps from suffocation, but they were also anxious, through resort
to legal proceedings, to restrict gin-drinking and gambling, and to extirpate
pornography or anything which they considered to be indecent. Morality

---

[1] Ann Dally, 'Anomalies and Mysteries in the "War on Drugs"', in *Drugs and Narcotics
in History*, ed. Roy Porter and Mikulas Teich (Cambridge, 1995), pp. 199–215.

should be enforced. The law should regulate not just public behaviour but private also. The weak should be protected not just from the evil of others, but from the evil within. Those of the lower classes who engaged in socially illicit behaviour would participate in other criminality as well.[2]

The main organ for their campaigning was the Society for the Suppression of Vice, which had been founded in 1801 to combat Sabbath-breaking, brothels and gaming houses, as well as blasphemous and licentious books and prints. Profanation of the Sabbath was at the core of the Society's work and absorbed most of its very considerable energy in the achievement of over six hundred convictions in London in the first year of its existence.[3] Yet it had still had time to spare to take on the provision of what it considered to be obscene material. It investigated, and discovered both that prosecutions for such offences at common law were almost unknown, and that a veritable conspiracy existed of rich foreigners based in London who employed about thirty agents – mainly Italians – to travel in pairs peddling their 'obscene books, prints, drawings, toys etc' throughout the land.[4] 'Toys etc' is, alas, not further elaborated. The Society swung into action, prosecuting traders in such articles for the indictable offence of obscene libel or under the Vagrancy Act of 1824, which provided for the summary punishment of publicly displayed obscenities. To be obscene the offending article had to outrage public decency and be injurious to public morals. By 1857 the Society had brought 159 cases to court, with only 5 acquittals.[5] Yet the Augean stable could not be cleansed, and 'the deluge of filth' continued, underground but unabated, aided by the inability of the authorities to seize

---

2   *OHLE*, XI, pp. 139f. For a succinct distillation of the arguments between proponents and opponents of the enforcement of morals, see Patrick Devlin, *The Enforcement of Morals* (Oxford, 1965) and H. L. A. Hart, *Law. Liberty and Morality* (Oxford, 1963). Later Victorians, such as Stephen in 1874, confronting the undermining of religious belief and the consequent erosion of Christianity's power of moral suasion, advocated increasing intrusion on the part of the state through the law. That largely happened, until the advent of the 'permissive society' in the 1960s. The immediate inspiration behind the Devlin/Hart debate was the 1957 Wolfenden Report on Homosexual Offences and Prostitution – a telling conjunction. Devlin, a senior judge, was erudite and elegant, but his argument is predicated on the contaminating and corrosive potential and 'self-evident' immorality of 'homosexualism'. As a result of the vast moral shifts in the last half-century, this now sounds like a voice from another age. Hart, an Oxford professor of jurisprudence, produced a short and lucid riposte which still resonates. As society secularises and diversifies it is increasingly difficult to justify the enforcement of morals, or even to define them.

3   *OHLE*, XI, p. 141.

4   Society Report of 1825, quoted in Thomas, *A Long Time Burning*, p. 189.

5   *OHLE*, XIII, pp. 364f.

the often 'immense stock' of those they prosecuted. With persecution, the pornography became only more extreme.[6]

This singular block to eradication led to the Lord Chief Justice, Lord Campbell, proposing an Obscene Publications Bill, which targeted not just the publisher or retailer but the obscene items themselves, which would be subject to summary seizure and destruction at the discretion of magistrates. He had been galvanised into action against the traffic in 'poison more deadly that prussic acid' by several trials over which he had presided, which had revealed to him the ready availability to members of the lower orders of 'licentious and disgusting periodicals'.[7] Despite express government disapproval, and opposition from two former Lord Chancellors – Brougham (who was more concerned about children of ten being sent to prison and pregnant women being set to the treadmill), and Lyndhurst (who denied having a 'zeal for filthy publications') – Campbell's measure passed into law in 1857.

Campbell did not intend it to apply to works of highbrow literature, and assured parliament that it would be deployed exclusively against those works 'written for the single purpose of corrupting the morals of youth and of a nature calculated to shock the common feelings of decency in any well regulated mind.'[8] The great fear was the easy corruptibility not of the governing, but of the working class. The former could safely be allowed to read Ovid or Suetonius in the original Latin, the latter only in expurgated translations. Macaulay found it 'difficult to believe that, in a world so full of temptation as this, any gentlemen ... will be made vicious by reading [Aristophanes and Juvenal]'.[9]

Critics wondered how 'obscene' would be defined, and how meritorious works of art would in practice be differentiated from merely corrupting pornography, problems of definition and differentiation compounded by the fact that the articles were subject to summary procedure, under which the gut reaction of magistrates would be decisive. They would not have to wonder long. Their reservations proved prescient.

In 1868, eleven years after the act came in, Campbell's successor, Lord Cockburn, sitting in the Divisional Court, had to review the case of *R. v. Hicklin*. This was a distasteful matter of an Evangelical metal-broker who

6 Thomas, *A Long Time Burning*, pp. 192f.

7 Campbell, *Lives of the Lord Chancellors*, X, p. 191.

8 Alan Travis, *Bound and Gagged: A Secret History of Obscenity in Britain* (London, 2000). p. 5.

9 Thomas Babington Macauley, *Critical and Historical Essays*, 3rd edn, 3 vols (London, 1844), III, pp. 256f. The Loeb classical library, founded in 1911, used to translate the salacious passages into Italian, providing a useful shortcut for many a pupil.

had produced a virulently anti-Catholic pamphlet exposing the methods supposedly used by priests to extract erotic details from susceptible women in the confessional. Ignoring the 'single purpose' principle, and interpreting the Obscene Publications Act in a much broader way than his predecessor had intended, Cockburn devised a test for obscenity that was to persist for a hundred years. It was 'whether the tendency of the matter charged as obscenity is to deprave and corrupt those whose minds are open to such immoral influences and into whose hands a publication of this sort may fall.' He acknowledged that illustrations in medical treatises such as Gray's *Anatomy* – first published in 1858 – 'may, in a certain sense, be obscene', but opined that, as they would not readily be seen by 'boys and girls', they would escape prosecution.[10] Cockburn's assurances were to ring hollow. His definition of obscenity was to give the Victorians a cudgel to wield against any work that might give offence, literary or even scientific, and it was to be employed throughout the English-speaking world for generations to come.[11] 'A tendency to deprave and corrupt' proved to be a low threshold to cross to establish an article's obscene nature.

In its application, the Obscene Publications Act 1857 has been arbitrary and unjust, and all too often ludicrous. It has done more to bring the law into derision than any other piece of criminal legislation. Categorisation according to simplistic formulae and transient ethical norms is a recipe for ridicule. If, in retrospect, it has added to the merriment of the nation, to those subjected to official censoriousness and condemnation it was depressing and discouraging. Fortunately, although its modern reincarnations – the Obscene Publications Acts of 1959 and 1964 – remain on the statute book, they are more of a curiosity than a threat, being rarely invoked.

The 1857 act's most notable early victim was a pioneering pamphlet on birth control entitled *The Fruits of Philosophy: An Essay on the Population Question*, first published in 1832. In 1877 the leaders of the National Secular Society, Charles Bradlaugh and Annie Besant, republished the tract. They did so cheaply, hoping for a mass distribution in the popular market. This, in itself, seemed proof of the work's potential to corrupt public morals. Wanting to provoke a test case they had given the authorities prior notification of their intentions, and declared 'we intend to publish nothing we do not think we can morally defend'. Morality may have been on their side. The law was not. Lord Cockburn himself heard the case, although he expressly deplored the fact that these 'injudicious proceedings' had greatly boosted circulation of a

---

10   *R. v. Hicklin* (1868) LR 3 QB, 360–74.
11   Travis, *Bound and Gagged*, p. 6.

work, now notorious, that until then had gone largely unnoticed. The jury found the defendants guilty of publishing a book that would deprave public morals, but not of any corrupt motives in so doing. Cockburn ignored the jury's disclaimer and so maintained that in obscenity cases motive was irrelevant.[12] Books about sexual activity especially for the mass market, even if not designed to titillate, were likely to be prosecuted.

And the basest form of sexual activity was 'inversion', 'the love that dare not speak its name': homosexuality, buggery and sodomy. Writing about it was bad enough. Practising it much worse. When a louche writer is a regular practitioner, that is worst of all.

In 1895 the Marquess of Queensberry, as illiterate as he was irate, left a card at the Albemarle Club addressed to 'Oscar Wilde posing as a somdomite'. The marquess, originator of the rules for boxing, had long harboured suspicions that this clever, witty and effete celebrity had an unhealthy interest in his wayward son, Lord Alfred Douglas. Spurred on by his young lover, Wilde took ill-advised legal action for criminal libel. Queensberry hired private detectives who uncovered all sorts of evidence about Wilde consorting with rent boys. The trial against the marquess collapsed and a prosecution under the Criminal Law Amendment Act 1885 was taken out against Wilde himself. The legislation was primarily intended to protect girls, raising the age of consent from thirteen to sixteen. A late amendment inserted as section 11 penalised what it termed 'gross indecency' between males in public or in private. It did not mention women, supposedly on the grounds that Queen Victoria did not believe that lesbians existed. Gross indecency was not defined in the act, but was generally interpreted as being any homosexual behaviour short of sodomy, which remained a separate and more serious offence. Section 11 was to prove a blackmailer's charter for decades to follow.

Wilde was given every opportunity to escape to the sunnier climes and less repressive atmosphere of France, but instead he awaited his fate, staying at the Cadogan Hotel in Pont Street, Kensington. This fashionable *fin-de-siecle* establishment was owned by Lillie Langtry, the famous actress and intimate of the future King Edward VII. While sipping 'at a weak hock and seltzer' Wilde was arrested there on 5 April 1895.[13] He was charged with twenty-five counts of gross indecency and put on trial in the Old Bailey.

---

12 Thomas, *A Long Time Burning*, pp. 265f; *OHLE*, XIII, p. 368.
13 Betjeman's 'The Arrest of Oscar Wilde at the Cadogan Hotel' perfectly evokes the ambiance of this tragi-comedy. A luxurious and leisurely breakfast can still be taken in the atmospheric Cadogan, where one can contemplate the 'wonders that might have been articulate' (Sir Alfred Douglas: 'The Dead Poet') amidst memorabilia of the man and his downfall.

Sir Edward Clarke QC, who had prosecuted Queensberry, now offered his services to Wilde, and waived his fee. It was an act of extraordinary generosity and, given the level of hostility being whipped up against Wilde, moral courage.[14] The trials became a *cause célèbre,* with Wilde putting up a spirited defence, eulogising the sort of love that existed between David and Jonathan in the Bible and Achilles and Patroclus in the *Iliad.* The evidence, however, that he was sexually consorting with boys was overwhelming, including the description from a chamber maid at the Savoy that she had found a stain like the map of Ireland on his sheets. After two trials (the jury had been unable to reach a verdict in the first), Wilde was convicted, and Mr Justice Wills, passed the severest sentence that the law allowed: imprisonment with hard labour for two years. Prostitutes celebrated the sentence in the streets, but the trial judge thought it 'totally inadequate for such a case as this'.[15]

Homosexual acts remained a crime for many years. Although they were made legal in 1967 by the passing of the Sexual Offences Act, even then there were qualifications. The participants had to be twenty-one or older, had to perform their acts in private, and while duets were allowed, trios and quartets were not. It was not until 1994 that the age of consent was lowered to eighteen, and in 2000 to sixteen, and it had to take the intervention of the European Court of Human Rights to regularise things in Northern Ireland. With the Sexual Offences Act 2003, gross indecency and buggery were deleted from the statute book, and sex between more than two men became legal. It had taken several thousand years finally to rebuild Sodom and Gomorrah in England's green and pleasant land.

The prosecution of 'sodomites' and the censorship of books went hand in hand. Home Secretaries and Chief Constables most eager to pursue deviants in their clubs and cottages were most ardent in their determination to rid the country of 'literary filth'. They were the twin of obsessions of the censorious. Books about homosexuality were obvious targets. Havelock Ellis published *Sexual Inversion* in 1898. Despite the fact that Ellis could marshal a legion of medical experts to prove the book's scientific merits, and had instructed Horace Avory, a silver-tongued silk, for the defence, it was to no avail. A prosecution was taken out not against the writer but against his publisher, Thomas Bedborough. Cravenly Bedborough pleaded guilty, circumventing a trial. He was fined. The work he had published was condemned unheard.

Inversion, even when not illegal, could still be pilloried. In 1928 *The Well of Loneliness*, a lesbian novel by Radclyffe Hall published by Jonathan Cape,

---

14 Montgomery Hyde, *The Trials of Oscar Wilde* (London, 1948), p. 65.
15 *Ibid.*, p. 339

was subjected to persecution. This was odd as it contained nothing sala-cious or raunchy. 'She kissed her full on the lips like a lover' is as erotic as it gets. It was a sentimental romance of little literary merit. On publication, Havelock Ellis and Vera Brittain praised its sincerity but not its style. Cyril Connolly thought it long and tedious, a brave book to have been written, which he hoped would 'pave the way for someone to write a better'.[16] It did, however, touch a raw nerve. It was daring. After the Great War the number of lonely spinsters was high, and it was feared that lesbian relationships would proliferate. Radclyffe Hall was almost a caricature of the genre: manly, sporting a monocle, smoking cigarettes, betweeded, and with a 'companion' called Una. It was also a time when morals were thought to be in steep decline. The young preferred to dance than to go to church. 'The *ancien régime* massed to defend the *status quo*', and unleashed a 'decade of state-subsidized prurience'.[17] An irate leader in the *Sunday Express*, denouncing *The Well* as contaminating and corrupting and calling for it to be suppressed, made Jonathan Cape take fright – or see an opportunity.[18]

He sought Home Office advice as to whether the work was obscene. Any fool could have predicted the answer, as the Conservative Home Secretary was none other than Sir William Joynson-Hicks, or 'the Preposterous Jix' as he was known, an evangelical moralist and the most self-righteous philistine ever to inhabit that office.[19] Cape was no fool and it is not inconceivable that he wanted the publicity of a ban to fan sales. He had made alterna-tive arrangements to cover that eventuality. The Director of Public Prosecu-tions, Sir Archibald Bodkin, was consulted on the merits of prosecution, and his deputy in turn consulted the Chief Magistrate, Sir Charles Biron, to see if he would be amenable. Jix wrote to Cape saying that *The Well* could be 'suppressed by criminal proceedings'.[20] Cape agreed to withdraw it from publication. The heated publicity, as usual, had generated unprecedented demand. The book was about to go into its third impression. Cape, eager to cash in on the sales notoriety engendered, sent the typeset to France for publication there. Customs were ordered to seize any copies entering the country. The chairman and members of the Customs Board decided to read the work themselves. When they did they concluded that it was not obscene,

---

[16] Diana Souhami, *The Trials of Radclyffe Hall* (London, 1998), pp. 173f.

[17] Ronald Blythe, *The Age of Illusion: England in the Twenties and Thirties 1919–1940* (London, 1963), pp. 16f.

[18] Souhami, *Trials of Radclyffe Hall*, pp. 176ff.

[19] Blythe, *The Age of Illusion*, pp. 15–42. Blythe may have been hilariously unfair to his subject, but the fact remains that Jix was a bumptious prude.

[20] Souhami, *Trials of Radclyffe Hall*, p. 181.

and told Winston Churchill so. As Chancellor of the Exchequer, he was responsible for Customs and Excise. Never a prude, Churchill despised and disliked Jix. He declared that he and his Customs would take no action on the matter.[21]

Mystified by the reaction of his senior colleague, Jix had to resort to the courts in his baleful attempt to reduce 'the whole content of English literature' to 'such stuff as [he] thinks it safe to put in the hands of a schoolgirl'.[22] Like Mr Podsnap in Dickens's *Our Mutual Friend*, he had indeed said that freedom of speech and writing must be limited and the test was 'whether what was written or spoken makes one of the least of these little ones offended'. If adopted, such a test would have outlawed Shakespeare's sonnets let alone Donne's elegies. Jix feared the matter going before a jury. He had copies of *The Well of Loneliness* seized and put before the Chief Magistrate, and summoned the publishers to appear before the Bow Street magistrates' court 'to show cause why the said obscene books ... should not be destroyed'. Silencing Norman Birkett who was acting for the publishers, and refusing to hear from the author or any of her array of distinguished witnesses, Biron condemned the book to be burnt as an obscene libel. It was to remain so categorised until 1949. The storm of publicity ensured that American sales of Hall's work soared to 40,000 a week.[23] A subsequent trial in New York concluded that the book violated no law.

Explicit heterosexuality was not exempt from official censure either. Female orgasms were a particular target, from Molly Bloom in *Ulysses*, to Constance Chatterley in *Lady Chatterley's Lover*. The actions brought against these books show the opposite ends of the persecutory spectrum. Given that James Joyce, the author of *Ulysses*, lived in France and the book was published there, no British prosecution of writer or publisher was possible. Copies of the book entering the country could be impounded by customs under the 1876 Customs and Excise Act. The work was condemned by officials who 'knew pornography when they saw it'. First and foremost was Bodkin who drafted a damning opinion based on the reading of 42 of its 732 pages. As a result, from 1922 to 1936 customs officials prevented some copies getting in, but they could never find and destroy all that the ban had generated. As ever, prohibition led to proliferation. Many a reader who might never have tried Joyce was enticed to secure a copy of this prohibited work. These curious readers must have been sorely disappointed with the

---

21 Travis, *Bound and Gagged*, pp. 57ff.
22 Geoffrey Faber, quoted in Souhami, *Trials of Radclyffe Hall*, p. 192.
23 *Ibid.*, p. 221.

weighty tome they had taken pains to smuggle into the country. Most of them would have been pushed to get past page three, and few indeed would have progressed to *Finnegan's Wake*.

Most shocking to the Home Secretary, however, was a matter-of-fact request that landed on his desk in 1926. Dr F. R. Leavis of Emmanuel College, Cambridge, wanted a copy of *Ulysses* for himself and another for the University Library, the latter for the use of undergraduates attending his lectures on Joyce. The reaction of the Home Office was incredulous. The Chief Constable of Cambridge was asked by the Director of Public Prosecutions to make inquiries into Leavis and to find out if the whole thing was a hoax. Far from being a hoax, the lectures would be given to 'girl undergraduates' as well as 'boys'. Bodkin next wrote to the vice-chancellor of Cambridge University, hoping that he had either the power to stop, or to persuade Leavis to cancel, the proposed lectures. In the event the vice-chancellor had neither the power nor the inclination.[24]

Perhaps even more disquieting for the Home Office was the revelation that the former Lord Chancellor, the late Lord Birkenhead, had a copy. Another figure of literary weight, T. S. Elliot, wanted publication in England to be allowed. He gave evidence before a court in New York, as a result of which the ban on importation into the United States was lifted, while Random House published a hugely successful unlimited edition in America. Finally, in 1936, John Lane of the Bodley Head brought out a British edition, advertising it as 'the banned book read by Lord Chancellors and the subject of Cambridge lectures'. The publishers made a large profit. The Attorney-General at last stepped in with his opinion that the book was not obscene. He went even further, stating that the *Hicklin* definition of obscenity was inadequate. The question of the intention of the writer had to be taken into account.

This more liberal view was not, however, sustained, and in the 1950s another wave of censoriousness was to sweep the land. The main perpetrator of this moral crusade was the then Conservative Home Secretary, Sir David Maxwell-Fyfe.[25] Under him the rate of prosecutions soared, the number of books seized increased exponentially, and even saucy seaside postcards were removed from sale under threat of the law. The nadir was when the Swindon magistrates ordered the destruction of Boccaccio's *Decameron*, despite the fact that it was readily available in the town's public reference library. The

24 Travis, *Bound and Gagged*, pp. 26f.

25 He was appointed by Churchill in 1951. In his autobiography he makes no mention of this aspect of his tenure.

Home Office bore the brunt of public ridicule. This was not the first literary classic to be confined to the flames by mediocrities: Flaubert's *Madame Bovary*, Defoe's *Moll Flanders*, and the works of Rabelais had joined them in the incinerator. The worst predictions of those who feared that the *Hicklin* test would castrate classics of world literature were coming true.

It was, however, a turning point. The Society of Authors, led by the MPs A. P. Herbert, Roy Jenkins, Michael Foot and Norman St John-Stevas, took action, and at Christmas 1955 presented Maxwell-Fyfe with a draft Obscene Publications Bill to replace its Victorian forebear and to substitute the *Hicklin* test with one that considered the prime purpose of the book. Expert evidence on its artistic and literary merit would be admissible. The proposal got nowhere at first but the fact that its sponsor was Roy Jenkins was significant. He would himself one day become Home Secretary, the most liberal in British history.

Before he assumed this office the pressure for reform did not diminish. In 1959 a new Obscene Publications Act, a private member's bill incorporating the Society's proposals, passed into law. It had been piloted through the House of Lords by Norman Birkett, who all those years before had tried in vain to prevent *The Well of Loneliness* from being denounced as obscene. No one would claim that *The Well* was a great work of literature, but the existing legal test, Birkett pointed out, would consign such undoubted literary masterpieces as Chaucer's *Reeve's Tale*, Shakespeare's *Romeo and Juliet*, and Pepys's *Diary*, to the gutter.[26]

Most importantly, section 4 of the new act introduced a new defence. Even if a book were found to have a tendency to deprave and corrupt, if it could be shown that publication was justified 'as being for the public good on the ground that it is in the interests of science, literature, art or learning, or of other objects of general concern', it would escape condemnation and seizure. Expert evidence was at last admissible. Birkett, recalling his own experience with Radclyffe Hall, told the house that he had 'a wild feeling of regret' that it had not been possible for him to address a jury in the first case brought before the courts.[27] It was, nonetheless, a very odd compromise. An article may indeed deprave and corrupt but all for the public good! The great test case on section 4 would come but a year later. Birkett would not appear for the defence as he had longed to do, but another legal titan did: Gerald Gardiner QC, who would one day, as Lord Chancellor, engineer the abolition of capital punishment.

---

[26] Hyde, *Norman Birkett*, pp. 584f.
[27] *Ibid.*, p. 586.

In May 1960, heartened by the new act, Allen Lane, the founder of Penguin Books, announced that he would publish in Britain 200,000 unexpurgated copies, in a cheap paperback edition, of a twentieth-century classic, *Lady Chatterley's Lover* by D. H. Lawrence. Throughout his career Lawrence's works – novels, poetry, paintings – had been subjected to almost unprecedented hostility and condemnation. *Lady Chatterley*, long banned in this country, was a challenge. Senior Treasury Counsel, Mervyn Griffith-Jones, opined that 'if no action is taken in respect of this publication it will make proceedings against any other novel very difficult'.[28] The fact that suppressing such a novel now seems absurd shows how rapidly mores change. The obvious of yesterday is the inconceivable of today.

Penguin Books Ltd was duly charged with publishing an obscene article. They were tried at the Old Bailey before Mr Justice Byrne and a jury. Under the new law the defence could call expert witnesses as to the literary merits of the book and the 'public good'. This they would do by battalions, from E. M. Forster to the bishop of Woolwich. In contrast, the Crown called no one. This was not for lack of trying, but none could be found to assist. In a delicious irony they even considered asking F. R. Leavis, who had written of *Lady Chatterley* that Lawrence's 'use of obscenity is an offence against taste'.[29] To disparage the book as literature, however, is not to encourage its prosecution and support its suppression. Leavis would not help.

Instead the prosecution decided to count the number of swear words in the work, a task as laborious as it was laughable. The farcical nature of the whole proceedings was revealed in the prosecutor's opening. Griffith-Jones solemnly informed the jury that the novel contained thirty occurrences of the word 'fuck' or 'fucking', fourteen of 'cunt', and four of 'cock'. Other than number-crunching he invited the jury of nine men and three women to apply, not the new legal test, but his own, to the work: would they approve of their sons or daughters – 'because girls can read as well as boys' – reading this book? Would they leave it lying around the house? Would they wish their wives or servants to read it?[30] It was the voice of another age trying to elicit outrage, but only provoking mirth. More mirth was later produced in the House of Lords when one of its members said he had no objection to his daughter reading the book, but the strongest objection to it being read

---

28 Travis, *Bound and Gagged*, p. 145.
29 *Ibid.*, p. 149.
30 C. H. Rolph, *The Trial of Lady Chatterley* (London, 1961), pp. 17–20. Rolph's account of the trial was banned in Australia – along with the novel – because it might in itself 'deprave or corrupt': Geoffrey Robertson, *The Justice Game* (London, 1998), p. 9.

by his gamekeeper. As counsel floundered so did his case. The jury, after less than three hours' deliberation, found Penguin Books Ltd not guilty.

No publicity is bad publicity, but this was great publicity as the publishers had anticipated. Within a year over two million copies of *Lady Chatterley* were sold, outselling the Bible. Thus was D. H. Lawrence's least-accomplished novel propelled into the halls of eternal fame. In 1990 it even became a 'Book at Bedtime' on Radio 4. In their efforts to stifle freedom by the deployment of repressive laws the authorities never seemed to learn.[31]

This was exemplified – and again cheerfully exploited by the defendant – seven years later in the only prosecution for obscenity where witnesses were called who acknowledged that they had indeed been corrupted. One such was David Sheppard, formerly England's cricket captain and then a bishop. The corruption came from his reading *Last Exit to Brooklyn*, a book published by John Calder, which regaled in some detail the seamier side of the lives of New York drug addicts and rent boys. After the publishers had been convicted at the Old Bailey and fined a paltry amount, the case went to the Court of Appeal. There the judges were persuaded by John Mortimer's argument that 'the descriptions of homosexual prostitution and drug-taking in the book were so revolting that, far from turning anyone to such practices, they would cause a sharp upswing in the marriage rate and the consumption of unadulterated "Old Holborn" tobacco'.[32] The conviction was quashed, not ostensibly on this ground but on the anomaly produced by the act: the trial judge had inadequately directed the jury that even if the book were obscene they had to determine whether publication was in the public good. *Last Exit* became a best seller. Publishers could make a good profit living off immoral earnings.

Mortimer developed a taste for such cases, defending the 'Schoolkids Issue' of the 'underground' magazine *Oz* in 1971. In it, amongst other instances of deliberately provocative adolescent erotica, the revered 'Rupert the Bear' had been depicted with a gargantuan erection ravishing a 'virgin granny'. The trial included surreal interchanges about the precise age of the cartoon character, and a defence witness, in response to a judicial query, telling the mortified Judge Argyll that cunnilingus was known in the navy as 'yodelling in the canyon'. Visiting American judges and their wives could not contain

---

31   In 1985 Mrs Thatcher's efforts to suppress the very mediocre *Spycatcher*, an indiscrete account of MI5 written by a former Assistant Director, Peter Wright, cost the Treasury £250,000, brought the law into international ridicule, ensured a wide readership for a pitiful book that would otherwise have passed without notice, and turned the author into a delighted millionaire.

32   John Mortimer, *Clinging to the Wreckage* (London, 1982), p. 182.

their mirth. One asked if they were 'running this thing right through the tourist season?' Meanwhile young protestors outside the Old Bailey carried placards bearing the legend, 'An Orgasm a Day Keeps the Doctor Away'.[33] Maybe so, but it could not keep a guilty verdict at bay. Another resounding defeat at trial met with success on appeal. It was becoming a habit.

The other aspect of moral delinquency that made a rare – and what may have been a final – appearance in court was blasphemy. In 1977 the redoubtable moral censor, Mary Whitehouse, 'ever on the lookout for material likely to cause her offence',[34] resurrected an arcane and archaic common law offence of blasphemous libel (which afforded legal protection solely to the sensitivities of the Established Church),[35] and proceeded to launch a private prosecution against Denis Lemon and his publication, *Gay News*. This niche newspaper had printed James Kirkup's explicitly homoerotic poem about Jesus's deposition from the cross, entitled 'The Love That Dares to Speak Its Name'.

Mortimer was instructed for Lemon. Geoffrey Robertson, a young Australian who had been instrumental in getting Mortimer for the *Oz* trial, represented *Gay News*. He confessed to having a soft spot for Mary White-house, ever since he had 'trodden on her toes at the Young Conservatives Ball'. In return she dubbed him 'the Devil's Advocate'. Mortimer, too, was a reluctant admirer of the redoubtable lady.[36]

Before the trial began at the Old Bailey there was legal argument of some significance. The defence submitted that the publication should be prosecuted under the Obscene Publication Acts of 1959 and 1964, rather than for the common law offence of blasphemy. This would have allowed expert evidence on the literary merits of the poem to be called. The judge, Alan King-Hamilton, recognised that in such circumstances an acquittal was likely, and ruled against this proposal. Blasphemy was the mischief here.[37] Literature was not to be an issue, but theology, you might think, was. Not for King-Hamilton, who ruled that as all the jurors had sworn on the New

33 Graham Lord, *John Mortimer: The Devil's Advocate* (London, 2005), pp. 150–7; Mortimer, *Clinging to the Wreckage*, p. 3.

34 John Mortimer, *Murderers and Other Friends* (London, 1994), p. 83.

35 In the seventeenth century the common laws courts assumed jurisdiction for what had previously been an offence cognisable only in the ecclesiastical courts. To attack or ridicule the Established Church was deemed to subvert the state. Blasphemy had last been prosecuted in 1922 and had long been thought obsolete.

36 Robertson, *The Justice Game*, pp.136f; Mortimer, *Murderers and Other Friends*, p. 87.

37 Alan King-Hamilton, *And Nothing But the Truth: An Autobiography* (London, 1982), pp. 174ff.

Testament and must be assumed to know what it said, neither side should call such evidence.[38]

There followed a surreal trial during which the jury heard the prosecution opening and were given a copy of the poem. The Crown called no evidence. It was a classic example of the legal maxim *res ipsa loquitur* – 'the thing speaks for itself'. The defence were restricted to calling character witnesses, one of whom shocked the judge by telling him that her sixteen-year-old son read *Gay News*. Then followed the closing speeches in which the barristers quoted more from the Bible than from their law books. The silver tongue of Robertson, that of a serpent though it be, was seductive. Mary Whitehouse later wrote:

> I shall never forget the dreadful sense of despair which overwhelmed me after hearing Geoffrey Robertson sum up for the defence. It was a truly remarkable performance. His manner was gentle and persuasive. In the silence that fell upon the court Robertson talked about God's love for sinners and for homosexuals who, like everyone else, might have hope of salvation and redemption … he picked up The Book of Common Prayer and drew the jury's attention to the words of the communion service: 'This is my Body – *eat* this. This is my Blood – *drink* this.' … God must have spoken through Robertson's words, whatever his intent.[39]

The Devil's disciple or the Wizard of Oz? John Mortimer was just as powerful an orator, but perhaps less in tune with this Bible-believing jury:

> The prosecution is this case appears on behalf of unknown supernatural forces and my learned friend Mr Robertson for a company without corporeal existence. I alone appear for a human being, who is in the dock in peril on this antique charge which has not been used for more than fifty years. The Sermon on the Mount tells us to love our neighbours, but Mrs Mary Whitehouse has put her neighbour in the dock.[40]

King-Hamilton had been chosen to try this case because, as a Jew, he was deemed impartial. Nonetheless he felt inspired by a power beyond himself. By all accounts – not just his own – he gave a masterly – and damning – summing up.[41] While the jury deliberated, the prosecutrix led prayers invoking divine assistance in securing a conviction. The jury duly obliged. *Gay News* and Lemon were fined. This time the appeal which went as far

38 Robertson, *The Justice Game*, p. 140.
39 *Ibid.*, p. 144.
40 *Ibid.*, p. 147; Lord, *John Mortimer*, p. 193. Mortimer conceded that Robertson's was the better speech: *Murderers and Other Friends*, p. 86.
41 Robertson, *The Justice Game*, p.148; King-Hamilton, *And Nothing But the Truth*, p. 180.

as the Law Lords was lost. Publication of the mediocre poem was banned as blasphemous. It was spitting in the wind. Every undergraduate in the country had access to copies distributed clandestinely by *Socialist Challenge* in a special July 1977 supplement, securing for the poem a readership way in excess of the norm for such a publication as *Gay News*. Many kept this exotic piece of illicit erotica as a precious memento of a bygone age. In 1983 the *Penguin Book of Homosexual Verse* listed the poem in the contents but, on the page on which it should have appeared, printed a disclaimer that it remained 'unavailable to the British public'. In reality, far more of the British public had access to the poem than if it had never received the oxygen of litigation and the inflammatory allure of martyrdom. The prohibition on its publication continues but is breached with impunity.[42]

Although the law against blasphemy is still extant it is hard to envisage its future use. In 1989 an attempt was made to prosecute Salman Rushdie's *The Satanic Verses*, but as the protection of the law did not extend beyond the Anglican faith, the prosecution was wholly misconceived and soon foundered. Had it gone ahead, a randomly selected jury would inevitably have acquitted, as anyone who had actually read the book, as opposed to burning it, would soon have realised how innocuous it was.[43]

In recent years, although the Obscene Publications Acts are still on the statute book, they are rarely invoked. Even the sale and possession of hardcore pornography has in effect become legal. Only what is called 'extreme pornography' – images of bestiality, of necrophilia, of genital mutilation, and of life-threatening acts – and pornographic images of children are actively prosecuted. All adults, not just Home Office or Customs officials acting on their behalf, are now responsible for what they choose to read and see. The public may well welcome the protection of the law, but is no longer so tolerant of its intrusion.[44]

The age of the legal suppression of homosexual activity, obscenity and blasphemy has ended in a whimper. The law could no more stem the moral 'slide' than could Canute the tide. We look back on its attempt with as much

---

[42] It is published in both Robertson, *The Justice Game*, pp. 145ff, and Travis, *Bound and Gagged*, pp. 258f.

[43] The public burning of *The Satanic Verses*, and a murderous *fatwah*, ensured its immortality.

[44] The law still intrudes into private life. Incest, bestiality and bigamy all remain crimes, and as recently as 1994, in the case of *Brown and Others*, the House of Lords narrowly upheld convictions on the basis that consent is no defence to the infliction of wounds or physical harm during sado-masochistic activity.

merriment as amazement, as no doubt future generations will look back on some of the moralistic and futile endeavours of our time. Meanwhile another, less amusing, relic of the past was also to be dispatched in the heady days of the 'permissive society'.

CHAPTER 33

Hanging in the Balance

The long and distressing controversy over capital punishment is very unfair to anyone meditating murder.

Archbishop Fisher, *Parliamentary Debates*, 1957

ENGLAND in the late eighteenth century had witnessed the highpoint of hanging. In the nineteenth century Peel and more radical reformers such as Romilly and Mackintosh had successfully restricted its ambit, until by 1861 only murder, treason, piracy with violence, and arson in the royal dockyards were deemed worthy of death. Progress thereafter stymied. In the eyes of public moralists such as Dickens and Thackeray, the worst excesses of public hangings – the lewd deportment of the crowds who came to gawk and get drunk – were removed after 1868 by confining all hangings behind prison doors. The process was sanitised, the procedure was carried out with solemnity and decorum and with the imprimatur and involvement of the Established Church, the numbers of those hanged were few, the offences for which they hanged were grave. It was Bill Sykes who was hanged for committing murder, no longer the Artful Dodger for picking pockets.

It was not until after the Great War that agitation to abolish the death penalty was revived, this time with political support. Newly elected MPs secured the establishment of a House of Commons Committee on Capital Punishment. The demise of the Labour government in 1931, however, put paid to further parliamentary progress. In the fraught and fear-filled 1930s such interest in abolition as persisted was kept alive by an unlikely duo: a leading socialist intellectual and future archbishop of Canterbury, and an eccentric millionairess with a suspect foreign name.

William Temple was a novelty: an eminent Anglican divine who actually opposed capital punishment. This was significant. Fines or imprisonment did not require religious sanction. Capital punishment always did. Both proponents and opponents relied on scripture. Its clerical defenders, from Archdeacon Paley in the eighteenth century to Archbishop Fisher in the twentieth, resolutely upheld its practical efficacy and its Old Testament imprimatur. Hanging was not just a deterrent; it was a moral and religious necessity. Abolitionists, predominantly Quakers, were prone to cite statistics

18. The indomitable 'V.D. Elsie', the eccentric and effective abolitionist, in characteristic pose.

and the milder tenets of the New Testament.[1] Temple, for the first time, managed to mount a coherent philosophical critique of capital punishment from the very heart of the Anglican establishment. His was a voice that could neither be ignored nor belittled. He had access to the corridors of power. He

---

1   For a full exposition of this theme see Potter, *Hanging in Judgment, passim.*

could command polite and respectful attention from politicians and jurists alike. Yet, in the prelude to another world conflagration, his was a voice speaking in the political wilderness. He was heard but not heeded.

Another more strident voice and one that shrieked for notice was that of the redoubtable Mrs Violet Van der Elst. A marvellous eccentric, largely lost to history, she was of considerable significance in keeping the issue of the death penalty 'alive' during a period typified by apathy. Of considerable means and indomitable perseverance, in 1935 she began a campaign of street protests against hanging. She engaged professional publicity agents and proceeded to develop her crusade on sensational lines. First she procured over 100,000 signatories for her petition urging the reprieve of a murderer called Brigstock. When that failed she hired two aeroplanes to trail black flags over Wandsworth Prison on the morning of his execution, while dozens of men with sandwich-boards patrolled outside the gates. At 9.00am, the time of the 'drop', ranks of women knelt in prayer and bared their heads. Promising to get 'worse and worse', she returned a fortnight later for a similar demonstration against another execution. This time the police were out in force and prevented her loudspeaker-vans from approaching the prison. Undeterred, Mrs Van der Elst, dressed in full mourning, drove her lemon Rolls Royce through the police cordon to the gates of Wandsworth Prison, going over one officer's foot in the process. The authorities were horrified by her antics but impotent. Her aeroplanes had committed no flying offences. So concerned with her activities was the Home Office that it told Special Branch to investigate her origins since her name suggested she might be an alien – she was in fact an Englishwoman who had married a Belgian.[2]

On another occasion she stopped a lorry and offered the driver £200 to ram his vehicle through the prison gates. The driver agreed, the attempt failed, but the door of publicity was opened to this strange little woman. Buoyed up by this, she capitalised on the attentions of the press – who dubbed her 'V.D. Elsie' – to book at the cost of £1000 the Queen's Hall, Langham Place, for a mass meeting in June 1935. The evening began with a concert of music composed by the impresario herself. She then regaled the large audience, calling for volunteers but not money – she had plenty – and claiming that she had received 'three million letters worldwide in support'. Two plain-clothes police officers had been sent to spy on this subversive gathering. They noted that all those attending were 'respectably dressed' and that the chairman was a colonel. Although at the end someone shouted 'Red Front', no obvious extremists were present other perhaps than two Salvation

---

2   Home Office Files HO 45 677344/2a; HO 45 677344/6; HO 45 677344/10.

Army officers in uniform. It was noted with relief that Mrs Van der Elst was not 'too well educated and sometimes used bad grammar'.[3]

Frustrated by the attitude of the Established Church, and determined to stimulate public interest, in 1937 she launched a new religion in which lives would be changed by hypnotism, criminals cured, and the campaign against hanging re-galvanised.[4] Her self-publicity knew no bounds. She even commissioned a pastiche of the crucifixion. On a hill several people hung from the gallows. On the left stood a red-robed judge, on the right a group of weeping figures, between them with arms outstretched, both guardian angel and Christ figure, was Mrs Van der Elst.[5] And on and on she went. Until the late 1950s she was to be seen with her supporters keeping vigil outside prisons on the eve on an execution and singing hymns on the morning of it. She never gave up, she never calmed down. She lived just long enough to see success, dying in 1966. Yet it was this strange woman that the Prime Minister, Clement Attlee, said had done more than anyone else to secure abolition.[6] She had certainly made capital punishment a laughing stock, and an institution that was based on solemnity and reverence could not long survive pantomime. As the 1930s receded and the 1950s advanced, momentum changed.

The ultimate demise of the death penalty, however, is attributable to a transformation in the views of politicians and the press, of church leaders and academics, and even of prison governors and judges. For the first time, the majority of all elements of the elite class would favour abolition, and so the days of the death penalty were numbered. What brought about this transformation? The year 1953 proved decisive, when the publication of the Royal Commission on Capital Punishment's long-awaited report coincided with two of the most notorious capital cases.

In 1948 a Royal Commission had been established, not to consider the abolition of capital punishment but whether its scope could be restricted and its operation refined. Finding a chairman was a problem, since obvious candidates such as Lord Birkett declined. It was not until April 1949 that the composition of the Commission was completed under the chairmanship of a cautious, diplomatic, and wise civil servant, Sir Ernest Gowers. A safe pair of hands and not the sort of man to rock the boat. For over four years the commissioners met in a stately first-floor room in Carlton House Terrace.

3   Home Office File HO 45 677344/16.
4   Charles Gattey, *The Incredible Mrs Van der Elst* (London, 1972), pp. 46ff, 150.
5   *The Times*, 30 October 1936.
6   Gattey, *Mrs Van der Elst*, p. 46.

Sitting at a horseshoe table they heard evidence from the most comprehensive range of expert witnesses, British and foreign, ever assembled on the subject. They included prison officials, criminologists, lawyers, and even a hangman. When Geoffrey Fisher, the archbishop of Canterbury, was giving his evidence that capital punishment was necessary but its carrying out should be solemn, a woman in a black coat and astrakhan collar stood up and enquired if he were a Christian, and asked if Christ would have spoken as he did that day. It was Mrs Van der Elst. The session was adjourned until it was safe to resume once she had driven off in her Rolls Royce. Most significantly the Commission examined the evidence for deterrence. They enquired into the experience of the United States, they looked to Europe, they considered the work of British criminologists. They found no convincing statistical evidence that capital punishment was a deterrent.

Gowers's report was finally presented to parliament in September 1953. The commissioners, restricted as they were by their terms of reference, nonetheless came down as near as they could in favour of abolition, although ultimately they could only tinker with the edifice of the criminal law. Only with abolition, they seemed to be hinting, could all the anomalies and ambiguities of the present system, which the Commission had been set up to rectify, be put right. Some saw this as an abolitionist conspiracy, an attempt to whittle down the gallows by indirect means. There was, however, no conspiracy: it was where the evidence led.

Perhaps the greatest importance of the Royal Commission lay in the clarity with which it mustered an enormous amount of evidence both for and against the imposition of the death penalty. Such a survey had the power to make converts, the most notable of whom was the chairman himself, Sir Ernest Gowers. He had started the enquiry without any strong feelings either way about the penalty but ended it 'as a whole-hearted abolitionist – not emotionally but intellectually'.[7] To win over the public, however, appeals to emotion as much as to intellect were necessary. The year 1953 would also provide the emotional stimulus to abolition. Earlier in that year two cases undermined the twin principal pillars upon which capital punishment was sustained: that mercy would always be shown to those meriting it, and that no innocent would ever be sent to the gallows.

In November 1952 two teenagers, Derek Bentley and Chris Craig, had set out to break into a shop in Croydon. Craig had a gun, Bentley some knuckle dusters. A neighbour living opposite had spotted them on the roof

---

7   Letter to Bishop Bell, Lambeth Palace Archives, cited in Potter, *Hanging in Judgment*,
    p. 159.

of the building, and telephoned the police. Officers got onto the roof, and quickly apprehended Bentley, who shouted to his accomplice, 'Let him have it, Chris.' Craig fired several shots, killing one of the officers, Sidney Miles. Craig continued to taunt the police with, 'come on you brave coppers. I am only sixteen.' The implication was that they were cowards if they could not take on a boy, or more chillingly that he had nothing to lose because he could not hang for killing them. The less-than cowardly police did take him on, disarming and capturing him.

Both young men were convicted of murder. The jury recommended mercy for Bentley. The trial judge and Lord Chief Justice, Lord Goddard, agreed that he was the lesser offender. Nonetheless, while the more culpable Craig was sentenced to be detained at Her Majesty's Pleasure (the equivalent of a life sentence for young offenders, although Craig spent a little over ten years in gaol), Bentley was sentenced to hang. He had to be: that was the sentence decreed by law.[8]

But surely he would not swing for it? Bentley seemed so obvious a case for respite: an unarmed mentally subnormal nineteen-year-old who had been in police custody at the time of the killing, and whose accomplice, the actual perpetrator of the crime, was, at sixteen, too young to die. Even his conviction on the basis of 'joint enterprise' was determined largely on a negative construction of the ambiguous phrase, 'Let him have it, Chris.' Did he mean that Craig should surrender the gun or shoot the officer? The murder of a policeman had rightly enraged public opinion, but Bentley's imminent execution in January 1953 generated unprecedented popular and parliamentary agitation for a reprieve. The public sense of guilt was stronger than its instinct for revenge. As one participant in the drama ruefully noted: 'sympathy was abruptly switched from the unfortunate policeman and his family to the youth who faced execution'.[9]

The decision on life or death rested with the Home Secretary, Sir David Patrick Maxwell-Fyfe ('the nearest thing to death in life' as the Bar jingle then had it).[10] He took soundings of Lord Goddard, who did not recommend a reprieve. Priding himself as the minister of the Crown least likely to bow to pressure, Maxwell-Fyfe sat stony-faced and with arms crossed in the Commons when abolitionist MPs launched attacks on his obduracy, one

---

8   On the above, see David Yallop, *To Encourage the Others* (London, 1971); Francis Selwyn, *Gangland* (London, 1988); C. B. Dee and R. Odell, *Dad, Help Me Please* (London, 1990); M. J. Trow, *Let Him Have It Chris* (London, 1990).

9   Kilmuir, *Political Adventure*, p. 207.

10   Ludovic Kennedy, *On My Way to the Club* (London, 1989), p.231.

calling him 'the man who rations mercy'.[11] The agitation to win this youth a reprieve may merely have dried the ink on the death warrant. Maxwell-Fyfe would not yield to what he considered to be 'hysteria'.[12] Derek Bentley had to die to uphold the morale of the police force. But he also had to die for the sins of his feckless generation and to deter other young hoodlums from hiding behind perpetrators too young to be hanged. Maxwell-Fyfe told a meeting of MPs that he accepted that Bentley was feeble-minded, illiterate and epileptic. This assessment merely confirmed him in his conclusion that 'he is a young man that society can well do without'. This cold rationale did little to dispel the feeling that his 'execution was a supreme indecency',[13] or that Maxwell-Fyfe was indeed 'the man who rations mercy'. His pusillanimous decision was counter-productive. Bentley had been executed as an example and had been made into a martyr.[14]

Within months the other, even more critical pillar undergirding the death penalty, was to be put under unprecedented pressure. Again Maxwell-Fyfe would play Atlas, not Sampson. In 1950 Timothy Evans had been executed for the murder of his wife and child, whose bodies had been found buried in the wash-house at the rear of 10 Rillington Place in London's Notting Hill. They had both been strangled. Despite having made confessions (later shown to be fabricated) admitting to his wife's murder, at trial and afterwards Evans had protested his innocence, and laid the blame on his former landlord and the chief prosecution witness, John Christie. Not only was Evans therefore believed to be a brutal killer, he had stooped so low as to try to cover up his own crimes by implicating a wholly blameless man. The revelation three years later that Christie was himself a necrophiliac mass-murderer, whose six victims were buried behind the wash-house and included his own wife, came as a bit of a shock. Christie even confessed to strangling Evan's wife – though not his daughter. He was duly executed in 1953, but not for the murders Evans was alleged to have committed. It was apparent to all but the blind and deaf that a psychopath had been allowed to carry on a killing spree while an innocent man had been hanged for crimes he did not commit.

---

[11] Kilmuir, *Political Adventure*, p. 206, who states that he was called this by the Labour MP Tom Driberg.

[12] *Ibid.*, pp. 206ff.

[13] R. T. Paget, *Hanged – and Innocent?* (London, 1953), p. 110.

[14] In 1993 Bentley received a royal pardon for his sentence, and in 1998 won a posthumous appeal against conviction on the basis of Goddard's summing-up which, in the words of Lord Bingham, the then Lord Chief Justice, was 'such as to deny the appellant that fair trial which is the birthright of every British citizen'.

The execution of the innocent would pose an insurmountable problem to the proponents of capital punishment. The Home Office knew this and did its best to maintain the infallibility of the system. Maxwell-Fyfe had once said that there was no practical possibility of an innocent man being hanged, and he still believed what he said. The problem was that others were losing their faith. In an attempt to quell doubts arising from the Evans and Christie cases, in July 1953 – the same month that Christie hanged – Maxwell-Fyfe instigated a brief private enquiry under John Scott Henderson QC. Within ten days a report was completed, concluding that Evans was guilty of murdering his wife and child, Christie's later confession to being the killer was false, and that there were, by coincidence, two psychopathic murderers living under the same roof at the same time. This conclusion may have assuaged the concerns of the Home Secretary – although in his memoirs he makes no mention of the Evans or Christie case, nor of the report he commissioned – but it carried little weight with the public or MPs. For them, if not for the Home Office, the case demonstrated beyond reasonable doubt that the possibility of a miscarriage of justice in a capital trial could not after all be wholly excluded and an innocent person might suffer death as a result.

Victor Hugo had written that he preferred to call the guillotine 'Lesurques' (the name of an innocent executed), not because he believed that everyone executed was innocent, but that one was enough to erase the value of capital punishment for ever. The debate over deterrence would always be clouded in the public mind by seemingly contradictory statistics, but one demonstrable mistake was enough to shake the gallows to its foundations. Thus in one year, a system predicated on infallibility had been smashed. The innocent could die; the venal might not receive mercy. Perhaps, in their deaths, Bentley and Evans did more to end hanging than any agitator or activist had done or would do. The death penalty had over another decade of life, but it was mortally wounded.

The momentum for its demise was quickened by the *cause célèbre* of the Ruth Ellis case. For what in other countries would be described as a *crime passionnel*, in which a jilted woman shot her unfaithful lover, this young mother was sentenced to hang. Fifty thousand people signed a petition for mercy, while the *Daily Mirror* led the press campaign against Ellis's hanging. In vain. The law would run its course, and Ruth Ellis would die. On the morning of 13 July 1955, in the last minutes of her life, as she prayed before a crucifix, the crowd outside Holloway Prison joined with Mrs Van der Elst in the chant 'Evans – Bentley – Ellis'. These were the names of the 'martyrs' – the Abolitionist Trinity – that would stalk capital punishment in its declining years, and help bring it down.

The 1957 Homicide Act, devised largely by the Lord Chancellor, Viscount Kilmuir as Maxwell-Fyfe had become, and backed by Archbishop Fisher, was the last ditch attempt to retain hanging as a judicial punishment while removing its most objectionable aspects. It was doomed to failure. The anomalies and injustices it engendered made capital punishment even more odious in the minds of many. The only remaining option was abolition. The moment came in 1965. The leaders of the Conservative and Liberal parties, and the Labour Prime Minister, were all abolitionists. The Lord Chancellor, Gerald Gardiner, was a Quaker who, because he might have had to pass a death sentence, had twice declined appointments to the High Court Bench. The new archbishop of Canterbury, Michael Ramsey, and a host of recently appointed diocesan bishops were wholeheartedly opposed to the death penalty. Prominent writers and academics wrote books and pamphlets in favour of abolition. Even an erstwhile executioner, Albert Pierrepoint, belatedly denounced his trade as futile. Sidney Silverman, the veteran Labour MP and inveterate campaigner, presented a private member's bill to abolish the death penalty, and the Cabinet allowed time for debate.

The greatest opposition came, as had always been the case, from the House of Lords. Archbishop Ramsey made a major speech in favour of abolition. Kilmuir was one of his most vigorous opponents. The turnaround in the Anglican Church bewildered and disturbed him. In over forty years in politics he never thought that he 'should see the day when public opinion would be sneered at from the Bench of Bishops and every other part of this House'[15] This was now a voice from the past, and represented a minority in the Lords. The bill passed by 204 votes to 104. The Murder (Abolition of the Death Penalty) Bill became law in November 1965. After an affirmative vote four years later, it remained, and remains, on the statute book. Later attempts to revive the ultimate penalty have all come to naught, and capital punishment has been consigned to the history books and to Madame Tussauds.

---

[15] *Parliamentary Debates (Lords)*, 5th series, vol. 268, col. 634.

CHAPTER 34

A Murder in Catford

A trial judge, a single appeal judge and a full Court of Appeal had all been
shown to have gone wrong. Every safeguard of our legal system had not only
proved itself to be ineffective, but had actually facilitated the tragic miscarriage
of justice that had occurred.

Christopher Price and Jonathan Caplan, *The Confait Confessions*

IN 1984, the single most important piece of criminal justice legislation in
modern times, other than the abolition of the death penalty, was placed
on the statute book. Just as the Adolf Beck scandal gave rise to the Court of
Criminal Appeal, so it took another miscarriage of justice before parliament
would act to protect suspects on the street and in the police station. The 1984
Police and Criminal Evidence Act for the first time ensured due process by
laying down the rights of those in police detention, as well as the criteria
governing the stopping, searching or questioning of suspects. That this provision was urgently needed is shown by the case that propelled it into being.[1]

At about 1.30a.m. on 22 April 1972 the body of Maxwell Confait was
found by firemen in his room at 27 Doggett Road, Catford, one of those
nondescript areas so common in south London. He had been strangled, and
an attempt to set fire to the premises had been made. Two doctors, on the
basis of *rigor mortis*, concluded that death had certainly occurred some hours
before the body was found and most likely between 8.00pm and 10.00pm.
Neither doctor deigned to employ the most accurate method of fixing the
time of death. They had both heard that the deceased was prone to indulge
in 'unnatural practices', and so they had declined to take the rectal tempera-
ture. This fastidiousness may have saved their blushes but it was to consign
three innocent boys to years of imprisonment.

Confait was twenty-six years old and from the Seychelles. He was a transvestite prostitute known locally as 'Michelle'. The trial judge, insensitively
even by the standards of the 1970s, was to refer to him as 'an odd creature
… and no great loss to the world'. Suspicion initially fell on his landlord,

---

[1] The account in this chapter is reliant on Christopher Price and Jonathan Caplan, *The
Confait Confessions* (London, 1976), *passim*.

Winston Goode. The circumstantial evidence against Goode was strong. A married man with five children, he was bisexual, and, it was thought, had been Confait's lover. The landlord and his tenant had certainly consorted together, and on several occasions had gone, both in drag, to West End clubs. Goode was also possessive and jealous. There was evidence that they had recently quarrelled and that Confait was intending to leave Doggett Road altogether. Goode gave inconsistent accounts to the police of what had happened on the night of the murder and was accused by them of the murder. He was not charged. Shortly afterwards he was admitted to a mental hospital. Two years later he would kill himself by taking cyanide.

The police suddenly changed tack. Whether through laziness, complacency or conviction, they diverted their attention onto three youths who had been arrested for arson in the locality. They were Ahmet Salih who, although the youngest at fourteen, was also the brightest; Ronald Leighton, who was fifteen but with an IQ of 75; and Colin Lattimore, who was eighteen but with the mental age of an eight-year-old. They were young, they were delinquent, they were fire-raisers, and most of all they were easy prey. Before 1984 the procedures under which suspects were detained or questioned was governed by the so-called 'Judges' Rules', judicial advice on the proper conduct of police investigations and the mode of questioning of suspects, the infringement of which might lead to evidence being excluded at trial.[2] At least in the eyes of the courts the police had a marvellous reputation for never breaking these rules, despite which confessions were surprisingly but gratifyingly commonplace. The three youths were questioned by the police at Ladywell Police Station and duly confessed. Colin Lattimore was the first, and his example seems to have led to a landslide.

On the basis of these confessions they were all sent to the Old Bailey in November 1972 to be tried by Mr Justice Chapman and jury, two for murder, and Salih for arson with intent to endanger life. Their lawyers included two Queen's Counsel (John Marriage and Cyril Salmon), and an experienced junior barrister later to become a QC and a circuit judge (Brian Watling). After a three-week trial they were convicted of a variety of offences by a unanimous jury. The trial judge passed sentences accordingly: Leighton, who had been convicted of murder, was detained during 'Her Majesty's Pleasure'; Lattimore, who had been convicted of manslaughter on the grounds of diminished responsibility, was detained under the Mental Health Act 1959; and Salih was given four years in youth detention for arson with intent. They had been tried in accordance with English law; they had been represented

---

[2]   These were first formulated in 1912, revised in 1918, and reformulated in 1964.

by eminent practitioners; their fate had been decided by an impartial jury of their peers. Justice for a poor, unfortunate, 'mixed-up' transvestite had been done.

The only problem was that justice had not been done for anyone, as those convicted were all demonstrably innocent. It was quite clear that the interviewees had been fed details by the officer in charge of the investigation, Detective Chief Superintendent Alan Jones. Even with such assistance their 'confessions' did not add up. The time of death precluded their involvement: Lattimore in particular had a rock-solid alibi until 1.00am. It also utterly destroyed the authenticity of their confessions which in any case were riddled with implausibilities and inconsistencies. At trial, however, Richard Du Cann QC, for the Crown, managed to undermine, with their ready compliance, the evidence of his own medical witnesses as to the time of death, and the combined effort of the defence barristers – all six of them – seemed unable to rectify the situation. The defendants had been badly served by their lawyers, however ostensibly eminent. The initials 'QC' after a name were often a reward for political success, or compensation for services rendered to the legal profession; they were not a guarantee of quality. Expecting an easy victory, confident that the timings would prove their clients innocent, the defence had done too little preparation, and had not even instructed their own expert. They were taken by surprise by events in court and did not have the resources or ability to fight back. They were far too deferential to the doctors who were fudging their evidence. Not one asked either doctor the vital question: 'could Confait have been killed as late as 1.00am on 22 April?' Both doctors later confirmed in a television documentary on the case that he could not. Too late. The barristers had put on a very poor show.

Nor did they do any better with other aspects of the case, including exploring the guilt of Winston Goode. Such efforts as were made were dismissed by the trial judge as 'defence tactics'. He too seemed determined to secure convictions against these defendants. The law was not blind but blinkered. With the exception of Salih's counsel, the only leader who was not a QC, no attempt was made to have the interviews excluded. The interviews were not just central to the prosecution case: they were the prosecution case. They were all open to challenge, but in the event only one was actively disputed. The judge even used the fact that no objection was made when he directed the jury on the reliability of the interviews. It was quite extraordinary. The defence barristers seemed to be in a trance, going through the motions – and some not doing even that – but with no vigour, no fire, and no forensic ability. Thomas Erskine or Marshall Hall they were not. The convictions were appealed, and the appeals dismissed.

After public campaigning, maintained by the strenuous efforts of Latti-more's parents, led by their local MP, Christopher Price, and involving widespread newspaper and television coverage, their case was eventually referred back to the Court of Appeal by the Home Secretary, only the sixth time this power bestowed by the Criminal Appeal Act of 1968 had ever been used. On 6 October 1975 the appeal began before Lord Justice Scarman and two other appellate judges. Du Cann, in the worst tradition of the prosecution, was determined to uphold the convictions at all costs. A new counsel, however, was instructed for all three appellants, Lewis Hawser QC.

This time the medical and other evidence of the time of death was fully explored, and even the Crown's original expert, when asked for the first time, conceded that the death could not have occurred as late as 1.00am. The two defence experts were adamant. Death occurred certainly before 11.00pm. and probably much earlier. Equivocation had been brushed away, and the expert evidence was seen in sharp focus. The death of Maxwell Confait could not have been caused by the appellants, whatever they may have said to the police; their confessions were false. The appeals were allowed. The young men walked free. As a corollary, the Confait murder, so badly mishandled by the investigating officer, has never been solved. The first suspect, Winston Goode, was almost certainly responsible for both the death and the arson. His widow thought so.

The treatment of these boys demonstrated the inadequacy of the legal protections for suspects, and convinced most of the judiciary of the need for reform.[3] Belatedly, the government was forced into action, resulting in the 1984 act. Under this, among many other important measures to guard proper procedure, strong safeguards were put in place for the questioning of suspects, including the tape recording of interviews. Over time, convictions based on contested confessions largely ceased, and so too have complaints about police malpractice in this area. It is now all on tape, and often on camera as well. The following year, in another major change parliament created the Crown Prosecution Service, which took over all prosecutions

---

[3] Not all, however. In 1980 Lord Denning, in *McIlkenny* v. *Chief Constable of West Midlands Police*, when stopping the Birmingham Six from taking civil action against the police, described the possibility of a court finding that the police had perjured themselves as 'such an appalling vista that every sensible person in the land would say: "It cannot be right that these actions should go any further".' Denning had abandoned Mansfield's maxim – but in vain. On his own reputation the heavens did fall when the convictions of the Birmingham Six were finally quashed by the Court of Appeal in 1991.

from the police, thus severing the unhealthy link between the investigation of offences and their prosecution.

These young innocents paid a high price, but their suffering was productive of something of lasting good: a fundamental change to pre-trial procedures. Over the years many others have benefited from that change – including the police – and the heavens have not yet fallen.

CHAPTER 35

The Rule of Law under Threat?

A land of settled government,
A land of just and old renown,
Where freedom slowly broadens down
From precedent to precedent.
                Alfred Tennyson, 'You Ask Me Why'

As well as substantial substantive changes to the law, such as the Police and Criminal Evidence Act 1984, there have been procedural changes, some of considerable significance. Foremost, the ancient assize courts and quarter sessions were replaced by the Crown Courts in 1971, and the judicial committee of the House of Lords by a newly constituted Supreme Court, established in 2005 and starting work four years later.

The symbolism of the newly constituted 'Westminster Triangle' is striking. On the south side of Parliament Square is Westminister Abbey, the royal chapel, the national shrine, the embodiment of the Established Church and of the monarchy at the heart of the state, both now more decorative than powerful. To the east stands the Palace of Westminster – the Houses of Parliament – which has replaced the monarch as the new absolute ruler and the maker of laws. To the west is the Supreme Court, the ultimate interpreter and protector of the law. This court was new in name and had to be rehoused to befit its dignity, and to distance it physically from parliament. Whereas the old judicial committee met in the House of Lords itself, the new Supreme Court moved into the refurbished Middlesex Guildhall in Parliament Square. The building housing it is impressive, but is dwarfed by both the Abbey and the Palace.

The symbolism seems to say that the monarch as source of law may have been replaced by parliament, but whoever makes the law still controls the law. The master has changed but master there is. This is not true. The law, as we have seen, has a life of its own. It has permeated English society with notions of justice and fairness which cannot be legislated away, however self-important the body trying to do so. The continuing supremacy of parliament is asserted – but not proved – by self-proclamation and long acquiescence. The common law saw off despotic kings. It would take up cudgels in the event of being confronted with a tyrannical parliament.[1] The law does not seek conflict with the legislature. It wants accommodation. But if ever the very principles of English – or British – justice were at stake it would have to stand its ground. Coke's dictum in Dr Bonham's case could have new life.

In recent years, in addition to those we have considered, there have been several major threats to British legal traditions and systems. The executive of the day is responsible for some or most, but parliament is often reprehensible in allowing an 'elective dictatorship', however benign its despotic intentions, to undermine intrinsic values.[2]

Torture

The most serious stain on Britain's reputation has been an ambivalence over, or even connivance in, torture, and complicity in that euphemism for illicit ill-treatment, 'extraordinary rendition'. Lord Bingham acidly commented that 'it cannot be said that the United Kingdom has shown that implacable hostility to torture and its fruits which might have been expected of the state whose courts led the world in rejecting them both.'[3] Fortunately the courts, despite popular and political displeasure, have remained unequivocally opposed to any compromise on the issue.

In *Othman v. Secretary of State for the Home Department*,[4] the deportation to Jordan of the radical Islamist Abu Qatada was prevented, in judgments that were both very detailed and fully reasoned, first by the Special Immigration Appeals Commission (SIAC), and then, on 27 March 2013, by the civil division of the Court of Appeal. In the latter, the Master of the Rolls and two Lord Justices of Appeal were well aware that Abu Qatada was 'regarded as a very dangerous person' and that there was 'a general feeling that his deportation was long overdue'. This, however, was not 'a relevant consideration' under human rights law. Despite dismissing some of the more egregious criticisms of the Jordanian state made by the appellant's lawyers, both tribu-

---

1   In such assertions I am not alone. Denning, *What Next in the Law*, pp. 319–20; Charles Stephens, *The Jurisprudence of Lord Denning: A Study in Legal History*, 3 vols (Newcastle, 2009), I, p. 1: 'One of the most important issues in contemporary British politics is whether the will of parliament, or the rule of law, should prevail.' T. R. S. Allen, *Constitutional Justice: A Liberal Theory of the Rule of Law* (Oxford, 2001) argues that an act which subverted basic democratic rights would not be enforced by the judiciary. Contrast this with Dicey's irenic nineteenth-century view.

2   Lord Hailsham, *The Listener*, 21 October 1976, p. 497.

3   Bingham, *The Rule of Law*, p.154.

4   [2013] EWCA CIV 277.

nals held that Abu Qatada's human rights would be breached were he to be returned. He had been convicted *in absentia* of conspiracy to commit acts of terrorism and would face a retrial – mandatory under the Jordanian criminal code – during which there was *a real risk* that evidence would be admitted against him that had been gained by torture. The European Court of Human Rights had ruled that this would be a 'flagrant denial of justice', rendering the whole proceedings 'automatically unfair and a breach of Article 6'. In their ruling the three British appellate justices did not equivocate either. A nation built on common law principles must be far distant from even a hint of the use of torture:

> Torture is universally abhorred as an evil. A state cannot expel a person to another state where there is a real risk he will be tried on the basis of evidence which there is a real possibility may have been obtained by torture.

A '*real risk*' – the same words as used by the Strasbourg Court in an earlier ruling on the same case – or even no more than a '*real possibility*' was enough for the courts to prohibit removal.

In another case decided on the same day, an Ethiopian national known as JI, who had settled in Britain but who had 'thrown in his lot with Islamic extremists who are committed to terrorism', won his appeal against the SIAC decision to deport him. The judges agreed that the Home Secretary was right to order his deportation on national security grounds, but JI was to be allowed to stay because of the risk of torture or degrading treatment if he were returned to Ethiopia. They held that the Commission had erred in allowing the combination of an undertaking from the Secretary of State regarding the timing of deportation and an improvement in the monitoring of human rights violations in Ethiopia to erode, in effect, the appellant's legal safeguards. The European Convention on Human Rights extended its protection to all, including those implicated in terrorism. Everyone in Britain must be equally protected by the law. This was consonant with common law. The judges, determined to uphold the rule of law, decided to allow his appeal, but 'with little enthusiasm'. These leading members of the judiciary may have had little enthusiasm for the beneficiary of their ruling, but they were enthusiastic about repudiating torture, and keeping the common law safe from its contamination.

Legislative Diarrhoea

When some unpleasant novelty arises – such as child pornography on the internet or credit card cloning – and society wants it proscribed and punished, there is no use looking to the common law for its prohibition or to earlier judgments for legal solutions. As the Victorians knew, a fast-changing society needs new laws. This is where parliament comes in, and over the last two centuries legislation rather than case law has been the predominant factor in criminal justice. When parliament enacts such laws as the 1861 Offences Against the Person Act, under which crimes of violence are still prosecuted, or the 1984 Police and Criminal Evidence Act, which provided for essential procedural protections during the arrest, detention and questioning of suspects, all is well. Some such laws were much needed and long overdue. Legislation that is concise, coherent and comprehensible is to be welcomed and will be long-lived.

But what was once a light dusting of legislation has become a snow storm, and finally an avalanche that threatens to overwhelm the legal system. Some call it overload, others legislative diarrhoea. In the seventeenth and eighteenth centuries, Coke and Blackstone respectively had bemoaned the deleterious effect of statutes on the common law, the latter complaining that it had 'been mangled by various contradictory statutes'.[5] In 1894 Maitland could write, contrasting the present with the Middle Ages, that 'the desire for continuous legislation is modern'. He bemoaned the fact that 'year by year, parliament must meet and pour out statutes [and] every statesman must have in his mind some programme of new laws'.[6] By modern standards even Maitland's over-active Victorians were quiescent. For instance, between 1861 and 1948 there were practically no criminal justice measures enacted, and those that were covered discrete offences, such as the age of consent or official secrets, and did so succinctly. In the post-war period, and in particular since the 1970s, governments have become increasingly addicted to enacting legislation, to tinkering, to changing, to regulating, to interfering.

Ignorance competing with ineptitude is no recipe for improvement. Almost all legislation these days comes too fast, is too complex and too indiscriminate. It is often badly drafted. Much of it is a hasty response by parliament to tabloid hysteria. England is surely not changing so much as to require new criminal legalisation every year, creating new offences, changing the law of evidence, or just the nomenclature of punishments. Turning 'Community Service' into 'Community Punishment' and then 'Community Pay-Back' is not a major advance in the way society copes with crime. The worst example of elephantine legislation is the 2003 Criminal Justice Act, with its 339 sections, 38 schedules and 1169 paragraphs, and 20 pages of

---

5   Stephens, *The Jurisprudence of Lord Denning*, I, p. 30.
6   F. W. Maitland, *Selected Historical Essays* (Cambridge, 1957), p. 122.

repealed statutes. Even High Court judges have admitted to being unable to understand some of its provisions, and, as a recent Lord Chief Justice has put it, its 'infinite complexity'.[7]

The result is that, perhaps for the first time, it has become impossible for anyone – even senior members of the judiciary – to know or understand the law in any area in its entirety. There is simply too much of it and much of that is confused, confusing, and sometimes plainly unintelligible. It will be enacted today, some of it will never be brought into force, some will inadvertently and catastrophically alter other laws, some will be abolished tomorrow. Members of parliament have too little understanding of the laws they are enacting. They will, of course, blame the judges and lawyers.

Today's criminal justice system is crying out for the intervention of a twenty-first century Robert Peel, someone able to reform and rationalise the law, and stem the avalanche of parliamentary intervention. The Law Commission and others have long been advocating a criminal code. No government has shown any interest.

Crime Does Not Pay

Precisely at a time when lawyers have to be more 'learned in the law', severe cuts in public funding, begun even before the recession, are likely to reduce the effectiveness of the Crown Prosecution Service and induce the better-qualified and more-gifted defence advocates to seek out the milk and honey provided by privately paying clients. Crime does not pay. Such cuts pose a serious threat to the administration of, and access to, justice, and to the quality of advocacy, not just in criminal and family courts but in mental health and immigration tribunals as well. More and more will the courts see lay people representing themselves, not through folly on their part but out of necessity.

Judges in criminal and civil courts, where poor standards of preparation or advocacy are observed, or where litigants in person are trying to represent or defend themselves, are thus faced with the prospect of reverting to a role in the trial process which has not pertained since before the nineteenth century. Once again they will be called upon to be more activist in trials, and to enter the adversarial arena, even at times taking over cross-examination: and this in the interests of justice, not from any desire of their own.

---

7   Lord Judge in programme 3 of *The Strange Case of the Law*, BBC 4, 2012.

Trials where lay people are representing themselves are inevitably going to be longer and more diffuse, and miscarriages of justice are more likely. Any savings in public expenditure are likely to be short-lived and ephemeral, and the damage already done to the justice system may be irreversible. This is the most serious threat to public justice ever experienced, trading in a Rolls Royce for a Trabant. Thus progress?

The Jury in Jeopardy

Trial by jury is fundamental to English liberty, and is as important in the present day as it was in earlier times.

> The first object of any tyrant in Whitehall would be to make parliament utterly subservient to his will; and the next to overthrow or diminish trial by jury, for no tyrant could afford to leave a subject's freedom in the hands of twelve of his countrymen.... Trial by jury is more than an instrument of justice and more than one wheel of the constitution: it is the lamp that shows that freedom lives.[8]

This is true, even if for a century and a half the remit of the jury has continued to narrow. With few exceptions civil actions are no longer tried by juries, but by judges. Nor do many criminal cases engage trial by jury. The majority end in guilty pleas, and of the rest a large proportion are tried by magistrates. But in many contested cases, where the stakes are high and the consequences serious, it is still lay jurors who sit in judgment on their fellow citizens. Serious offences are always sent to the Crown Court, and defendant still has the right to elect for trial by jury for some less serious offences, particularly those in which dishonesty is alleged.

The jury, though not the norm, is still the bulwark of justice. Popular participation is one hallmark of the common law system. Jury service provides a unique opportunity for ordinary members of the public to gain an insight into the workings of the criminal justice system and to make important and informed decisions about their fellow citizens based on serious consideration of evidence. A beneficial side effect of the jury system is that it is good for democracy as well as for defendants.

It is, however, under threat from a number of sides. Trial by judge alone was established in Northern Ireland during The Troubles by the creation of so-called 'Diplock Courts'. More recently the Criminal Justice Act of 2003 made provision for judge-only trials in exceptional circumstances. The most

---

8   Patrick Devlin, *Trial by Jury*, rev. edn (London, 1970), p. 164.

obvious of these is jury-tampering – in days past, one of the reasons for the establishment of the Court of Star Chamber.

But the main threat to the jury system comes from within and from another modern development: the internet. A number of recent cases have revealed that some jurors, despite judicial direction to the contrary, have embarked on their own investigations or have even communicated with parties in the case. The Court of Appeal, presided over by the then Lord Chief Justice, Lord Judge, recognising the danger to the integrity of trial by jury, has passed deterrent sentences on offending jurors. Their irresponsible actions, their inability not to tell all on Facebook or Twitter, pose a real danger to the whole jury system. If it cannot preserve its integrity it cannot survive.

Last Words

The English common law has made a long and eventful journey from first gestation in Anglo-Saxon England, through its coming to birth in Plantagenet times, to its full flourishing from the sixteenth century to the present day. Its growth has been organic, and shaped by conflicts and wars. Its development has been aided by the perpetuation of myths, the ingenious interpretation of precedents, and by sheer necessity.

It persists as one of the great legal systems of the world, the greatest where the preservation of liberty is concerned. In its public guise it has overcome great dangers before, and is so ingrained in the very fabric of English society as to make for cautious optimism that it will survive these current challenges, and that its guiding principles of equality before the law, the independence of the judiciary, the right to jury trial, and the right to equality of arms in the adversarial system will survive. So much of what the English are and cherish depends upon it.

The rule of law is fundamental to lives and liberties, a constant feature in the unwritten constitution of Great Britain, and one that safeguards rights and freedoms from the over-reaching despotism, however benign, of either kings or elected governments. The remedy against the abuse of power is the rule of law. As it preserves us, we must preserve it.

Bibliography

Allen, T. R. S., *Constitutional Justice: A Liberal Theory of the Rule of Law* (Oxford, 2001).

Anstruther, R., ed., *Chronicles of Ralph Niger* (London, 1851).

Aston, Robert, *James I and his Contemporaries* (London, 1969).

Bacon, Francis, *Bacon's Essays*, ed. Richard Whatley (London, 1892).

Baker, J. H., *The Reports of John Spelman*, Selden Society, 94 (1978).

—— *The Order of Serjeants at Law* (London, 1984).

—— *The Legal Profession and the Common Law* (London, 1986).

—— *The Common Law Tradition: Lawyers, Books and the Law* (London, 2000).

—— *The Law's Two Bodies* (Oxford, 2001).

—— *An Introduction to English Legal History*, 4th edn (London, 2002).

—— *The Inner Temple: A Community of Communities* (London, 2007).

Bartlett, Robert, *Trial by Fire and Water, the Medieval Judicial Ordeal* (Oxford, 1986).

—— *England under the Norman and Angevin Kings, 1075–1225* (Oxford, 2000).

Bede, The Venerable, *History of the English Church and People*, Folio edn (London, 2010).

Benson, A. C., *The Letters of Queen Victoria*, 3 vols (London, 1907).

Bingham, Thomas, *The Rule of Law* (London, 2010).

Birkett, Norman, *Six Great Advocates* (London, 1961).

Blackstone, William, *Commentaries on the Laws of England*, 4 vols, (Oxford, 1765–69).

Blair, Peter Hunter, *Anglo-Saxon England* (Cambridge, 1956).

Blythe, Ronald, The Age of Illusion: England in the Twenties and Thirties 1919–1940 (London, 1963).

Bogdanor, Vernon, *The New British Constitution* (Oxford, 2009).

Bowker, A. E., *Behind the Bar*, 3rd edn (London, 1951).

—— *A Lifetime with the Law* (London, 1961).

Boyer, Allen, *Sir Edward Coke and the Elizabethan Age* (Stanford, 2003).

Brand, Paul, *Origins of the English Legal Profession* (Oxford, 1992).

—— *The Making of the Common Law* (London, 1993).

Brougham, Henry, *Historical Sketches of Statesmen*, 6 vols (London, 1845).

—— *Life and Times*, 3 vols (New York, 1871).

Burke, Edmund, *Correspondence*, ed. Thomas Copeland, 10 vols (Cambridge, 1958–78).

—— *Writings and Speeches*, 12 vols (New York, 2008).

—— *Reflections on the Revolution in France* (1791), Folio Society edn (London, 2010).

Burnet, Gilbert, *Death and Life of Sir Matthew Hale* (London, 1682).

—— *History of His Own Time*, 6 vols (Oxford, 1823).

Calendar of State Papers Domestic, Elizabeth, 1581–90, ed. Robert Lemon (London, 1865).

Campbell, Lord, *Lives of the Lord Chancellors*, 7th edn, 10 vols (New York, 1878).

Carlyle, Thomas, *Historical Sketches* (London, 1898).

Carpenter, David, *The Struggle for Mastery: Britain 1066–1284* (London, 2003).

Cash, Arthur, *An Essay on Woman* (New York, 2000).

—— *John Wilkes, The Scandalous Father of Civil Liberty* (New Haven, 2006).

Cavendish, George, *Thomas Wolsey*, Folio Society edn (London, 1962).

Chadwick, H. Munro, *Studies on Anglo-Saxon Institutions* (Cambridge, 1905).

Chibnall, Marjorie, ed., *The Ecclesiastical History of Orderic Vitalis*, 6 vols (Oxford, 1969–80).

—— *The Debate on the Norman Conquest* (Manchester, 1999).

Clanchy, M. T., *Early Mediaeval England*, Folio Society edn (London, 1997).

Clarendon, Earl of (Edward Hyde), *The History of the Rebellion and Civil Wars in England*, 6 vols (Oxford, 1721).

Coke, Edward, *Institutes of the Laws of England*, 4 parts (London, 1817).

—— *Selected Writings of Sir Edward Coke*, ed. Steve Sheppard, 3 vols (Indianapolis, 2003).

Cooper, R. W., *The Nuremberg Trial* (Harmondsworth, 1947).

Cowper, Francis, *A Prospect of Gray's Inn*, 2nd edn (London, 1985).

Danziger, Danny and John Gillingham, *1215: The Year of Magna Carta* (London, 2003).

Dee, C. B., and Odell, R., *Dad, Help Me Please* (London, 1990).

Denning, Alfred, *What Next in the Law* (London, 1982).

—— *Landmarks in the Law* (London, 1984).

Devlin, Patrick, *The Enforcement of Morals* (Oxford, 1965).

—— *Trial by Jury*, revised edn (London, 1970).

Dicey, A. V, *Lectures Introductory to the Study of the Law of the Constitution* (London, 1886).

Downer, L. J., ed., *Leges Henrici Primi* (Oxford, 1972).

Elton, G. R., *England Under the Tudors*, Folio Society edn (London, 1997).

English Historical Documents,

  I, *c.500–1042*, ed. Dorothy Whitelock, 2nd edn (London, 1979).

  II, *1042–1189*, ed. David Douglas and G. W. Greenaway (London, 1953).

  III, *1189–1327*, ed. Harry Rothwell (London, 1975).

  IV, *1327–1485*, ed. A. R. Myers (London, 1969).

  V, *1485–1558*, ed. C. H. Williams (London, 1967).

  V(a) *1558–1603*, ed. Ian Archer and F. D. Price (London, 2011).

  V(b) *1603–1660*, ed. Barry Coward and Peter Gaunt (London, 2010).

  VIII, *1660–1714*, ed. Andrew Browning (London, 1966).

  X, *1714–1783*, ed. D. B. Horn and Mary Ransome (London, 1969).

  XI, *1783–1832*, ed. A. Aspinall and E. A. Smith (London, 1969).

Erskine, Thomas, *Speeches*, 4 vols (Chicago, 1876).

Fletcher, Richard, *Bloodfeud: Murder and Revenge in Anglo-Saxon England* (Oxford, 2003).

Foot, Sarah, *Aethelstan, The First King of England* (New Haven and London, 2011).

Fortescue, Sir John, *De Laudibus Legum Angliae* (Cincinnati, 1874).

Foss, Edward, *Biographia Juridica* (London ,1870).

Gannon, Anna, *The Iconography of Early Anglo-Saxon Coinage* (Oxford, 2003).

Gardiner, S. R., *History of England*, 18 vols (London, 1863–97).

Gash, Norman, *Mr Secretary Peel* (London, 1961).

Gattey, Charles, *The Incredible Mrs Van der Elst* (London, 1972).

Geoffrey of Monmouth, *History of the Kings of Britain*, Folio Society edn (London, 2010).

Gerard, John, *The Autobiography of a Hunted Priest*, trans. Philip Caraman (New York, 1952).

Gest, John, *The Lawyer in Literature* (Boston, 1913).

Gibbon, Edward, *Miscellaneous Works of Edward Gibbon, Illustrated from his Letters, with Occasional Notes and Narrative, Complete in One Volume*, ed. John, Lord Sheffield (London, 1787).

Gibson, William, *James II and the Trial of the Seven Bishops* (London, 2009).

Gilmour, Ian, *Riot, Risings and Revolution: Governance and Violence in Eighteenth-Century England* (London, 1992).

Green, Thomas, *Verdict According to Conscience: Perspectives on the English Criminal Trial by Jury, 1200–1800* (Chicago, 1985).

Gregg, Pauline, *Free-born John: A Biography of John Lilburne* (London, 1961).

Guy, John, *The Cardinal's Court: The Impact of Thomas Wolsey in Star Chamber* (Hassocks, 1977).

Hale, Matthew, *Pleas of the Crown*, 2 vols (London, 1736).

Hall, G. D. G., ed., *The Treatise of the Laws and Customs of England commonly called Glanvill* (London, 1965).

Halliday, Paul, *Habeas Corpus from England to Empire* (Cambridge, MA, 2010).

Harding, Alan, *The Law Courts of Medieval England* (London, 1973).

—— *Medieval Law and the Foundations of the Modern State* (Oxford, 2001).

Harris, Tim, *Revolution: The Great Crisis of the British Monarchy, 1685–1720* (London, 2006).

Hart, H. L. A., *Law, Liberty and Morality* (Oxford, 1963).

Havery, Richard, *History of the Middle Temple* (London, 2011).

Hawes, Francis, *Henry Brougham* (Edinburgh, 1957).

Hawkins, William, *A Treatise of the Pleas of the Crown*, 3rd edn, 2 vols (London, 1739).

Hibbert, Christopher, *King Mob: The London Riots of 1780* (London, 1958).

—— *Charles I* (London, 1968).

Hill, Christopher, *Liberty against the Law* (London, 1997).

Hoare, P., *Memoirs of Granville Sharp*, 2 vols (London, 1828).

Holt, J. C., *Magna Carta*, 2nd edn (Cambridge, 1992).

Hoppitt, Julian, *A Land of Liberty? England 1689–1727* (Oxford, 2000).

Hostettler, John, *A History of Criminal Justice* (Hook, 2009).

Hostettler, John and Richard Braby, *Sir William Garrow* (Hook, 2009).

Howell, T. B., ed., *State Trials*, 33 vols (London, 1809–26).

Hudson, John, *The Formation of the English Common Law* (London, 1996).

—— ed., *The History of English Law: Centenary Essays on 'Pollock and Maitland'* (Oxford, (1996).

Hudson, William, *A Treatise on the Court of Star Chamber* (London, 1792).

Huntingdon, Henry of, *History of the English People 1000–1154*, ed. D. Greenway (Oxford, 2002).

Hurd, Douglas, *Robert Peel* (London, 2007).

Hyde, Montgomery, *The Trials of Oscar Wilde* (London, 1948).

—— *Norman Birkett* (London, 1964).

James I, *King James VI and I: Political Writings*, ed. Johann Sommerville (Cambridge, 1994).

Jardine, Lisa and Alan Stewart, *Hostage to Fortune, The Troubled Life of Francis Bacon* (London, 1998).

Johnson, Cuthbert, *Life of Sir Edward Coke*, 2 vols (London, 1837).

Kantorowicz, Ernst, *The King's Two Bodies* (Princeton, 1997).

Keane, John, *Tom Paine: A Political Life* (London, 1995).

Kennedy, Ludovic, *On my Way to the Club* (London, 1989).

Kenyon, J. P., *The Stuart Constitution* (Cambridge, 1966).

Keynes, Simon and Michael Lapidge, eds, *Alfred the Great: Asser's Life of King Alfred and Other Contemporary Sources* (London, 1983).

Kilmuir, Earl of, *Political Adventure* (London, 1964).

King-Hamilton, Alan, *And Nothing But the Truth: An Autobiography* (London, 1982).

Langbein, John, *The Origins of Adversary Criminal Trial* (Oxford, 2003).

—— *Torture and the Law of Proof* (Chicago, 2006).

Langbein, John with Lerner, Renée Lettow and Smith, Bruce, *History of the Common Law* (New York, 2009).

Lawson, J. P., *The Life and Times of Archbishop Laud*, 2 vols (London, 1829).

Locke, John, *Two Treatises of Government*, ed Peter Laslett, 2nd edn (Cambridge, 1967).

Lockyer, Roger, ed., *The Trial of Charles I*, Folio Society edn (London, 1959).

Lord, Graham, *John Mortimer: The Devil's Advocate* (London, 2005).

Macaulay, Thomas Babington, *History of England*, 12th edn, 5 vols (London, 1856).

—— *Critical and Historical Essays*, 3rd edn, 3 vols (London, 1844).

Mackie, W. S., *The Exeter Book*, 2 vols (Oxford, 1934).

Maitland, F. W., *Pleas of the Crown for the County of Gloucester 1221* (London, 1884).

—— *Selected Historical Essays*, Cambridge (1957).

Malmesbury, William of, *Gesta Regum Anglorum*, ed. R. Mynors, R. Thompson and M. Winterbottom, 2 vols (Oxford, 1998).

Manning, William, *The Key of Liberty: The Life and Democratic Writings of William Manning, 'A Laborer,' 1747–1814*, ed. Michael Merrill and Sean Wilentz (Cambridge, MA, 1993).

Marjoribanks, Edward, *The Life of Edward Marshall Hall* (London, 1929).

Marvell, Andrew, *The Poems and Letters of Andrew Marvell*, ed. H. M. Margoliouth, 3rd edn, 2 vols (Oxford, 1971).

Mazzulla, F. and Mazzulla, J., *Al Packer: A Colorado Cannibal* (Denver, 1968).

McCormick, Donald, *Blood on the Sea* (London, 1962).

McDougall, Ian, ed., *Cases that Changed our Lives* (London, 2010).

Megarry, Robert, *A New Miscellany-at-Law* (Oxford, 2005).

Mitchell, Charles and Mitchell, Paul, *Landmark Cases in Equity* (Oxford, 2012).

Mortimer, John, *Clinging to the Wreckage* (London, 1982).

—— *Murderers and Other Friends* (London, 1994).

Muddiman, J. G., *The Trial of King Charles the First* (includes *King Charls, His Case*) (Edinburgh and London, 1928).

Mullin, Christopher, *A View from the Foothills* (London, 2009).

Munro Chadwick, H., *Studies on Anglo-Saxon Institutions* (Cambridge, 1905).

New, Chester, *The Life of Henry Brougham to 1830* (Oxford, 1961).

O'Brien, Conor Cruise, *The Great Melody* (London, 1993).

Oliver, Lisi, *The Beginnings of English Law* (Toronto, 2002).

Orwell, George, *Collected Essays, Journalism and Letters*, 4 vols (London, 1968).

Oxford History of the Laws of England (Oxford, 2003–)

    I, *The Canon Law and Ecclesiastical Jurisdiction from 597 to the 1640s*, by R. H. Helmholz (2004).

    II, *871–1216*, by John Hudson (2012).

    VI, *1483–1558*, by John Baker (2003).

    XI, *1820–1914: English Legal System*, by William Cornish *et al.* (2010).

    XII, *1820–1914: Private Law*, by William Cornish *et al.* (2010).

    XIII, *1820–1914: Fields of Development*, by William Cornish *et al.* (2010).

Paget, R. T., *Hanged – and Innocent?* (London, 1953).

Paine, Thomas, *Political Writings*, ed. Moncure Conway (Pennsylvania, 1978).

Pattenden, Rosemary, *English Criminal Appeals 1844–1994* (Oxford, 1996).

Peacey, Jason, ed., *The Regicides and the Execution of Charles I* (Basingstoke, 2001).

Plucknett, Theodore, *A Concise History of the Common Law*, 5th edn (London, 1956).

Pollock, Frederick and Maitland, Frederic, *The History of English Law before the Time of Edward I*, 2nd edn, 2 vols (Cambridge, 1899).

Porter, Roy and Teich, Mikulas, eds, *Drugs and Narcotics in History* (Cambridge, 1995).

Poser, Norman, *Lord Mansfield, Justice in the Age of Reason* (Montreal and Kingston, 2013).

Potter, Harry, *Hanging in Judgment: Religion and the Death Penalty in England from the Bloody Code to Abolition* (London, 1993).

Prest, Wilfred, *William Blackstone* (Oxford, 2008).

Price, Christopher and Caplan, Jonathan, *The Confait Confessions* (London, 1976).

Reynolds, Andrew, *Later Anglo-Saxon England: Life and Landscape* (Stroud, 1999).

—— 'Crime and Punishment', in *The Oxford Handbook of Anglo-Saxon Archaeology*, ed. Helena Hamerow, David Hinton and Sally Crawford (Oxford, 2011), pp.891–913.

Robertson, A. J., *Anglo-Saxon Charters* (Cambridge, 1939).

Robertson, Geoffrey, *The Justice Game* (London, 1998).

—— *Crimes against Humanity* (New York, 1999).

—— *The Tyrannicide Brief* (London, 2005).

Rolph, C. H., *The Trial of Lady Chatterley* (London, 1961).

Roper, William, *The Life of Sir Thomas More*, Everyman edn (London, 1963).

Roughead, William, *Trial of Oscar Slater*, 4th edn (Edinburgh, 1950).

Rude, George, *Wilkes and Liberty* (Oxford, 1962).

—— *The Crowd in History, 1730–1848* (London, 1981).

Russell, Conrad, *The Fall of the British Monarchies, 1637–1642* (Oxford, 1995).

Scarman, Leslie, *English Law – The New Dimension* (London, 1974).

Schama, Simon, *Rough Crossings* (London, 2005).

Schwoerer, L. G., *The Declaration of Rights, 1689* (Baltimore, 1981).

Selden, John, *Table Talk* (London, 1689).

Selwyn, Francis, *Gangland* (London, 1988).

Shyllon, F.O., *Black Slaves in Britain* (London, 1974).

Simpson, A.W. Brian, *Cannibalism and the Common Law* (Chicago, 1984).

—— *In the Highest Degree Odious: Detention without Trial in Wartime Britain* (Oxford, 1992).

Souhami, Diana, *The Trials of Radclyffe Hall* (London, 1998).

Spence, Joseph, *Anecdotes* (London, 1820).

Stephen, James Fitzjames, *Liberty, Equality, Fraternity*, 2nd edn (London, 1874).

—— *A History of the Criminal Law of England*, 3 vols (London, 1883).

Stephens, Charles, *The Jurisprudence of Lord Denning: A Study in Legal History*, 3 vols (Newcastle, 2009).

Stryker, Lloyd, *For the Defence* (New York, 1947).

Stubbs, William, *The Constitutional History of England*, 3 vols (Oxford, 1880).

Thomas, Donald, *A Long Time Burning* (London, 1969).

Thomas, Peter, *John Wilkes: A Friend to Liberty* (Oxford, 1996).

Thompson, E. P., *The Making of the English Working Class* (London, 1963).

Thompson, Faith, *Magna Carta, its Role in the Making of the English Constitution, 1300–1629* (Minneapolis, 1948).

Thorne, S. E., *Sir Edward Coke 1552–1952*, Selden Society (1952).

—— ed. and trans. *Bracton on the Laws and Customs of England*, 4 vols (Harvard, 1968–77).

Townsend, William, *The Lives of Twelve Eminent Judges*, 2 vols (London, 1846).

—— *Modern State Trials*, 2 vols (London, 1850).

Travis, Alan, *Bound and Gagged: A Secret History of Obscenity in Britain* (London, 2000).

Trevelyan, G. M., *England under the Stuarts* (London, 1946).

Trevor-Roper, Hugh, *Archbishop Laud* (London, 1962).

Trow, M. J., *Let Him Have It Chris* (London, 1990).

Tusa, Ann and Tusa, John, *The Nuremberg Trial* (London, 1983).

Van Caenegem, R. C., *The Birth of the English Common Law*, 2nd edn (Cambridge, 1988).

Vogler, R., *A World View of Criminal Justice* (Aldershot, 2005).

Wallace-Hadrill, J. M., *Early Germanic Kingship in England and on the Continent* (Oxford, 1971).

Walvin, James, *England, Slaves and Freedom* (Mississippi, 1986).

Warren, W. L., *Henry II* (London, 1991).

—— *King John* (New Haven and London, 1997).

Watson, E. R., *Trial of Adolph Beck* (Edinburgh, 1924).

Weaver, Gordon, *Conan Doyle and the Parson's Son* (London, 2006).

Wedgwood, C. V., *The Trial of Charles I*, Folio Society edn (London, 1981).

West, Donald and Walk, Alexander, eds, *Daniel McNaughton: His Trial and the Aftermath* (Ashford, 1977).

Whitman, James, *The Origins of Reasonable Doubt: Theological Roots of the Criminal Trial* (New Haven and London, 2008).

Wilkes, John, *The North Briton, XLVI Numbers Complete*, 4 vols (London, 1772).

Willock, Ian, *The Origins and Development of the Jury Trial in Scotland*, Stair Society (Edinburgh, 1966).

Willson, David, *King James VI and I* (London, 1956).

Wilson, H. A., ed., *The Pontifical of Magdalen College* (London, 1910).

Winston, Richard, *Thomas Becket* (London, 1967).

Wise, Steven, *Though the Heavens May Fall* (Cambridge, MA, 2005).

Wormald, Patrick, *The Making of English Law: King Alfred to the Twelfth Century* (Oxford, 1999).

Yallop, David, *To Encourage the Others* (London, 1971).

Index

Page numbers in bold type refer to illustrations and their captions.

Printed in the United States
By Bookmasters